A SATELLITE EMPIRE

ROMANIAN RULE IN SOUTHWESTERN UKRAINE, 1941–1944

Vladimir Solonari

CORNELL UNIVERSITY PRESS
Ithaca and London

First published 2019 by Cornell University Press

Printed in the United States of America

Library of Congress Cataloging-in-Publication Data

Names: Solonari, Vladimir, author.
Title: A satellite empire : Romanian rule in southwestern
    Ukraine, 1941–1944.
Description: Ithaca [New York] : Cornell University Press,
    2019. | Includes bibliographical references and index.
Identifiers: LCCN 2019002500 (print) | LCCN
    2019003651 (ebook) | ISBN 9781501743191
    (pdf) | ISBN 9781501743207 (epub/mobi) |
    ISBN 9781501743184 | ISBN 9781501743184 (cloth)
Subjects: LCSH: Transnistria (Ukraine : Territory under
    German and Romanian occupation, 1941–1944)—Politics
    and government. | World War, 1939–1945—Ukraine—
    Transnistria (Territory under German and Romanian
    occupation, 1941–1944)
Classification: LCC DK508.9.T73 (ebook) |
    LCC DK508.9.T73 S64 2019 (print) | DDC 940.53/
    4772—dc23
LC record available at https://lccn.loc.gov/2019002500

To my wife and children, Anastasia, Elizaveta, and Alexei

CONTENTS

ACKNOWLEDGMENTS

My research was made possible by generous support from the United States Holocaust Memorial Museum, Yad Vashem, the Holocaust Educational Foundation, the National Endowment for the Humanities, and the Imre Kertész Kolleg at the Friedrich Schiller Universität, Jena. My home institution, the University of Central Florida, also generously supported my research travel to archival sites through the Pauley Endowment and otherwise encouraged me in my efforts. I express the deepest possible gratitude to all these institutions. Numerous scholars, who at various occasions commented on papers that led to this book, provided me with insightful comments and offered invaluable advice as to how I could improve my work, among them Amir Weiner, Norman Naimark, John-Paul Himka, Omer Bartov, Per Rudling, Alexander Prusin, Holly Case, Harris Mylonas, Irina Livezeanu, Leon Volovici, Jean Ancel, Mikhail Tyaglyy, Michael David-Fox, Peter Holquist, Diana Dumitru, Nathalie Moine, Catherine Goussef, Tanja Penter, Joachim von Putkamer, Stephen Lovell, Kenneth Slepyan, Ben Torne, Marius Turda, Paul Weindling, Flavius Solomon, Zvi Gittelman, Tal Bruttmann, Andrew Kornbluth, Alexandru Moraru, Liviu Carare, Luis Martinez-Fernandez, Joanna Michlic, Martin Dean, Peter Haslinger, Marine-Janine Calic, Béla Bodó, Eric Steinhart, Wendy Lower, and Radu Ioanid. Special thanks go to Dmitry Tartakovsky, who helped me get rid of many typos and otherwise strengthen my text. Needless to say, all errors and omissions are my own. I am also indebted to my colleagues at the Department of History at the University of Central Florida, who invariably showed their interest in my work, helped me in ways too numerous to remember, and encouraged me to trudge on. Archivists in Washington, DC, Jerusalem, Kyiv, Odessa, Freiburg, and Chişinău deserve the most effusive praise for their professionalism and tenacity in helping me identify and obtain necessary documents. Finally, my mom, Elvira, my aunt Nelli, and my sister Olga and her family provided me board and warmth during my research trips to Moldova, Ukraine, and Germany, while my family in the United States, my wife Anastasia, daughter Elizaveta, and son Alexei, helped me weather various storms along the road by extending their love and care.

Abbreviations

BBT	Bessarabia, Bukovina, and Transnistria
CBBT	Civil-Military Cabinet for Bessarabia, Bukovina, and Transnistria, an agency subordinated to the chairman of the Council of Ministers (Romania)
CC CP(B)U	Central Committee of the Communist Party (Bolshevik) of Ukraine
CFR	Romanian Railways state company
CM	Council of Ministers (Romania)
CP(B)U	Communist Party (Bolshevik) of Ukraine
CPOS	Council of Patronage of Social Work (Romania), a quasi-governmental philanthropic agency
CPSU	Communist Party of the Soviet Union
GULAG	Main Board of Corrective Labor Camps, network of the Soviet penal camps
KGB	Committee of State Security (USSR)
NKGB	People's Commissariat of State Security, successor to NKVD
NKVD	People's Commissariat of Internal Affairs (USSR)
NSDAP	National Socialist German Workers' Party (NSDAP), also known as the Nazi Party
PCM	Office of the Chairman of the Council of Ministers, Romania
PNL	National Liberal Party (Romania)
PNȚ	National Peasant Party (Romania)
POW	prisoner of war
Raikom	raion Communist Party committee (Soviet Union)
RKKS	"Notes of the Reich Credit Offices," German quasi-currency issued exclusively for circulation in the occupied territories during World War II
SMERSH	"Death to Spies," Soviet umbrella counterintelligence unit coordinating activities of the eponymous agencies within the People's Commissariats of Defense, of Internal Affairs, and of the Navy

SS	"Protection Squads" of the NSDAP
SSI	Special Service of Information, an intelligence-gathering agency, subordinated to the Council of Ministers (Romania)
SS SK-R	Special Detachment-Russia of the SS
USB	Ukrainian Security Service
VoMi	Coordination Centre for Ethnic Germans of the NSDAP

Note on Toponyms

Many locales mentioned in this book changed their names several times during and after World War II: from Russian into Romanian then back to Romanian (in the eastern part of today's Republic of Moldova, which during the war belonged to Transnistria), then to Ukrainian. Even if the name stayed the same, if transliterated from Cyrillic, whether Russian or Ukrainian, into English, it would appear differently from when transliterated into Romanian. For obvious reasons, I refrained from using the occupiers' names for Transnistrian locales and preferred transliterating them from Russian Cyrillic, as current at the time. However, some territorial entities, such as județe, were created by the Romanians and did not exist either before or after the war. They were usually named after the main towns or cities in their territory. In such cases, I used Romanian names for județe but kept Russian names in Latin transliteration for the towns themselves. The same was true of the concentration camps created by the Romanians. While this rule may create some difficulties (for example, the town of Tulchin but Tulcin judeţ or Berezovca judeţ but the town of Berezoka), it has the advantage of being both fair and true to the sources. The name of the Buh River I used in its current Ukrainian form. I did the same with regard to some of the most important cities in the area, such as Vinnytsia and Mykolaiv.

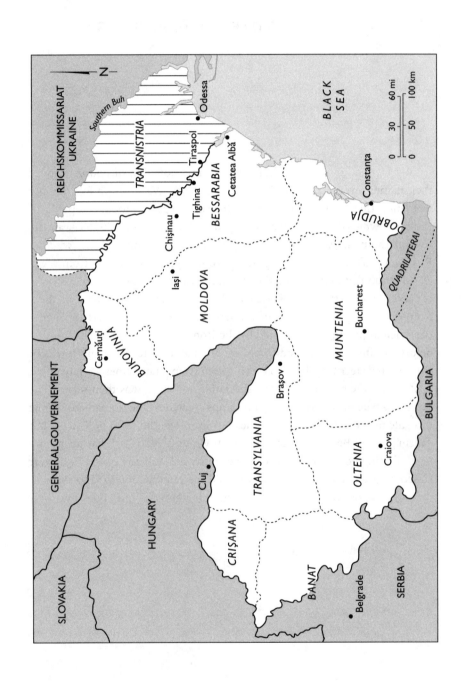

MOGHILAU

TULCIN

JUGASTRU

BALTA

SOUTHERN BUH

RABNITA

GOLTA

DNIESTER

ANANIEV

DUBASARI

BEREZOVCA

Romania

OCEACOV

TIRASPOL

TIRASPOL

ODESSA

OVIDIOPOL

ODESSA

Reichskommissariat
Ukraine

A SATELLITE EMPIRE

Introduction

This is a book on the political and social history of a region of southwestern Ukraine that was under the Romanian occupation during World War II. Known at the time as Transnistria—that is "land beyond the Dniester (or Nistru) River" in Romanian—it comprised the whole of Soviet Odessa oblast, the western part of Mykolaiv oblast, and southern part of Vinnytsia oblast of Ukraine, its western border being the Dniester River and eastern border the southern Buh River. With an area of around 40,000 square kilometers, a population of about 2.3 million people, and the major Black Sea port city of Odessa, Transnistria was somewhat an anomaly in the wartime organization of occupied Soviet territories as the rest of them were ruled by the Nazi German occupiers.[1] This fact alone makes the Transnistrian story fascinating, not only in its own right but also as a foil against which to try and better grasp societal dynamics in the occupied USSR as a whole. Indeed, tracing Romanian policies in Transnistria while understanding the means by which locals in Transnistria tried to make sense of, accommodate, resist, and subvert these policies can shed valuable light on the role of cultural, ideological, and institutional factors that determined the ways in which the "occupation worked (or did not work)" all over the USSR.

This book investigates the conditions in Transnistria under the Romanian occupation from different perspectives. First, from the perspective of the Romanian national government: what aims it pursued in occupying the region and establishing its administration there; how it designed institutions of occupation in ways that were both typical and particular, both for Romania and occupied Eastern Europe; what ideologies of rule over foreign territories drove the government's policy in that region; and how and why its priorities shifted over time. Second, the book adopts the perspective of local administrative and military personnel: who were these people, what were their backgrounds, and how did Romanian governmentalities (political, administrative, legal, and cultural) as well as realities on the ground shape their practices in the region. Finally, the book explores the ways in which the local population perceived, experienced, and reacted to the occupation. While situating itself at the intersection of several traditions of inquiry, the book's primary aim is to contribute to the historiography of occupied Europe during World War II.

The beginning of Western scholarship of Transnistrian wartime history belongs to the first decade of the Cold War. As early as 1957, the doyen of Soviet World War II social history scholars, Alexander Dallin, published the first English-language scholarly book on the subject of wartime Transnistria, titled *Odessa, 1941–1944: A Case Study of Soviet Territory under Foreign Rul.*[2] Based almost exclusively on the interviews with refugees from the region who resided at the time in the West, some of whom might have been perpetrators of crimes against humanity, *Odessa* paints a picture of an incompetent, deeply corrupt, immoral but at the same time rather benign occupation regime, substantially milder than the one established in the rest of the Soviet Union by Nazi Germany (the subject of another influential book by the same author), and certainly more agreeable to his interviewees than the Soviet system.[3] Given that Dallin did not have access to Soviet and Romanian archives, his achievement was indeed impressive and his insights still relevant for our understanding of Odessa's city life during the war. Still, Dallin's casual treatment of the persecution of Jews in the city whose very name became synonymous with some of the worst anti-Jewish atrocities is alarming to our contemporary sensitivities.

For several decades after the publication of *Odessa*, Transnistria dropped off the radar of Western scholars, probably because of changing agendas, the advent of the revisionist trend in historiography, as well as the continuous inaccessibility of archives in the Soviet Union. The situation started to change after the downfall of communism. In 1996, a slim volume published by renowned German historian Ekkehard Völkl was the first Western scholarship based on the newly opened Soviet-era state regional archive in Odessa that houses the collection of the Romanian provincial administration's documents.[4] This book's major achievement is a clear and concise reconstruction of the institutional setup and the evolution of economic policy. However, its treatment of the dynamics of collaboration and resistance in their various forms is rather cursory. The major recent publication is the book by a young German historian, Herwig Baum, titled *Variants of Terror: A Comparison between the German and Romanian Occupation Rule in the Soviet Rule, 1941–1944.*[5] As the title suggests, Baum treats major topics, such as Romanian occupying forces' institutional set-up, economic exploitation, together with resistance toward it and combat against it by locals, as well as the occupiers' war crimes in a systematic, comparative framework. In each chapter, he first summarizes the findings of major German- and English-language works of scholarship concerning developments in the German zone of occupation, and then does the same with respect to Transnistria, this time basing his narrative on his own extensive archival research in Germany, Romania, and Ukraine. These presentations are followed by an informed discussion comparing the two zones. Baum's contribution to the study of wartime Transnistria is of first-rate importance and I concur with most of his conclusions. Unfortunately, Baum used Russian-language sources only occasionally and for that reason his account of local resistance needs some revising. Baum did not research collaboration in Transnistria.

Soviet historiography invariably painted the period of the occupation in only two colors—black and red. Black was used to describe the crimes of the occupiers (Soviet historians, as a rule, refused to see differences between German and Romanian occupation policies) and the suffering of the local population at their hands. Red was applied to account for partisans and their exploits; they were meant to be expressions of the "all-people" patriotic war struggle against hated enemies. In independent Ukraine, historians still face difficulty transcending the language of the Soviet era when it comes to writing the history of World War II in the region.[6] This may explain why publication of a book on the conditions in Odessa under Romanian rule by an amateur historian and writer, Alexandr Cherkasov, which emphasizes mildness of the Romanian administration, the economic improvements supposedly felt widely by Odessans, and the rich cultural life in the city, generated heated debates with accusations of national betrayal and selling out.[7]

The design of this book has been influenced by the recent spate of monographs on the occupation policy and social developments in various regions of the occupied Soviet Union and Eastern Europe.[8] Many of them have been written by German historians and heavily based on German archival materials, although increasingly scholars rely on materials in multiple languages. The proliferation of regional studies stems from the realization that German occupation policy as well as local reactions to it varied greatly from country to country and from one territorial-administrative unit to another.

Partially this was a result of conditions on the ground, in particular perceptions of cultural proximity or remoteness from the German *völk* of a population group over which Germans exercised their power. Partially this was a matter of sheer chance since much depended on the personality of the local Nazi leader and his position within the Nazi hierarchy. Within the increasingly fragmented and poorly coordinated Nazi state, each particular individual's connections in Berlin and with the powerful bonzes at top of the state defined his room for maneuver at the local level. His own understanding of what order of priorities in his fiefdom maximized his career chances was often crucial in defining his policy. Further, changing conditions at the front often required revisions and adjustments in the occupation policy, and the way it was done in each individual region varied greatly. Thus, regional studies of occupation policy and their impact on the local population are crucial for a better, more nuanced, and precise understanding of the history of World War II and its consequences.

There are marked variations in these books' designs and emphases, with some scholars more interested in institutional and political history, others in the history of the Holocaust, and still others in the history of collaboration or resistance. Some books combine analysis of the German institutional set-up in a region, the personnel recruited, their aims and ideological framework, and the evolution of their policy, with accounts of the local population's perceptions of the occupiers, their strategies of survival, the reasons and forms of accommodation, as well as their resistance in its various forms. I see this book as belonging to this group of scholarship, although it is devoted not to the German but to the Romanian zone of occupation.

Two major themes run through this book. First is the contradictory nature of Romanian occupation aims and methods, stirred by the nationalistic imagining of the province as an "oriental space" awaiting its civilized colonizers but tampered by a pragmatic urge to pump as many resources from it as possible with the least administrative and military cost. This theme of fantasy versus pragmatism is central to the recent research of Nazi occupation policies in various parts of Eastern Europe and I show how it can be fruitfully developed with respect to the Transnistrian case. Scholars usually see Nazi fantasies as stemming from their racial worldview and colonial experience in Africa. Romanians were unenthusiastic of Nordic racism and obviously never had colonies. Nevertheless, they were keen to prove their worthiness by administering this "oriental" province in an exemplary manner as bearers of a supposedly superior civilization.

The second theme, suggested to me by Michael David-Fox to whom I am profoundly grateful, is continuity between wartime and pre–World War II

Transnistrian society. World War II (or the Great Patriotic War, as it is commonly known in Russia and among pro-Russian circles in Ukraine) is usually thought of as a great divide in the Soviet history, as an ordeal from which the Soviet regime emerged transformed and legitimized in the eyes of its own population and beyond to a previously unattainable degree. Its social base widened on account of the millions of returning front-line soldiers, many of whom identified themselves with the official myth of the war as the ultimate proof of the superiority of the Soviet system. Being promoted into positions of authority at various levels, they would become the backbone of Soviet power for decades to come.[9]

It is not my intention to question this fundamentally correct and highly productive interpretation. Nevertheless, I believe that it is important to bear in mind that Soviet citizens who lived under, collaborated with, suffered at the hands of, and fought back against the occupiers did not possess the foreknowledge of the war's outcome. The mental framework that they used to comprehend their reality, the ways in which they reacted to events and interacted with authorities and with each other were profoundly shaped by their previous life experiences. Whatever their perceptions of the occupiers and their regime, whatever their attitudes, strategies, and actions, they were conditioned, perhaps in equal measure, both by the "facts on the ground" in occupied Transnistria and by lessons they had learned from the Soviets. To understand these people, who lived just several decades before us but whose world seems almost as strange as that of the Middle Ages, is a difficult task. I admit that it has a mesmerizing appeal for me. Other themes I discuss are specific to individual chapters, but it would be premature to discuss them at this stage. I hope that taken together they comprise a coherent whole.

This book does not explore the persecution and fate of Jews and Roma in Transnistria. This was not my original intention. In fact, I initially planned to put these stories in the very center of the book. The more I worked on this project, however, the more aware I became of the extraordinary complexity of the story of the Jews and Roma.[10] To try and cram this analysis into the present book would make it lose effect among the other subjects covered. I would like to emphasize that in this respect, too, I follow an established norm in the regional studies of occupation, which tend to focus *either* on the Holocaust *or* on the occupation policies, collaboration, and resistance rather than on all these issues simultaneously.[11]

This book is based on several years of archival research all over the world. Since September 2008 when I started to work on this project, I researched relevant collections in the archives of US Holocaust Memorial Museum in Washington, DC (USHMM) that houses microfilm copies of documents from various countries, including Romania and Ukraine; in Yad Vashem, an Israeli government institution in Jerusalem that is a museum, a research institution, and an archive (functioning mostly along the same lines as USHMM); in Kyiv and Odessa (Ukraine); and in Chişinău, Moldova. Archival documents I consulted can be divided into several categories. The first comprises various texts generated by the Romanian occupation administration in Transnistria, the gendarmerie, police, and troops deployed there, as well as supervisory bodies in Bucharest. Naturally, these documents are, in the broad sense, of paramount importance for the reconstruction of Romanian policy in the province, but they are also indispensable for the study of the local population's attitudes toward the occupiers reflected in various reports "on the mood of the population," as well as of resistance movements, both nationalist and communist.

The second category covers activity reports and investigations of partisan groups and underground communist organizations held in Kyiv and Odessa former party archives. Upon the province's liberation by the Red Army, all partisan and underground resistance groups were requested to present activity reports which were to be verified by the NKVD and approved by the party. These documents reveal an atmosphere of paranoia and intense fear that hovered over their authors. Since members of the party and political police knew only two types of former partisans: heroes and traitors to the motherland, while in reality many resisters widely practiced dissimilation and some form of accommodation to the occupation regime, the reports were intended to reveal as much as to conceal. Authentic stories of resistance were too complex and ambiguous to be told in such a setting. Written in stridently clichéd Soviet speak and in a self-glorifying manner, these reports often cannot be taken at their face value. Fortunately, they are sometimes accompanied by depositions of individual partisans and "interviews" (in fact, interrogations) conducted with them by party officers; some of these documents reveal important details about life under occupation. In the 1960s and 1970s, the party reopened investigations into the activity of partisan movement. Unlike first postwar years when the party's and police's priority was to filter out dubious and unreliable elements, in the later years the emphasis shifted to the myth-building of resistance as a phenomenon of the "all-people" struggle against the enemy. Consequently, the investigators were often inclined to reverse previously issued condemnatory decisions, rehabilitate pronounced "traitors," embellish officially sanctioned tales of resisters' exploits, and add new names to the rosters of Soviet heroes. They probably erred as much on the side of gullibility as their predecessors on the side of suspicion. Still, since the times were now more relaxed, some depositions of former participants and eyewitnesses collected in these later decades appear less formulaic and more persuasive. They are probably more reliable and offer unique insights into the social history of resistance.

The third category comprises Soviet and Romanian investigative files concerning war crimes committed in Transnistria, mostly the mass murder of Jews. Coming from the archive of the Ukrainian security service (former KGB archive) and the Romanian Information Service (former Securitate), they were identified and microfilmed by the USHMM and Yad Vashem staff. Soviets vigorously prosecuted war criminals from the first days following the liberation to the end of their regime. In Romania, investigations were mostly confined to the second half of the 1940s and early 1950s after which they stopped.[12] The reliability of both Soviet and Romanian investigative files can be legitimately questioned based on the long records of the communist regimes' use of the judiciary for political ends, as well as of torture for the extraction of preconceived "evidence." Nevertheless, recent research seems to have proven beyond a reasonable doubt that the facts established by Soviet postwar investigations are usually corroborated by other sources.[13] This finding suggests that investigative records of war crimes were, generally speaking, free of blatant distortions of truth, if one ignores the obligatory Soviet-speak which investigators routinely put into the mouths of perpetrators and eyewitnesses alike. It is hard to see what political benefits the regime could have derived from distorting the records of individual lower-ranking perpetrators, whose number was legion in the immediate postwar years. It is more than probable that the investigators tried to establish the guilt of each accused as truthfully as they could, even if their own definition of what constituted guilt, in particular high treason in the occupied territories, was quite different from our perspective today, as well as from the norms established in Western Europe.[14] The same was even more true for Romanian postwar trials of war criminals, with the possible exception of the trial of very top leaders of the wartime regime in 1945, which was highly politicized. In 1945–1946, when most Romanian trials of Transnistrian criminals took place, the communist regime was still not completely established, and the judicial system still possessed a degree of press autonomy, if not independence.

This is not to say that all communist-era files are of the same quality. Soviet files, in particular, tend to be of higher quality the later they are. As a rule, investigations carried out by the army and its counterintelligence agency Death to Spies (SMERSH) were rather summary, involved a limited number of eyewitnesses, and resulted in harsher sentences. As time went on, investigations gradually became more detailed and aimed to establish the exact circumstances of the crime, the motives of perpetrators, and their individual responsibility in each act of mass murder. At the same time, however, eyewitnesses' accounts became less precise and less reliable. Earlier files can thus be more valuable because they often contain precious information from survivors (who sometimes voluntarily sought out teams of investigators to supply their information) and other eyewitnesses, whose memories were still fresh. Romanian investigative techniques were different from those employed by the Soviet in that the files would not contain transcripts of interrogations but declarations of the accused and eyewitnesses that were, in all probability, composed by the secretary or interrogator himself, and then signed by the person interrogated. In that way, they were likely to have omitted important details, which otherwise would have been recorded. Romanian files, while indispensable, suffer from the lack of access of Romanian interrogators to the eyewitnesses who at the time of the investigation resided in the Soviet Union. For reasons that remain obscure, little cooperation existed between the Soviet and Romanian investigative teams, and no Soviet citizen was ever interrogated by Romanian investigators. Thus, Romanians were left to rely on a much narrower selection of eyewitnesses, a fact that substantially hampered their efforts and, correspondingly, the value of their Transnistria-related files.

Another problem is posed by the great variety of situations and individual stories, the full complexity of which cannot, as a rule, be grasped from the available sources. The researcher thus confronts an overwhelming amount of evidence that exists in fragmentary form. Under such conditions, the most one can hope to achieve is to establish recurring patterns of the pressures and motives that conditioned local choices in favor of collaboration and participation in massive killing operations. Even so, these materials offer great insights into the recruitment practices, social composition, and motivations of perpetrators that cannot be gleaned from other sources.

Among my other sources are occupation-era newspapers, memoirs of former Romanian and German officials and clergymen in Transnistria, and testimonies and memoirs of survivors and eyewitnesses. All of these and some other, less prominent types of sources that I used have their own strengths and weaknesses. Although considerations of space prevented me from discussing them at any length, I used them to the extent of their reliability, as I understood it, and, as far as possible, in conjunction with other sources.

The book is divided into three parts. The first explores the process of Transnistria's creation as an occupation zone and administrative entity. Here, I explain the place of Transnistria in the Romanian government's grand strategy, the aims of the occupation and its limits, the design and personnel of its institutions and the culture-determined practices of the day-to-day business of governing the province. In the second, I trace the Romanian actions intended to simultaneously transform Transnistria—in terms of both its demography and the "culture" of its population—and exploit its economic resources. I show how the latter preoccupation quickly overrode the other two and demonstrate the consequences of this development. Finally, in the third part I explore reactions to Romanian occupation on the part of the local non-Jewish population. I define those reactions as belonging to two broad categories: accommodation and collaboration, on the one hand, and resistance, on the other; I also trace their evolution throughout the occupation period. This structure thus speaks broadly to my intention to combine the exploration of political, institutional, and social history of the region during World War II. In conclusion, I sum up my findings and make wider inferences from them by putting them into the context of wartime experiences in the occupied Soviet Union.

Part 1

Creating and Running Transnistria

CHAPTER 1

Conquering and Delimiting Transnistria

Before the Romanian occupation, Transnistria did not exist as a territorial-administrative entity. Meaning "the territory beyond the Dniester River" in Romanian, the term had a half-mystical connotation as the region in which lost ethnic Romanian "brothers" resided. In the interwar period, this notion was popularized by ethnic Romanian émigrés from southern Ukraine who escaped the trepidations of the Russian Civil War in Romania. The Romanian government secretly supported their propaganda, possibly as a counterweight to Soviet claims over Bessarabia, but did so intermittently and unenthusiastically. Romania never laid official claims to the region. Thus, the decision to occupy the region militarily and administer it during the war was a novelty in Romanian statecraft. This chapter explores the context within which Transnistria emerged as a legal and administrative reality as well as the Romanian policymakers' visions and calculations that culminated in its formation.

The Conquest

Romanian occupation of Transnistria was an outgrowth of the country's participation in the war against the Soviet Union alongside Nazi Germany. Although initially there was a wide consensus in Romanian society behind such participation, Romanian troops' role in the conquest of the territory to the east of the Dniester River—a de facto Soviet-Romanian border between 1918 and 1940—was controversial from the beginning. This fact cast a shadow over Romanian rule in the province from 1941 to 1944.

When on June 22, 1941, Romania went to war against the Soviet Union, the country was united behind its leader's, General Ion Antonescu, decision to align the nation to Nazi Germany in order to exact revenge on Soviet empire. The previous summer, Romania suffered a series of humiliations at the hands of its neighbors who forced her to cede parts of her territory: first, Bessarabia and northern Bukovina to the Soviets, then northern Transylvania to Hungarians, and finally, southern Dobrudzha (Dobrogea) to Bulgaria. After the fall of France, Romania's principal ally in the 1920s and 1930s, Germany and Soviet Russia remained the only serious military powers on the European continent. Although it was Germany who forced Romania to cede its territories to Hungary and Bulgaria, Romanians saw the Soviets as a more immediate danger than the Germans. After the annexation of Bessarabia and northern Bukovina in late June 1940, the Soviets continued to threaten Romanian interests claiming special rights in the Danube Delta. Romanians feared a full-scale Russian invasion, and they might have been correct about it.[1]

Under such conditions, both the last government under King Carol II headed by Ion Gigurtu, and Ion Antonescu who was appointed by Carol as dictator (Conducător) on September 4, 1940 and then ousted the unpopular king from the throne on September 6, chose an alliance with Germany as the only way to protect the country from continuous Soviet threat.[2] Ion Antonescu decided to join Germany in the war against the Soviet Union in late 1940 or early 1941 single-handedly but the decision had unanimous support in his own government, most of Romania's political class, and the country at large. Almost everybody agreed that the country needed to use this moment to avenge its humiliation at the hands of the Soviets and take Bessarabia and northern Bukovina, annexed the previous summer by the country's eastern neighbor, back. Besides, Romanian propertied classes hated Bolshevik system and preferred, in their great majority, fascist dictatorship to Soviet-type communism.[3]

This is why when, on July 5, Romanian troops entered the capital of Bukovina, Cernăuți, and on July 16, the capital of Bessarabia, Chișinău, the country was euphoric. Ion Antonescu was on the peak of his popularity and quickly rose through the army ranks, conferring upon himself the rank of marshal on August 21, 1941. Eulogized as a liberator of the enslaved provinces, he claimed to his credit the role of a commander of the "Army Group General Antonescu" that drove the Soviets from eastern Romanian lands. The group combined the Third Romanian Army (under General Petre Dumitrescu) that acted in northern Bukovina and northern Bessarabia, the Fourth Romanian Army (under General Nicolae Ciupercă) that acted in southern Bessarabia, and German Eleventh Army (under General Eugen Siegfried Erich Ritter von Schobert) that acted in northern and central Bessarabia. This arrangement, suggested by Hitler during his meeting with Antonescu on July 12 in Munich and clarified in the following exchange of letters between the two, ostensibly put German troops under the Romanian command for the first time in history. However, it was devoid of real substance: German Eleventh Army's High Command served as "work staff" of the "General Antonescu Army Group" with its orders to the Romanian units overseen and signed by Antonescu who, in turn, answered to the High Command of Wehrmacht and Hitler. The General Antonescu Army Group lasted only as long as the troops operated within the 1939 Romanian borders. As soon as they passed the Dniester River on July 17, the group was shut down.[4]

If this act was intended to signify the end of the Romanian army participation in the war, the reality proved otherwise. Romanian troops continued their advance eastward in the steps of their mighty ally. It is not exactly clear when the decision to pass the Dniester River was made by Antonescu but

FIGURE 1.   The Soviet prisoners of war taken in the first weeks of the war by the Romanians. Photo: Army Propaganda Department. Original caption reads, "This riff-raff stripped of their humanity by indoctrination and alcohol just yesterday was Stalin's army's best. Today the guards drive them into the camps." Courtesy DANIC.

on July 27, 1941, Hitler in his letter to Conducător commended him for his determination to wage the war "alongside Germany until the very end."[5] At the time, the Third Army was already advancing toward the southern Buh River in what was to become northern Transnistria. A day before the Fourth Army completed the reconquest of southern Bessarabia and was advancing across the Dniester River in the direction of Odessa, to which they lay siege on August 5. On July 31, Antonescu, in a letter to Hitler profusely and grovelingly thanked him for his appreciation of Romanian bravery and confirmed his resolve to "go to the end in the action that I started in the east against the great enemy of civilization, of Europe, and of my country: Russian Bolshevism."[6] During his meeting with Hitler on August 6 in the Ukrainian town of Berdychiv, Antonescu explained his immediate military plans more precisely: to occupy not only Transnistria but also Crimea from which Soviet air force threatened Romanian port city of Constanţa.[7]

Although Romanians agreed that their eastern provinces had to be taken back from the Soviets, and Germany's attack on the USSR was the right moment to do so, they were not in accord on the participation in the war farther to the east. As Romanian losses mounted, doubts increased. On August 8, 1941, Ion Antonescu ordered the Fourth Army to capture Odessa "on the march." This, as it turned out, was an unrealistic order since by that time the Soviets heavily fortified the city from the attack from the north by land troops (before the war's outbreak, Soviet plans appreciated the likelihood of such an attack as low and consequently, the city was fortified on the shores only). Three defense lines of barbed wire, trenches, dugouts, machine gun and artillery nests ran around the city in three semicircles starting from as far away as thirty kilometers. The city was defended by the force of no less than 90,000 troops constantly reinforced by fresh compliments transported by sea and supported by gunfire from the Soviet naval force.[8] Romanian intelligence failed to alert the Romanian High Command to the strengths of the Soviet defenses and their determination to retain the city. When on August 20, General Eugen Siegfried Erich Ritter von Schobert, commander of the Eleventh German Army offered German assistance to the Fourth Romanian Army charged with capturing Odessa, Ion Antonescu turned down this offer on the ground that Romanian forces were sufficient to accomplish the task and assured his counterpart that Odessa would be taken "by early September *as the latest.*"[9]

Two Romanian assaults, between August 8–24 and August 28–September 5, were poorly prepared and badly executed. As the result, they failed to produce the desired success and instead resulted in casualties of no less than 58,859, of whom 11,046 dead, 42,331 wounded, and 5,478 missing in action.[10] On September 3, 1941, commander of the Fourth Army General Nicolae Ciupercă forwarded a memorandum to Ion Antonescu in which he opined that "nearly all our divisions have exhausted their offensive potential, both physically and morally," while the enemy was "taking full advantage of his control of the sea to reinforce Odessa." He advised the Conducător against further frontal attacks.[11] In response, on September 9, Antonescu dismissed Ciupercă "for lack of offensive spirit" and appointed in his stead his Minister of Defense general Iosif Iacobici who revised Ciupercă's plan of assault on the city. However, the third offensive carried out by Iacobici on September 12–21, was no less disastrous than the previous two, leading to further enormous casualties.[12]

Further Romanian setback came when the Soviet combined land, marine, and airborne forces launched a surprise attack against their positions on the seashore to the east and west of the city on September 21 and October 2. Romanian troops retreated, sometimes in panic. Many gains attained in the previous months were lost and Antonescu had to request, to his chagrin, support in infantry and air force from the Germans. Seeing Romanian humiliations at Odessa, the Germans honored this request and dispatched an infantry division and heavy artillery contingent freed after their crushing victory over the Soviets at Kyiv.[13] By the time their reinforcements arrived in early October, the Soviets had already abandoned Odessa. Soviet plans changed under the pressure of developments on the fronts farther to the east in southern Ukraine. The German victory in the battle of the Perekop Isthmus, which connects the Crimean Peninsula with mainland led to a drastic deterioration of Soviet positions in Crimea. With Sevastopol, the main naval Soviet base, threatened on land by the quickly advancing German troops, Odessa lost its strategic importance for the Soviets. Consequently, the Soviet High Command decided to concentrate all available forces on Sevastopol's defense. From October 2 through October 16, the bulk of the Soviet forces successfully evacuated from Odessa into Crimea by sea. Romanian forces resumed their attacks on the city on October 15 and, without encountering serious resistance, entered Odessa the next dat. Their third major offensive scheduled to start on October 20 never took place. Romanian losses in the battle of Odessa reached staggering 90,020, of whom 17,891 dead, 63,280 wounded, and 8,849 missing in action. The number of losses at Odessa represented an unsustainable 26.46 percent of the total forces engaged there, 340,223 out of 583,930 men of the overall Romanian land force. This was substantially higher than the share of German losses on the Eastern Front as a whole by September 30, 1941—17.22 percent.[14]

General Ciupercă was not the only military top brass opposed to Antonescu's reckless strategy at Odessa. According to Ioan Hudiţa, deputy secretary general of the oppositional National Peasants Party (PNŢ)—that was ostensibly banned alongside all other parties and political organizations but in reality continued to function in a semi-clandestine fashion—this was also the opinion of the under secretary of state at the Ministry of National Defense general Gheorge Jienescu. As Hudiţa wrote in his diary on July 10, Jienescu felt that the cost of front assaults ordered by Antonescu contrary to German advice was too high and that many other generals believed the same but, minding Antonescu's vengefulness, were loath to confront him over the issue.[15] According to the assessment by the Romanian General Staff, the morale of the troops engaged at Odessa was considerably lower than the one they displayed during fighting in Bessarabia. The recovery of Bessarabia and northern Bukovina was worth the fight, whereas the rationale of the war beyond the Dniester was beyond them.[16]

Inordinately high Romanian losses dampened societal support for the war. On August 13, Hudiţa wrote in his diary during his father's visit to Bucharest. A schoolteacher from the village of Bogdăneşti in northern Moldova, he told his son that in this village and others around it residents were mourning the death of hundreds of young men killed at Odessa. People "were cursing Antonescu [and] the alliance with Hitler."[17] During his visit to Bogdăneşti on September 7, 1941, Hudiţa confirmed widespread popular resistance to the continuation of the war beyond the Dniester.[18]

In Hudiţa's party opinions were divided as to the wisdom of continuing military operations beyond the Dniester, but its leader Iuliu Maniu, a well-respected nationalist democrat from Transylvania and former prime minister, as well as Hudiţa himself, resolutely opposed this policy. On July 23, Maniu sent a memorandum to Antonescu in which he, in the name of his party, praised the dictator for regaining Bessarabia and northern Bukovina but warned him against waging the war to the east of those provinces. "It is inadmissible for us to appear as aggressors against Russia, today an ally of England, which will probably be a victor [in the war]," he wrote prophetically.[19] In the other powerful opposition party, the National Liberals were more in favor of Antonescu's policy of continuous war but its leader Dinu Brătianu was in full agreement with Maniu on the issue.[20]

On the international arena, Romania's actions beyond the Dniester had grave consequences. On November 30, 1941, Great Britain presented an ultimatum, requesting withdrawal of Romanian military back to the 1939 borders within five days. When the Romanians did not budge, Great Britain declared war on Romania on December 6; British dominions of Canada, New Zealand, Australia, and South African Union followed suit.[21] This was a nightmare—a Western power and traditional ally of Romania, now at war with their country—that even some members of the ruling circle wanted to avoid. According to General Jienescu, who desperately tried to persuade

Antonescu to accept the British ultimatum, even General Iosif Iacobici wanted to withdraw troops west of the Dniester (he was dismissed from the post of chief of the General Staff in January 1942 and then transferred to army reserve), and this view was supported by a majority of generals.[22]

FIGURE 2. Romanians greet German ambassador in Bucharest, Manfred Freiherr von Killinger (standing on the balcony of the embassy), on the fall of Odessa. Courtesy DANIC.

Still, even at the height of fighting at Odessa, popular opinion was still largely supportive of the war and an alliance with Germany. When the news of the fall of Odessa were announced by the Romanian media, there was no shortage of publicly expressed enthusiasm from all sectors of Romanian society.[23] Antonescu thus withered a temporary crisis of confidence caused by the lackluster performance of his troops at Odessa. In January 1942, under pressure from Hitler, he decided to drastically increase Romania's contribution to the war on the Eastern Front. In the summer of 1942, the Romanians were fighting in Crimea, Caucasus, and in the Don region, advancing toward Stalingrad, twenty-six divisions in all. In November 1942, 380,103 Romanian troops were engaged on the Eastern Front. Until then, the Romanian troops refrained from taking part in offensive operations and were instead conducting mopping up and other anti-partisan actions, as well as protecting warehouses and communication lines. They would avoid devastating losses until the destruction of their Third Army at Stalingrad.[24]

Still, neither the Conducător nor his top subordinates could escape the bitter realization that the capture of Odessa was due to German military successes, not their country's battlefield prowess. Intended as an ultimate proof of Romania's status as an important force in Southeast Europe, the battle demonstrated the country's humiliating dependence on its all-powerful and feared ally. Conditional nature of Romania's rule over Odessa and the surrounding areas was an indisputable reality from the moment the Romanian flag was foisted there.

Diplomatic and Political Origins of Romanian Occupation Zone[25]

Conquering—with crucial German support—Odessa and the surrounding areas was one thing, establishing Romanian administration there was another. This section explores rationales that led Romanian and German leaders to this decision and the reaction to it by Romanian elite circles. From the Conducător's standpoint, the Romanian troops' preeminent role in the conquest of Transnistria, and in particular of Odessa, had to boost its claim of territories in the east. For Antonescu, the question was not whether such expansion was desirable, but only how far east it should go.

The issue of territorial compensation of Romania in the east was first raised by Hitler on June 12, 1941, during his talks with Antonescu in Munich. He used it as a bait to secure the Romanians' extensive cooperation in his anti-Soviet war. Initially, Hitler pretended that he had no particular interest in Romania taking part in military action on the Eastern Front; his primary concern was stability in the country and regular delivery of Romanian oil and agricultural produce to Germany. If Romania would honor her obligations in those domains and possibly even join Germany on the battlefield, the Führer added, then at the end of the conflict she could count on "boundless" territorial acquisitions in the east.[26] The only surviving (German-language) transcript of this conversation does not contain evidence of further discussion of this issue, but it is possible that such talks did take place, as later developments suggest. On July 16, at a conference in Berlin dedicated to the organization of administration of the occupied Soviet territories, Hitler insisted that Odessa and territories north of it would be apportioned to Romania (he probably meant after the war). This idea encountered resistance on the part of the Reich Ministry for the Occupied Eastern Territories (Reichsministerium der Besetzten Ostgebieten), whose representative, Georg Leibbrandt, argued that such arrangement would antagonize Ukrainian nationalists, whom he considered Germany's allies. Leibbrandt was also worried about the possible negative consequences for a sizable ethnic German community in this region. Hitler, however, asserted that fastening Romania to Germany by putting it in charge of an occupied region (Bezatzungsgebiet) far outweighed any possible negative consequences.[27]

Antonescu was certainly interested. In a letter to Generalmajor Arthur Hauffer, chief of the German Military Mission (Heeresmission) in Romania, dated July 22, 1941, he raised the issue of territorial expansion of Romania beyond the Dniester, putting forward two arguments in favor of this proposition: the perceived necessity to prevent the creation, after the war, of a "politically and militarily uncontrollable Ukraine" that could threaten Romanian interests in the region, and the existence of numerous ethnic Romanians (known as Moldovans) in the territory to the east of the Dniester for whose protection Antonescu intended to create a special "fortified zone." To make this idea more appealing to the Germans, Antonescu added that it would help them secure direct access to northeast Balkans through the Dniester River and the still-to-be-built canal that would connect the Dniester with Vistula River in the north.[28]

The Wehrmacht, which experienced the shortage of security troops necessary for the protection of its rears, in the early August considered employing the Romanian troops for that purpose but by August 9 the German High Command ruled this option out.[29] Hitler, however, again showed more willingness to satisfy the Romanians' vanity in order to get more of their cannon fodder. On August 14, 1941, in a letter to Antonescu he suggested that the latter accept the responsibility for safeguarding, with the bulk of his forces, the territory between the Dniester and Dnieper rivers, while some more mobile

and better trained big units continued to fight, alongside their German counterparts, east of the Dnieper.[30] The Conducător responded on August 17,
acceding to Hitler's military requests to enforce security between the Dniester and Dnieper rivers but declining the responsibility for "administration
and economic exploitation" of this territory as a whole. He reasoned that
since Romania, and especially Bessarabia, faced the necessity of "total economic and administrative reorganization," they simply did not have enough
resources for this task. He could only accept responsibility for "administration and economic exploitation" of the territory between the Dniester and
southern Buh rivers.[31] This territory was at least two times smaller than the
one suggested by Hitler.

Antonescu's response suggests either a malentendu or a deliberate manip-
ulation on his part. Indeed, nothing in Hitler's letter implied the intention
to create a separate Romanian administration between the Dniester and
Dnieper rivers. Rather, Hitler envisaged a purely auxiliary role for the Romanian troops in this region, subordinated to the German High Command.
Antonescu, however, pushed the arrangement to a considerably higher
level: the territory between the Buh and Dniester rivers would become a
Romanian zone of occupation, which Romania alone would administer and
"exploit economically." As if to drive this point home, in the last paragraph
of his letter Conducător added a request to the Führer to issue instructions to
German authorities clearly establishing Antonescu's authority on the issues
concerning the territories both between the Dniester and Buh rivers and
between the Buh and Dnieper rivers. An alternative explanation presupposes
that before writing his message, Antonescu received Hitler's agreement to
his vision via diplomatic channels (indeed, he refers to his conversations with
the German ambassador Freiherr Manfred von Killinger at the beginning of
his message). Either way, it appears that Hitler acceded to the Conducător's
demand for the territorial expansion of Romania at the beginning rather
than at the end of the conflict, as the Führer initially envisaged.

Initially, the Conducător and his lieutenants foresaw that Transnistria's
occupation would be followed by its eventual annexation, cleansing of ethnic
"aliens," and repopulating it with ethnic Romanians. Antonescu's expansionist striving in the east found considerable support both in the upper echelons
of his administration and in the Romanian society. On June 17, 1941, the
Council of Ministers discussed measures to be taken in case of an impending
war. Mihai Antonescu, who presided over this meeting, expounded his and
the Conducător's vision over the future administrative organization of soon-
to-be liberated provinces of Bessarabia and Bukovina as well as "the territories beyond the Dniester" (teritorii transnistriene). He made it clear that all

of these territories "would be incorporated into the Romanian sovereignty" and that the authorities "would have to apply there a policy of purification of race through the phenomenon of emigration."[32] Mihai Antonescu referred to the same idea in the meeting of June 25, 1941, where he explained that some of the ethnic Romanian refugees from Hungary-occupied northern Transylvania could be settled "on the Bessarabian or Transnistrian properties" (meaning those properties whose owners would have been evicted).[33]

The government did not hide its expansionist plans from the public. On July 27, 1941, Hudiţa noted in his journal that the Romanian government-controlled newspapers started to publish information about ethnic Romanians residing to the east of the Dniester River and he immediately realized that this campaign aimed at preparing the Romanian public opinion for territorial conquests in the east.[34] Some ministers leaked the news to their friends of various political hues.[35] Iuliu Maniu, Hudiţa, and some other PNŢ leaders grew increasingly concerned and attempted to persuade Antonescu to withdraw troops behind the Dniester River and to renounce his expansionist plans. On July 18, Iuliu Maniu sent a memorandum to Ion Antonescu in which he emphasized that the return of northern Transylvania had to be an absolute priority and that eastward expansion might endanger attaining this goal.[36] PNŢ leaders were alarmed by persistent rumors circulating in Romania that the Hungarians were considering to "transfer" ethnic Romanians from northern Transylvania into Ukraine in order to ethnically cleanse the territory. They suspected that the Hungarians were in cahoots with the Germans who enticed the Romanians to occupy Transnistria in order to claim later that in this way Romania received compensation for northern Transylvania and the issue was thus closed.[37] Besides, they worried that Romania's participation in the military operations beyond the Dniester and the occupation of Transnistria would alienate Britain and the United States and thus endanger Romania's diplomatic and military positions.[38]

The National Peasants Party leaders used different ways to impress this vision on Ion and Mihai Antonescu, who sometimes met with them on the latter's request, but all their efforts failed. The fundamental issue here was their mutually exclusive judgments as to the likely outcome of the war. Maniu and Hudiţa never wavered in their conviction that Germany would lose the war (other leaders of the party sometimes dithered but mostly followed their lead), whereas Ion Antonescu was no less certain that the opposite was true. As he explained to Nicolae Lupu, another prominent member of PNŢ inner circle who paid him two visits on August 25 and 27, 1941, the German army was "invincible" and it functioned "as a clock." "Paralytic [Franklin Delano] Roosevelt will not be able to create [such] an army in even ten years," he went on. "Just wait and see how in a few weeks Hitler will be in Moscow and Leningrad."[39] "If [after that] England will try to resist," he added, "it will be occupied in less than a week. Wow to the nations that would attempt to resist this army." Two days later Antonescu was a little more pensive but still insisted that "Even if beaten, Germany will still remain powerful enough to protect her European allies."[40] From this assessment—which at the time seemed realistic to a great many people in Romania and beyond—it followed that Romania should prove its loyalty to Germany and become its most valuable ally. Thus, participating full force in the war east of the Dniester River and occupying and administering Transnistria was in complete accord with Romania's best interest.

As is clear from the proceeding account, the creation of a separate Romanian zone of the occupation was Ion Antonescu's initiative. In that, he had firm support from his council of ministers, most of them hard-core nationalists. At least some of the pro-Western opposition leaders were adamantly against it on legal and political grounds. They tried to dissuade Antonescu from this endeavor but failed. German leadership was divided as to the wisdom of allowing their junior ally such privilege and even Hitler, who encouraged the Romanian dreams of eastward expansion, initially meant to award them eastern territories after the war. It was the Conducător's stubborn insistence that eventually swayed the Germans. Now the Romanian leaders had to define the legal basis of their rule over Transnistria.

Occupation or Annexation? Legal Status of Romanian Rule in Transnistria

During the first weeks of the war, Ion Antonescu and his closest entourage believed that occupation would soon be followed by annexation that would establish full sovereignty over the province, but they soon walked back from this position. The pivotal problem here was Transylvania because Antonescu's government was in agreement with the pro-Western opposition and practically everybody else in the Romanian political class: Transylvania was the number one priority. This might seem counterintuitive since, after all, in the war against the Soviet Union Romania was fighting alongside its archenemy Hungary who had just snatched northern Transylvania. Antonescu, however, believed that proving Romania's loyalty and prowess on the battlefield was the only way to persuade the Nazis that they made a mistake in Vienna in the summer of 1940 when they decreed transfer of this region to Hungary. Regretting their mistake, he dreamed, the Nazis would either order the Hungarians to give northern Transylvania back to Romania or let the Romanians take it by the force. In fact, Antonescu told Lupu that after the war the Romanian troops would return back home "via Transylvania."[41] That Romanian leader could sincerely believe in such ludicrously naive proposition may constitute an ultimate proof of his political inaptitude—the point PNȚ leaders would repeat time and time again—but the bigger issue is that, as Holly Case has recently demonstrated with an abundance of evidence, Romanian grand strategy in 1941–1944 was predicated on this same assumption.[42]

But why were the Romanians of all political hues obsessed with northern Transylvania? After all, there was almost no interest toward returning southern Dobrudzha, lost to Bulgaria approximately at the same time as northern Transylvania to Hungary. The answer lies in the central place Transylvania occupied in Romanian historical imagination that formed the very foundation of what Katherine Verdery aptly called their "national ideology."[43] According to the dominant "theory of continuity," Romanian ethnic nation resulted from the intermarriages of "autochthonous" Dacians and Roman settlers that occurred between Dacia's conquest by Emperor Trajan (101–106 AD) and the Romans relinquishing it under Emperor Aurelian (270–275). Following Aurelian's withdrawal, Dacia suffered a series of "barbarian invasions" but Romanized population survived by hiding in the Transylvanian mountains from which they descended in the twelfth century when they were first mentioned in the written sources.[44] Thus, Transylvania was, as the Romanians would put it, "the cradle and the heart of the Romanian nation." To this one should add that in the decades preceding the Great War, the interethnic strife in Transylvania, which at this time was ruled by the nationalistically inclined Hungarian elite in what was Austria-Hungary, reached its apex. In 1916, Romania went to war with Central Powers for the sake of Transylvania, which it eventually gained, in 1919, at the astonishing human and economic price. Thus, losing northern Transylvania in the summer of 1940 was seen as the greatest national humiliation. And so, all Romanians seemed to agree that regaining it must be an absolute priority.

Seen from this standpoint, the regime faced a difficulty. Although Antonescu did not sign the Vienna accord, he acquiesced and implemented it. Fighting alongside the Hungarian troops against the Soviets could be construed as a sign of relinquishing claims over Transylvania forever—an accusation that a self-professed "integral nationalist," as Antonescu called himself, desperately wanted to avoid. Striving to avert being seen as a traitor to the national cause would later lead Romanian leaders to make gestures that would create serious problems in German-Romanian relations. This happened, for example when Mihai Antonescu, in October 1941, announced to the stunned Ribbentrop that he considered the Vienna accord "null and void" or when on March 27, 1942, in a public speech he violently attacked the Hungarian policy in northern Transylvania and its conduct in the war.[45]

Although the Antonescus refused to heed the opposition's request to stop at the Dniester and limit Romania's war efforts to liberating Bessarabia and northern Bukovina, they made it clear that the annexation of Transnistria would never happen at the price of losing Transylvania forever. In the meeting of the Council of Ministers on August 20, 1941, Mihai Antonescu declared: "[While] the Romanian army [is] operating in Ukraine, it has been agreed with the German High Command and Führer Hitler that administration of some territories beyond the Dniester . . . will be entrusted to the Romanian State. . . . In this moment . . . [W]e have agreed to occupy these territories military . . . We do not make any declaration of annexation."[46]

The vice chairman of the Council of Ministers made no bones explaining this about-turn. He referred to the unsolved Transylvanian issue that he defined as the number one priority of Romania's foreign policy. Under no circumstances would Romania agree to get Transnistria in exchange for permanently losing Transylvania, which meant for Romania much more than any other region:

> The Romanian Nation [*neam*] is a Carpathian nation; . . . here we were born and here we will die . . . this is why there is no connection between our extension in the east—while we are awaiting decisions which will be given to the Russian peace—and the Romanian Nation's rights over Transylvania . . .
>
> The Romanian Nation is not even discussing any compensation [for northern Transylvania] because nothing can compensate the sacred rights of a nation.[47]

Such strong rhetoric would be commonplace during the Antonescu regime. Perhaps the fact that both Antonescus and the great majority of their ministers and other appointees were *regățeni*, that is hailed from the so-called Old Kingdom or *Regat*, which existed from 1866 to 1918 and was approximately two times smaller than Greater Romania of 1918–1940, goes some way toward explaining this phenomenon. *Regățeni* ruled over Greater Romania for most of the interwar period but their near-monopoly on power caused tremendous consternation on the part of the elites in Transylvania, Bessarabia, and Bukovina. The antiestablishment coalition led by PNȚ stormed into power in 1928 riding on a wave of popular protest but was soon ousted from office. Regional tensions, mutual suspicions, and divided loyalties remained a constant in Romanian politics.[48] In 1941, with 140,000 refugees from northern Transylvania flooding Romanian cities, and PNȚ spreading its anti-Hungarian propaganda, being seen as sacrificing Transylvania for the sake of an alliance with Germany who decreed the Vienna diktat was something the regime simply could not afford.[49] Mihai Antonescu's message thus was, quite logically, first return of Transylvania, then talk about the future of Transnistria. When pressed, he would even state that he was ready to relinquish Transnistria in order to get Transylvania back: "But if in the future I will tell Germany: Romanian soldier has died for the future of Europe; I refuse the territory beyond the Dniester River for the sake of Transylvania, I need this diplomatic freedom of maneuver."[50] Ion Antonescu, too, probably following the advice of his Foreign Minister, firmly refused to declare annexation of Transnistria otherwise than within a framework of general peace after the war.[51] On February 11, 1942, on the occasion of Ion Antonescu's visit to Hitler's Wolfsschanze (Wolf's Lair; military headquarters on the Eastern Front), he remitted to his host a memorandum in which he affirmed the Romanian claims over Transylvania and her refusal to subordinate them to the common struggle in the east.[52]

If Romania was not annexing Transnistria, at least not immediately, what were the aims of its occupation? At the end of the day, occupation was costly and hazardous. The Hungarians, fighting side-by-side with the Germans and Romanians, did not create their own zone in the Soviet territory. Nor did the Italians, whose contribution to the war in the east was at least as important as that of the Romanians. Facing the necessity to explain his government's thinking on this issue, Mihai Antonescu offered, while speaking to his ministers in August 1942, a few rather disjointed and self-contradictory ideas. First, he envisaged using this region as a sui generis pawn in future negotiations over the general peace that would follow the defeat of the Soviet Union. The Romanian control over Transnistria would help persuade Moscow to return Romanian gold reserves evacuated to the Russian Empire in 1916, which the Bolshevik government refused to give back, as well as to pay compensation for damages inflicted by the Soviet occupation of Bessarabia and northern Bukovina in 1940–1941. It could also obtain better protection for all ethnic Romanians residing east of the Dniester River.[53] Had Mihai Antonescu stopped here, it might have appeared that the Romanian occupation of Transnistria was intended to be temporary and designed to obtain rather limited gains, but he went further, using this time quite ominous language.

Superior Romanian interests in the east, which, the vice chairman of the Council of Ministers intoned, coincided with their pan-European interests, consisted in preventing the formation of a new powerful Russian or, still worse, Ukrainian state. Either Russian or Ukrainian, such a state would be expansionist since the expansion was a fixture of the Slavic nature. Such a state would instinctively aim to reunite itself with Slavs in the Balkans. Thus, all Europe had to realize that the "Slavic mass threatened all institutions of civilization, that Germany had today been fighting a battle for the conservation of Europe, that beyond the struggle of nationalities and states, there has already started the struggle of races, envisioned by [Oswald] Spengler." Consequently, measures had to be taken to "break the unity of the Slavic race" and "to destroy the Slavic world . . . to reduce the power and biological potential of the Slavic race, that biological potential which, filled with primitive venom, etc."[54] This magniloquent nonsense, of which Mihai Antonescu was a great practitioner and fan, demonstrates how powerful was the attraction exercised by the Nazi racism over this Romanian leader, former pro-Western public intellectual. It also suggests that at that stage he saw the annexation of Transnistria as a necessary step in this struggle of the races and as the most likely outcome of the war.

The decision not to declare the annexation of Transnistria upset many a Romanian nationalist intellectual who rushed to express their enthusiasm over the region's occupation as soon as the Romanian troops' entry into Odessa was announced. On October 25, 1941, Hudița noted with indignation that the public lecture on the subject of German philosopher and educator Johann Friedrich Herbart—delivered by the Romanian philosopher and Minister of Culture and Cults Ion Petrovici at the Romanian Academy—was transformed into the obsequious demonstration of loyalty to the regime and its military successes. Public intellectuals of all stripes—left, right, and center—hurried to take part in it. Given the timing of the conference—barely a week after the fall of Odessa—the event was seen as an expression of public support for the German-Romanian brotherhood-in-arms in the east.[55] Hudița's own party, too, was divided over this issue so much so that it was only due to the tremendous moral authority of Maniu, who was unflinching in his conviction that Hitler would ultimately lose the war, that the party refrained from expressing its support for the conquest.[56] This stance, however, was so unpopular with the populace that, according to some, party members risked to be lynched if they tried to defend it publicly.[57]

Some ministers in the government were impassioned with the Antonescus' apparent caution and demanded an immediate declaration of annexation. As Minister Petrovici put it during the meeting of the Council of Ministers on January 23, 1942, "Up until today Romania has pursued a policy of defense . . . It did not stand us good stead. Now, if we have a chance of [territorial] expansion, let us do it. This is a sign of vitality." State Secretary at the Ministry of Finance and noted Romanian sociologist, Mircea Vulcănescu, supported Petrovici suggesting that the country could present this policy as the fulfillment of its "civilizing mission."[58] Governor of Transnistria Gheorghe Alexianu was also pressing for a speedy clarification of the territory's legal status saying that his employees wanted to be assured that they were laying the foundation of the Romanian rule in the province for many years ahead. The Conducător, however, would not budge. He told Alexianu that "many people" were petitioning him to annex the region without realizing full consequences of such action and that he would not follow such foolish advice.[59] The Romanian government-controlled press stacked with nationalistically minded journalists felt confused about the official stance on Transnistria and requested clarification. Mihai Antonescu's instruction—to emphasize "civilizing action" but keep silence over "political action of sovereignty"—did not seem to have satisfied them.[60]

The Conducător's stance on this issue was inconsistent. While refusing to declare annexation, he instructed Governor Alexianu to work in Transnistria "as if Romania has been installed in those territories for two million years"[61] On February 26, 1942, he went even further and talked about the future of the province as if it has already been decided: "It is no secret that I am not disposed to let go anything I have already grasped by my hand. Transnistria will become a Romanian province, we will make it Romanian and will get all foreigners [that is, nonethnic Romanians] out of there. I will bear this entire burden on my shoulders [but] make this desideratum a reality."[62]

Ion Antonescu was likely unaware that his instructions were contradictory: the territory could not be administered both as if it already were a part of Romania and as if under it were military occupation only. The problems were arising at every step. Because the occupier could not change the property relations, for example, the Romanians refused to return immovable property in the cities to the former owners from whom the Soviets confiscated them. Nor could the authorities disband the hated kolkhozes, although the local population was clamoring for the introduction of private property over land. The Soviet civil and criminal codes remained in force in Transnistria and in general, as Mihai Antonescu instructed Governor Alexianu on January 23, 1942, the occupation regime had "to take into account the transitional situation [of Transnistria]."[63] In practice, however, this latter instruction could not and was not followed consistently. For example, while in the cities the real estate was not returned to the former owners, in the countryside the former dekulakized peasants did get back their houses—to do otherwise was not politically feasible and such alternative was not even discussed.

The legal nature of the Romanian rule over Transnistria was thus only vaguely determined and to the extent that it was determined, it was not meant to be strictly applied. As will be shown throughout the book, both the Conducător and his ministers and appointees in the province were unwilling to remain within the limits defined by international law for military occupants. In the minds of the Romanian policymakers, refraining from declaring outright annexation did not necessarily entail providing protections envisaged in the international law for the local population. It was a figure of speech more than an exposition of governing philosophy.

CHAPTER 2

Defining Aims and Experiencing the Limits of Occupation

The idea to use Transnistria as a pawn to obtain various gains at the end of the war, either in bargaining with Russia, or Ukraine, or with Hungary and Germany, was part of Romania's grand strategy. Its application was supposed to wait until the end of the war. Mihai Antonescu's apocalyptic vision of "the destruction of the Slavic mass" was also of little practical use. What, then, about Romania's immediate aims there? Ion Antonescu gave two different answers to this question.

The first was, simply, that his task was to establish such an efficient and forward-looking administration capable of obtaining spectacular results in all spheres that "everybody"—by which he meant primarily Westerners, mostly Germans but also British, Americans, and French—would see that Romania was worthy to be raised to the higher level in the pecking order of European states. Ion Antonescu suffered from an acute inferiority complex, namely from a perception that his beloved Romania was looked down upon by other European states. He complained to his ministers that even his German allies would sometimes tell him that Romanians "were not capable of administering themselves."[1] He would sometimes go as far as to say that Romania was "an Abyssinia of Europe"—quite an astonishing declaration for a self-professed Romanian nationalist.[2] From his perspective, as well as from the perspective of other nationalists such as his minister Petrovici, raising his country's ranking required it ruling over other peoples, and ruling in an orderly, efficient, and "civilized" manner, comparable to how other European powers were supposedly ruling over their Asian and African subjects. This is what he said to the Council of Ministers on November 13, 1941. When Governor Alexianu raised the issue of methods of economic exploitation of Transnistria, the Conducător interrupted him: "We pursue in Transnistria an important political scope. . . . we need to demonstrate in the face of history, in the face of humanity, and in the face of even of our own country, that we are able to administer ourselves. . . . to demonstrate in the face of history and of Europe that we are able to administer a larger country."[3] Two days later, in a note scribbled on Alexianu's request to send to Transnistria the best civil servants from Bucharest's government departments, he wrote: "Yes. The whole prestige of this country is engaged in Transnistria. We have to demonstrate that we are able to administer a larger country. For that, we need [there] select people, in whom we can trust because they are energetic, perspicacious, conscientious, and honest.[4]"

Paradoxically, the quality of civil service in Romania—a serious problem, given the shortage of trained personnel on all levels—was to rank second after that employed in Transnistria. Indeed, Ion Antonescu took Transnistrian project close to heart. He wanted to make Transnistria a showcase or, as he put it, a "model" province both for the outside world, as proof of the Romanians' calling to the higher civilizing mission in Eastern Europe, and for Romanians, as evidence that his administration was capable of working miracles where others failed.

FIGURE 3. Opening of the exhibition "Transnistria" in Bucharest, October 1942. Transnistria's new coat of arms is on the top of the column. Inscription on the column reads "Through storm and fire, on the wings of sacrifice, work, and calling, a new world is being forged (zeește)." Courtesy DANIC.

Still, as was often the case with the Conducător, having issued these categorical instructions about the primacy of political over economic aims in Transnistria, he almost immediately directed his administration in the opposite direction. In the same meeting of the Council of Ministers on November 13, 1941, while addressing Alexianu, Ion Antonescu said:

> As I told you, this Transnistria has to live from her own resources . . . because in Romania we do not have any kind of resources to support it: neither agricultural, nor industrial, nor commercial.
>
> In the second place, this province has to cover costs of provisions and other needs of troops deployed there.
>
> In the third place, Transnistria has to cover, in the largest possible measure—neither me nor you are not [yet] aware of how big these possibilities are—our war expenses . . . the war has cost us 170 billion lei and we will exert efforts to pull out 10–15–20 or 40 billion lei from Transnistria. If we stay longer and pull out more from there, then even better.[5]

The cited numbers were indeed astonishing. In 1941, Romania's population (without Bessarabia and northern Bukovina) was about 13,250,000. By November 1941, Romania spent on war—at the tremendous cost to its economy and standard of living—170 billion lei. Now he expected that a province with 2,500,000 residents and the economy ravaged by the Soviet scorched-earth policy, war actions, and the breakdown of economic ties with the rest of the USSR, would support an occupation army of 170,000 and, on top of that, contribute up to 40 billion lei to Romania's war effort.[6]

Evidently, this could be achieved, if it could be achieved at all, solely by means of ruthless exploitation of the local population, and Ion Antonescu made no bones that he was fully aware and approving of that. At the December 16, 1941 meeting of the Council of Ministers, Governor Alexianu complained that he was "disappointed" that the local population had not accorded necessary "assistance" for carrying out agricultural work and suggested that he needed to apply force to "pull them out to work," since this is how they are used to be treated. The Conducător immediately agreed:

> You pull out people to work even with a whip if they do not understand.
>
> . . . If a peasant does not come to work, pull him out even with a bullet. For this, you do not need my authorization.
>
> We made them a favor by saving them, and if they do not understand, then treat them as animals, with a lash.
>
> Ahead of their interests, there stand interests of the Romanian State, and these interests require that we pull out as much as we can

[from Transnistria] for the economic needs of the war, and especially for the future operations, so that we could support ourselves by pulling out from there. I do not bring there any food supply from Romania.[7]

That "pulling out as much resources as possible from Transnistria" by violent means and regardless of the costs to the local population, was hardly conducive to transforming Transnistria into a showcase for his regime, did not occur to the Conducător. As will become evident below, such *governmentality* was shared by many an administrator in Transnistria. In reality, the perceived need to ruthlessly exploit the province economically would eventually overwhelm all other aims of Romanian occupiers in the region.

The Issues of Sovereignty

On November 26, 1941, Mihai Antonescu had a conversation in Berlin with Hermann Göring, Reichsmarschall and the second most powerful man in Germany at the time. Exhilarated by the supposedly sincere expressions of Göring's sympathy for Romania's continued claims to northern Transylvania, vice chairman of the council of ministers recalled in his dictated report on the meeting that Reichsmarschall expressed his grief over that loss: "For the time being, you have Transnistria. Use it as you want and as long as you want. Its borders are not determined yet." The next day Hitler repeated this sentiment almost verbatim, "You have in the east unlimited rights and powers: take there as much as you want."[8] Had Mihai Antonescu been less prone to self-delusion, he could have retorted to his interlocutors that reality on the ground had already belied their pretended generosity. Not only were the borders of Transnistria delimited by this time, but the Romanians' rights and powers in that region had been checked by their ruthless ally. As time progressed, the situation got worse for them.

The exact borders of Transnistria were defined in German-Romanian negotiations in Bessarabia city of Tighina (Bender/Bendery) on the Dniester River, on August 28–30. Generalmajor Hauffe represented the German side, and General de Brigadă Nicolae Tătăranu, the Romanian side. Two problems caused some tension. The first was Transnistria's northern border—Romanians wanted to push it up to the north of the strategically important railway hub of Zhmerynka (Jmerinca in Romanian transcription), together with the nearby town of Bar, but the Germans resisted this proposal. The rest of the borders—the coast of the Black Sea, the Dniester River in the west and the southern Buh River in the east—were self-evident. Representatives failed to agree on the northern border and left the issue to the heads of state. Although the exact date of Hitler-Antonescu agreement is not known, it is certain that by the end of October both sides considered Transnistria's norther border defined in accordance with earlier Romanian requests.[9] The second point of contention was Antonescu's decision to create civil administration of the region, directly subordinated to himself as the head of the country's armed forces, rather than to the local military command. This effectively removed Transnistrian administration out of Wehrmacht control. Despite their consternation, the Germans could but acquiesce.[10]

On August 30, Hauffe and Tătăranu signed an "Agreement Concerning Security, Administration, and Economic Exploitation of the Territories between the Dniester and Buh Rivers (Transnistria) and the Buh and Dnieper River (Buh-Dnieper Region)" also known as the Tighina Convention. Art. 1 defined responsibilities in the following manner: in Transnistria, the Romanians were responsible for security, administration, and economic exploitation, with the exception of transmissions and communications, whose regime was subject to regulations provided for in art. 3; in the Buh-Dnieper region, administration and economic exploitation were Germany's responsibility while Romania was responsible for security. Art. 2 defined the strength of the Romanian military responsible for security in both regions. Two to three army corps were expected to be entrusted with this task, out of which one would always be deployed in Transnistria and another in the territory between the Buh and Dnieper rivers. The overall strengths had to be of approximately seven infantry divisions and two cavalry brigades. Romanian forces in the territory between the Buh and Dnieper rivers were to be "utilized" on the orders of the commander of the German Army Group "South," but they were to be "subordinated" to the commander of the Romanian Army Corps. What this would mean in practice had to be determined in a separate convention. The involvement of the local civil residents in enforcing security and order was deemed desirable under the proviso that they would not be armed. German "Liaison Units" subordinated to the German Army Mission in Romania would remain under the Romanian army command.

Art. 3 was the longest and the most detailed. It established German almost total control over railway communications in Transnistria. A German "Board of Transportation" in Odessa was to be set up with the mission to exercise such control. Most important, railway stations were subordinated to local German boards functioning under the supervision of German board in Odessa. Romanians were supposed to have their representatives alongside those boards. Germans committed themselves to remake Odessa-Balta railway into one of European size (Russian tracks are wider than European) and expected Romanians to do the same with respect to tracks Odessa-Razdelnaia and Râbniţa-Balta. River transportation was also to be under German control. Maritime transports on the Black Sea were to be governed by mutual agreement of the two sides' respective maritime authorities. Highways and bridges were to be maintained by the Romanian army rear services, with the advice of the German Commander of Pioneers entrusted with such mission by the German Military Mission in Romania. Telephone lines were to be maintained by the Romanians who were also expected to build a new line from the Romanian city of Bacău to Odessa and farther eastward to Mykolaiv across the Buh. Romanians were responsible for the security of railways, highways, and transmission lines.

Art. 4 dealt with economic exploitation of Transnistria. Romanian administration had to be subordinated to a head who, "in the interests of common prosecution of the war, in areas of decisive importance depended on the directives received from the Supreme [Romanian] Military Commander in Transnistria." This chief could request a counselor from the Germans. Economic exploitation of the region was to be the responsibility of the Romanian army rear services, which was supposed collaborate with the "Liaison Office of the German Wehrmacht in Odessa" (Verbindungsstelle der Deutschen Wehrmacht in Odessa). This office would be responsible for the provisioning of German troops deployed in the region and for "helping the Romanian army rear services to collect and share materials necessary for carrying out common operations and to determine, by a common agreement, the means necessary for the conduct of war, according to the following principles: all stocks would be ascertained jointly. Romanian occupation troops, administration, and population would get their share. Surplus quantities would be put at the disposal of common operation. In case of operational interests, the needs of the operative troops would prevail over those of the army of occupation, administration, and population."

Art. 5 regulated distribution of war trophies. The general principle was, "What Romanian troops ceased, remains Romanian war trophies; what German troops ceased, remains German war trophies," although the Germans promised to transfer to the Romanians four stocks of captured goods in Transnistria (no further details provided). Art. 6 provided for speedy replacement of German agricultural managers in Transnistria imposed by the Eleventh Army by Romanian managers. Art. 7 dealt with the issue of deportation of Jews to the east (this issue is discussed later in this chapter). Art. 8 noted that the Romanians would control the Transnistrian border in the west, along the Dniester River; while the Germans would control it in the north and east, along the Buh River. Art. 9 stated: "Clearing of accounts of goods shipped out of Transnistria would be accomplished later by Romanian and German local authorities."[11]

As this summary suggests, the Convention severely limited the sovereignty of Romania in Transnistria in all matters, not only military. In fact, the Germans used the pretext of military necessity to have their prying eye in the collection and distribution of military booty, deliveries of provisions to the troops stationed there and elsewhere, as well as in seizure of assets found in the province. They also laid claim to a part of Transnistrian produce. Finally, under the apparently innocuous pretext of giving "advice" in administrative matters, the Germans intended to influence Romania's decision making. Stretching the provisions of the Convention, German would manage to maintain substantial presence in Transnistria throughout the whole period of occupation. German construction company operated in Transnistria, and German air and naval bases were built and maintained in Odessa, Ochakov, and Golta.[12] One of the most sensitive issues was that of control over the railways, the key transportation arteries in the region.

Controlling Communications in Transnistria

At the November 13, 1941 meeting of the Committee of Ministers, Governor Alexianu and Minister of Public Works and Communications Constantin Buşilă complained of German control over the railways that severely limited their ability to ship agricultural goods from Transnistria into Romania—an urgent issue at the time. As Buşilă explained, every shipment had to be coordinated with the German central office in Berlin that was not fully appraised of the situation in the province. The Conducător's reaction was swift and energetic: "This administration [of the railways] has to be transferred to us. This was an omission in the Convention; it was my omission. Now we came across difficulties and in order to overcome them, we need a Romanian administration . . . because otherwise we cannot have a good administration there, being at Berlin's discretion. . . . the administration must be Romanian in its entirety."[13] He ordered for the issue to be renegotiated via diplomatic channels, that is bypassing Wehrmacht High Command, and even threatened that in case the Germans would be recalcitrant, he would withdraw from Transnistria back to the west of the Dniester. The negotiations lasted approximately four months and the convention was signed probably in early March 1942 with railways transferred by the end of that month into the Romanian hands.[14] The particulars of this negotiations and a copy of the convention did not seem to have surfaced so far but it is clear that it provided for the railway takeover by the Romanian state Railway Company CFR.[15] Thus, the Germans ceded to the Romanians demands on this important issue.

The same happened with control over the ports, primarily over the great port of Odessa: with the exceptions of military installations, commercial facilities were eventually transferred into the Romanian hands. As Ion Antonescu interpreted the Tighina Convention in the meeting of the Council of Ministers on March 27, 1942, the Romanians agreed to the German control over Odessa port because they did not have enough trained engineers to repair damages caused by the Bolsheviks' scorched-earth policy; German control was thus intended to be provisional. He referred to his (otherwise unknown) conversation with the Führer, in which Hitler asked him to let the Germans use the port for their own purposes, thus implicitly recognizing Romania's sovereignty.[16] This, however, was not the impression of the Romanian officials in Odessa, who complained that initially the Germans showed no intention to cede control over the port of Odessa.[17] Nevertheless, on June 10, 1942, the Romanians did obtain control over the port from the Germans.[18] Tensions over this issue would continue to flare up periodically. In the meeting of the Council of Ministers on August 27, 1942, under secretary of state of the Ministry of National Economy responsible for the supplies for the army and civil population, General Constantin Constantin complained about German kommodore (also referred to as Colonel) Astmann (also rendered as Hastmann, Hausmann) who not only refused to assist the Romanians in their effort to ship grain collected in Transnistria to Romania from Odessa but even stated that they needed not to worry since all grain from the region would be shipped to the German troops fighting on the Eastern Front.[19] In the eyes of the Romanians, this was one more sign that the Germans interpreted the Tighina Convention differently: as a kind of condominium with equal participation instead of territory under the Romanian sovereignty.[20] Mihai Antonescu raised the issue in his negotiations with the German foreign minister Joachim von Ribbentrop on September 22–23 in the latter's Feldquartier in Zhytomyr, Ukraine. As Antonescu bragged to the ministers on September 29, 1942, when he handed over his memorandum to Ribbentrop on this issue, the latter—"with loyalty that deserves specials thanks"—immediately concurred and ordered Karl Ritter, his liaison officer for Wehrmacht, to let German General Staff know that these issues surpass the army's competence and "that in any case Colonel Astmann could not communicate in such terms with the Romanian Government." Ribbentrop assured the Romanian that "all necessary forms would be found to guarantee you . . . indispensable transports."[21] The pompous and self-congratulatory tone with which vice chairman of the council of ministers recounted this story suggests that he considered this confirmation of Romanian rights from Ribbentrop an important diplomatic victory. Nevertheless, as he told the ministers on October 6, 1942, he still had to meet two more times with the same German commodore of the Odessa port and to threaten him with a complaint to the Führer for the latter to comply. Mihai Antonescu believed from that moment on the Germans would adhere to the interpretation of the Tighina Convention to the Romanians' satisfaction. Indeed, Romanians did not seem to have major problems of this kind through the end of their rule over the province.[22]

Dividing Transnistrian Booty

As these episodes suggest, control over communication lines was tied up with the issue of extracting economic resources, primarily agricultural goods, from Transnistria. German strategy in World War II was predicated on the extraction of food from the occupied eastern territories—particularly from Ukraine, which was considered a "breadbasket of Europe"—both for the troops and for Germany's civilian population. German planners perceived ruthless extraction of agricultural resources as a conditio sine qua non for victory.[23] No wonder then that the German army rear services were scouring for local resources for their own use.

The problems between Romanians and Germans in Transnistria started as soon as their troops entered the region. Although both Romanian and German army commanders issued orders strictly forbidding "savage requisitions"—that is, requisitions exceeding what was strictly necessary for the provision of troops without leaving the necessary minimum for the survival of the locals—evidence abounds that these regulations were not observed.[24] In late summer or early fall of 1941 (the exact date is not indicated in the document), the Office of the Studies of the newly appointed Governor Alexianu reported that in Ovidiopol județ "operational troops seized every-thing, including seed reserves."[25] According to the German sources, Roma-nian troops requisitioned local food reserves without regard to the existing regulations, with quotas being regularly exceeded due to the multiple requi-sitions from the same localities, and Romanian soldiers resorting to plunder whenever they felt they were under-provisioned by their own rear services. Since, as Baum suggests, Romanian rear services were severely underde-veloped and could not cope with logistical difficulties of waging a war far away from their national territory, under-provisioning of Romanian troops was more the norm than the exception. Acts of physical violence and rape of local women often accompanied disorganized requisitions and outright plunder by individual Romanian soldiers. Baum suggests that some of these "excesses" were due to the traditions of warfare in the Balkans according to which violence against civilians was a legitimate means of retribution and intimidation of the enemy but whether that was indeed so or a sheer lack of discipline was a sole and sufficient reason for Romanian "excesses" is anyone's guess.[26]

As soon as Transnistria had been conquered by the Axis powers and operative troops left its territory, it was the Romanians' turn to complain about wild requisitions by the Germans. On November 20, 1941, Governor Alexianu requested that the commander of the Third Romanian Army increase border troops along the Buh River because the existing garrisons had so far been unable to stop German and Hungarian servicemen from crossing the river from the east into the Romanian zone. There, they "loaded and shipped away animals, foods, cereals, and all other sorts of goods without having any approval [for this from the Romanian authorities] and without leaving any receipt or payment for the seized goods."[27] According to the data composed by prefect of the Balta judeţ, by November 17, 1942, Germans illegally shipped from this territory about 348 tons of cereals, about 313 tons of barley, 1,502 cows, 1,812 sheep, 426 pigs, and other products. Farmers complained to Romanian authorities about such incidents, often accompanied by threats and beatings, but the latter could effectively intervene only when plaintiffs could indicate the names of the soldiers involved and numbers of their units, which apparently was possible only in exceptional cases.[28] At the December 16, 1941 meeting of the Council of Ministers, Ion Antonescu also grumbled about the lack of proper "supervision" in Transnistria that allegedly led to the Germans requisitioning "as many [cereals] as they could."[29] "You should not let things like this happen any longer," the Conducător ordered Governor Alexianu. "Transnistria is ours and nobody is allowed to interfere there."[30]

From the end of 1941, the number of complaints about the German troops' requisitions decreased dramatically but soon another issue came to the fore. In the spring of 1942, Hermann Neubacher, German Nazi diplomat stationed in Bucharest with the title of "Special Representative for the Economic Transportation Issues" (Sonderbevollmächtigte für Wirtschafts- und Transportfragen), visited Transnistria and suggested to Governor Alexianu to sign a special export-import agreement with the Reich, to which the Romanian responded positively.[31] Alexianu's report to Mihai Antonescu on this issue provoked a strong reaction on the part of the latter, who saw in German initiative not only a breach of Romania's sovereignty but also a backdoor attempt by Romania's powerful ally to divert Transnistria's resources from Romania's pressing needs for Germany's benefits.[32] This was an entirely plausible interpretation, given that trade between Germany and Romania was conducted on the basis of negotiated prices heavily skewed in favor of Germany and on the exchange rate that artificially inflated Reichsmark's value. Mihai Antonescu immediately banned any such dealings without preliminary clearance from the government in Bucharest. Soon after, however, he faced renewed German pressure to share Transnistrian resources.

As Antonescu explained to the ministers and governors of the "liberated" provinces on August 16, 1942, Romanian government had of late been facing demands to supply Axis powers' troops, which at the time were fighting in Crimea and the northern Caucasus, with provisions from Transnistria. That ran against the Germans' practice of supplying their troops from the territories under their military, as opposed to the civilian, occupation. Provisions from the regions under civilian administration were shipped to the Reich. The problem was further complicated by the rudimentary character of the Romanians' supply services that made their troops at the front dependent on the supplies they received from Wehrmacht rear administrations. By attempting to shift this onerous obligation onto the Romanians, the Germans intended to free these resources for their own use. Mihai Antonescu resolutely resisted this venture. He perceived behind it an attempt to reinterpret the Tighina Convention in a way that would transform Transnistria into a condominium that would allow Germany full access to its resources. Instead, the vice chairman of the council of ministers argued that Transnistria, although not part of Romania proper, was under the Romanian sovereignty. As an occupier, Romania had the right, in conformity with international law, to appropriate all war trophies in the territory.[33] It should be noted that Romanian rulers loosely interpreted the concept of "trophy," including in it all goods they might, for any reason, find useful for their country. (I will return to this problem in chapter 7). The Conducător was particularly outspoken in this regard, ruling that as an occupier Romania could take "all it wanted" from Transnistria.[34]

Following this logic, Mihai Antonescu insisted that if anything was left in the region, which Romania could appropriate and ship away but did not do so, it should be considered a Romanian investment there. Besides, Romanian state did invest in the repair and improvement of roads, railways, bridges, as well as restoration of factories damaged by the Soviets during their withdrawal and/or by military action when Romanians were interested in the products the factories manufactured. All of this meant that all of the region's resources rightfully belonged to Romania, otherwise they were not interested in administering a region at their own expense. Transnistria belonged to Romania and Romania only and if Germans wanted to get any goods from it, they could receive them solely within the framework of overall clearing agreement with Romania, so that exports from Transnistria would be assimilated to the exports from Romania proper, and German payments in goods and services would be delivered to Romania, not Transnistria. That was the meaning, Mihai Antonescu insisted, of a protocol signed with Carl Clodius, head of the commercial policy section of the German Foreign Ministry (Leiter der Handelspolitischen Abteilung des Auswärtiges Amtes), which designated Transnistria as part of the Romanian "economic space."[35] According to Mihai Antonescu, during his talks with Ribbentrop, it was decided that provisioning of Romanian troops on the Eastern Front was not the Romanians' responsibility and that they would be provisioned by the German rear services from the territory in which they were deployed. On that occasion, Ribbentrop confirmed that Romanians' occupation rights over Transnistria were unquestionable.[36] Vice chairman of the council of ministers ruled that goods could be exported from Transnistria to Germany but only within a special quote for the region shown on the export page of the clearing agreement between the two countries.[37]

For the time, it seems, Romanians obtained what they wanted. Even when, in January 1944, German operative troops, in their endeavor to stop the Soviet advance across the Buh in the direction of Vinnytsia and the Dniester, entered northern Transnistria where they conducted successful defensive operations, they carried out requisitions for their own provisioning in full cooperation with Romanian administration. For the goods received, they issued required receipts to the satisfaction of Governor Alexianu, thus giving the Romanian government a reason to believe that they would include these deliveries within Romanian exports to Germany.[38] Such hopes would soon prove illusory. When on February 23, 1944, Mihai Antonescu informed his ministers of the ongoing negotiations with Clodius on a renewed accord on commercial and financial cooperation, he described them as "the most difficult" he ever conducted with the Germans. His counterpart flatly refused to promise any deliveries to the Romanians while insisting that the latter increase the volume of theirs. The Germans' blood sacrifices in the war against the common enemy, he claimed, gave them the right to demand as much.[39] As to Transnistria, the Germans invoked the Tighina Convention, which they interpreted in the sense that this province "being an element of military occupation was left, in accordance with the Führer's letter, to Romania; this, however, did not mean that it stopped to be occupied by the German troops as well. In other words, Germany [did] not consider itself obliged to pay for anything it received from Transnistria." The Germans refused to accept as a subject of discussion even the expenses that the Romanian railways incurred while transporting their troops within Transnistria.[40]

By this time, German-Romanian relations had deteriorated to the point that all traces of earlier trust and cordiality disappeared. Between October 25 and December 15, 1943, Hitler and Ion Antonescu exchanged remarkably frank and unfriendly letters, which brought the existing tensions to the forefront and, in all probability, made matters even worse. When Hitler, citing the deteriorating situation at the front, requested the Romanian troops' more active participation in the defense of Transnistria, Antonescu refused, claiming the lack of sufficiently trained and armed troops—a circumstance he attributed to Germany's failure to live up to its obligation to deliver the necessary materiel and instructors. He reminded Hitler of Romania's previous sacrifices in the war, which were higher than of any other German ally (he meant primarily Hungary) but which were not adequately valued by Berlin. To add insult to injury, Antonescu declined Hitler's request to transfer Transnistrian railways to the German administration. Hitler answered by asserting that Romania's very existence was due to Germany's protection against Bolshevism. Romania's national interests would be better served, he maintained, by active participation in the common war effort, not by petty squabbles over financials particulars.[41] Clodius's brazen claims thus not only represented a reversal of a previous German stance on the issue but also reflected a fundamental change in the Nazi leadership's policy toward Romania.[42] No agreement was reached on this issue, as well as on many others during these negotiations, so that Ion Antonescu's insisting that Romania's position on the accounts between Germany and Transnistria remained unchanged and that "the issue was not closed as long as our troops fight alongside the German soldiers," was no more than a face-saving gesture.[43]

By the time these discussions were taking place, legal status and institutional set-up in Transnistria underwent a transformation. On January 29, 1944, the Conducător dismissed Alexianu from the position of governor and abolished civilian administration of Transnistria. This decision was as much due to the deterioration of the region's strategic position, which led to its de facto transformation in operational troops rear area, and thus made existence of a separate civilian administration a nuisance to the unified military control as to the increased tension between the governor's office known as *guvernământ* and Bucharest ministries. The latter grew increasingly suspicious of what they perceived as Alexianu's opaque dealings and creative accountancy which, they felt, concealed gross financial mismanagement (I will return to this subject in the next chapters).[44] One of the issues that came up during the investigations of Transnistrian accounting records was a sloppy recording of deliveries to the German troops whose growing numbers in the region consumed a constantly increasing share of its resources. As it turned out, Alexianu's numbers were invariably much higher than those shown by the Germans, and the governor had no proof that would substantiate his claims.[45] Still, the Conducător was loath to humiliate his erstwhile favorite administrator by publicly firing him for mismanagement. Instead, using the military situation as a pretext, he abolished the *guvernământ* and replaced it by a military administration of the territory between the Dniester and Buh rivers (even the name of Transnistria was thus dropped).[46]

General Gheorghe Potopeanu, who was put in charge of this newly created administration, oversaw the "evacuation" of Transnistrian industrial assets to Romania (code-named "Operation 1111"), starting in March 1943.[47] That remained his major preoccupation through March 15, 1944, when he issued an order to withdraw all remaining personnel from the province and to end "Operation 1111."[48] By that time, the German troops were in full control of the province and were requisitioning provisions without any regard to the Romanian claims to its still overtly recognized sovereignty over it and the local population's needs.[49]

Volksdeutschen in Transnistria

Another thorn in the side of Romania's administration's in Transnistria was a rather numerous, about 130,000-strong minority of ethnic Germans (a little more than 5 percent of the province's overall population).[50] Targeted by the Nazi leaders and in particular Himmler—in his capacity of the Reich commissioner for the Consolidation of German Nationhood (Reichskommissar für die Festigung deutschen Volkstums)—for the reeducation, strengthening, and transformation into bastion of "Germandom," this community was transformed into a veritable "state within a state," to the chagrin and constant irritation of the Romanian authorities in the region.

Descendants of "colonists," invited by the Russian Imperial government to settle in the newly acquired and sparsely populated territories to the north of the Black Sea, they lived mostly in tightly knit rural communities with a minority of them residing in the cities. Ethnic German villages varied in size widely, from small hamlets to townlets with thousands of residents. Their exact number is not known. When in mid-1942 the *guvernământ* requested from prefectures information to that effect, eleven out of twelve replied, providing names for 185 localities overall.[51] The real number was probably a little higher. When in late September 1941, SS Sonderkommando-R (SK-R), tasked by Himmler with organizing, protecting, and reeducating the Soviet

Volksdeutsche, arrived at Transnistria, they found an impoverished and deeply traumatized ethnic group.[52]

In the early twentieth century, the Volksdeutsche farmers were—because of the privileges they were granted by the tsarist authorities and because of their higher educational level and agricultural skills—the most prosperous part of the region's rural population. However, the Great War marked the beginning of their decline both in terms of social status and material well-being. First discriminated against and repressed by the tsarist authorities during World War I as part of the "enemy nation," they found themselves on the wrong side during the Russian Civil War in which they supported the Whites. Under the Bolsheviks, the Black Sea Germans (*Schwarzmeerdeutschen*), as they were also known, suffered disproportionally, first as "class enemies" due to their relative prosperity, and, in the late 1930s, as members of a politically unreliable minority that was potentially spawning ground for the Nazi spies. According to the data collected by the Sonderkommando-R and cited by Eric Steinhart, no less than 17 percent of this population were deported by the Soviets by the time they withdrew from the province, with heads of households predominating among the deportees.[53] With their religious leadership decimated, most churches closed (85 percent of the Black Sea Germans were Catholics, the rest Protestants), all independent political and cultural activity forbidden, their communities' social fabric was irreparably damaged. Besides, their previously notoriously closed settlements became increasingly heterogeneous due to the influx of ethnic outsiders provoked by the unprecedented social upheaval of the 1930s and encouraged by the Bolshevik regime.[54]

Sonderkommando-R, led by SS-Oberführer Horst Hoffmeyer and numbering about 250 men and women (the latter serving mostly as nurses) had responsibility for all Volksdeutsche communities in the Soviet Union—an obviously impossible task. Of those, Transnistrian Volksdeutschen were the most compact and numerous community. Consequently, Hoffmeyer appointed his deputy SS-Obersturmführer Dr. Klaus Siebert head of the Transnistrian Volksdeutsche administration in the region; approximately one-half—120 to 150 members—of Hoffmeyer's men were to assist Siebert in this gargantuan job.[55] Faced with deplorable conditions of their charges, Siebert's men proceeded to 1) ethnically purify their communities; 2) consolidate their settlements; 3) protect them from Romanian pillaging and what they saw as excessive demands of the Romanian administration; 4) improve their material conditions; and last but not least, 5) reeducate in National Socialist ideology.[56]

Some of the SK-R policies had a direct bearing on the Romanian interests in Transnistria. For example, ethnic purification of the Volksdeutsche villages started with apprehension and murder of Jews and their children from mixed marriages. By the time SK-R established its headquarters in the town of Landau, Berezovca județ, and Siebert appointed district commanders (Bereichskommandoführer) to police ethnic German settlements, most Jews there were murdered by SS-Einsatzgruppe D that ravaged Transnistrian Jewish communities in July–August 1941.[57] However, ethnic Germans often hid those Jews who were married into their families. SK-R was determined to complete this unfinished business. They invested considerable efforts in ferreting out and murdering Jewish survivors, as well as their offspring, an "operation" that lasted well into the fall of 1941.[58] This campaign was of no consequence to the Romanian authorities, who never protested or as much as mentioned it in their bureaucratic correspondence. Perhaps this is unsurprising, given that the Romanians' own anti-Semitic violence reached its peak during that same period. When, however, SK-R turned against Christian aliens residing in predominantly ethnic German settlements, the Romanians protested. True, Germans were not murdering these people, at least not en masse, as they did Jews; they were "just" expelling them but because many of the expellees had nowhere to go, they turned to the Romanians for protection. The authorities felt obliged to respond, perhaps not so much because of their sympathy toward the victims' plight as owing to the Germans' acting without prior consulting them, thus undermining their prestige in the eyes of the locals. The situation was especially humiliating when the Germans victimized ethnic Romanians, or Moldovans, whom the Romanians considered their brothers worthy of special protection.

For example, on September 29, 1941, Berezovca județ prefect colonel Loghin reported to Governor Alexianu that the ethnic German mayor (installed by either the German army or SK-R) in the village of Șevcenco (Shevchenko) expelled local Romanians from the village.[59] In fact, as follows from the reports the prefect received from his subordinates on the accident, the ethnic German mayor expelled not only ethnic Romanians but Ukrainians and other non-German Christians, too. Moreover, he showed some leniency toward ethnic Romanians, letting them stay through the spring while other "aliens" had to leave immediately. The mayor explained that ethnic Germans were expropriated during collectivization and were now reclaiming what was legitimately theirs. One Ukrainian resident ordered out of the village explained that he had relocated there on the Soviet authorities' orders during collectivization as a kulak. Now he had nowhere to go.[60] In the village of Veselinovo, Berezovca județ, German militiamen executed one ethnic Moldovan, and when the Romanians requested explanations, refused to as much as talk to them. A gendarmerie lieutenant who reported this case to

Prefect Loghin opined that such actions could lead "to an uprising against Romanians, who no longer commanded any respect from the local population."[61] From conversations with ethnic German residents, Prefect Loghin got the impression that the "Germans were preparing colonization of Transnistria." Authorities installed by SK-R took no orders from the Romanians while their Volksdeutsche charges learned from them arrogant ways toward the Romanians whom they called "Gypsies," a highly insulting ethnic slur.[62] Likewise, complaints came from Tiraspol județ.[63] When ethnic Germans were in an insignificant minority in a village, they were ordered into a locality with a preponderance of ethnic Germans from which nonethnic Germans were mercilessly expelled. In a particularly egregious case, in Grosulovo raion of Tiraspol județ, sixty-five Ukrainian families were expelled to make room for eight German families[64] While being transferred, ethnic Germans took with themselves a disproportionate share of kolkhoz property but while expelling ethnic Ukrainians, they let them take only their personal belongings.[65]

On October 5, 1941, Alexianu reported these problems to Mihai Antonescu and requested their clarification with the German government.[66] The issue came for discussion in the meeting of the Council of Ministers of November 13, 1941. There, Ion Antonescu ruled, "nobody can interfere in [ethnic] German communes—not even SS. . . . We have to make a written presentation to Mr. [Ambassador of Germany von] Killinger in which it should be made clear that under such conditions I am not able to take responsibility for the organization of good administration in Transnistria. Either there is a single rule, or I withdraw from there."[67] Those were, however, just words. Expulsions and purifications along the lines prescribed by SK-R continued unabated. When on November 21, 1941, Oceacov județ prefect lieutenant colonel Vasile Gorschi requested instructions as to how to react to such actions in the localities under his jurisdiction, Alexianu responded that "the German population exchange is an issue that pertains to them; you must look past it in order to avoid any conflict."[68] Such operations lasted well into 1942. In March 1942, Alexianu complained to Hoffmeyer that in Berezovca județ violent expulsions of the "Ukrainians and even Moldovans" to whom no share of the kolkhoz property was allotted taking place every day.[69] All things considered, the Germans succeeded in ethnic consolidation of Volksdeutsche villages on their terms because the Romanians abandoned their policy of protecting the Transnistrian Christian non-ethnic German population.

With regard to the other problems created by the SK-R policies, the Romanians were more successful in defending their own interests. First among them was the issue of a fiscal obligation of Volksdeutschen vis-à-vis the Romanian administration. Initially, ethnic Germans, incited by the Wehrmacht troops, refused to fulfill any obligations before the Romanian administration and troops, including payment of any taxes or deliveries. Ethnic Germans, empowered by the German troops and armed by SK-R, pillaged kolkhoz assets, both those whose members they were and in the neighboring settlements. For example, in the village of Raidolna (probably wrong spelling), Berezovca județ, according to the report of a gendarme officer of October 3, 1941, an unidentified German officer accompanied by armed ethnic German civilians, seized fifteen horses, thirteen cows, and sixty-five sheep whom they then brought to the neighboring German villages and distributed to the residents. When the Ukrainians protested this seizure, a German officer threatened them with a revolver.[70] At the same time, ethnic Germans refused to submit to the Romanian troops' demands for requisition, even if it was carried, as far as one can rely on the Romanian accounts, with legal formalities. On August 17, 1941, Ion Antonescu complained to General Eugen Ritter von Schobert, Commander of the Eleventh German Army (whose commanding officer Antonescu ostensibly was) that in the territory to the east of the Dniester, "German military organs . . . prevented the Romanian troops from requisitioning animals and provisions, particularly in [ethnic] German localities."[71] More often than not, they simply refused to obey the Romanian authorities' orders or allow billeting their troops in ethnic German villages or surrender 50 percent of their harvest to the authorities as all agricultural producers were supposed to do.[72]

In the late fall of 1941, tensions between the two allies escalated, requiring urgent diplomatic mitigation on the national government level. On November 14–15, Mihai Antonescu negotiated an agreement with German minister (ambassador) in Bucharest, Manfred Freiherr von Killinger, based on proposals submitted by SS-Oberführer Hoffmeyer. Its conditions, laid out in an exchange of letters between Mihai Antonescu and von Killinger, were defined in an agreement signed on December 15, 1941. This understanding provided for broad autonomy for the Transnistrian German communities that were to be governed by an office of Volksdeutsche Mittelstelle (VoMi), or Main Welfare Office for Ethnic Germans in Odessa. Headed by SS-Obergruppenführer Werner Lorenz, since 1939 VoMi was subordinated to Heinrich Himmler in his capacity of the Reich Commissioner for the Consolidation of German Nationhood. In Transnistria VoMi was equivalent, for all practical purposes, to SK-R. Mayors and other authorities in the German settlements were to be appointed by VoMi and "confirmed" by the Romanian prefects. Armed ethnic German militia was to be under the exclusive control of VoMi, too. Public school instructors in German localities were to be appointed by VoMi, and education was to conform to VoMi's instructions. However, the costs of maintenance of schools, churches, hospitals, cinemas, public baths, and other institutions of similar character in German localities were to be defrayed by the Romanian state. In turn, the Romanians obtained VoMi's agreement that ethnic Germans would deliver 50 percent of their crops to the Romanian state and would allow billeting the Romanian troops there and conducting requisitioning of goods for their needs. However, unlike everywhere else in Transnistria, previous requisitions by the troops were to be deducted from this quota, as were seeds necessary for the new season. It was tacitly assumed that redistribution of the kolkhoz property in favor of ethnic Germans, which had taken place prior to that time, would not be revised and the Romanians even promised to transfer to them some horses that were at their disposal (probably trophy). Inventory of goods and garnered crops in German villages would be conducted jointly by the Romanian and ethnic German authorities. Ethnic consolidation of the German settlements by means of expulsions and resettlement was explicitly sanctioned.[73]

Hoffmeyer-Alexianu understanding, as it would be referred to in the Romanian correspondence, established ethnic Germans' highly privileged status and large administrative autonomy within Transnistria—a situation that developed against the Conducător's explicit ruling issued on November 13, 1941, and repeated in the Council of Ministers meeting of December 16. Probably unaware that the understanding had already been signed, the Conducător ruled, yet again, that "until the problem of Transnistria was resolved," the Romanian administration had to treat ethnic Germans, Romanians, and Ukrainians with equanimity. Only ethnic Romanians were to be accorded privileges, "but nothing should be done in a visible way," otherwise there would be difficulties.[74] There is no sign that this ruling had any effect. As Transnistrian gendarmerie colonel Mihai Iliescu reported on May 15, 1942, the German population of the region followed orders issued by the SS who bestowed on them a whole series of favors, on account of other ethnic groups, and demonstrated little subordination and respect toward the Romanian authorities. In fact, Iliescu intoned, the Romanian gendarmes and policemen could not even pursue criminals within the German settlements.[75] The Romanians' lack of oversight over ethnic Germans' villagers made a mockery of the understanding's provision concerning their inhabitants' duty to deliver one-half of their garnered crops to the Romanian state. As Siguraţa (intelligence unit within the gendarmerie and police that relied on undercover agents) bureau in Berezovca judeţ related in March 1943, ethnic Germans made a point of delivering as much as they liked claiming that they had met a quota of 50 percent while preventing the Romanian administration from verifying the real volume of their collected harvest.[76] Nor were the Romanian troops allowed to requisition much-needed horses from ethnic Romanian settlements, according to Alexianu's complaint of November 17, 1943.[77] The Conducător's stern reminder to the governor that he, and not the Germans, was sovereign in Transnistria had, in all probability, the same effect as his previous injunctions.[78]

Controlling Population Movements In and Out of Transnistria

A source of deep frustration for the Romanians was their limited ability to control the in- and out-migration from Transnistria. As a big shock came the realization that deportation of Jews from Bessarabia and Bukovina into the rump Russian state, as envisaged by the Romanian leaders in the first weeks of the war against the Soviet Union, would not be allowed by the German High Command. In the summer and fall of 1941, the Romanians deported more than 164,000 Jews from those two provinces.[79] Their initial intention was to deport them farther east, possibly "across the Ural Mountains," as Ion Antonescu put it.[80] But because the German army command protested citing communication and other logistical problems such massive deportations would create for the German operational troops, and pushed most of the deportees back across the Dniester, murdering about 1,200 of them in August 1941, the Romanians had to delay further deportations.[81] As has already been noted, the issue was discussed during the Tighina Convention negotiations. Art. 7 of the Convention stated: "The evacuation [euphemism for deportation] of Jews across the Buh River is presently not possible. They, thus, have to be concentrated in work camps and used as a labor force until, pending termination of operations, their evacuation to the east would be possible."[82] This provision obviously referred to the Romanian intention to resume deportation of Bessarabian and Bukovinian Jews across the Dniester River; it had the effect of transforming Transnistria into a temporary dumping ground for Romania's ethnic undesirables.

According to Alexianu's declaration during the postwar pretrial investigations, such transformation was not part of the Conducător's original vision for the region. Alexianu first heard of the plans "to transfer" Bessarabia and Bukovina Jews into Transnistria in September 1941 from three unidentified colonels from the General Staff who also indicated three routes for their convoys. At that time, it was still expected that the Jews would be soon deported so that "the German administration would receive them in order to push them farther east."[83] By November 1, 1941, after first 65,000 Jews had arrived in Transnistria, Alexianu realized that the actual number of Jews slated for "transfer" was "much higher" than he expected, their sanitary conditions were "very bad," threatening with the spread of contagious diseases everywhere they went, while his resources were so meager that he literally "could not give them a loaf of bread."[84] As he related to Antonescu on December 10 of the same year, the actual number of Jews who had arrived in Transnistria was 115,000 while the initial estimation was 50,000. Besides, there were local Jews whose number he estimated as being anywhere between 30,000 and 100,000, and that was only in Odessa. Alexianu was convinced that unless the Tighina Convention's provision concerning the Jews' transfer into Germany-occupied Ukraine was fulfilled as early as possible, "there would be no tranquility in Transnistria."[85] Although Alexianu, according to his own admission, at that time conducted negotiations with the Germans and was optimistic as to their outcome, the latter definitively refused to accept "Romanian" Jews and instead insisted on a series of much more sinister local "solutions," to which the Romanians eventually agreed.[86]

Another group of people whom the Romanians desperately wanted to see leave Transnistria into the German zone of occupation were approximately 10,000 families of Ukrainians and Poles from eastern Galicia whom the Soviets brought into southern Bessarabia and settled on the former properties of ethnic Germans. (Ethnic Germans from Bessarabia and northern Bukovina were relocated into the Greater Reich [annexed western Poland] in the fall of 1940, according to the German-Soviet convention and the Nazi policy of consolidation of Germandom).[87] As soon as the German and Romanian troops cleared Bessarabia, these people expressed strong desire to return to their homeland; the Romanian authorities interested in keeping the former German properties ready for the settlement of ethnic Romanians were happy to oblige but were not ready to defray any expenses for their repatriation. In early November 1941, Ion Antonescu resolved that these people be left to travel to Transnistria on their own risk and account, while the Ministry of Foreign Affairs was to intervene with the German authorities in Generalgouvernement to whom eastern Galicia belonged.[88] The Germans, however, refused suspecting that among them there might have been "politically unreliable persons" and proposed to create an ad hoc commission to verify the identity of each settler. The Romanians turned this suggestion down since they believed that this would be only a "partial solution" of the problem.[89] While the negotiations dragged on, about 1,200 Polish settlers reached, in early 1942, the town of Moghilev in northern Transnistria. According to the note composed by Antonescu's secretariat (secretariatul Preşedenţiei Consiliului de Miniştri or PCM), they "were in miserable hygienic conditions, living 300–400 persons in a school hall and in a theater hall, surviving on a ratio of 600 grams of bread [per person] provided by the prefecture."[90] Of this group, only thirty-three families were allowed entry into the Generalgouvernement in the spring of 1942. Despite this crisis and notwithstanding the Ministry of Foreign Affairs opinion that continuous negotiations with the Germans were "inopportune at the moment," on September 1, 1942, the same secretariat suggested that the rest of the settlers from this group be transferred from Bessarabia into Transnistria "in order to get them out of the national territory and be ready to repatriate them at any moment."[91] General Constatin Voiculescu, governor of Bessarabia, supported this proposal while Alexianu resisted it saying that he had no resources to provide for them. In the meeting of the Council of Ministers of March 17, 1943, Ion Antonescu resolved in favor of Alexianu, citing lack of resources and the danger of the spread of diseases and the settlers' premature deaths due to the strain of travel. "They are also humans," the Conducător ruled. Since the Germans refused to accept these people, "invoking all kinds of pretexts," the Romanians had to keep them in their own territory, creating "humane conditions for them." Attempts to deport them into Transnistria had to stop.[92] About one month earlier the Conducător had already ruled that those Polish settlers who were already in Transnistria, should not be encouraged to pass through the border into the German zone of occupation without the latter's prior agreement. Instead, they should have been "grouped by families and put to work."[93] In this way, he was probably responding to Alexianu's earlier suggestion that they be interned in concentration camps in the areas "where there is a noticeable lack of labor force."[94] From the surviving evidence one cannot gather whether and how this order was carried out and what the subsequent fate of these victims of Soviet, German, and Romanian callous social engineering was.

While the Romanians could not persuade the Germans to help them get rid of some of the ethnic undesirables in Transnistria (and Bessarabia), they equally had to acquiesce to the arrival of other persons whom they saw as an imminent danger to their interests and security. In the fall of 1941, the Germans initiated a policy of mass release of the Soviet prisoners of war (POWs) of Ukrainian nationality who were from the areas occupied by the Axis powers. These POWs had to present a proof of their place of origin and of nationality, whether in the form of Soviet papers or depositions of eyewitnesses and sometimes to sign a document committing themselves to refrain from any anti-Axis activity. Following that, they were issued laissez-passers to their domiciles, which frequently included Transnistria. From the German perspective, this policy was aimed at securing a sufficient labor force in the rural areas to help harvest the crops—a task of first-rate importance for the

Wehrmacht.[95] The Romanians had no control over this policy and generally considered such persons and especially the former Red Army officers security risks. Tellingly, the Romanians did not replicate this policy with respect to the Soviet POWs held in their own camps, with the exception of those of the Romanian ethnic origin.[96] In October 1941, the Second Army Corps deployed at the time in Transnistria informed its subdivisions that the Germans released from captivity "a number of those [POWs] who are from Transnistria. [They are] to be let go to their places of origin." Only those in possession of German-issued certificate were to be allowed to travel through the region. All weapons found on them were to be confiscated and those without certificate had to be arrested and sent to the prisoners' collection centers.[97] Despite these instructions, in the first months of occupation, the Romanian gendarmes routinely arrested such persons and interned them in camps with the other POWs.[98] In February 1942, the German Military Mission in Romania protested against such practice to the Romanian General Staff.[99] Under the German pressure, the Romanians had to agree and let these POWs reside in the Transnistrian countryside where they had to register with the authorities and appear before them for verification twice a month.[100] According to the Transnistrian governorship's data, on August 1, 1943, there were 74,854 Soviet POWs released by the Germans, apparently of mostly Ukrainian ethnic origin, residing in their putative places of origin in Transnistria.[101]

Keeping these persons under close supervision presented a logistical problem to the anxious authorities. So, on March 6, 1942, Golta Gendarmerie Legion requested permission to intern in concentration camp POWs released by the Germans; they were especially concerned about the Red Army "intelligentsia officers."[102] It appears that the Romanians' fears were justified because when in early spring of 1943 the Romanian gendarmerie and secret police (siguranța and Serviciul Special de Informații or SSI) discovered a wide communist-led network of subversive cells, they identified the POWs as the main recruiting ground for them.[103] In the fall of 1943, when partisan activity in the Transnistrian countryside flared up again, General Subinspectorate of Gendarmerie for Transnistria proposed, and the Third Army Corps agreed, that officers and NCO-Soviet POWs be rearrested and interned in concentration camps.[104] In January 1944, the SSI reported to the Romanian Third Army deployed in Transnistria that in accordance with the order of Odessa Gendarmerie Inspectorate, the gendarmerie and police started arresting and interning persons of this category in concentration camps.[105] It is not clear to what extent this order was carried out.

As this chapter shows, the Romanian occupation's aims were contradictory from the beginning. Torn between the declared imperative to demonstrate the Romanian capacity to rule in a civilized manner over the purportedly benighted "easterners" and urging to extract as many resources as possible from the province, the Romanian administration had to decide which priority to pursue and chose the latter one. To the Romanians' frustration, their sovereignty and freedom of actions in Transnistria were severely limited by their ruthless German allies who never completely relinquished their claims over a share in economic resources of Transnistria. In a never-ending tug of war with Berlin, Bucharest did obtain some successes, such as control over the railways, but they were largely temporary and conditional. The Germans succeeded in extracting a share of resources from the region, the full extent of which the Romanians were not even able to ascertain, let alone control. No less humiliating to their pride and ability to economically exploit the region for their own benefit was the special status of the Volksdeutsche community in Transnistria, transformed by the SS Sonderkommando-R and VoMi into a veritable state within a state, with enormous economic privileges, administrative and fiscal autonomy, and an independent police force. The Romanian's limited ability to control population movement out of the region into the rest of the occupied Soviet territories—despite promises made by Hitler to Antonescu on the eve of Germany's attack on the Soviet Union—and from the German zone of occupation into Transnistria led to the region's transformation into something it was not originally intended to be: the dumping ground for Romania's ethnic undesirables. This fact had enormous implications for the fate of the deportees and constrained the Romanian ability to change the ethnic composition of its population.

These observations should come as no surprise. From the moment the Romanian leaders decided to bring their country into the German sphere of influence, they had to forfeit a substantial share of control over their country's economy and foreign policy in favor of their all-powerful and ruthless ally. While planning to expand their country's borders on account of its eastern neighbor, they had to contend with their subservient position vis-à-vis Germany. Although the Romanian leaders did argue, sometimes heatedly, with the Nazi rulers for their country's interests as they understood them and sometimes did obtain concessions, they could not change the fundamental reality of two powers' comparative material forces.

CHAPTER 3

Configuring Transnistrian Administration

Until the conquest of Transnistria, Romania did not have the experience of a long-term occupation of enemy territory (although it did occupy most of Hungary in July 1919–February 1920). Now the country's leaders faced the question of how to organize their administration in Transnistria. The most obvious solution was to follow German example, particularly since the Germans were only too happy to offer one. Two German officials with the title of "advisers" (Beräter) were particularly important in this regard, Karl Pflaumer (1896–1971) and Theo (or Theodor) Ellgering (1897–?).

Learning from the Germans

German advisers' arrival in Romania coincided with that country's reorientation toward Berlin in the summer of 1940. Their arrival, in itself a sign of a new foreign policy alignment, followed an established Romanian tradition of learning from their Western patrons and allies by employing their experts in various government departments and agencies. It was the last government of King Carol II, under Prime Minister Ion Gigurtu, that initiated the invitation of German experts. The number of advisers grew under the National Legionary State when Ion Antonescu shared power with the pro-Nazi fascist party of the Iron Guard (or Legionaries), in September 1940–January 1941.

For a short time following the suppression of the Legionaries' rebellion in late January 1941, the number of German experts was rolled back since Ion Antonescu suspected them (correctly) of secretly supporting the Legionaries, but this number climbed back up again once his fears of Legionaries' peril subsided. Pflaumer and Ellgering belonged to this last group of German Nazi experts to arrive in Bucharest.

A professional policeman in Baden, Pflaumer was an early member of NSDAP, probably from as early as 1922, and of SS from 1931. After the Machtergreifung, he was appointed minister of the interior in Baden and gradually rose in the SS ranks to become SS Brigadeführer (equivalent to Generalmajor in Wehrmacht) in April 1940. From the summer of 1940, he served as a counselor to the chief of civil administration (Chef der Zivilverwaltung) in the newly annexed Alsace. Pflaumer arrived in Bucharest in February 1941 to help Romanians reorganize their state administration, and in March 1941 was conferred the title of "Adviser for Domestic Administration" (Berater für Innere Verwaltung).[1] Ellgering hailed from Duisburg in whose municipal government he served from 1914, initially as a trainee and finally, since 1934, as Beigeordnete, a post that in other cities and towns was known as Burgermeister or mayor. Simultaneously he served as NSDAP-Kreisleiter für Kommunalpolitik. Following the downfall of France, Ellgering served, as did Pflaumer, in Alsace. From June through March 1941 he was Oberstadtkommissar in Strasbourg. From March 1941 through 1942 Ellgering served as an Adviser on Issues of Communal Administration (Berater für kommunale Verwaltungsfragen) to the Romanian government.[2]

Pflaumer's and Ellgering's initial mission in Romania consisted of helping the government reform local administration according to the German model. After having examined the Romanian system—built on the French model of prefects, appointed by the national government, who were in charge of all substantial issues at the county or județ level—German advisers concluded that the system was too centralized and did not allow for local initiative. Their solution was to create larger provinces with governors appointed from the center but with greater autonomy in matters provincial. Beyond provinces, powers should be redistributed from county to district levels (plasă) ruled by pretors; lowest units or communes, comprising individual towns or clusters of villages, were also to receive more powers and responsibilities.[3]

When in May–June 1941 these ideas were first presented to Ion and Mihai Antonescu, both enthusiastically supported them.[4] Soon, however, Mihai Antonescu was seized by doubts as to the applicability and desirability of transferring German system unto Romanian soil, lock, stock, and barrel.[5] Some of his subordinates vociferously opposed such plans as early as

July 1941.[6] Nevertheless, acting on the suggestion of German experts, the government appointed a commission for administrative reform with the participation of Pflaumer and Ellgering. The commission, whose first meeting took place in December 1941, was tasked with working out a number of draft laws to reorganize both the central and the local administration. This work was conceived as one of the most important aspects of "national revolution," which was supposed to lead, to quote Mihai Antonescu, "to a moral, economic, and technical remaking of the population as a whole." As his instructions to the commission demonstrate, at that time German ideas were still assimilated by the Romanian government.[7]

I was not able to trace further work of this commission, but in any case, it had no influence on the administration in Romania as a whole. By the time it started its work, the Romanian leaders' attention had already shifted to military, economic, and foreign policy developments. In the two eastern provinces, Bessarabia and Bukovina, however, both of which returned to Romanian rule in July–August 1941, German advisers' ideas had an immediate application. Pflaumer explained in his July 15, 1941 memorandum to the governor of Bukovina, Colonel Alexandru Rioșanu, that initially the Conducător intended to introduce military rule in the two provinces, but Pflaumer suggested to him that the provinces' liberation offered "a unique occasion to introduce some useful and necessary reforms into the Romanian administration."[8] Ion Antonescu agreed, if one is to believe Pflaumer, with the Germans' perception that the Romanian administration suffered from excessive centralism. It was in Bessarabia and Bukovina that this problem had to be first confronted.

This was the origin of a project of Bessarabia's and Bukovina's transformation into the "model provinces" that were supposed to demonstrate to the rest of the country the benefits of new territorial arrangements. Initially, Ion Antonescu was determined to make this plan work and, accordingly, the role of the German advisers in the two provinces was particularly prominent. By the order of July 23, 1941, that appointed General Constantin Voculescu a plenipotentiary of the Conducător for the administration of Bessarabia, Ion Antonescu also appointed as his adviser "from all points of view (that is, with regard to all problems), Minister Pflaumer."[9] According to Vasile N. Florescu, an important civil servant in the provincial administration of Bukovina (from February 1942 through the end of Romanian rule there in April 1944 he would serve as its secretary general), in his instructions to Rioșanu Ion Antonescu stated that Pflaumer's "orders were to be followed without murmur."[10] Perhaps the most radical arrangement introduced on that occasion by Ion Antonescu was to forbid Bucharest ministries and other officials to correspond with administrative entities in the provinces other than via offices of his plenipotentiaries (from September 3, 1941, they would be called governors). For the purposes of supervising and coordinating such correspondence, a special entity called the Civil-Military Cabinet for Bessarabia and Bukovina (Cabinetul civico-militar pentru Basarabia şi Bucovina) was created within "The Office of the Chairman of the Council of Ministers" (Preşedenţia Consiliului de Miniştri), in effect, Ion Antonescu's chancellery.[11] In response to Mihai Antonescu's doubts as to the feasibility and desirability of such strict shielding of provincial administrations from the supervision of Bucharest ministries, the Conducător sent a long telegram on August 19, 1941 from Tighina—a Bessarabian town on the western bank of the Dniester River from where he commanded military operations on the front. He made it clear that he fully supported the new administrative arrangement and was not disposed to concede an iota of it: while ministers were free to come to the provinces at any time, they could not order or even supervise provincial administrations in any way, as was a norm in the rest of Romania. The Conducător referred to such practices as the "stupid mentality of those whose heads had been warped by old habits," which he was determined to eradicate.[12]

It is possible that the real reason for Ion Antonescu's strong support for the strict separation of the eastern provinces from the rest of the country was his desire to preside over their reconstruction in the spirit of "integral nationalism," as he called his own personal philosophy.[13] As he put it in the meeting of the Council of Ministers in October 1941, upon his return from Bessarabia, he believed that in two to three years it was possible to transform Bessarabia into "the model province to serve as an example to follow for the country as a whole; and so from the periphery I would start straightening out things in the rest of the country."[14] Although the law on the organization of Bessarabia and Bukovina did provide for the elevation of plasă and pretors (called prim-pretor in this context) over judeţ and prefects, no indication exists that this provision had any effect on the administrative realities in the provinces. The exceptional powers of the governors, however, did remain their distinctive feature, despite numerous protests from Bucharest bureaucrats, supported by Mihai Antonescu, who rightly saw in this extravaganza an attack on the long-standing traditions of Romanian state philosophy.[15]

Another aspect of Pflaumer's and other German advisers' expertise that elicited the Romanian leaders' enthusiasm was their experience in organizing what Mihai Antonescu called "population exchange and forced migrations [in] Alsace, Loraine, and in some parts of Prussia."[16] The available information on their role in the organization of deportations of Jews from the two provinces is contradictory. Pflaumer and Ellgering are known to be the first to propose the creation of the Jewish ghetto in Cernăuți no later than August 1941. It was they, too, who invited the Cernăuți mayor, Traian Popovici, to visit Krakow to acquaint himself with the Jewish ghetto there; this visit did not take place.[17] However, there is no evidence that German experts either advised or encouraged the deportation of Jews from the two provinces. On October 17, 1941, Ellgering, in his report to German ambassador Manfred Freiherr von Killinger, expressed surprise about Antonescu's order to deport the Jews of Bukovina and doubts about its rationale. He supported the suggestion of German Consul in Cernăuți, Franz Gebhard Schelhorn, that deportation of Jews "useful" for Bukovina's economy should be postponed until their replacements from among ethnic Romanians were trained. This proposal helped save about 20,000 from deportation.[18]

Although Pflaumer and Ellgering's initial mandate was confined to Romania proper, their ideas had a significant bearing on the design of the occupation administration in Transnistria. The future governor of Transnistria, Gheorghe Alexianu, first entered into contact with German advisers in the summer of 1941, when he tasked the committee of experts with creating a new arrangement for Bessarabia and Bukovina. Prior to northern Bukovina's cession to the USSR in June 1940, Alexianu was professor of administrative law at the University of Cernăuți and in 1939–1940 he served as the governor (*rezident regal*) of the region (*ținut*) of Suceava (roughly coinciding with Bukovina), during the short-lived regional administrative system introduced by King Carol II. On friendly terms with Mihai Antonescu, vice chairman of the council of ministers recommended him to the Conducător for the post of the governor of Bukovina.[19] Ion Antonescu preferred his friend Colonel Rioșanu for this position. However, when he later searched for a candidate for the governor of Transnistria, Minister of National Economy Ion C. Marinescu recommended Alexianu again, and this time Antonescu agreed.[20] He appointed Alexianu his plenipotentiary for the administration of the territory between the Dniester and Buh rivers on August 19, 1941, when heavy battles were still going on in and around Odessa.[21]

Judging from the handwritten note of Alexianu to Mihai Antonescu from July 14, prior to his appointment as Transnistria's head of the administration, Alexianu had serious disagreements with Pflaumer. Although unidentified, it is likely that they concerned Pflaumer's vision, rooted in German federalism, to which Alexianu, raised in the tradition of French-Romanian centralism, was opposed. After his appointment as governor, Alexianu continued to work with the German advisers. In a telegram dated November 26, 1941, he profusely thanked Pflaumer for his undeclared counseling services.[22]

Another German adviser, Baron von Malchius, "indefatigably worked" with Alexianu for a year and a half until he was recalled back to Germany "for another assignment" on March 6, 1943.[23] Malchius's sphere of expertise was, according to Alexianu's testimony in the 1945 pretrial investigation, the "administrative organization" of a region.[24]

There are reasons to believe that in his new position, Alexianu became more amenable to German advice. In a letter to Ion Antonescu of September 12, 1941, while explaining the basics of Romanian administration in Transnistria, he stated that he intended to give more powers to pretors because, with the larger than in Romania județe planned, prefects in Transnistria would have no possibility to exercise effective control over them. This was one of the main concepts German advisers insisted on. The provincial administration would be based on *Führerprinzip*, he added.[25] It is likely that this latter idea was suggested to Alexianu by Baron von Malhius who, according to Alexianu's testimony, advised him to apply to Transnistria arrangements decreed by Alfred Rosenberg, Reich Minister for the Occupied Eastern Territories, to the German administration in the occupied USSR. Despite Alexianu's postwar claim that he resisted von Malhius's advice, it is obvious that he liked at least this one element of it.[26] He thus cherry-picked those aspects of German practices that suited his own immediate interests, which themselves depended on his position within the government.

What proved to be the most significant and enduring aspects of German influence on the design of Transnistrian institutions was the enormous powers with which the office of the governor (*guvernământ*) was invested, as well as its virtual insulation from control and interference by Bucharest ministries. Nor were the laws of the country—which the Germans saw as too cumbersome and restrictive to allow for a provincial and local initiative—applicable in Transnistria.[27] What German advisers initially suggested for Bessarabia and Bukovina was implemented, to a considerably larger degree and in a purer form, in occupied Transnistria. The common origin of the administrations of the two eastern Romanian provinces and Transnistria was underscored by the decision to include the latter in the purview of the Civil-Military Cabinet for Bessarabia and Bukovina. Following the creation of the Romanian administration in Transnistria, it became the Civil-Military Cabinet for Bessarabia, Bukovina, and Transnistria (Cabinetul civico-militar pentru Basarabia, Bucovina și Transnistria, or CBBT). This arrangement gave rise to the widespread practice of referring to Transnistria as one of the provinces of Romania although, as has been already discussed, it was not annexed by this country, and its legal status and internal organization differed from the two eastern Romanian provinces. For lack of a better term, from now on I will also refer to Transnistria as "a province," without implying the similarity of its legal status to that of Bessarabia and Bukovina.

Initially, Ion Antonescu resolutely defended the administrative autonomy of the three provinces. For example, in the Council of Ministers meeting of November 13, 1941, he again prohibited the ministries to issue regulations with direct applicability in the province, without first receiving his sanction via CBBT. Addressing his ministers, he ruled: "None of you have the right to communicate directly with the provinces, because otherwise you generate this cacophony, when, as Mr. Alexianu has said, everybody comes with different methods and gives different orders." He next addressed the governors thusly:

> I ask you to take note of what I tell you, Messrs. Governors: tear everything you receive from the authorities and send it torn apart back. Just as I said: tear all the papers you have received directly from the ministries into forty pieces and send them back. Give the order to your subordinates to do the same . . .
>
> All orders which are to be sent to the provinces are to pass through the CBBT, where they are to be triaged. All dispositions sent are not to be fulfilled.[28]

Just what that "triage" should amount to was not properly explained. The CBBT statute issued shortly after Mihai Antonescu ordered its creation on July 25, 1941, provided for the creation of the Council of Coordination, which was comprised of delegates from all government ministries and under secretariats of state (in effect, separate departments). Alongside it, an administrative service was created that was supposed to guarantee fulfillment of the Council's orders. The CBBT was supposed "to triage all correspondence, both one that was addressed by the ministries to the governors' cabinets or guvernământe, and that addressed by guvernământe to the ministries, and to guarantee resolution of all problems in a consistent (unitar) fashion, in conformity with legal provisions and orders issued by the Leader of the State."[29] This was a gargantuan task that the CBBT was given no powers to fulfill. It could not subject legal or administrative acts of the governors to any kind of expertise, nor could it abrogate or even recommend their abrogation or modification. Nor could it do the same with respect to dispositions of the ministers regarding the provinces. Although the statute gave the CBBT the power to ascertain "in what measure the ministries' programs are applicable in the provinces," this provision contradicted art. 39 of the Law of September 3 that obligated the guvernământe's directorates to carry out such programs and gave the ministries the right to verify their execution in the provinces. Again, while the *guvernământe* were obligated to submit monthly reports "concerning all achievements and all local problems and needs," the CBBT was given no indication as to what it was supposed to do with such information.[30] All things considered, the CBBT proved little more than a storing facility for bureaucratic correspondence between the Bucharest government and the *guvernământe*, with no real powers to initiate, carry out, or verify the implementation of any disposition concerning actions to be taken in the provinces.

Transnistria as a "Model" for Romania

Since its inception, the place of Transnistria in Ion Antonescu's government was thus tightly entwined with that of Bessarabia and Bukovina. These two eastern provinces had a particular distinction that Transnistria initially lacked in that they were supposed to become "models" for the rest of the country. They were Conducător's pet projects, designed to bring to fruition his vision of Romania reconstructed on the principles of integral nationalism. Both the wide provincial autonomy and exceptional powers of the governors were conceived as means to that end. However, the privileged status of Bessarabia and Bukovina and Conducător's fondness with their supposed achievements did not last and to the extent that their fortunes declined, Transnistria's standing grew. For a short time, in the summer of 1943, Ion Antonescu even promoted Transnistria to the position of a "model" for the rest of the country, thus placing it on the pedestal from which he had just removed Bessarabia and Bukovina. This is how this unlikely development unfolded.

From the moment of the two provinces' creation, their administrations came under continuous attack from Bucharest ministries whose heads could not stomach an anomaly of autonomous units in an otherwise centralized unitary state. Under such conditions, the extent of the two governors' freedom of action ultimately depended on Ion Antonescu's resolve to uphold his initial vision of wide provincial autonomy. This resolve, in turn, depended on the governors' ability to impress Antonescu with their achievements. Benefitting from subsidies from Bucharest and relying on the forced labor of the locals mandated to help restore public buildings and infrastructure damaged by the war and retreating Soviets, the governors created a number of "model institutions," such as schools, hospitals, and administrative offices, which exhilarated Antonescu during his inspection in April 1942. Speaking in the meeting of the Council of Ministers upon his return from inspection on April 30, he told his ministers that the situation in the eastern provinces was much better than in the Old Kingdom, still ruled according to old habits.[31]

It soon became clear, however, that whatever the governors achieved in Bessarabia and Bukovina, they did in large measure at the expense of the national budget. Severely damaged by the violent destruction of Jewish communities in the summer and fall of 1941, provincial economies failed to recover and running and repairing the provinces required large subventions. As Mihai Antonescu stated in an angry exchange with the governors of Bessarabia and Bukovina in the Council of Ministers meeting of September 29, 1942, the country as a whole had to carry a financial burden in order to support the "privileges" that the two provinces had arrogated to themselves.[32] Financial insolvency of Bessarabia and Bukovina presented a problem in view of the ever-increasing war burden, and it gave powerful ammunition to the governors' critics in Bucharest. A series of decree-laws and other regulations issued in the summer and fall of 1942 reinstated most of the ministries' prerogatives in the provinces.[33] Finally, on January 13, 1943, by decree-law #18, the Conducător cut the provincial autonomy of Bessarabia and Bukovina so severely that it remained in name only.[34]

Thus, long before *guvernământe* of Bessarabia and Bukovina were de facto liquidated by the Red Army's advance beyond the Dniester River into Romanian territory on August 20, 1944, the project of using Bessarabia and Bukovina as a testing ground and "models" for a new, reconstructed and reeducated postwar Romania in a New Europe was quietly abandoned.[35] Exactly at the same time when Bessarabia's and Bukovina's fortunes as "model" provinces sank, the Conducător's eyes increasingly turned toward Transnistria as a new and more promising candidate for this role.

In mid-April 1943, Ion Antonescu dismissed the governors of Bessarabia and Bukovina, Generals Constantin Voiculescu and Corneliu Calotescu, respectively.[36] The Conducător's displeasure was apparently caused by the governors' supposed mismanagement of the former properties of deported Jews and "repatriated" ethnic Germans.[37]

In the spring of 1943, Transnistria's governor Gheorghe Alexianu was also under increasing pressure from Bucharest ministers supported by Mihai Antonescu and for a time he seemed to be in danger of sharing the fate of Voiculescu and Calotescu. The attack on Alexianu was led by the Minister of Finance Alexandru Neagu, who accused him of systematically inflating the numbers of Transnistria's deliveries to the army and to Romania. Neagu might have been unaware of how many deliveries went unregistered, according to Ion Antonescu's instructions.[38] The full extent of Minister Neagu's disagreement with Alexianu became evident in the Council of Ministers meeting of March 17, 1943, when the former stated: "Mr. Alexianu does not believe in our principles [that is, following regulations on public accountancy]. When he sends us every week [reports] showing surpluses of 13–14 billion lei, but according to our data we have a few million lei, it means we do not think in the same way."[39]

On that occasion, Mihai Antonescu suggested that the Directorate of Finance of the *guvernământ* be subordinated to both Alexianu and Neagu, which would have severely undermined the *guvernământ's* insulation from oversight by Bucharest's bureaucracy. The Conducător, even if concerned by the substance of Neagu's accusations, declined this proposal.[40] While agreeing that Transnistrian public accountancy had to be made "orderly," he insisted that complete transparency and registration of all requisitions from the region were undesirable because they could strengthen Moscow's claims that Romanians were conducting an unrestricted plunder of the region. "We have to take as much as we can from Transnistria, Ion Antonescu ruled, but without receipts since otherwise the Russians will pick these documents up tomorrow and bring them to the Green Table [of the peace conference]."[41] Thus, application of legal regulations to public accountancy in Transnistria had to be avoided.[42] The Conducător nevertheless ruled that a special commission with representatives from the Ministry of Finance and of Transnistrian *guvernământ* had to be set up to figure out how to comply with these contradictory imperatives: instill order in Transnistrian accountancy without full transparency and adequate registration of deliveries from the region.[43]

For the next several months, the Conducător continued to issue contradictory rulings on the matter. On April 15, 1943, he supported Alexianu's request that the frequency of inspection teams' visits from Bucharest to Odessa should be limited to once per three months.[44] At the same time, he insisted that the work of the government commission tasked with the verification of stores created by the *guvernământ* for the sale of Transnistrian produce in Romanian cities at lower-than-market prices be continued, despite protestations and hurdles put up by the governor for its work. When commission's findings indicated irregularities in the stores' accounts, he ordered, in late May 1943, that Secretary General of PCM Ovidiu Vlădescu oversee verification, "starting from harvesting, handling, shipment, and through sale" of Transnistrian products.[45] This was a sign of the Conducător's displeasure. Still, Alexianu managed to survive this crisis of confidence and for a time even improve his standing with the Conducător.

On June 21, 1943, Ion Antonescu visited Transnistria for several days. Upon his return, he took Alexianu's side in the ever-deepening dispute with Minister Neagu over balancing accounts between Odessa and Bucharest:[46]

This is a silent work of subversion. It is regrettable. I would have been happy if all Romanian territories were in the same situation from the point of view of administration, education, industry, authority, and contribution to the national economy, as I found during my inspection in the entire territory of Transnistria. In the future, no decision should be taken without first consulting Mr. Alexianu and without my approval. . . . Before making accusations, one should go there and see for himself. The same directives given by me were executed there in their totality while here I meet a silent resistance from everyone up to the ministerial level. Once again, I would be happy if all villages, schools, institutions, and factories had the same life [*suflet*] in them as they have in Transnistria, where they were raised from ruins.[47]

In the Council of Ministers meeting of July 1, 1943, Ion Antonescu pointed to the Transnistrian *economate*—distribution centers of goods in short supply to which solely persons with ration cards had access—as models for the rest of the country. Cooperative stores in Romania, he added, were in worse shape than shops open by Russians in Transnistria.[48]

As to what exactly happened during Ion Antonescu's visit to Transnistria in June 1943, one can learn from the memoirs of Nichita Smochină, a self-appointed leader of Transnistrian Moldovans. This is how he described what he called Alexianu's *Potemkeniad*:

In the vicinity of Odessa, in a mansion [*castel*], they set up a nursing home for the elderly. Having visited this mansion, Ion Antonescu liked how it was organized. A little later, landowner Râmniceanu [who was in the Conducător's retinue], returned to learn more about this institution, since he was interested in creating a similar one on his own estate. To his great surprise, he learned that there was neither a sign of a nursing home, nor a nursing home as such. At the entrance, a guard told him, "No nursing home here. It was here solely for inspection." Along the road to [the town of] Balta were old trees on both sides. The governor explained to the marshal that people planted those old trees. In fact, though, they chopped them down [in another place] and installed them there for just two to three days. En route, the governor showed that all fields were sowed, but in fact they were sowed only along both sides of the road. Minister of Agriculture Pană, who was a good producer of grains, [saw through this subterfuge]. Still, he had no courage to say so to the marshal.[49]

If Smochină's testimony can be suspect because of his resentment of Alexianu, whom he saw as unduly awarded the post that should have rightfully belonged to him, the governor's instructions to the local level administrators issued on June 20, 1943, on the eve of the Conducător's visit, substantiate Smochină's claim of a massive window-dressing exercise. They also provide an insight into how Alexianu, and Ion Antonescu, understood what constituted signs of good governance. The governor started by instructing his administrative personnel on the proper way to greet dignitaries inspecting their locale. They had to line up according to their rank and salute by raising their right hand ("Roman salute"). They had to introduce themselves succinctly, by indicating their position within the administration but without mentioning their names. Everybody had to have handy reports with graphics showing Romanian achievements, preferably in comparison with the Soviet rule. The local population also had to learn how to properly greet Romanian dignitaries—hats off, their right hands up. Everybody had to stop working and listen in silence until the dignitaries departed, and then promptly resume their tasks. All public spaces had to be cleaned, fences painted "to give an impression to a person entering a village of the cleanliness and health of its residents." All this was necessary in order "to show everywhere that the civilization that we have installed here is based on cleanliness and order."[50]

The Alexianu-Antonescu Nexus

Alexianu's brazen showmanship and Ion Antonescu's vast capacity of self-deception were important reasons of Governor Alexianu's longevity. Another reason was his toughness in defending his prerogatives to single-handedly rule over the province, to appoint, promote, and dismiss his subordinates as he pleased, and to control the flow of information in and out of Transnistria. On December 11, 1941, he reported to Ion Antonescu that there were in Transnistria "too many" intelligence services who bothered him and the Conducător with "unfounded denunciations." He gave a number of examples, the first being the mayor of Odessa, Gherman Pântea, "who conducted the most laudable activity . . . together with his subordinates." Pântea declined a request by an unnamed intelligence officer that all appointments in the municipal administration be made following security clearances, and Alexianu firmly supported the mayor. Since this and other denunciations had been proven wrong, the governor concluded that he "had no need" for so many intelligence agencies in Transnistria. He was fully capable of guaranteeing tranquility and order there without their unwanted presence.[51] In April 1943, the intelligence agency within the Ministry of the Interior, also known as siguranța, reported to Ion Antonescu that numerous positions of authority on the local level in Transnistria were occupied by former communist functionaries who presented a threat to Romanian interests and security. This report was forwarded to Alexianu who took almost three months to respond to it. When he finally did, the governor claimed that upon verification, all information was shown to have been wrong and asked not be bothered by such trivial matters in the future. His administration, he claimed, was capable of guaranteeing security and order in the region, and for the attainment of this objective, "there was no need to collect so much useless information, especially given that it often turns out to be wrong."[52] Nor was Alexianu willing to admit that his administration was corrupt, a fact that was a general knowledge in Transnistria. This is what he wrote, in July 1943, in response to the SSI reports on the corrupt dealings of Odessa's deputy mayor, Constantin Vidraşcu:

> Following investigations, it was established that not one single shred of information submitted to you is true. I hold it my duty to draw your attention to the fact that I continue to receive numerous notes of this kind. Faced with this campaign of denigration of everything that is Romanian prestige and authority, I ask you to communicate to me the source of this information. I would then ask Mr. Marshal [Ion Antonescu] to impose the most drastic punishment on those defamers who seek to inflict damage on the country and its administration, which makes everything possible to do good in the spirit of the marshal.[53]

The most powerful argument Alexianu invoked in favor of the alleged necessity not to allow outside bureaucratic oversight in his region was undesirability to register the full extent of the Romanian plunder of Transnistrian economic assets. This argument was accepted by the Conducător when he ruled against the introduction of public accountancy regulations in the province during the Council of Ministers meeting of March 17, 1941. Moreover, by refusing to register all deliveries from the region, or to indicate their real value, Alexianu was simply following Ion Antonescu's instructions. In fact, the Conducător would sometimes rebuke Alexianu for registering too much. As he angrily noted on March 12, 1943 on the margins of a CBBT report for the Radio Moscow broadcast that accused Romanians of the illegal shipment of assets from Transnistria: "Mr. Alexianu takes imprudent steps. One takes administrative measure in this region not by means of publications and written orders but by means of local [read: oral] administrative directives. . . . I have already alerted Mr. Alexianu to this issue. This order will be read to him and he will come to discuss the issue with me again."[54] The Conducător sided with Alexianu in December 1943, when he requested that ministerial departments be ordered to stop requesting further information on the shipment of goods from Transnistria "so that the enemy will not immediately discover this."[55]

Still another, more personal, reason existed for Ion Antonescu to keep some of the shipments from Transnistria underreported. The fact of the matter was that Alexianu offered, and Antonescu accepted, to ship substantial amounts of goods and render important services to various groups and institutions in Romania as the marshal's charitable gifts, all of these on Transnistria's account. Charitable activity under Antonescu was centralized under the organization called the "Social Work Patronage Council" (Consiliu de Patronaj al Operei Sociale, or CPOS). Created by the decree-law of April 10, 1941, it was headed by the Conducător's wife, Maria Antonescu, with Veturia Goga, widow of Transylvanian nationalist poet and former prime minister Octavian Goga (December 1937–February 1938), as Maria's deputy. Goga was a close friend of the Antonescu family, and through the marshal's wife exercised what many Romanians believed was an undue influence over him. The CPOS was thus a personal fief of the Conducător, impervious to outsiders and unaccountable to anybody but him. Its powers were enormous since, according to its statute, it was tasked with "coordinating the activity of all institutions, public or private . . . in the sphere of social welfare."[56] Although there is no evidence that either Ion or Maria Antonescu embezzled CPOS funds, it is quite likely that Veturia Goga did.[57] Ion Antonescu had enormous trust in the CPOS and often claimed that it was the only absolutely "clean" and efficient public institution in Romania, to whom management of any economic asset in the public interest could be entrusted with complete confidence.[58]

FIGURE 4. Maria Antonescu distributes packages to the sick at a hospital, 1941. Courtesy DANIC.

The "gifts" offered by Alexianu were sometimes channeled via the CPOS, whose close association with the Conducător's family made those disbursements appear as acts of Ion Antonescu's personal generosity and evidence of his care for the "deserving poor."[59] Sometimes they were disbursed in Ion Antonescu's own name, without letting the beneficiaries know where the funds were coming from. Either way, they tended to boost Ion Antonescu's social capital and legitimacy in the eyes of Romania's still largely traditional society with strong expectations of political patronage. From numerous examples of such gifts, I will cite just three. In February 1943, Alexianu requested the Conducător's permission to sell 40,000–50,000 liters of fruit brandy brewed in Transnistria on the Romanian domestic market. Alexianu added that 200 lei from the proceeds of the sale of each liter would be transferred into the CPOS account. Ion Antonescu's response was: "Very good."[60] In March of the same year, Alexianu suggested that the construction of a school building in Predeal, a resort area where Ion Antonescu's villa was located, should be completed—using the province's funds by the beginning of the new academic year. The Conducător's response was: "Yes. [Governor Alexianu] will be thanked for his initiative."[61] In early April 1943, Alexianu wrote an even more revealing letter to Antonescu: "In view of the approaching Easter holiday, the *guvernământ* has considered opportune, *as it did in the past*, to send to the Romanian soldiers in Crimea and on the front, gifts in the name of the Marshal of the Nation to show that the Conducător never forgets, even for a moment, to care about those who fight for the glory of their nation." Alexianu added a list of goods intended for distribution that included 300,000 eggs, 15,000 kg of candy, 5,000 bottles of brandy, and 5,000,000 cigarettes. Antonescu's response was identical to the previously cited.[62] As Alexianu's letter suggests, only a part of such transfers of funds from Transnistria left any paper trail. For that reason, their overall amount is impossible to assess with any certainty. None of the archival collections contain a single instance of Ion Antonescu's refusal to accept the distribution of Transnistrian products in his name, thus suggesting that he expected such services from the governor as a matter of course.

Perhaps it would not be an exaggeration to describe the Alexianu-Antonescu relationship as "special," based on their mutual understanding, possibly reached even before Alexianu was appointed to that position, that some of Alexianu's actions in the province would be of a rather legally dubious nature, that they should not be reported in their totality, and that Ion Antonescu would provide necessary "cover" for such practices. By invoking the necessity of keeping silence over many aspects of Transnistria's exploitation, and manipulating the Conducător's gullibility and his inclination to

take his own fantasies for reality, Alexianu managed not only to survive longer than his counterparts in Bessarabia and Bukovina, but in the process to
consolidate his control over the Transnistrian administration and to stave off
attempts of Bucharest ministries to foist their oversight on "his" province.

How much of Alexianu's success in preserving his single-handed rule in
Transnistria was due to personal as opposed to structural factors? Herwig
Baum, who emphasizes differences between the Romanian and German
rules in occupied Soviet territory, contrasts the "polycratic system" in the
German zone with Romanian rule in Transnistria, which he dubs "patrimonial domination." According to the widely held view among German historians, the "polycratic system" was characteristic to Nazi rule in the occupied
eastern territories, rife with acute rivalry between provincial administrations
(Reichskomissariate), the Ministry of Occupied Eastern Territories in Berlin
headed by Alfred Rosenberg, and Heinrich Himmler, who in his multiple
capacities exercised control over security forces there. Baum is inclined to
see "patrimonial domination" in Transnistria as determined by such structural and cultural factors as the lack of a fascist-type mass party in Romania
and the Conducător's mistrust of the Romanian bureaucracy on which he
nevertheless had to rely absent any alternative. Ion Antonescu carved his
own "administrative patrimony" in Transnistria as a compensation for his
frustrations in Romania, where he had to refrain from repressing all opposition parties and felt constrained by bureaucratic regulations and institutions
he disliked.[63]

This view is no doubt largely correct and grasps important aspects of
Romanian administration and policy in Transnistria. It might nevertheless be useful to recall that there was nothing uniquely "Romanian" in the
design of Transnistrian provincial administration, in particular its unprec-
edentedly large autonomy. In fact, this idea came from the German advisers.
Both Pflaumer and Ellgering advised Romanians to follow German experi-
ments with large provincial autonomy coupled by management based on
Führerprinzip as practiced at the time in the newly conquered provinces in
the west (Alsace-Loraine) and east (East Prussia and Warthegau).[64] Inciden-
tally, there too, the degree of real freedom of action enjoyed by individual
provincial administrators largely depended on the strength of their personalities and their standing with Hitler and other Nazi leaders in Berlin.[65] The
German advice was assimilated by Antonescu and Alexianu for different
but mostly personal reasons, such as their lust for power and vainglory.
Seen in this context, Transnistrian "patrimonial domination" appears as
less of a fixture determined by cultural and structural characteristics of the

Romanian state—real as they were—as by the dynamic of the Alexianu-Antonescu relationship and the ability of the governor to manipulate the Conducător. That, as will be discussed in chapter 7, Ion Antonescu ultimately changed his opinion of Alexianu's administration and withdrew his support from him testifies to the unstable and essentially situational nature of this arrangement.

CHAPTER 4

Ruling Transnistria

The structure of the low- and mid-levels administrative apparatus in Transnistria closely followed that in Romania. The *guvernământ* was composed of departments (*direcții*), which closely corresponded to Bucharest ministries. Five of them—administration and communication; agriculture and economy; education, culture, and propaganda; public health; and finance—were already mentioned in the Antonescu's decree of August 19, 1941, which established the Romanian administration of the territory between the Dniester and Buh rivers.[1] Later on, the number of the departments grew exponentially, mostly by divisions, such as the department of agriculture and economy branching off into the department of agriculture and the department of economy, and later the department of economy fragmenting into the departments of economy, industry, transportation, constructions, agricultural engineering, and commerce. By the end of the Romanian rule, the number of departments grew to at least thirty.[2] This extraordinary growth reflected both the highly centralized and bureaucratic nature of the Romanian rule in the region and the increasing demands placed on the Transnistrian administration by the government in Bucharest. The governor was assisted by his Secretary General Emanoil Cercavschi who simultaneously was his deputy. He also relied on the assistance of his cabinet, headed by Olivian Verenca and on the services of the Bureau of Studies (oficiu de studii) and the Bureau of Statistics (oficiu de statistică).[3]

The legal basis of the Transnistrian administration constituted law-decrees and decrees (the differences between these types of legal acts were largely philosophical, the former being issued in the name of the king and the Conducător, the latter of the Conducător only). The governor himself issued ordinances (*ordonanţe*), in effect, local laws; decisions (*decizii*), which are similar to executive orders; rules (*rugulamente*); and guidelines (*instrucţiuni*).[4] The ordinances were issued in the name of Antonescu as commander-in-chief of the army, "acting via the Governor Professor Gheorghe Alexianu," while acts of the other aforementioned categories in the name of Alexianu only. Various departments also issued their own *decizii* and *instrucţiuni*.

Below the *guvernământ* level, the administration also followed the established Romanian administrative traditions. On the county or judeţ level, the highest authority was the prefect. Prefects performed the tasks of "supervision, coordination, and management of administrative activity." Each prefect was "assisted by two subprefects" as well as by an agricultural, a mechanical, and an economic adviser with the title of an engineer and "a number of functionaries necessary for the fulfillment of secretarial tasks."[5] Prefects appointed mayors of villages and towns, as well as their deputies and advisory councils. They confirmed appointments of all public functionaries at the judeţ level. The police (with the responsibility in the towns) and gendarmerie (with responsibility for the countryside) "stood at the orders of prefect."[6] There were thirteen judeţe in all, each composed of three to eight raions.[7] Raions were Soviet-era administrative units that closely resembled the Romanian *plase* (singular: *plasă*). It is not clear why in this instance, the Romanians decided to keep the Soviet-era administrative term. As with *plase* in Romania, raions were headed by pretors, who oversaw the activity of nine administrative sections that roughly corresponded to the departments of the *guvernământ*.[8] They were supposed to be manned by "a necessary number of specialized personnel."[9]

The lowest administrative unit was the *comună* (pl.: *comune*). *Comună* could be a village, a cluster of villages, or a town (*oraş*, pl.: *oraşe*), or even a *municipiu* (pl.: *municipii*, approximate translation: city; henceforth, I will use "city" for *municipiu* and "town" for *oraş*). *Comune* were headed by *primari* (sing.: *primar*), or mayors (henceforth I use "mayor" for *primar*). In the rural commune, mayors were assisted by "village councils," or advisory bodies composed of three members. Both mayors and members of the councils were "designated" by the village assemblies (this procedure did not necessarily mean elections, sometimes candidates were "proposed" by representatives of the occupying authority) and confirmed by pretors. In the towns, mayors and their deputies, whose number dependent on the number of residents,

FIGURE 5.   Orthodox Christian Metropolitan Visarion (Puiu) (center), flanked by Mayor Gherman Pântea (on his left) and Governor Gheorghe Alexianu (on his right) followed by General Gheorghe Gheorghiu during Christmas festivities, December 1942, Odessa. Courtesy DANIC.

were appointed by the prefects, while in the cities they were appointed by the governor.[10] In the city of Odessa, Mayor Gherman Pântea, appointed by Alexianu on October 18, 1941, immediately divided the city into three sectors, each run by its own assistant mayor (*ajutori de primari*). Later on, in 1943, Pântea was given the title of mayor-general (*primarul general*) and assistant mayors became "mayors of the sectors" (*primari pe sectoare*). Pântea was assisted by two vice mayors.[11]

Administrative Personnel

Alexianu, a son of an Aromanian émigré from the Balkans, distinguished himself not only as an important legal scholar but also a convinced hard-core nationalist and anti-Semite.[12] During his tenure as a royal resident in (in effect, governor of) Bukovina he oversaw the application of anti-Semitic law-decree #169/1938 on the revision of Romanian citizenship, which targeted those Jews who entered Romanian territory following World War I in an allegedly "illegal" manner.[13] On the other hand, Alexianu was a sworn enemy to the Legionaries, a fascist-type party to whom Ion Antonescu was once sympathetic and with whom he shared power from September 14, 1940 to

January 23, 1941 (the period known as National Legionary State), but whom the Conducător severely persecuted after their failed rebellion of January 21–23, 1941. In late November 1940, the Legionaries even attempted to abduct and kill Alexianu but he was saved by the officers of the artillery battery deployed at the time near his residence.[14] Thus, Alexianu, although seriously wounded in the incident, escaped the fate of the other prominent members of the Romanian elite assassinated by the Legionaries, who held them responsible for their and their leaders' murderous persecution in the 1930s, under King Carol II. It should be noted that it was not unusual for Romanian elites to be both hard-core nationalists and anti-Semites, on the one hand, and anti-Legionary, on the other, since many of them supported Kind Carol in the 1930s, while the Legionaries resolutely opposed the monarch. Alexianu's background made him an ideal candidate for the post of Transnistria's governor from Ion Antonescu's perspective since after the Legionaries' rebellion Antonescu considered them the greatest domestic threat and for that reason made peace with the former Carlists.

Gherman Pântea, a Bessarabian Romanian, played a role in the events leading up to the union of Bessarabia with the Romanian Kingdom, which was voted for on March 27, 1918, by the local self-appointed assembly, of which he was a member. Pântea does not appear to have received a formal university education, but in 1919, at the behest of Prime Minister Ion C. Brătianu, the University of Iași granted him the lowest law degree (*licență în drept*).[15] In the 1920s, he was a prominent member of the Bessarabian provincial organization of the National Liberal Party (NLP), which governed Romania with a strong hand for most of the decade, and in 1923 and 1927–1928 was mayor of the provincial capital, Chișinău. At the end of the decade, NLP lost power, and Pântea left its ranks but still managed to be elected (by the city council) for a short term as Chișinău mayor in 1932, when a short-lived government "of technicians" he supported was in power in Bucharest. He was a member of ten consecutive chambers of deputies of the Romanian parliament, and in 1938–1940, during King Carol's dictatorship, served as a member of the senate.[16] Pântea was a typical Romanian politician of the interwar period—opportunistic and ever-ready to adjust to the constantly changing circumstances. However, in contrast to Alexianu, nothing in his record suggested prominent legal expertise or extremist political proclivities. His fortes were his knowledge of Russian language and Russian ways, as well as his ability to cultivate friendships with persons from different circles and of different political views. If one accepts Pântea's assertion that he was recommended to Ion Antonescu by Ion Mihalache, one of the prominent personalities in the National Peasants Party, the main rival of the

NLP, that fact in itself testifies to Pântea's remarkable political versatility. According to the same source, during his first meeting with Ion Antonescu, the Conducător explained his choice by pointing out that he made some inquiries and found out that Pântea had been "the best mayor" of Chişinău. Antonescu, who resided in the Bessarabian capital in 1938–1939 as a commander of the Fourth Army Territorial Corps deployed there, no doubt made inquiries among his contacts in the province, which also suggests that local elites there remembered Pântea fondly. Given how different Pântea's and Alexianu's backgrounds and personalities were, the former's assertion that the Conducător first offered the post of Transnistria's governor to him is surprising. Only after he expressed his doubts as to the advisability of having a civilian as head of the Romanian administration in Transnistria while Bessarabia and Bukovina were entrusted to military generals did Antonescu turn to Alexianu.[17] Is it indeed conceivable that Antonescu seriously considered Pântea for the position of governor, or was that conversation just his ruse meant to sow distrust and heighten rivalry among the two? This is not a frivolous question, since Alexianu's personal convictions and policy would leave a deep and gory imprint in Transnistria, whereas Pântea's record in Odessa would be a substantially more moderate one. On the other hand, Antonescu would develop much closer relations with and place greater trust in Alexianu than Pântea, thus suggesting that perhaps their politics had more in common and that Alexianu's appointment was not as accidental as Pântea's account suggests. It wasn't long before Pântea, conforming his reputation of conviviality, managed to overcome Alexianu's initial hostility and turn him into a powerful protector.

In matters of personnel selection, Alexianu had final say on the provincial and judeţe levels, although Bucharest ministries presented candidates from among their employees for the directories overseeing areas under the ministries' purview.[18] According to Alexianu's Ordinance #8, art. 6 from September 12, 1941: "For the sake of securing the unity of leadership, the whole administration of Transnistria receives its orders from the High Commander of the Army, who carries out his decisions and issues instructions via the Civil Governor."[19] This potent formula presupposed Alexianu's full control over the appointment and promotion of civil servants in the province but in practice it was circumscribed by the legal provisions regulating civil service, which established strict requirements for appointments and promotions (in particular, passing tests or *concurs*) as well as by a severe shortage of qualified personnel.

Civil servants posted in Transnistria were considered *detaşaţi*, that is, on a special assignment from the respective government departments. Since the Romanian economy and society became increasingly regulated during the war—as was the case in other belligerent countries—the workload on most bureaucrats grew correspondingly; although their numbers likewise expanded, it was not sufficient to meet the new obligations. Administering Transnistria added substantial stress to the heads of various government agencies that were reluctant to see their employees depart. According to Smochină, while waiting for to meet with Ion Antonescu in Tighina on August 15, 1941, the inspector general of the Romanian gendarmerie, General Constantin (Pichi) Vasiliu, expressed his concern over his increased duties in no uncertain terms. "Look, gentlemen," he told Smochină, Alexianu, and Pântea, "I barely stand up to the [threat posed by] communists and Soviet agents in the country, while Antonescu wants to extend our administration up to the Dnieper River. Under no circumstances can this be done." "What are my gendarmes doing in Transnistria?" he asked looking in Smochină's eyes, thus suggesting that he held him responsible for this unnecessary and unwise measure.

Bucharest bureaucrats were not thrilled by the prospect of leaving their homes and families to serve in an unknown country. To overcome this obstacle, on August 19, 1941, Ion Antonescu decreed that *detașați* civil servants would receive double salary in lei and a "supporting allowance" (*alocație de întreținere*) in RKKS up to double salary in lei.[20] According to Alexianu's note of September 3, 1942, salary in lei was paid by the institution from which a civil servant was *detașat* and transferred into his bank account in Romania. The salaries in RKKS were paid by the *guvernământ* and one of them was convertible into lei with the proviso that it will remain in Romania. This money came from goods shipped from Transnistria and sold to Romania's population in specially created government-owned stores at lower-than-market prices.[21] Since RKKS quickly lost its purchasing power and the *guvernământ's* efforts to control prices had only limited success, many goods in Transnistria shortly after the installation of the Romanian administration became obtainable only on the black market and at inflated prices. To offset the effect of their policy on their own civil servants, the *guvernământ* created special stores for them called *consum general* in which basic goods such as foods, soap, and cloth were available at the officially set prices.[22] Special canteens were also established for them.[23] Workshops subordinated to *guvernământ* produced wares primarily for the Romanian military and only after that for the local population.[24] Those with higher ranks and better connections were allotted villas built during the tsarist era by the Russian upper classes in the tsarist era, which under the Soviets were populated by members of communist nomenklatura. Lining up the Odessa littoral, they were often surrounded by gardens or orchards. In order to make them available to the new residents, the authorities had to evict squatters from the lower classes who had occupied them following the Soviet withdrawal.[25]

Romanian administrative personnel in Transnistria was exempt from mobilization into the acting army. In December 1942, on the request of Alexianu, who complained of difficulties recruiting qualified cadres, and against the opinion of his General Staff, Ion Antonescu decreed that such personnel was to be considered "as if serving at the front."[26] In June 1942, the governor proposed the introduction of military-type uniforms for civil servants in Transnistria, with the letters "G.T." (Guvernământul Transnistriei) embroidered on the power part of the sleeves. It is unknown whether this proposal was approved and there is no evidence that it was ever implemented.[27] In 1942–1943, Alexianu requested more and more bonuses and decorations for his subordinates, while the Conducător sometimes supported and on other occasions turned down such initiatives.[28] Transnistrian civil servants' high remuneration and bonuses induced resentment among civil servants in Romania.[29] In December 1943, the General Staff, supported by the Ministry of Finance, complained to Antonescu that these salaries were higher than those of the frontline officers; the Conducător was outraged and ordered an investigation into this issue.[30]

The prefects were selected from a list composed by General Vasiliu from among active gendarme officers, usually in the rank of major, lieutenant colonel, or colonel. Vasiliu, who experienced a shortage of trained personnel, was slow to send his men into the occupied territory. On September 22, 1941, Alexianu related to Ion Antonescu that he needed "more officers to be appointed prefects."[31] He had to wait four more months, however, to receive from Vasiliu a list of ten candidates. While sending this list the inspector general of the gendarmerie simultaneously requested that Major Modest Isopescu be relieved of his duty as prefect of Golta județ since "he was badly needed as a commander of the Balta Gendarme Legion."[32] Alexianu, who by this time had developed a particularly close relationship with Isopescu, refused to budge, reminding Vasiliu his promise to appoint "another officer" as commander of the Balta Legion.[33] This case shows that despite the shortage of qualified gendarme officers and divergent priorities between Vasiliu and Alexianu, the governor enjoyed considerable leeway in appointing prefects he personally trusted.

Pretors were selected from among Romanian public servants with law degrees who passed qualification exams for appointment as prefects in Romania and were awaiting vacancies.[34] According to Romanian historian Pavel Moraru, "a considerable part" of pretors were of Transylvanian origin, probably refugees from the northern part of this province, which in the summer of 1940 had been transferred to Hungary.[35] Each județ had one or two subprefects appointed from among Romanian civil servants with law degrees. One more subprefect per județ appointed from among local Moldovans (often émigrés to Romania) was exempt from such qualification requirements.[36] Although on September 23, 1941, Alexianu complained that "not all positions of subprefects could be filled since the bulk of the proposed candidates turned the appointment down or did not come," shortly afterward the situation seemed to have improved and no trace of this problem's persistence surfaces in the extant sources.[37] According to Alexianu's report of March 3, 1943, each prefect "was assisted by a limited number of public servants, such as an agricultural engineer, a mechanical engineer, an economics specialist, an inspector of education, a limited number of administrative personnel, and a chief medical doctor. There [was] a special section for composing and notarizing documents."[38] If one is to judge from the detailed data of *prefectura* (prefect's office) employees from Berezovca județ, dated January 1943, Alexianu's claim that the number of administrative personnel was "limited" was not exactly correct: at that time, in addition to the four pretors, one subprefect, two medical doctors, two lower-level medical, one veterinary personnel, and five teachers, there were twenty-six other administrative personnel.[39]

Several factors seem to have contributed to this exponential growth—despite Alexianu's declared intention to impede it—of administrative personnel at the lower level. First, high salaries and perks in the province constituted a proverbial pull, while a shortage of jobs in Romania pushed the Romanians to look for employment elsewhere. In 1941–1943, the human resource section of the *guvernământ* (Direcția administrativă) was inundated with requests for appointment in various positions—from a subprefect to a stenographer. The language utilized by some of the job seekers makes it clear that they considered employment in the Romanian administration in Transnistria as a sui generis social welfare for underpaid but patriotic Romanians and that they were convinced that the government shared such sentiments. For example, writer-journalist Valeriu Olaniuc argued his case for an appointment "in the departments of propaganda or missionary activity" by indicating that he was burdened by a family of two children and had to take care of his parents. Olaniuc stated that he "had a soul that strove to have a position of responsibility and initiative, inspired by the love of King, Nation, and Conducător," and that his fourteen-year record of practicing his métier had proven his devotion "to the Romanian Nation and its spirituality."[40] Tellingly, Alexianu or the director of the human resource department, to whose attention such requests were submitted, usually turned them down or directed their authors to follow legally established procedure, starting with taking qualification tests at the PCM.[41] Clearly, the *guvernământ* did not suffer from a shortage of volunteers to serve in its administration.

Nepotism and Corruption

Some prefects, whose responsibilities included appointing județ-level civil servants, were only too happy to increase the number of their subordinates, abusing the lack of clear guidelines on the organization of *prefecturas*. For example, in November 1941, Alexianu ratified the appointment of eighteen civil servants in Dubăsari județ, whose list was suggested to him by the prefect.[42] It seems that sometimes Alexianu suspected that some prefects were not motivated by local needs as much as by the desire "to make arrangements" for their friends and relatives but found it difficult to resist the prefects' pressure. For example, on January 8, 1942, Prefect Isopescu from Golta județ requested permission to appoint functionaries in his office from among those "lawyers and civil servants" from Romania whose numerous petitions for appointment he had received.[43] Alexianu's first reaction was negative: he wrote back to Isopescu indicating that "all appointments had to be made within the approved limits and only following the creation of administrative positions."[44] Nevertheless, when Isopescu repeated his request in a slightly different form in a new cable—"to appoint and summon from the country [Romania] functionaries whom we badly need"—Alexianu, instead of reprimanding him for insubordination, answered that he would respond at the conference to which all prefects were to be summoned. A handwritten note on this cable reads that the decision "was communicated [to Isopescu] verbally."[45] It is likely that this decision was positive since this seems the only way to explain Alexianu's unwillingness to leave a paper trail—such permission would violate the established rules. In August 1943, Alexianu again showed readiness to accommodate the request of the newly appointed prefect of Dubăsari județ, Alexandru Batcu, to employ additional functionaries in his service.[46]

Owing to the postwar investigation into Modest Isopescu's crimes (he was the chief organizer of the massacres of Jews in the camp Bogdanovca in late 1941–early 1942 as well as other atrocities), we know that Alexianu's suspicions regarding Isopescu's hiring practices were well-founded. According to a deposition of Dragoș Isopescu, Modest Isopescu's nephew, who in 1946 was a student at the Commercial Academy in Bucharest, not only did he "obtain a post" in Golta *prefectura* at the time his uncle headed it, but the chief of the bureau of information at the same *prefectura* was Manole Isopescu, another member of the prefect's extended family.[47] According to a well-informed Jewish survivor Mihail Cvitco, Modest Isopescu was godfather to Golta's subprefect Aristide Pădure. Another Jewish survivor, Vasile Nemeș, testified that Golta judeţ was run in a corrupt and brutal manner by "Isopescu's clique," which included "his brother, cousin, gossip [*cumnat*, considered a member of family in Romanian culture] . . . [so that] local population . . . lived under his family's control."[48]

Because the situation in the other judeţe was not investigated as thoroughly as it was in Golta, there is no way to know whether and to what extent Isopescu's model of family rule was replicated elsewhere. Many Romanian civil servants in Transnistria saw placing their relatives and friends in lucrative positions as their duty dictated by age-long customs and cultural norms. For example, on August 1, 1942, the *guvernământ* secretary general, Emanoil Cercavschi, sent a letter to a female friend in Germany (Cercavschi hailed from Bukovina, an Austrian province before World War I). The letter, which was intercepted by military censors despite an official stamp "not to be censored," contained what censors assessed as "offenses to the honor of the Romanian State and Nation." They forwarded its Romanian translation to Alexianu, together with a note registering their opinion. Cercavschi's obsequious expression of joy at being decorated by a German order, which he purportedly held higher than any Romanian distinction he had ever received indeed sounded unbefitting a Romanian civil servant. After noting matter-of-factly the deportation of Jews into the province, with a note that "of course" he could not help those who asked for help (among the deportees were probably common acquaintances of his and his German friend's), Cercavschi added an invitation to somebody identified as Rudi, probably a physician, to come to Transnistria. He promised to find him "a lucrative occupation, especially given [current] shortage of doctors." He went on to add that it would be even better if both of his German friends could come to Romania "for fattening" since "there were still plenty of pickings."[49] The military censors' remonstrance, however, failed to produce any effect on Alexianu, who simply ignored it. To the governor, it seems, such attitudes and assumptions were as natural as to Cercavschi.

Cercavschi's letter suggests that the "lucrative" character of Transnistrian positions included not only, and perhaps not primarily, official salaries—triple the amount paid in Romania—but also shady incomes. Some other contemporary observations confirm this impression. This is what, for example, SSI's (Romania's intelligence and counterintelligence service) office in Tiraspol related in October 1942: "A considerable part of Romanian civil servants currently employed in Transnistria have low professional skills, are too young, inexperienced, and lacking sufficient education; a majority of them have already compromised themselves due to their striving to enrich themselves quickly and by any means, considering their appointment in Transnistria as a once-in-a-lifetime stroke of good luck."[50] Indeed, the evidence of official corruption on all levels and in various forms—black trafficking of goods, extortion and taking of bribes, embezzlement of public goods—abounds in Romanian, German, Soviet, and Jewish sources. Enumeration of individual cases can cover dozens of pages, but I will confine myself to several pieces of evidence, which I deem the most informative. Primarily, there was massive speculation of goods and currency brought from Romania by the military and civil servants, who were the only people with permission to cross the Dniester River into Transnistria. In March 1943, the Second Bureau of the Third Army Corps (intelligence) reported that "on the occasion of one single search in a Bucharest-Odessa passenger train on February 7, 1943, we found 14,000 lei in cash, 62 meters of silk, 23 pairs of female stockings, 490 reels of thread, 60 bottles of lamp gas, 1,500 boxes of matches"—all articles of great value strictly prohibited from importation into the province.[51] On February 9, 1943, Alexianu issued Ordinance #9, instituting severe customs control on the borders as well as ordering the internment of contrabandists in concentration camps.[52] By August 1943, the authorities confiscated contraband merchandise valued at 292,340 RKKS.[53] In November 1943, Reserve Colonel Mihai Botez, the prefect of Ovidopol județ, was under investigation for contraband, and Ion Antonescu ordered him court martialed.[54] Still, all of this was just a drop in the bucket since many basic necessities, such as clothes and shoes, could be procured only on the black market as contraband merchandise from the local industries working almost exclusively for the Romanian troops.[55] Alexander Werth, who as a BBC correspondent in Russia visited Odessa days after its liberation by the Red Army in April 1944, noted that at that time, one could still buy such items as "German pencils, Hungarian cigarettes, German cigarettes, and even perfume and stockings," on the black market. Werth attributed this bounty to the legacy of the Romanian domination since, as he remarked, probably relating rumors collected from the locals, "Romanian generals used to bring whole truckloads of ladies' underwear and stockings from Bucharest and get their orderlies to sell them on the market."[56] According to Werth's local informer, Romanian soldiers, too, "always had a variety of things to sell."[57]

Bribery was endemic. As Werth's same informer put it, "with a little money [one] could buy anything from the Romanians, even a passport in the name of Richelieu."[58] The Extraordinary State Commission for the

Determination and Investigation of Nazi and Their Collaborators' Atrocities in the USSR (ChGK) collected, following the liberation of Odessa, testimonies on atrocities in Odessa and the Odessa oblast, most of which came from Odessa intelligentsia, often Jews who survived by bribing the Romanian officials. As one lawyer, Lukashov (no first name and patronymic provided) put it: "Every Romanian functionary, from the lowest to the highest, took bribes. . . . They arrested a lower-level employee of the mayor's office and put him in front of the city hall with a sign, 'bribe-taker,' while at that very time every employee of the mayor's office was accepting bribes."[59] In September 1943, the SSI (Romanian intelligence and counterintelligence service) reported from Ananiev that "bribery is accepted by absolutely all authorities" and "is considered customary."[60]

Embezzlement of public funds, of goods considered "war booty," and of things belonging to murdered Jews or other victims was another widely reported practice. For example, Pretor Vasile Mânescu, under whose jurisdiction tens of thousands of Jews interned in the Bogdanovca camp were first dispossessed of their meager valuables and then murdered, was denounced and charged, in 1942, with the appropriation of the majority of their valuables (although not of the murder as such). On par with Mânescu, other local Romanian officials participated in this embezzlement.[61] According to Pretor Pădure, his boss, Golta județ prefect Isopescu used to send farm animals from Transnistria to the farms in Romania owned by other officials on assignment in Transnistria, who then paid "compensation" to him. According to the same source, Isopescu "once traveled to Kiyv to procure spare parts there, and returned with Persian rugs, saying that he needed them as a memento."[62] Persian rugs as coveted objects of illegal appropriation are mentioned in other depositions, including in that of Alexianu, who asserted that after one (unnamed) siguranța commissar had been "caught with Persian rugs," he was tried. Perhaps tellingly, Alexianu failed to indicate the verdict.[63] As already mentioned, Odessa mayor's office (*primaria*) was often seen as extremely corrupt, and among its officials the most infamous was Gherman Pântea's deputy Constantin Vidrașcu.[64] According to his brother-in-law's deposition, Vidrașcu occupied a ten-room apartment in Odessa, and when he left the city, he brought with him back into Romania two railcars filled with furniture.[65] Alexianu, who during his stay in office resolutely defended his administration's reputation by refuting most of the accusations of wrongdoing, changed his tune during the 1945 pretrial investigations and acknowledged that despite his best efforts he was unable to prevent massive pillage of murdered Jews' movable properties. "They used to ship [into Romania former Jewish] pianos in military trucks," he said. Displacing his responsibility on the supposed Romanian national character, he noted melancholically, "Unfortunately, our nation [*neam*] has inclinations to thievery."[66]

Police, Gendarmerie, and Intelligence Services

Romanian law enforcement bodies, the police and gendarmerie, were organized along the French model and were both subordinated to the Ministry of Interior, Direcția jandarmeriei (Department of Gendarmerie) and Direcția poliției (Department of Police), respectively. The gendarmerie had its responsibility in the rural areas while the police in urban centers. The basic territorial unit of the gendarmerie was the legion (*legiune*), whose boundaries coincided with the județ. The legions were under the orders of their commandants, typically a gendarmerie officer in the rank of major, who in turn was subordinated to the prefect. In December 1941, the Transnistrian police was unified into a separate inspectorate headed first by Colonel Emil Broșteanu and later, from April 1942, by General Mihail Iliescu. In June 1943, this inspectorate was divided into the Balta and Odessa Inspectorates, which united into the General Subinspectorate Chișinău-Odessa (still headed by Iliescu).[67] Transnistrian inspectors (and, respectively, subinspectors general) had double subordination: to the inspector general of gendarmerie (simultaneously vice minister of internal affairs) and to the governor of the province.

On the lower level, each județ had its own gendarmerie *legiune* (pl. *legiuni*, henceforth I refer to this unit as legion) commanded by the gendarme officer in the rank of major. In Transnistria, legions were initially divided into five sectors patrolled by gendarmerie platoons (each legion numbered five platoons) and commanded by a lieutenant. Gendarmes were supposed to patrol by either walking in groups or riding horse-drawn carts.[68] According to the postwar testimony of Ioan Popescu, commander of the Berezovca Gendarmerie Legion in 1941–1942, each sector included about forty *comune*, so that the gendarmes visited a *comună* once every fifteen days. Because telephone connections were "nonexistent," communications were carried out by couriers, so that it took two to three days for a report from a far-flung village to reach the legion commander.[69] Small wonder then, that legion commanders felt that their manpower was insufficient in view of the tasks they faced.[70] Alexianu tried to improve the situation, and on December 10, 1941, he requested additional gendarmerie units for the purposes of creating gendarmerie posts in each village, following the practice in Romania. Starting on May 1, 1942, sectors were divided into gendarmerie posts, each headed by a gendarmerie NCO, usually in the rank of corporal, and staffed by up to ten men. Each post was provided, at least in theory, with two machine guns.[71] Setting up a post in each village proved impossible, as Transnistrian Gendarmerie Inspector Iliescu's report, dated December 9, 1942, to Inspector General Vasiliu indicates. Iliescu explained that the gendarmes were in no position to provide permanent guards for the Jewish ghettoes, 133 in all, owing to the insufficiency of their numbers. Under such conditions, the gendarmes could supervise interned Jews solely by periodic patrolling, otherwise their numbers should be increased.[72] Vasiliu, who was reluctant to spare "his" gendarmes for Transnistria, claimed that this situation was satisfactory, as proved by the "absence of any serious case of terrorism or sabotage" in the province.[73] By the fall of 1943, however, partisan activity intensified, and requests for increasing the gendarmes' numbers became more frequent. By the end of that year, the strength of the gendarmerie units in the two most threatened județe, Balta and Tulcin, was doubled.[74]

Because of the difficulties associated with recruiting professional police officers in Romania, the town police and the village police in Transnistria consisted of local residents—volunteers or appointees. This police force was under orders of the gendarmerie legion commanders and was called "communal police" (usually referred to as "local police").[75] The same kind of arrangement pertained to the city police of Tiraspol. Only in Odessa, the maintenance of order was entrusted to professional policemen from Romania, whose overall number in December 1941 totaled 150. Considered too small for policing a city with an estimated population of 350,000, 800 gendarmes (probably soldiers who passed through a short training program) were added to supplement their effective.[76] As in Romanian cities, Odessa police was considered a *prefectura poliției* headed by a police officer in the rank of captain or major. Odessa police was originally subordinated to the army and the governor but, following its chief's complaint that double subordination was creating problems, it seemed to have been transferred under the governor's exclusive control.[77]

The Transnistrian gendarmerie included "security police," or poliția de siguranța, commonly known as siguranța. That service was subordinated to the Transnistrian inspector and each legion had its own siguranța bureau. Prefectura poliției in Odessa also included a bureau of siguranța.[78] Besides its commanding officer, usually a lieutenant, each siguranța bureau included three to seven agents (*agenți*), whose mission was defined as "collection and diffusion of specific information." In practice, the siguranța's mission was detection, penetration, and neutralization of clandestine resistance groups, whether pro-Soviet or Ukrainian nationalist. The siguranța's immediate task was the recruitment of "trustworthy persons (Moldovans)" who had to serve as informers.[79] Rules provided that siguranța officers and agents had to be under cover and always clad in civilian clothes; siguranţa offices had to be located in a building away from the gendarmerie quarters. These regulations were not always followed, however, and one is struck by how widely the agents were known as such by the locals.[80] Since siguranţa agents were professionals on a mission from Romania, they often were hampered by their insufficient command of local primary languages (Russian or Ukrainian).[81]

Alongside the siguranţa another Romanian secret service was active in Transnistria, known as the Special Service of Information (Serviciul Special de Informaţii), or SSI. The SSI was an heir to the army intelligence and counterintelligence service, which until September 1940 was known as the Secret Service of Information (Serviciul Secret de Informaţii). This earlier SSI was subordinated to King Carol II, who used it to spy on and intimidate his opponents.[82] One of the first acts of the newly minted dictator Ion Antonescu was sacking SSI's long-standing director and Antonescu's personal nemesis Mihail Moruzov. Simultaneously, Antonescu ordered the renaming of the service, its reorganization, and subordination to the prime minister's office (Preşedenţia Consiliului de Miniştri), that is to himself. From November 12, 1940 and until the end of Antonescu's regime, Eugen Cristescu served as its head (director). An experienced civil servant with a law degree and a distinguished career in the Ministry of the Interior, Cristescu was also Ion Antonescu's confidant. A series of decrees and regulations issued in September–November 1940 clarified the SSI's tasks and structure. According to Moraru, the SSI mission "was strictly of intelligence and counterintelligence (not repressive) character." Its personnel was recruited from both active and reserve military officers as well as civil servants. Although in theory independent from the army, it still was expected to closely collaborate with the second section (intelligence) of its general staff, as well as with police, gendarmerie, and border guards. Although the SSI's network of spies and informers spread both inside and outside of the country, since Romania's entry into the war much of its activity was focused on the territories occupied by the Romanian army.[83] In particular, the SSI created a special unit called the "Mobile Echelon," which followed the Romanian troops into the Soviet territory and supplied its information to the second sections of general staffs of various army units.[84]

In the first half of October 1941, Colonel (later General) Ion Lissievici, head of the first section (intelligence) of the SSI and of its Mobile Echelon, initiated the formation of what would become the Odessa Intelligence Center. In agreement with the heads of intelligence sections of various large units (division and up) of the Fourth Army, he issued regulations concerning its structure, personnel, and tasks. The Odessa Intelligence Center, set up the following month, was composed of three active military officers and fourteen to sixteen civil servants. Subordinated to it were initially two (Tiraspol and Moghilev) and later five subcenters (additionally in Ovidiopol, Ochakov, and Berezovca), which were called counterintelligence, rather than intelligence, subcenters. Each subcenter had *rezidenţe* in each judeţ and, in Odessa, *circumscripţii*, which in effect coincides with raions. Subcenters consisted of heads and their assistants, to whom sometimes were added temporary employees on a mission from Romania. *Rezidenţe* included a resident or two—one for information and another for counterinformation. They had limited funds at their disposal for the hire of local informers. SSI employees wore civilian clothes and used false names. Similar to the gendarmerie and siguranţa reports, the SSI reports from Transnistria are filled with complaints of insufficient funds, lack of vehicles and draught animals, as well as the unreliability of telephone and telegraph services. Another problem was limited knowledge of local languages. Nevertheless, a specific feature of the SSI organization in Transnistria was that its officers were not on Alexianu's payroll and their promotion did not depend on provincial power holders. In fact, there was substantial tension between the SSI, which sometimes supplied critical information on the governor and provincial state of affairs in general, and the *guvernământ*. The SSI reports tended to be more frank and informative than any other official agency's reports in the region. Its antipartisan activity also proved more professional and effective than any of its institutional competitors.[85]

Administration of Justice

Administration of justice in Transnistria was entrusted to the military. According to the Romanian legal experts, following the occupation, the Soviet judiciary ceased to exist. Consequently, it was the army that exercised what the Romanian jurists called "repressive justice, prompt and severe," on the basis of the Romanian Code of Military Justice. There were two levels of military courts, pretorial courts at the level of judeţe, and two martial courts: in Odessa for the southern part of Transnistria and in Tiraspol for the northern part. Gendarmerie legion commanders performed functions of pretorial courts, serving as prosecutors, grand jurors, and deciding judges. They were guided by the provisions of the Romanian Code of Military Justice and by the decrees on the organization of Transnistria, together with its governor's ordinances and other regulations.[86] They also imposed sentences for breaches of their own judeţe-wide regulations. Initially, according to Alexianu's Ordinance #37 from December 20, 1941, military pretors (otherwise known as legion commanders) could impose sentences for up to two years in prison and a 20,000 lei fine, or a combination thereof. Ordinance #10 from January 4, 1944, extended their sentences to up to twelve years in prison and/or equivalent fines.[87] Martial courts, presided by military magistrates, imposed sentences from these thresholds up to the death penalty, for crimes provided by the Code of Military Justice in all matters pertaining to state security and by the governor's ordinances. There was no legal recourse for appealing such sentences, except petitioning for their suspension on probation. Local residents could request a suspension in the same court that sentenced them, while Romanian citizens sentenced by military pretors could request suspension from martial courts. Decisions pronounced on the requests for suspension were definitive and no further appeal was allowed. Alexianu's Ordinance #133 from September 9, 1943, established an unprecedented procedure of prosecution of civil servants in Transnistria, both on mission from Romania and local residents. Their administrative bosses could initiate an investigation into their supposed wrongdoing, both on their own volition and following a lead from a denunciation and send their cases to the pretorial or martial court, depending on the rank, for sentencing, obviating prosecutors.[88] Needless to say, such provisions put local civil servants in the situation of full dependence on their prefects, who could both initiate their prosecution and sentence them at will. Governors' powers over employees of the *guvernământ* were also increased, even though not as thoroughly since sentencing depended on magistrates in the courts over which he did not preside.

Romanians, following the international legal norms on military occupation, intended to adjudicate private law disputes according to the Soviet legal norms. On January 17, 1942, in a memorandum to Ion Antonescu, Alexianu noted that "in principle," an occupying authority keeps local laws (he specifically meant the Soviet Penal Code) in force, with the exception of matters of public order and state security, in which it enforces its own legal norms.[89] Although Alexianu hasted to add that "nothing hinders an occupying power from extending its penal laws over the occupied territory, even pending conclusion of the peace treaty," when this issue came up for discussion in the Council of Ministers, Mihai Antonescu, who presided over the meeting, ruled out such option. As he explained, his overriding concern was to avoid giving the Hungarians any pretext for claiming that Romania has already extended its sovereignty over Transnistria.[90] In view of the nonexistence of Soviet courts of law in Transnistria and the inability of Romanian judges to apply Soviet law, the application of Soviet private law (in Soviet legal parlance, it referred to a substantial part of the Penal, Civil, and Administrative codes that were not available in Romanian translation) inevitably caused difficulty. Perhaps tellingly, the Romanian archival sources seemingly contain no information on how this task was performed. According to noted Odessan lawyer Iakov Borisovich Brodskii, a surviving member of the liberal-minded and cosmopolitan Odessan upper middle class and a lawyer with a record of service stretching all the way back to prerevolutionary Russia, there were no courts to adjudicate civil cases, but "interested parties could resort to the services of mediators whom Romanians quasi-recognized, that is, one could obtain enforcement of their decisions."[91] Brodskii failed to provide further information as to who these mediators were, but Lukashov who also spent the war years under occupation, noted in his deposition to ChGK that in Odessa "civil cases were litigated either in the legal *direcția* of *primaria* (mayor's office) or in the board of arbitration (*arbitrazh*)." Lukashov then went on to add that the "process of law in arbitration boards was extremely simplified, procedural norms were not followed. All proceedings were held in Romanian."[92] This suggests that arbitration functions were performed, in Odessa at least, by Romanian officials who were not necessarily lawyers, and that the application of Soviet legal norms was rather "theoretical."

All Odessan lawyers who lived in the occupied city and deposited their testimonies to ChGK after the war, unanimously condemned the Romanian judiciary in Transnistria for its abuses and its insatiable, insolent, and shameless venality. To quote Brodskii again, the most eloquent, informative, and surprisingly nuanced eyewitness: "Bribery thrived everywhere . . . Among martial court magistrates and employees, all but three persons used to take bribes, including stenographers and guards." Brodskii told the story of another lawyer, Baranovskaia (in fact, his mistress with whom he had fathered a son), who was denounced as a Jewess hiding under an assumed name. Following her arrest, she managed to transmit negotiated bribes to siguranța chief Porumbescu and prosecutor Gavrilovich via Romanian lawyer Sârbu. The latter, however, failed to deliver the bribe to the addressees (presumably appropriating it), and on April 20, 1942, Baranovskaia was executed by firing squad. Another Jewish lawyer, Kaidman, who was also denounced and arrested, bribed Gavrilovich. When Gavrilovich requested additional payment and Kaidman was unable to gather the necessary funds, he was sentenced to death and executed. Still another Jewish lawyer, Bogopol'skii, while interned in a ghetto together with other Jews, transmitted a bribe to Odessa siguranța chief Răzvan. The latter, however, did nothing for his release. Bogopol'skii then submitted a complaint to the prosecutor Ionescu, whom Brodskii characterized as a decent man of liberal views. Ionescu summoned both Bogopol'skii and Răzvan to his office where they negotiated a price for the Jew's release in Ionescu's presence. With all this, continued

Brodskii, the majority of Romanian prosecutors were liberals, Anglophiles, and Russophiles (this latter assertion seems unlikely, added in order to divert probable NKVD attention to Brodskii's ties to the pro-Western Romanians); they did not believe in the Axis powers' victory and considered the war a mistake; and they despised "Antonescu's men." When confronted with evidence of abuses in the Romanian law enforcement, they explained it by a shortage of trained personnel during the war, so that Bucharest authorities assigned the worst cadres to the mission in Transnistria.[93] Still, whether "liberal" or not, that same Ionescu was mentioned by at least one other eyewitness as a brutal and cynical bribe-taker.[94]

Preliminary investigations, conducted by the police and gendarmerie as well as by lower-ranking military prosecutors, routinely included cruel methods such as beatings, both with fists and rubber hoses; wrapping in wire; breaking fingers by squashing them between the door and the doorframe; burning the heels with flaming coals; and even a local invention, the "electric chair," which, according to Brodsky, did not kill but caused serious burns. Its inventor was none other than Răzvan himself, and the chair was reportedly so popular among the Romanian investigators that they would borrow it from the Odessa office for use in outlying Transnistrian territories (they called its use a "scientific treatment").[95] According to the same source, these methods were not practiced by prosecutors in the "highest" martial court (probably meaning Odessa). What was more, according to those Soviet resisters who survived arrest and investigation, during the trial some defendants would renounce their depositions, claiming that they made them under duress, causing such depositions to be dismissed.[96] A former SSI investigator Constantin Hariton independently confirmed such accounts during his interrogation in April 1945.[97]

That the Romanian version of "repressive justice" was not the same as complete lawlessness and the arbitrary application of lethal violence against anybody suspected of hostile attitudes is further confirmed by instances of the release of individual resisters when martial courts concluded that the prosecution had failed to prove their guilt. Summarizing the SMERSH's findings on the Soviet resistance in Transnistria and the Romanian fight against them, deputy head of the Organization and Instruction Department of the Central Committee of the Communist Party of Ukraine (CC CP(B) U), Viktor Alidin reported in April 1945 to the CC CP(B)U's first secretary Nikita Khrushchev that, following a transfer of cases to martial courts, "they would accept the defendants' complaints about torture, would treat them with respect during interrogations, and even release some of the less active members of the underground." Perplexed by these practices, as well as by rather lenient sentences that some of the leaders of the Soviet underground received—such as various terms in prison or of forced labor (*katorga*) instead of the death penalty—Alidin explained these practices as a form of the Romanians' "cunning" (*ukhishchrenie*).[98]

What for Alidin appeared as a subterfuge, for some Romanian magistrates on the mission in Transnistria was the carrying out of their professional duty. According to Colonel Chirilă Zoltan, who in 1942–1944 served as chief prosecutor of the Odessa martial court, there was a constant tension between the gendarmes and prosecutors "due to the illegalities committed by the gendarmes." In particular, when in February or March 1943, following the arrest of a group of "terrorists" in Berezovca judeţ, the Odessa martial court was scheduled to try ten of them, Zoltan's subordinate, Lieutenant Dumitru Leşeanu, who was in charge of this case, discovered from the materials in the file that eighty other suspected members of the group were shot to death by the gendarmes "while trying to escape from under the escort." Suspecting foul play, Leşeanu, "a brave man," as Zoltan characterized him, raised the issue with Zoltan, but the latter refused to follow up. As he explained, General Vasiliu and Governor Alexianu had by that time warned him not to interfere in such matters, for fear of being sent to the front. This threat was issued on the occasion of the Odessa martial court prosecutors' arresting several police officers, who murdered suspected members of the Odessa communist underground.[99] When interrogated in 1949, Leşeanu stated that according to his observations, "all so-called killings due to attempts to escape from under escort were nothing more than pretexts systematically used by the police and gendarmerie bodies to justify acts of extermination committed by them."[100]

The Romanian police and gendarmerie were empowered in their policy of murder of all suspected partisans by Ion Antonescu himself. According to General Ion Lissievici's memoir, he received an order to that effect from the Conducător in response to a proposal to modify the policy toward suspected partisans in Transnistria; although Lissievici failed to provide the date, in all probability he was referring to the fall of 1941. According to his account, the initiative came from the Odessa martial court magistrates who, seeing that due to the high number of arrested suspects they were unable to process all their cases while the city prison had no capacity to house them, suggested that from now on only "active partisans would be tried by the martial court." Those whom the magistrates labeled as "proven simple accomplices" were to be interned in a concentration camp in Romania. When this proposal reached Ion Antonescu in a report submitted to him by the SSI Odessa Information Center, he turned it down, adding that "all partisans—those active and their accomplices—had to be shot. This order will be also transmitted to *guvernămante* of Bessarabia and Bukovina." Lissievici claimed that he decided not to implement this order, and although he did inform the military commandant of Odessa of its existence, he let him know that he recommended that all partisans continue to be tried by the martial court, which presupposed sentencing them to less severe punishments than death penalty.[101]

Whether Lissievici did indeed conceal the order or not is less important than the fact of its issuance. There is no doubt that the gendarmerie commanders were aware of its existence and acted accordingly, even if not with respect to each and every suspect. Soviet sources mention numerous instances of extrajudicial killings of suspected resistance members by the gendarmes. To cite just one particularly notorious case, in February 1943, the gendarmes arrested thirty members of an underground Komsomol cell in the village of Krymka, Golta judeţ. Despite the fact that this cell had failed to achieve much of anything except killing one of its own for reasons that remain obscure and carrying out a failed raid on the gendarme post, all of the arrested were escorted to jail in Golta, where they were beaten and tortured. Shortly afterward, twenty-three of them were sent back to the village, presumably for lack of evidence and with the purpose to reside there under gendarmerie surveillance. En route to the village, all of them were shot by the escort under the pretext of attempting to escape. The remaining seven were transported to Tiraspol martial court, which, having found no evidence of their subversive activity, sent them back to the village with the same purpose. Instead, the gendarmes shot and killed this group, too, under similar circumstances and the same pretext.[102]

Evidently, the Romanian magistrates routinely caved in under political and administrative pressure and acquiesced in what they themselves called abuses by the police and gendarmerie against suspected partisans. They also refused to prosecute perpetrators of mass extrajudicial killings of Jews, although they did sometimes investigate the appropriation of Jewish possessions by their murderers for personal use.[103] At the same time, the Romanian magistrates often refused to impose the death penalty on Jews arrested for violating the ban on leaving their concentration camps and ghettoes, a "crime" for which the notorious Ordinance #23 established such a punishment. This follows from the postwar prosecution of Dionisie Fotino, who in 1942 served as a commander of the gendarmerie legion and was a military pretor in Iampol judeţ. Fotino interpreted the ordinance in the sense that the sentencing and execution of Jews who escaped from designated areas had to be accomplished by him. Consequently, he both sentenced and personally executed tens of victims, evidently deriving pleasure from such actions.[104] In his defense, Fotino claimed that his actions followed directly from the ordinance's text and that, being unwilling to execute it, he initially sent arrested Jews to the martial court, which however refused to try the accused and sent them back to him. He then requested the interpretation from the grand pretor (prosecutor) of the Romanian Army, General Ioan Topor, who responded that the ordinance had to be applied on the spot, without trial by the martial court. Thus, according to Fotino, he simply followed the ordinance's provisions, which left him no room to maneuver.[105] These arguments were, however, turned down by the prosecution and judge on the grounds that Fotino's was an exceptional case among other pretors and that his successors did not interpret the ordinance in this way so that executions stopped once he was transferred to another assignment.

It would thus be an exaggeration to conclude that the repressive Romanian justice system in Transnistria was a complete sham. Rather, it was institutionally weak, corrupt, and muddled, and only sporadically did it provide some protection to the victims of the Romanian arbitrariness and brutality. So vulnerable were the magistrates to the administrative pressure that only in cases when demonstrative lenience was deemed in Romania's best interest (such as in trials of leaders of the party underground) or when a defender was such a small fish that even gendarmes had no interest in their fate, did the magistrates' inclination to mete out sentences roughly proportionate to the proven guilt had a real effect on the defendants' fate.

Romanian occupation authorities were created following native administrative traditions as modified by the Nazi German advice and Ion Antonescu's vision of establishing a "model" province under his personal guidance. Although the Romanian laws were not enacted in the province and the Soviet laws were barely enforced, the Romanians intended to base their rule on properly enacted legal regulations issued by the governor of the province. In his endeavor to highlight the Romanians' supposed administrative abilities, the Conducător wanted to man the Romanian administration, gendarmerie, and police with the best cadres available. In reality, however, these plans were compromised by the shortage of trained personnel at all levels, the unwillingness of Bucharest ministers to part with their best employees, and the Conducător's inclination to obviate proper legal procedures where the circumstances, as he understood them, demanded as much. Illegal policies were enacted by the governor on the verbal orders of the Conducător, or sometimes preempting them, via the governor's trusted underlings and without leaving behind a paper trail. Another channel through which such policies were enacted was the Gendarmerie inspector general, General Picky Vasiliu, who acted via provincial gendarmerie inspectors and further down the line of subordination. The Romanian magistracy failed to apply the law against perpetrators of grave crimes from among the Romanian state's agents.

This culture of lawlessness and lack of accountability facilitated the spread of corruption at all levels. Inefficient and unrealistic local currency regime presented countless opportunities to the Romanian state functionaries for enriching themselves via murky, shadowy schemes. For many, the temptation proved too strong. To the contemporary observers, the Romanian administration in Transnistria often appeared as the embodiment of petty-minded venality. Still, one should bear in mind that the German occupation regimes and practices in the European East were also notoriously corrupt.[106] It was not so much the vices of the Romanian administrative culture "in general" that manifested itself in the repugnant aspects of Transnistrian occupation as the incongruities of its tasks, design, and circumstances under which it was conceived and exercised.

Part 2

Transforming and Exploiting Transnistria

CHAPTER 5

Making Transnistria "Romanian"

The Romanian rule in Transnistria was informed by two philosophies of rule over foreign territory, which I designate as nationalist and orientalist. Although they share basic assumptions, these philosophies differ substantially in some important respects. According to Ernest Gellner, nationalism postulates "culture" as the basic social bond and holds that the only "natural" social form is the one in which all members of the group belong to and are ruled over by the persons of the same culture. In its extreme version, Gellner's argument goes, nationalism requires that *"only* members of the appropriate culture . . . join the unit in question, and *all of them* . . . do so."[1] What Gellner calls "culture" should be more appropriately called "ethnicity" in the case of wartime Romania, since the official Romanian ideology of that era merged culture and "blood" or "biology" in a supposedly "organic" whole.[2] Thus, according to the nationalist precept, in order to secure Romanian domination over Transnistria, it had to be made ethnically Romanian. Whether Slavs could be assimilated and become Romanians was a moot question.

Since this aim could not be achieved immediately, and as long as Transnistria remained culturally foreign, the orientalist imagining appeared as a more relevant way of ruling the province. It may appear as somewhat counterintuitive that I resort to the notion of "orientalism" to conceptualize the Romanian policy. After all, Edward W. Said spoke of Orientalism as pertaining almost exclusively to Western European—in particular British, French, and American—ways of understanding, discoursing, and ruling over the Middle (or Near) East, not any other "east."[3] Nevertheless, other scholars have shown how Western European and German views of Eastern Europe were in many ways akin to Orientalism, as Said defined it.[4] As Vejas Gabriel Liulevicius argued, Orientalism was just one of the ways to elaborate on the supposedly "intrinsic opposition" between "the East" and "the West." Just as the orientalist discourses presented "the Orient" as a realm of passion and indolence to be mastered by Western rationalism, the Germans tended to conceptualize Europe's east, in particular Slavs, as the "natural" sphere for the application of their *Ordnung* and *Kultur*.[5] Russian empire builders also widely employed the orientalist tropes while talking about their "mission in the East."[6] Modern Romanian culture exhibited some of the fundamental assumptions of orientalist thinking, in particular in reference to Eastern Slavs.[7]

Orientalist governmentality, unlike the nationalist variety, did not require purification, assimilation, and eventual blending of the Transnistrian population into the mass of Romanians. To the contrary, it posited and tended to reinforce a gap between the supposedly superior rulers and their inferior subjects. Both philosophies and techniques of government bred arrogance of power and reinforced their rulers' assumption that violence if applied for the attainment of the higher good was justified. Neither lent legitimacy to the voices of their subjects. In this chapter, I focus on those aspects of the Romanian rule in Transnistria that could be better understood within the framework of ethnic nationalism. In the next, I concentrate on the orientalist aspects.

As was discussed in chapter 1, on February 26, 1942, Ion Antonescu declared his firm intention to annex Transnistria. He wanted "to make [Transnistria] Romanian," to rid it of all ethnic non-Romanians living there and to repopulate it with ethnic Romanians from the country that supposedly did not have sufficient land to sustain its citizens.[8] The idea that any annexation, in order to be secured, had to be followed by changes in the given territory's demography to make it "an organic whole" with the rest of the country was an article of faith among Central and Eastern European nationalists.[9] The Romanians had their own experience in changing the ethnic character of a province—Dobrogea.[10] Ion Antonescu's vision of postwar Romania included its total "purification" from ethnic "foreigners." This had to be achieved either by means of population "exchanges" with a neighboring country, or expulsions in the territories of the supposed losers of the war, such as Serbia and Ukraine. As for the Jews and Roma, ethnicities without their own states, they had to be deported in the vaguely identified regions (beyond the Ural Mountains).[11]

"Purification" of the eastern provinces—Bessarabia and Bukovina—of Jews by means of mass murder and violent deportation at the beginning of the war was part and parcel of this plan and fit into the concept of these provinces' supposed "model" status. Expelled initially into Transnistria, the Jews were slated to be deported farther east. But because of the continuous—well beyond original expectations—military actions on the Eastern Front, the deported, as well as local, Jews and Roma were interned and kept in the Transnistrian concentration camps. Their presence in Transnistria was deemed "temporary." Other ethnic minority residents of Bessarabia and Bucovina—ethnic Ukrainians, Bulgarians, Russians, and Gagauz—were expected to follow the Jews' fate shortly after the end of hostilities. A year earlier, in 1940, some 195,000 ethnic Germans left Bessarabia and Bukovina for the Third Reich, in line with Hitler's vision of consolidation of "Germandom."[12] All of these "population movements"—if one is to put migrations carried out in organized conditions, as was the case with ethnic Germans, under the same umbrella with the murderous actions of the Romanian army and gendarmerie against the Jews—had the effect of "freeing" enormous amounts of arable land and other immovable properties for the "new owners." To reverse the effective depopulation of the eastern provinces, particularly because of their supposed strategic importance as "bastions" against the ever-expansionist Russia, the Conducător decided to settle war veterans and other healthy and vigorous farmers of procreative age from the Old Kingdom in Bessarabia and Bukovina in order to build what he called "an impenetrable wall in the east."[13]

As soon as Antonescu came into contact with eastern Romanians, however, he began doubting their usability for the purpose of ethnic homogenization of Romania. In mid-October 1941, the director of the Central Statistics Institute (CIS), Sabin Manuilă, drafted a plan for the complete ethnic homogenization of Romania by means of population exchange, prepared in based on the Conducător's instructions. Manuilă's draft included eastern Romanians among other ethnic Romanians to be brought into the country to Romanianize it.[14] A mere month later, at the meeting of the Council of Ministers on November 13, 1941, Ion Antonescu opined that it would make more sense to bring ethnic Romanians from the east of the Buh River into Transnistria, not Bessarabia and Bukovina, whose "freed" lands were to be reserved for war veterans.[15] And on February 26, 1942, he explained to his ministers that ethnic Romanians in Transnistria were so heavily Russified that "a titanic . . . well-coordinated, and intense struggle" would be needed to recuperate, by means of national education and religious services conducted in Romanian, these alienated "elements" for their own nation. Unless more reliable ethnic Romanians from Romania were settled in Transnistria, the province would never become truly Romanian.[16] Thus, Transnistrian Romanians first had to be Romanianized themselves, and their brethren from the country settled among them to guarantee the success of this process. As for the ethnic Romanians from beyond the Buh, they would not be permitted to settle to the west of Transnistria, so doubtful was their reliability. On November 6, 1942, the Conducător instructed Titus Dragoş, state under-secretary for Romanianization, Colonization, and Inventory, to extend its work on plans for resettlement in Bessarabia and Bukovina onto Transnistria. Antonescu added: "In Bessarabia, [ethnic Romanian] Bessarabians and war veterans will be given land. . . . In Transnistria, [ethnic] Romanians from the east of the Buh and war veterans [will be given land]."[17] As these words demonstrate, Antonescu's change of heart vis-à-vis eastern Romanians was dramatic. They also explain why he was ready to invest substantial resources in researching these communities, even during the war.

Eastern Romanians: A Solution or a Problem?[18]

In July 1941, Ion Antonescu instructed Sabin Manuilă to carry out a census of ethnic Romanians residing east of the Dniester River.[19] The first task was to correctly assess their overall numbers. At the time Antonescu believed that "a great number of Romanians" lived there.[20] This assessment was introduced into the Romanian public discourse by a group of Transnistrian ethnic Romanians who immigrated to Romania following the Russian Revolution and Civil War. These immigrants, surviving at the margins of the Romanian nationalists' circles with the support of the government's subsidies, maintained public interest in the Transnistrian Romanians' cause by harping on the latter's supposed great numbers, ancient origin, and the purity of blood. According to Nichita Smochină, the de facto leader of this group, the number of Moldovans in Transnistria alone was about 1,200,000, which effectively meant that they comprised more than one-half of the province's population of 2,200,000–2,300,000.[21] A more cautious Manuilă assessed their number in the whole USSR at about 800,000.[22]

These numbers flagrantly contradicted the Soviet censuses of 1926 and 1939, which indicated that the Moldovans comprised 30.1 (1926) or 28.5 (1939) percent of the overall population of the Moldavian Autonomous Soviet Socialist Republic (MASSR)—572,000 and 599,000, respectively. The MASSR existed from 1924 to 1940, comprising the territory between the Dniester and Buh rivers but was smaller than Transnistria.[23] Since the MASSR's borders were defined based on the ethnographic principals, the Moldovans comprised a much smaller share of the population of the territory between the Buh and Dniester rivers as a whole, if one were to follow the Soviet data.

In pursuance of Antonescu's instruction, Manuilă created two teams, one for Transnistria headed by Henri H. Stahl and another for the territory to the east of the Buh River, headed by Anton Golopenția. Stahl's team's mission, besides taking stock of ethnic Romanians, was to count the entire population in the region, as well as to "inventory" all properties and goods found there. Because of the strong Soviet resistance in and around Odessa, the team started its work only in December 1941. The team consisted of 143 employees of the CIS. According to Alexianu's Ordinance #25 from November 21, local authorities from the *pretura* down to the *primaria* levels, both in urban and in rural locales, had to create a commission for *inventory* headed by delegates appointed by the *guvernământ*. These commissions were to "work under the supervision of the administrative bodies and under the technical leadership of the Central Statistics Institute."[24] Census takers let people identify their ethnic belonging themselves, although a special effort was made to make sure that ethnic Romanians residing in predominantly Ukrainian villages would be encouraged to identify themselves as such, despite the possible social pressure to assimilate into the majority. They came up with 197,685 ethnic Romanians or 8.4 percent of the overall population. Although second only to the Ukrainians (76.3 percent) and ahead of the Russians (6.5 percent) and ethnic Germans (5.4 percent), ethnic Romanians represented only a small minority, predominantly residing in rural settlements. They were concentrated in the west of Transnistria, where in five raions along the Dniester River they constituted a majority, and in the center, where they were in a minority of 5 to 15 percent.[25]

The team led by Golopenția was much smaller—between fourteen and seventeen people.[26] In addition to professional census takers, it also included sociologists, folklorists, and musicologists. The team arrived at Tiraspol on December 20, 1941, and immediately proceeded eastward into the German-occupied zone across the Buh River. To their chagrin, however, they learned that their authorizations for crossing into the German zone, promised by the Germans, had not yet been issued, and they had to return to Transnistria where they spent the following winter and spring conducting detailed research in several Romanian villages along the Dniester. Authorizations finally arrived in June and the work began in August 1942. Through the end of that year, the team focused on the area between the Buh and Dnieper rivers, roughly commensurate with Generalbezierk Nikolajew.[27] Its task was limited: to identify and register ethnic Moldovans as well as to evaluate their level of national consciousness, not to take stock of *all* residents. During this time, small groups of two to three members of the team searched each locale, both in the rural areas and in the cities, in Generalbezierk Nikolajew.

A special methodology designed for this purpose was intended to provide local ethnic Romanians with incentives for registering as such with the team. The ultimate purpose of registration—eventual "transplantation" into the territory under the Romanian sovereignty—was not disclosed to the population. To encourage registration, the census takers solicited from the army and a philanthropic organization called the Council of Patronage over Social Action (Consiliu de Patronaj al Operei Sociale), headed by Ion Antonescu's wife Maria, the creation of 15,000 packages of gifts. Each package included two kilograms of salt, one kilogram of soap, ten boxes of matches, five packages of tobacco, and, for families with small children, one kilogram of sugar. All of these were precious commodities in a war-ravaged country. Only those locals who registered as Moldovans received these packages, accompanied by a leaflet containing an appeal from the Conducător to "The Moldovan Brothers," in Romanian but printed in Cyrillic script with which Moldovans were familiar. Suspecting that "out of the desire to get these packages, even those locals who otherwise would not declare themselves Romanians would [now] offer proof of their Romanian ethnicity," Golopenția developed an elaborate questionnaire designed to gauge the degree of an individual claimant's national consciousness. It included queries about the language spoken in the family, with further queries as to whether it was used in communication among parents only or among them and their children, and about the ethnic belonging of the claimant's spouse and of the spouses' parents. If a head of the household was able to provide enough evidence of his Romanianness, the whole family was registered, and he received a package.[28]

With the work in Generalbezierk Nikolajew mostly completed by mid-November 1942, the team decided at a conference in Odessa to transfer their activity farther east and north, into Generalbezierk Dnjepropetrowsk, as well as south into Generalbezierk Krim, which included not only the Crimea but also the northern Black and Azov sea coasts adjacent to the peninsula. Another 15,000 packages were requested and received for distribution in this area. In early 1943, having received permission from Genralfeldmarschall Erich von Manstein, Golopeția's men traveled into the military zone of occupation, reaching as far as sixty kilometers to the east of Stalino (as the city of Donetsk was known at the time), where they found a few more ethnic Romanian villages.[29] Their work continued through September 1943. Due to the enormous size of the area to be investigated, the low density of its Moldovan population, and the strain on the team's personnel and other resources, the census takers refrained from visiting each locale. Instead, they visited only those villages about which they had previously received information that people speaking Romanian (or Moldovan, as it was known locally) resided there.[30] According to Golopenția's 1950 summary, researchers identified about 200,000 ethnic Romanians between the Dniester and Buh rivers, and another 120,000 between the Buh and Donets. Golopenția concluded that these findings confirmed the Soviet censuses, according to which there were about 360,000 Moldovans in the USSR before the war, the differences being caused by the presence of additional numbers in the northern Caucasus and in the Far East (migrants from the tsarist era), as well as war losses.[31] As Golopenția commented, all of previous Romanian "deductions" were useless since they "were made in response to the momentary political requirements and with ulterior motives."[32]

The research of Moldovans residing in the territory beyond the Buh River was by necessity hasty and rather superficial, but the Romanian researchers studied more thoroughly several large and relatively ethnically homogenous villages in the western and central parts of Transnistria. The initiative belonged to Governor Alexianu, who on November 20, 1941, in a telegram to Professor Dimitrie Gusti, head of the Bucharest Institute of Social Sciences, requested "a specialist" to be sent to him in order "to conduct scientific work about the soil, people, and life in Transnistria."[33] Alexianu's addressee was the most important Romanian sociologist in the interwar era. His and his institute's influence reached its apex in the late 1930s, mostly due to the support of King Carol II. By 1941, they had seventeen years of experience in conducting "monographic research" in various Romanian villages. During the summers, Gusti's students under his supervision lived in, observed, and described all aspects of individual villages' lives. The collections of essays resulting from such work, some published, others not, were known as "sociological monographs."[34]

From Gusti's perspective, Alexianu's invitation came in handy at a time when he was still "out in the cold," where he found himself following King Carol's resignation. However, Gusti's methodology, requiring a minute description of all aspects of social reality in each locale, did not fit well into Alexianu's agenda of describing his province as a whole, and during a rather limited time span at that. Eventually, instead of sending one specialist, a commission was set up under the leadership of Gusti's appointee, sociologist and instructor (conferențiar) at the department of philosophy and literature at the University of Bucharest, Dr. Traian Herseni. The commission included a geographer, two physical and one cultural anthropologist, a linguist, a folklorist, a musicologist, and administrative personnel.[35] While waiting for the Germans' permission to travel across the Buh River, Golopenția's team studied a large village called Valea Hoțului in the center of Transnistria (Ananiev județ) with a mixed population, which also was the administrative center of an eponymous raion. Golopenția, who unlike his mentor Gusti appreciated the impracticality of minute descriptions of each locale and insisted on the necessity of looking for repetitive patterns of social interactions, selected this village as representative of the whole province, although Moldovans were a majority there, unlike in the other Transnistrian locales. Following Golopenția's methodology, his team focused on the investigation of the Soviet administrative practices at the local level and the "practical problems that the Transnistrian reality presented to Romanian administration."[36] Finally, the third team, under the supervision of Henri H. Stahl, studied a village in Tiraspol județ.[37]

Romanian researchers collected an enormous amount of information, some of which was published while the rest perished during the war or afterward when the communist authorities considered this activity problematic due to its association with the anti-Soviet war of 1941–1944.[38] Much of the team's effort was devoted to the evaluation of the eastern Romanians' "national consciousness." Although the opinions were not uniform, and some researchers tended to be more upbeat than others, generally speaking what they found belied the wild claims of the self-appointed east Romanians' spokespeople, such as Nichita Smochină. This is, for example, how sociologist Paul Mihăilescu described the worldview of a typical Moldovan from Valea Hoțului: "A Moldovan from Valea Hoțuluii is "a Moldovan from Valea Hoăului," not 'a Moldovan from Transnistria,' nor 'a Moldavan,' much less 'a Romanian.' [Outside of clearly distinguishing Jews from everybody else], "any differentiation based on ethnicity is perceived by him as irrelevant."

Mihăilescu went on to quote a nineteen-year-old teacher from a local Moldovan school: "We do not think of the nation since people are not different according to which nation they belong to, they are different according to how they are. This we believe in and I do not know how it can be changed." He concluded, "A Moldovan from Valea Hoțului, if measured by a criterion of [national] consciousness, can be called 'a Romanian' in the same way in which one can call thusly a chair, a cow, or a pipe. That is, without meaning anything."[39] Constantin Gheorghe Pavel, who studied ethnic Romanians from Crimea, was even more skeptical, writing that "the idea of repatriation does not preoccupy them otherwise than as a way of [finding a good job] and . . . [obtaining] a material advantage."[40] Golopenția tried to strike a more positive note. He suggested that this lack of national consciousness was a relatively recent phenomenon, engendered by a process of accelerated economic development in the late tsarist period and social upheaval during the Soviet era. "By transplanting these families in the Romanian milieu and granting them various advantages," he opined, "[their] latent Romanian-ness would be completely reactivated."[41]

Racial research, conducted by Iordache Făcăoaru, a member of the Traian Herseni team, a former Legionary, a vociferous proponent of "scientific" racism, and a partisan of ethnic cleansing, led to ambiguous findings.[42] On the one hand, Făcăoaru claimed, he found that the share of the "Eastern European race" was higher in Transnistria than among Transylvanian Romanians, whom he, a Transylvanian Romanian himself, believed to have been the most "biologically worthy" among all Romanians. The most "valuable" Nordic and Atlantoid (his invention) races were underrepresented among Transnistrians, which put them below Transylvanians. On the other hand, the same criteria put Transnistrians on a higher level of "biological worthiness" (valoarea biologică) than that occupied by Bessarabians. And, to make matters even messier, Romanians from eastern provinces (Transnistria, Moldova, and Bessarabia) were better "racially endowed" than Romanians from southern provinces (Oltenia, Muntenia, and Dobrogea), although less endowed than Romanians from western provinces (Bukovina, Banat, Transylvania, and Crișana-Maramureș).[43] Făcăoaru's findings were disturbing to the established Bucharest-based Romanian elites since they suggested that ethnic Romanians from the very core of the Old Kingdom, Oltenia and Mutenia, where Bucharest is located, were somehow less worthy biologically than their benighted brothers from Transnistria, who experienced centuries of Slavic domination.

Serological research of Transnistrian Romanians, conducted on Făcăoaru's initiative by a group of Romanian physicians, among whom Manuilă's son Alexandru was particularly prominent, led to different but equally surprising conclusions. This population's blood indices supposedly indicated their biological distance from the Eastern Slavs and their great proximity—almost sameness—to ethnic Romanians from the center of the country. To the latter group, Transnistrian Romanians' blood was even closer than that of Bessarabian ethnic Romanians. This meant, the researchers claimed, that for centuries Transnistrian Moldovans had guarded their separate ethnic individuality from the surrounding Slavs and this fact, they hypothesized, should have also found expression in the particularities of their way of life, although they were unable to point to anything specific.[44]

It should be noted that racial research was not particularly popular among the Romanian academic circles and had only limited support from the government. This was so because the Romanian elites were aware that "scientific racism" prevalent in the German-speaking world, with its emphasis on the Aryan race as the most biologically advanced one had the potential to undermine the Romanians' own standing, among whom the ratio of individuals with Aryan features was rather low.[45] For a short time in 1942, Transnistria became the center of such research, which is impressive especially against the background of scarce resources. Alexianu's sponsorship was of central importance for the successful implementation of this project, as was Herseni's initial inclusion of Făcăoaru in his group. Indeed, the very absence of physical anthropologists in either Stahl's or Golopenția's teams underscores the significance of Herseni-Făcăoaru's personal nexus, both of them being former legionaries, hardline nationalists, and biological racists.[46] While in Transnistria, Herseni established friendly relations with Alexianu, who made him head of the department of culture (*direcia culturii*) and defended him against the SSI's attempts to send him to the front as a suspected legionary.[47] In the fall of 1943, Alexianu appointed Herseni director general of the administration, a position in which Herseni would remain through the end of the Romanian occupation. Before leaving the region, he would order the destruction of "confidential" archival files, including those pertaining to "Jewish issues" and the plunder of the region's productive assets (Operation 1111).[48]

No matter how much importance Alexianu, Herseni, and Făcăoaru attributed to their racial studies, no evidence exists that they influenced Bucharest decision makers. When in November 1943, Ion Antonescu vetoed plans of the massive transfer of Romanians from beyond the Buh River into Bessarabia, he acted on his suspicion of their supposed alienation from the Romanian nation because of the influence of the surrounding Slavs and his fear of their infiltration by the Soviet agents. As is clear from the preceding, on the issue of their supposedly low level of national consciousness the Conducător was in agreement with most Romanian experts who studied these populations. He also kept to his earlier decision to reserve arable lands in Bessarabia and Bukovina for war veterans.[49] Nevertheless, while unsuitable for "placement'" in the older Romanian provinces, eastern Romanians were acceptable for settlement in Transnistria.

Transplanting Eastern Romanians into Transnistria

Initially, Ion Antonescu's vision of Romanizing Transnistria by changing its population was enthusiastically shared by many experts, bureaucrats, and the army's top brass.[50] Some of them were not disposed to wait until the end of hostilities (Ion Antonescu's preference) and advocated immediate action. For example, in July 1942, Major General Gheorghe Manoliu, commander of the Fourth Mountain Division deployed at the time in Crimea, urged Ion Antonescu to allow repatriation from the peninsula of ethnic Romanians who expressed such desire. In anticipation of this permission, Manoliu urged them to sell their belongings, which they proceeded to do.[51] Although the Conducător often blocked such initiatives, occasionally he gave in. In November 1942, General Cristea Pantazi, serving as the minister of defense, while on a visit to the front in the northern Caucasus, came across the Romanian-speaking village of Moldovanskaia and ordered that they were transferred to Transnistria, and Ion Antonescu confirmed his minister's order. The total number of these "refugees," as they were officially called, was 3,300. In addition, about 2,000 ethnic Romanians from the village of Dunaevka on the Azov Sea coast and still more from Crimea, about 8,000 altogether, were transferred into Transnistria.[52] Pantazi might have intended that they be eventually settled in Bessarabia, but Ion Antonescu, who believed that ethnic Romanians from east of the Buh River were not reliable enough for the settlement in Romanian proper, ordered, in November 1942, that "not a single Romanian who resided in the territory to the east of Buh River be colonized in Bessarabia. All [of them] were to be placed in Transnistria, in groups, forming Romanian villages."[53] He reaffirmed this position in January 1943, in an instruction written on the report on the problems of repatriation.[54] In the meeting of the Council of Ministers of February 4, 1943, Mihai Antonescu again stated that eastern Romanians were to be colonized only in Transnistria. The army should refrain from organizing or encouraging further transfers of populations which had to be carried out only in "in the framework of the [preapproved] plan."[55]

Alongside the issue of the "repatriation" of ethnic Romanian-residents of the "old" (before 1939) Soviet territories, there was a problem of returning former residents of Bessarabia, Bukovina, and Transnistria who had left these territories during the Soviet rule. Unlike ethnic Romanians of the former category, whose repatriation the government postponed indefinitely, the people of this category could return to their homes during the war, but only if they met a number of conditions. First, they had to be ethnic Romanians; second, they had to have no history of active support of the Soviet regime or collaboration with its repressive organs; and third, they had to be free of all contagious diseases. For the implementation of this policy, the Central Commission of Repatriation was set up under the State Under Secretariat of Romanianization, Colonization, and Inventory, a powerful government agency whose head held the rank of cabinet minister. With its headquarters in Bucharest, the Central Commission instituted the Commission of Triage, composed of the representatives of the *guvernământe* of the three provinces, of the army of occupation, and of the Transnistrian gendarmerie, with its seat in Tiraspol. Two additional triage subcommissions were set up in Varvarovka and Golta, on the Buh River.[56] This policy was also meant to contribute to the Romanianization of the three provinces.

Extant fragmentary and confused statistics as to the results of the commissions' work suggest that the implementation of this policy was inconsistent and somewhat at odds with the prescribed guidelines, for reasons that remain obscure. According to the report of the Commission of Triage to the Department of Labor of the Transnistrian *guvernământ*, from November 25, 1942 through October 11, 1943, the Golta subcommission had screened 9,406 refugees, of whom 7,732 were Moldovans, 1,444 "of various nationalities," and 230 were "passed [back] over the Buh River." These data suggest that not all ethnic non-Romanians were turned away, at least not immediately.[57] On at least one occasion, Alexianu did approve immigration of seven Ukrainian families into Transnistria, on the request of the Department of Labor, where it was argued that their heads were industrial engineers necessary for the provincial economy and otherwise unavailable in Transnistria. Still, this could hardly account for the large number of non-Romanians who were not immediately sent back across the Buh.[58] Despite the Romanians' best efforts, Transnistria's borders remained porous. In August 1943, the Triage Commission estimated that since Transnistria's occupation by the Romanian troops, as many as 30,000 persons had clandestinely crossed into the territory from the rest of the occupied Soviet territories. As many as 8,000 of them were believed to have been hiding in Odessa; 3,000 had been identified as illegal migrants and the Triage Commission urged an intensification of efforts to identify the rest and deport them all, but there is no evidence that this memorandum produced any effect.[59]

On February 1, 1943, the SSSRCI advised Alexianu to set up a group of experts tasked with the elaboration of an exact plan for the resettlement of ethnic Romanians from east of the Dniester in Transnistria, with the understanding that the order to start the operation would be issued "when political conditions would make it possible."[60] According to the government guidelines, the newcomers were to be settled compactly, that is in villages in which only ethnic Romanians would be allowed to reside. Undoubtedly, this provision was designed to guarantee the preservation and strengthening of the Romanian ethnic consciousness and culture among the settlers. The non-Romanian population had to be expelled from their dwellings and resettled in "centers with a predominantly ethnic Romanian population."

The provisions in this letter made little sense since there were just too few such localities in Transnistria. This was the reason why the SSSRCI called such an arrangement "provisional"; apparently, it meant that in the future ethnic non-Romanians had to be expelled east of the Buh. The placement of newcomers had to start along the western bank of the Buh River and then extend westward.

In the following months, Ion and Mihai Antonescu continued to hold their own against the never-ending initiatives from all quarters requesting permission to begin immediate population transfers. In March 1943, the Conducător turned down Golopenția's memorandum, insisting that the transfer of eastern Romanians into Bessarabia and Bukovina and the expulsion of the Slavs from those provinces into Ukraine had to be carried out during the war, and in April of the same year he reaffirmed this policy.[61] All studies of population transfer, Ion Antonescu ruled, had "theoretical character" only and "no practical measures could be taken at the moment. If [Romania] would win the war, [I] would solve the problem by bringing together all Romanians scattered around in the course of centuries. . . . The space within which an integral Romanian bloc would be reconstituted" depended on the outcome of the war.[62] It is likely that in addition to the practicalities of massive population transfers during the war, Ion Antonescu's awareness that such actions would contravene international law with regard to the rights of occupiers also affected his thinking on this issue.[63] In June 1943, the Conducător turned down Hoffmeyer's proposal to bring into Transnistria all eastern Romanians from Germany-occupied Ukraine, while "giving back to the Germans an equal number of the [non-ethnic Romanian] population from Transnistria [Germans needed them as labor force in their zone of occupation]." His explanation was that "the issue has not been sufficiently studied."[64]

In the meantime, Gheorghe Alexianu was enthusiastically "placing" ethnic Romanians dispatched into his province by Minister of Defense Pantazi. On April 21, 1943, he ordered that eastern Moldovans had to be "colonized" in the villages along the Dniester River in Râbnița and Moghilău județe in order to Romanianize them. Ukrainian residents of those villages had to be "evacuated" to Oceacov județ in the southwestern corner of the province (that is, at its opposite end), where they were to be "placed" in the houses of local Ukrainian residents.[65] The villages where Moldovan refugees were to be "placed" were to be allotted additional resources so that they would become "model" settlements, demonstrating to the surrounding Slavs ethnic Moldovans' superiority.

The operation was poorly planned and badly executed. Initially, the governor ordered that refugees be "placed" in Jugastru județ but then suddenly and without explanation changed his mind, ordering that they be settled in Moghilău județ. When he became aware of this order, a couple of days before the "refugees" arrived, the prefect of Moghilău județ asked Governor Alexianu to reconsider. The governor refused. That brought the situation to a breaking point. The Moghilău prefect requested 300 gendarmes to "secure order both among the [ethnic Ukrainian deportees] and [Moldovan] refugees," a completely unrealistic number, given the shortage of gendarmerie personnel in the province. The governor turned this request down but relented a little, advising that refugees be "placed" without "evacuating" the owners of the houses in which they were to be sheltered.[66] It is not clear whether this advice was followed since it was issued after the operation was already well underway. In the meantime, on June 4, 1943, army intelligence (Section II of the General Staff) related to Alexianu that deportations of Ukrainians from Râbnița județ had been "carried out hastily and produced great dissatisfaction among the evacuated Ukrainians because they were allowed to take with them only a minimum of their belongings. . . . Fears are spreading among the locals that deportations will be extended to other districts."[67]

Governor Alexianu dismissed this information, noting that the locals' dissatisfaction was inherent in any forced deportation operations, which were necessary if the resettlement of (ethnic) Romanians was to be carried out. On June 8, 1943, the SSI informed the government that ethnic Romanians evacuated from Râbnița județ had arrived at their destination in Oceacov județ in the most miserable state, "having been dispossessed of their belongings by abusive officials." "The first evacuations," the SSI note said, "resulted in rumors that all locals would follow suit"; such rumors had even "resulted in the delay of agricultural works."[68] If Ion Antonescu was aware of this experience, it surely only strengthened his negative attitude toward plans of further population transfers.

The purported beneficiaries of this transfer did not fare much better. As secretary general of Ion Antonescu's office (PCM), Ovidiu Vlădescu related to Alexianu on September 22, 1943, they were "profoundly dissatisfied." They "peregrinated from one office to another with petitions and requests" complaining that at the moment of their departure they were promised to be brought into Bessarabia and be supplied "with everything necessary." In reality, "they received almost nothing." "Many of them having neither clothing nor shoes were horrified by the approaching winter." Public expressions of this dissatisfaction, Vlădescu noted, "produced a negative impression on the locals and gave additional impetus to the communist propaganda."[69]

While the Romanian officials were learning how difficult and contentious population transfers were, they faced increased pressure from refugees who tried to escape into the territory under the Romanian sovereignty. Some of them were fleeing the brutal policy of recruitment for work (in effect, slave labor) in Germany; others fled for fear of the Soviet reprisals for their collaboration with the occupiers; still others hoped to escape harsh conditions of the Soviet rule.[70] The refugee flow increased manifold in the aftermath of the German defeat at the battle of Kursk in July 1943 and the rapid Soviet advance into Ukraine. Cognizant of the swiftly deteriorating strategic situation of their country, a few Romanian officials in the Ministry of Foreign Affairs concluded that instituting an immediate "exchange" of Bessarabian and Bukovina Slavs for ethnic Romanians from Ukraine would consolidate the Romanian claims to the retention of the two eastern provinces at the end of the war, which they estimated to end in a compromised peace. Mihai Antonescu was initially unreceptive to such entreaties, but on August 20, 1943 he convoked an inter-ministerial commission with the participation of representatives of the governors' offices of the two provinces to deliberate on such proposals. On August 28, the commission adopted a plan that envisaged the expulsion of 930,000 Slavs from Bessarabia and Bukovina and the bringing in of 350,000 ethnic Romanians from Ukraine, including Transnistria's residents. This plan meant, inter alia, that 580,000 "excess" Slavs from Bessarabia and Bukovina would be dumped into Ukraine without any care for providing resources for them.[71] Ion Antonescu, too, appeared to be gradually moving toward the idea of permitting settlement of the Romanian refugees from the east of Bessarabia. On September 22, he issued an order to General Olimpiu Stavrat, governor of Bessarabia, and to Alexianu to organize their placement in the former German territories in southern Bessarabia.[72] On October 16, the Conducător decreed the creation of a central body charged with organizing these persons' placement in Bessarabia.[73]

Approximately at the same time, and in pursuance of Alexianu's requests to appoint a group of specialists from the CSI to help him organize a "repatriation" of eastern Romanians (Alexianu's primary concern appears to have been separating ethnic Romanians from the other refugees), Manuilă sent eight of his employees under the leadership of Golopenția to Transnistria.[74] Probably utilizing personnel of the existing triage subcommissions Golta and Varvarovka, three "commissions on passage" were created with seats in Golta on the right bank and Voznesensk and Mykolaiv on the left bank of the Buh River, that is, in the German zone of occupation. Simultaneously, other members of Golopenția's team worked with guvernământe of Transnistria and Bessarabia to help organize the transfer of Moldovans from Kuban and Crimea—previously settled in Râbnița and Moghilău județe of Transnistria—into southern Bessarabia.[75]

By early November 1943, the refugee crisis reached catastrophic propor-
tions. In a dispatch to Golopenția of November 5, 1943, Manuilă advised him
to resign himself to the idea that "our ideal" (that is, the creation of ethnically pure Romania via massive transplantation of populations) could not be
realized and concentrate on saving the refugees.[76] According to Golopenția's
response to Manuilă, by that time the retreating German troops had pushed
the local population of all nationalities ahead of them (probably to avoid
them being drafted into the returning Red Army). Because the Germans had
already requisitioned their cattle, the expectation that each refugee family
would bring at least a cow with them could not be met.[77] Golopenția evidently implied that these people were in need of immediate help. As Prefect
Isopescu related to Alexianu, desperate ethnic Romanian refugees crowded
together on the left bank of the Buh River, requesting permission to enter
Transnistria and offering to sell to the Romanian authorities their belongings "at extremely advantageous prices" if they were allowed to do so.[78] The
German military put pressure on the Romanian authorities to let ethnic
Romanians into the territory under their control and even offered the much
needed logistical support to help carry out this operation. Golopenția and
Manuilă, who shared their deputy's point of view, insisted that the Romanian
authorities had to organize ethnic Romanians' immediate resettlement in
southern Bessarabia.[79]

On November 15, 1943, Governor Alexianu added his voice to the growing
chorus, requesting immediate resettlement. Persuaded by the developments
at the front that Transnistria would soon be lost to the Soviets, he insisted
that not only ethnic Romanians from beyond the Buh River but also those
from Transnistria had to be immediately resettled in Bessarabia and Bukovina. All Ukrainians and other Slavs had to be expelled from there. Alexianu
opined: "Provided the *guvernământe* of Bessarabia and Bukovina would fully
cooperate, we could bring, and in a very short time at that, all this irredentist,
lazy, disobedient to the authorities Ukrainians, and . . . in their stead settle the
entire Moldovan population from the Dniester River villages."[80]

These arguments produced exactly the opposite effect from the one
Alexianu intended. The Conducător was horrified by the specter of masses
of politically dubious and impoverished people flooding into his country. On
November 13, 1943, he vetoed the CIS proposal, stating that it "would pro-
voke a disaster." This time, he cited the lack of resources to house and feed
the potential newcomers, as well as the threat of epidemics they were likely
to bring. If Alexianu preferred, he could allow the refugees into Transnistria, but under no pretext could they go any further.[81] In the meeting of the
Council of Ministers on November 16–17, 1943, the Conducător reaffirmed

his determination to restrict the influx of refugees as much as possible, even those of ethnic Romanian origin, although he conceded that a limited number of persons of the latter category could be allowed to settle on abandoned German and "freed" Jewish properties in the south of Bessarabia. He added that such refugees would be settled in the nonethnic Romanian villages, which in such cases had to be divided into two halves, one reserved for refugees, and the other for the original residents. The original residents from the former half were supposed to be expelled from their homes and settled in the houses in the other half of the village, alongside the owners. Refugees were to be settled in the houses emptied in this manner. In either case, the arrangements had to be temporary in nature: "Under no circumstances . . . should they [ethnic Romanian refugees] fancy that they have been settled permanently." The settlement in Transnistria could continue "at least in order to change its ethnic aspect."[82]

Even these more modest plans of resettlement remained largely on paper. Although Alexianu and his German counterpart in Mykolaiv reached an agreement concerning the resettlement, it was not implemented because, as Golopenția explained in his 1950 deposition, "just a few hundred families, most of whom arrived on their own to the points of passage over the Buh, were [eventually] triaged [and allowed to pass the river]."[83] When in August 1944 the Red Army entered Bessarabia, only about 1,500 eastern Romanians were living in the southern part of the province.[84] Thus, the Consuducător's stubborn refusal to let "not Romanian enough" Moldovans into his own country prevented the implementation of the initial ambitious plans of resettlement. It is more than likely that if the Soviets' returned, they would have ordered the resettled people back to their places of origin. Ironically, by refusing to follow the experts' advice, Ion Antonescu helped prevent needless suffering of many thousands.

Nationalizing and Organizing of the Transnistrian Moldovans

Whether the Transnistrian Moldovans would eventually be "transplanted" into Bessarabia and Bukovina, as the more moderate politicians, experts, and administrators suggested, or remain in Transnistria, as Ion Antonescu and the more radical nationalists demanded, everybody agreed that they were in dire need of education to raise their "national consciousness." Following an established Eastern European tradition of nationalizing the peasant population with vague ethnic consciousness via schools and churches, the Romanian administration invested in the reeducation of Moldovan school teachers and priests.[85] According to the activities report of the Department of Culture for 1941–1943, in the summers of 1942–1943 the authorities organized "general culture courses" in Râbnița, Dubăsari, and Tiraspol, which were frequented by 1,500 Moldovan teachers. These classes were offered by Tiraspol Moldovan high school (*liceu*) teachers, as well as lecturers from Romania. All attendees traveled to Romania, with costs defrayed by the *guvernământ*, and the authorities believed that this trip "gave excellent propagandistic results." College for the training of teachers (*școala normală*) and a Christian Orthodox theological seminary were opened in Tiraspol. In addition to the "didactic material" imported from Romania, 30,000 "Romanian-Russian ABCs" had been printed and distributed among the Moldovan students.[86] At the elementary level, the Romanians financed education for all children in Transnistria, regardless of their mother tongue. However, at the *gimnaziu* (middle) and *liceu* (pl. *liceuri*, equivalent to high school) levels, they favored education in Romanian, as the following data for early 1943 reveals: the total number of elementary schools was 2,220, of which 327 or 14.7 percent were Romanian; 1,677, or 75.5 percent were Ukrainian; 156, or 7 percent were Russian; and 60, or 2.7 percent were German. At the *gimnaziu* level, the percentage of the Romanian schools rose to 40; at the "practical *liceuri*" level it was 17.2, and among the "theoretical-practical *liceuri*" (the most prestigious type of high schools), the Romanian establishments comprised 91.3 percent.[87]

The authorities propagated both the Romanian high culture and folklore. Two national (Romanian) theaters were opened in Transnistria: one in Tiraspol, shortly following its occupation by the Romanian troops, and another, in June 1942, in Odessa. The former was quartered in the former Soviet theater building, which used to produce plays in Russian, Ukrainian, and Moldovan (its Soviet-era troupe moved to Chișinău in 1940 and at the beginning of the war was evacuated to the east). The latter moved into the building of the Soviet-era Ukrainian theater, which had been shut down by the governor's order on the pretext that its productions were low-quality. Both local artists and those from Romania performed in these theaters, as well as organized "patriotic festivities." To counter what the authorities saw as disappearance of "national costumes," they imported such costumes from Romania and distributed them among university students of Moldovan ethnicity.[88]

Granting material and status privileges was another way of instilling a sense of separate identity and entitlement into the Moldovans with the ultimate purpose to tie them to the occupation regime. On September 16, 1941, the commander of the Fourth Army, Lieutenant General Iosif Iacobici, issued instructions on the treatment of the local population beyond the Dniester River, requiring that each ethnic Romanian household be issued, and that they display, the following written sign: "This house belongs to a Romanian. Trespassers will be shot."[89]

Established in imitation of German policy, which issued similar certificates to members of the Volksdeutsch community in the occupied Soviet territories, consistency and resoluteness of its application is doubtful since no instances of severe punishment for trespassing on Moldovan property was ever reported.[90] The authorities distributed to Moldovans, but not to their Slavic neighbors, agricultural implements from kolkhozes; significantly reduced their taxation burden; and systematically preferred Moldovan vendors whenever public procurements were made. Moldovan farmers were allowed to own twice as many animals as farmers of the other ethnicities (except Germans), and were allotted a monthly allowance of 50 RKKS "for the protection of [the] autochthonous Romanian element." Ethnic Romanian applicants were admitted to Odessa University hors concours and were granted stipends and guaranteed places in student hostels; a limited number of Moldovan youth were enrolled in the universities in Romania.[91] Local Moldovans were promoted into administrative and managerial positions. One subprefect in every Transnistria județ was ethnic Moldovan. As a rule, Romanians appointed the Transnistrian Moldovans as mayors of mixed villages and towns and made them heads of local police units. Members of other nationalities were appointed in these positions only if no Moldovans were available.[92] Small wonder, then, that ethnic non-Moldovans resented this policy as discriminatory and felt that they were treated as second-class people.[93]

The local press, controlled by the authorities, exalted the Moldovans' ancient presence in the regions and their supposedly higher level of culture, implying their special rights in Transnistria. For example, the newspaper *Transnistria*, published in Bucharest and distributed in the province, reported verbatim a speech by a University of Bucharest history professor and former government minister, Constantin C. Giurescu, delivered in Tiraspol on the occasion of the Romanian national holiday on May 10, 1942. In the speech, Giurescu claimed that local Moldovans hailed from the most ancient inhabitants of the region, the Gets and Dacians, and thus had historical rights over Transnistria.[94] A few months earlier *Odesskaia gazeta*, the mouthpiece of the *guvernământ*, explained that the planned exhibition about Transnistria in Bucharest would "contrast the Slavic world and communist ideology, on the one hand, and vital interests of the Romanian people and European civilization, on the other" and would show that the life of Moldovans was based on "centuries-long traditions inherited from the Gets and the Dacians."[95]

In addition to using the Transnistrian Moldovans as props of the occupation regime, the Romanian leaders allotted to them one more task: they had to demand the annexation of the region to Romania after the end of hostilities, thus strengthening the Romanian claims over it. The orchestration of the purportedly spontaneous outpouring of popular enthusiasm had to be arranged by the Transnistrian Moldovan émigrés in Romania and refugees from the Russian Civil War and Bolshevik oppression. In the interwar period, those of them, mostly young men, who possessed even an elementary education benefitted from stipends, subsidized housing, and other forms of government support designed to help them receive degrees from Romanian and, at least in one case, Western European universities. Most of them eked out a modest living, having been employed in various low-paid bureaucratic posts. Others participated in government-sponsored periodicals designed to keep the "Transnistrian problem" in public view. The Romanian governments in the interwar era did not seriously consider laying claim to Transnistria; rather they were interested in utilizing arguments produced by the Transnistrian militants as a counterweight to the Soviet claims on Bessarabia.[96]

The most successful of this group of Transnistrian refugees turned nationalist activists was Nichita Smochină, who successfully graduated from the University of Iași in 1924, majoring in philosophy and law. In 1930–1935, he continued his studies at the Sorbonne in Paris. Although he failed to obtain a doctorate there, he managed to collect rich materials on the history of the Transnistrian Moldovans, some of which he later published in Romania. His leadership among the Transnistrian refugees in Romania was constantly challenged by his numerous detractors, but nobody could rival his energy and publishing record. In 1938, Smochină started his service in the government in Bucharest, initially at the commissariat for minorities, then at the Ministry of Propaganda and, following Antonescu's coup d'état, as a liaison officer for issues concerning refugees from Transnistria, Bessarabia, and Bucovina, whose numbers increased dramatically following the Soviet annexation of the latter two provinces in June 1940.[97] According to Smochină's account, which cannot be independently verified, by early 1941 Antonescu's trust in him increased so much that he tasked him with preparing a collection of documents meant to discredit the Legionaries, which was published shortly following their revolt. Smochină even accompanied Antonescu to Munich, where on June 11–12 the latter held a summit with Hitler.[98]

On August 12, 1941, Antonescu announced to a group of would-be appointees in the newly "liberated" provinces his decision to appoint Smochină as Transnistria's governor but soon reconsidered because of Smochină's insistence. The latter had a different ambition for himself: he wanted to enter history as a man who brought Transnistria into Romania's fold. If he were governor, Smochină explained, the legitimacy of such a proclamation, in the eyes of the international law, would likely be dubious. "At the end of the day," Smochină recollected after the war, "they accepted my idea, that is, that I would not be appointed the governor but instead would take care of political issues while the governor would follow my advice and that we would collaborate. They asked me to prepare the people [of the region] for unification with Romania, to proceed to the election of the Moldovan National Council with me as chairman, with the intention to vote union with the Romanian Motherland, following the example of Sfatul Țării in Bessarabia and of Consiliul Dirigent in Transylvania [in 1918]."[99] Based on this account, one may suspect that Smochină was either politically naive, for having passed up the post of the governor, and instead settling for a position without real power, or that he lied in his memoir, inflating his role in the events. Nevertheless, if one recalls that the Romanian leaders, to whom Smochină was indeed close at the time, were so dazzled by the massive German victories that they were sure of a quick victory in the war, Smochină's choice does not appear to be irrational. Preparing to play a leading role in solemnizing Transnistria's union with Romania, Smochină reckoned that his post would bring him more fame and long-term political benefits than serving in a powerful but transitory position as the province's governor.

Together with Smochină, numerous other Transnistrian refugees returned into the region, among whom there were, inevitably, his bitter rivals. Old animosities flared up again, fanned by greed, rent-seeking and moral depravity of many a member of this motley crowd. When on September 3, 1941, the first meeting of the self-appointed National Council of the Transnistrian Romanians took place in Tiraspol, it was in its entirety devoted to the distribution of lucrative positions in the province's administration, which the Council members hoped to receive from the governor.[100] In response, Alexianu, upset by what he understandably considered its members' impudence, put the Council on hold.

Much of Smochină's memoir's pages devoted to wartime events are filled with descriptions of his rivals' misdeeds, some of which are so egregious that they almost defy imagination. For example, Ștefan Bulat, a felon convicted of embezzlement in Bessarabia shortly before its occupation by the Soviets, was released from prison when the Soviets entered the province. Having escaped into Romania, he settled as a refugee in Bucharest, and became a Legionary. Soon, he appropriated a farm illegally "confiscated" by the "movement" from a Jew. During the meeting of September 3, 1941, in Tiraspol, Bulat requested appointment as head of the police in Transnistria and later continued to pester Smochină and the governor with innumerable requests for compensation for the property he lost under the Soviets. Worst of all, he smuggled an eighteen-year-old Jewish girl from a concentration camp in exchange for forced concubinage. Eventually, the story became public; the girl was denounced to the Germans, arrested, and interned in a concentration camp.[101] Medical doctor Ilie Zaftur was reportedly so enthused by the German and Romanian anti-Jewish measures that he even worked on a project of gassing them in specially created chambers (it is unknown whether he was aware of similar German practices).[102] Smochină himself was not immune to the allure of rent, and among his first actions he secured his son Alexandru's appointment both as a member of the National Council and a subprefect in Berezovca județ.[103] Later on, he was reported to have received "gifts" from the Department of Culture of the *guvernământ*, consisting of art objects looted from Odessa museums.[104]

The tension between Smochină and his rivals in the community of the Transnistrian returnees from Romania was so intense that in mid-October 1941 he tended his resignation from the post of chairman of their association. Mihai Antonescu refused to accept it, stating that the government still considered him as the only authorized representative of the Transnistrian Romanian refugees.[105] Alexianu, who suspected Smochină of intentions to undermine his authority, supported the convocation of a Romanian Transnistrians congress on December 15, 1941, the main purpose

Figure 6.   Ilie Zaftur, Onisifor Ghibu, Ştefan Bulat, Pantelimon Halippa, and Nichita Smichină. Tiraspol, 1941. Ghibu and Halippa were long-time nationalist activists who played an important role in preparing Bessarabia's unification with Romanian in 1918. Courtesy DANIC.

of which seemingly was to create a committee under the chairmanship of Smochină's nemesis, Ştefan Bulat, under the pretext that Smochină spent most of his time in Bucharest. The organizers obviously did not inform Smochină of the event, but Mihai Antonescu helped him again by making sure he arrived at the congress just in time to be elected—triumphantly, and to Alexianu's chagrin—to the chairmanship of the newly created committee whose main purpose was "to give representation to the Transnistrian Romanians and to endow them with a possibility to work, in collaboration with provincial authorities, for the attainment of unification [of Transnistria with the motherland]."[106]

Smochină's success was overshadowed by the creation of the Romanian Scientific Institute of Transnistria (later renamed Institute of Transnistria), headed by Ştefan Bulat. The initial draft statute for the Institute, dated early December 1941, defined its aims as "studying all the problems relating to Transnistria and guiding them [sic] along the road of Romanianism." The means for achieving these aims were "studies and demonstrations by all allowed and possible ways."[107] This definition would give the Institute powers far beyond its putative "scientific" character, including the right to speak on behalf of the Transnistrian Moldovans, thus replacing the committee headed by Smochină. Suspecting intrigue against his power in the region, Alexianu vetoed the draft and ordered that it would be rewritten by his research bureau (Birou de Studii). He added that the Institute would have two sections only, historical and literary.[108] The final version of the statute, approved by Alexianu on February 26, 1942, defined the Institute's aims thus: "To study all problems . . . and spread [its findings] by all means among the Transnistrians and everywhere."[109] In this way, the governor made sure that the Institute's sphere of responsibility would be circumscribed to the study of local folklore and the waging of national propaganda among the Moldovans.

Following the adoption of the Institute's statute by the governor, its new chairman, Ştefan Bulat, proceeded to convoke meetings of the Transnistrian Moldovan intellectuals, such as teachers, agronomists, and local civil servants—anyone of Romanian ethnicity with a minimal education and some notoriety at the district level, to create the Institute's chapters (filiale) in each judeţ. Bulat acted through the newly appointed subprefects of Moldovan extraction, thus appearing to be in agreement with the guvernământ but at the same time representing as a fledging parallel power in the region.[110] Following the creation of such chapters, the Institute's activity was effectively reduced to lobbying the Transnistrian Moldovans' interests with the governor. For example, on April 17, 1942, Bulat forwarded a memorandum

to Alexianu requesting pay raises for all civil servants from among the Transnistrian Romanians, as well as a one-time bonus of 1,000 RKKS for all of the
ethnic Romanian households—quite a substantial sum at the time. Irritated,
the governor, while agreeing to the former request, noted that the Institute
was allowed to intercede solely on behalf of "the neediest children and wid-
ows" (this looks like a concession on Alexianu's part since such rights did not
follow, strictly speaking, from the Institute's statute).[111]

Throughout its existence, the Institute continued to busy itself with
similar memoranda, which seemed only to augment the governor's displeasure.[112] Bulat's ambitions were indeed grandiose. On February 16, 1943,
at the time when enthusiasm for the immediate population transfers was
growing among the Romanian governing circles, the Institute forwarded a
memorandum to Mihai Antonescu proposing the creation of the National
Eugenics Council subordinated directly to the PCM. The suggested title
of this institution seemed to have been a misnomer since its only would-
be aim was to oversee the planned population transfer, and in the process
provide Bulat with a voice in it.[113] Besides repeating the usual arguments
in favor of such transfers of eastern Romanians into Transnistria, Bessarabia, and Bukovina, the authors added several others that are indicative of
their ideological inclinations. First, they opined that the moment for the
operation was opportune since "Slavs were in an impasse: Serbia, Poland,
Czechia, and Ukraine did not even exist." Second, they theorized that due
to the abolition of private property and political repression in the Soviet
Union, "the population of Ukraine lacked initiative and energy to resist." As
such, they "could be easily transferred from one part into another."[114] Mihai
Antonescu's response to the initiative is not known, but Alexianu's opinion
was that "under the circumstances [the creation of such a body] was not
opportune."[115]

Alexianu not only saw to it that the Institute had no statutory authority but also denied it any financial support. In despair, the Institute's leaders attempted to organize the sale of fruits from Transnistria in Romania
through an office under its supervision, in cooperation with the municipality of Tiraspol. Judging from the fact that in December 1942 this office was
transferred to the municipality of Tiraspol, this initiative was also blocked
by the *guvernământ*.[116]

The increasing tensions between the self-appointed leaders of the
Transnistrian Moldovans and the governor came to a head in April 1943.
After having received a positive response from Ion Antonescu to their initiative to start registering volunteers from among the Transnistrian Moldovans for service in the Romanian armed forces, the Institute's leaders

proceeded to implement their plan in a provocative manner. Widely over-stretching its newly acquired prerogatives, the Institute proclaimed on April 22, 1943, the creation of the Military Council of Transnistria, with Ştefan Bulat as its head. The same day, the new Military Council ordered the creation of a center for recruitment, two military schools for officers and NCOs in Odessa, and the supply and sanitary services for what they called the Voluntary Corps, or the Army of the Moldovan Republic. All of these and other administrative bodies were to be headed by members of the Military Council. Judging from the language of the decisions adopted, Bulat and his group imagined themselves as leaders of a separate military force fighting against the approaching "invasion of Judaic communism" alongside the other Axis powers' armed forces. All military officers resid-ing at the time in Transnistria, both former Red Army prisoners of war released from camps because of their Moldovan nationality and former Tsarist army officers, were to be mobilized in this corps and serve under the orders of the Military Council. Financing of the newly created institu-tions was to come from Transnistrian kolkhozes, which were obligated to pay an additional tax.[117]

As Bulat and his supporters later explained in a memorandum to Ion Antonescu, they intended to follow the example of the Russian Liberation Army, which was being created at this time by General Andrei Vlasov from among the Soviet prisoners of war.[118] On April 30, 1943, Alexianu met with Bulat and another member of the Military Council, who handed over to the governor minutes of the meeting of April 22 and the decisions adopted. Alexianu immediately interpreted the document as an attempt to create a separate military force in the province, outside the Romanian government's control. He also suspected that the scheme was designed to carry out some-thing akin to a coup against him and his administration. Alexianu made his views known to people in his entourage, and the next day "the whole Odessa" was talking about an attempted coup. Without any delay, the Trans-nistrian Moldovans' leaders were arrested, interrogated, and released, then rearrested and expelled, one by one, from Transnistria into Romania, "for activities incompatible with Romanian interests in the region."[119] The gov-ernment terminated their employment and by the end of 1943, they were living in Romania in desperate material circumstances, Ion Antonescu stub-bornly refusing to allow their reintegration in the civil service.[120] In an infor-mation note prepared by the SSI, these leaders were evaluated as corrupt, scheming, incapable of sound judgment, and generally unreliable (neserioşi). The reason for their expulsion was, according to this note, "their conspir-atorial initiative and separatist tendency to transform Transnistria into an independent state."[121] Although somewhat of a stretch, the note adequately captures the quixotic nature of the Institute leaders' self-chosen role.

This chapter contrasts the initially grandiose vision of an ethnodemographic transformation of Romania's eastern borderlands with the inconsistent, petty-minded, and ultimately failed policy measures intended to achieve it. It also highlighted the tensions between more radical and more moderate brands of ethnic nationalism promoted by Ion Antonescu and some of his government experts, respectively. It should be noted that the experts' views were close to those of the leaders of Romanian pro-Western democratic opposition. Most Romanian wartime elites, both those who supported Antonescu's regime and those who opposed it, espoused the idea of population exchange as a means of consolidating the Romanian nation-state. The difference between the government and the opposition, supported by most experts lay in that the government intended to extend Romania's borders eastward, incorporating Transnistria, while the opposition rejected this idea as impractical and dangerous folly. The government's vision included the ethnic cleansing of Transnistria and its repopulation by ethnic Romanians, and thus it implied that the Transnistrian Moldovans should remain in the province. Opposition from the start of the war advocated their relocation to Bessarabia and Bukovina, which had to be cleansed of national minorities (which did not mean that the opposition condoned the physical destruction of local Jewry).[122] Despite the obvious fact that this measure contrived international law, opposition leaders and government experts saw it as an acceptable means to secure the two provinces for Romania. They also hoped that these measures would put an end to Antonescu's attempts at territorial annexations in the east.

Antonescu's supporters and more moderate nationalists shared the ethnonationalist concept of the Romanian nation-state, but their understanding of the Romanian national identity differed in yet another important respect: Antonescu, who called his type of nationalism "integral," saw the Romanian nation as a solid entity that had to be homogenized ethnically and culturally. The Romanian moderate nationalists, however, tolerated limited cultural heterogeneity. Mindful of what he saw as a low level of national consciousness among eastern Romanians, Antonescu and his government abhorred the idea of bringing them within the borders of prewar Romania. The maximum to which they agreed was transforming Transnistria into a sui generis reservation for these "not really Romanians," and even then, they had to be intermingled with the war veterans in order to facilitate their reeducation in the national spirit. Persistent requests of Golopenția and Manuilă, both of whom were close to the democratic opposition, to organize eastern Romanians' transfer into Bessarabia and Bukovina and the Conducător's stubborn refusal to heed their advice testify to the depth of tension between philosophies and political options espoused by the two camps.

It is likely that this tension goes some way toward explaining the noted inconsistencies in Romanian policy toward eastern Romanians. Ironically, it was Ion Antonescu's deep suspicion of eastern Romanians that helped prevent a costly and chaotic—in the conditions of the constantly deteriorating war situation—population exchange. Not only would it have led to the unnecessary suffering (as the limited experience of settlement in Râbnița and Mogilev județe showed) of hundreds of thousands, but it would have given the Soviets a strong pretext to impose even harsher conditions on Romania after the war.

It is more difficult to assess the effectiveness of the Romanian efforts to raise the level of "national conscientiousness" of eastern Romanians. The shortness of time within which such a policy was pursued made it virtually impossible for it to achieve a lasting effect. Nevertheless, it is probable that by systematically granting to the Transnistrian Moldovans numerous privileges the Romanians elicited some loyalty on their part, even if for a short time. The fact that by the end of the occupation the Romanian surveillance bodies did not distinguish ethnic Moldovans and local Slavs in their reports on the "moods of the population" (see chapter 10) suggests that this loyalty disappeared as soon as the Moldovans realized that the Soviets would soon return and that the Romanians would not allow them to relocate to Romania. As for the attempts to mobilize eastern Moldovans to demand annexation of Transnistria to Romania, they quickly imploded under the weight of ineptitude and the boundless ambitions of their self-appointed leaders. By the fall of 1943, the changing fortunes of war made this project irrelevant.

CHAPTER 6

"Civilizing" Transnistria

Changing the province's ethnic demography was a long term policy; in the shorter term, the Romanians ruled over an ethnically foreign solid majority. Predicated on the idea that the (ethno)national state was the only "natural" form of modern political organization, their "national ideology," to borrow Catherine Verdery's term, did not prepare the Romanian government for such situation.[1] Nor had they ever ruled over any colonies whose population would be explicitly excluded from the national body politic. Nevertheless, the Romanians were exposed to the European discourse on the need to rule over backward "oriental" populations as a supposed duty of civilized nations. For the development of his guidelines on the colonization of the eastern territories, Ion Antonescu heavily relied on two Romanian agricultural experts, Aurel Talaşescu and Agricola Cardaş, who in 1941–1942 published brochures that referenced their visit to the Italian colony of Libya in 1938, on the invitation of Mussolini's government. There they witnessed the triumph of "Italian civilization" and labor over "oriental barbarism." It was from teachers like these, as well as the Nazis, they implied, that the Romanians had to learn if they wanted to accomplish their mission as descendants of the ancient Romans.[2]

Ion Antonescu showed a considerable affinity for this kind of thinking when he insisted, in mid-November 1941, that Transnistria had to serve as proof that Romania was able "to administer a bigger country."[3] The

Conducător suffered from a pronounced inferiority complex, namely from a perception that other European states looked down on his beloved Romania. From this perspective, administering Transnistria in an orderly, efficient, and "civilized" manner—as other European powers were supposedly doing in ruling over their Asian and African subjects—would help Romania raise its rank in the pecking order. Governor Alexianu was perfectly in tune with his boss. He, too, saw "order" and "civilization" as major planks of the Romanians' mission in Transnistria. This is, for example, how he defined the essence of the Romanian policy in the region in his order to the prefects on June 20, 1942: "We have to show everywhere that the civilization that we bring here is based, first and foremost, on discipline and order."[4] Employing tropes of the "accursed Russian steppe" and "Slavic shapelessness," redolent of the orientalizing Kulturträger discourse, he strongly implied that the Romanians had to perform that role to the benefit of benighted and recalcitrant locals.[5]

Order, discipline and the use of violence to enforce them feature widely in the internal correspondence between various bureaucracies, gendarmerie, police, and army units in Transnistria. "Civilization" was a buzzword in the province's official propaganda, too. In his first address to the Transnistrian population, Alexianu defined the Romanian mission in the region thus: "[The Bolsheviks] first destroyed your soul [meaning religion] . . . and then wanted to take your life [a reference to the scorched-earth policy the Soviets practiced in retreat], but an allied Christian state has come just in time to save you and give you the possibility of enjoying light, civilization, and life based on the fear of God and your ancestral faith."[6] In his speech at Odessa University on August 26, 1942, Mihai Antonescu declared, "Our revenge against Russia is building European civilization on this land."[7] A little later, in a speech at the opening of the exhibition "Transnistria" in Bucharest, the vice chair of the Council of Ministers stated, "This exhibition testifies that the war in the East is not only a military campaign, it is also a civilizing, constructive action for the defense of the basic norms of the continent and of our Nation."[8]

Another recurrent phrase was "European culture." For example, in its activity report for 1941–1943, the Division of Arts at the Department of Culture stated: "In this war, the Axis powers in general, and Romania in particular, defend the values of a European culture, a moral style of life gained through the historical experience of continuous civilization."[9] In the self-image that the Romanian leaders, administrators, and government-controlled press propagated, Romania was a bastion of European civilization on its easternmost endangered border, where it fulfilled the role of a guardian against barbarians of all sorts. True to its historical mission, Romania now joined Nazi Germany as the main defender of European civilization and culture against the "Yids" whose "Asiatic" spirit was embodied in Soviet communism, which was inimical to the very essence of "Europe." Romanians gave the "Russians" (understood in this context as all non-Jewish locals) a choice of either joining in the battle against the "Yids' communism" or facing tough consequences.[10] Educated Odessans easily discerned the arrogant tone and humiliating meaning of the Romanian official discourse. For example, one Pavel Krapivnyi, a documentary movie producer (*rezhissër*) who lived in Odessa under the occupation regime, testified to the ChGK that "the Romanians used to declare everywhere that they were bearers of Western European culture and civilization, that they were the crusaders, that they have brought faith, love, and peace."[11] According to the university docent Nikolai Sokolov, Transnistria attracted numerous Romanian Kulturträgers who waged propaganda "exalting natural resources and 'culture' of the Romanians."[12] According to the lawyer N. Lange, the Romanians claimed that their Prince Dimitrie Cantemir and his son Antioch Cantemir, as well as Metropolitan Petru Mohyla (Movilă), were the "fathers of Russian culture."[13]

Despite this in-your-face self-aggrandizement, Romanians were stunned by the distinctly "European" look of the metropolis of Odessa. By the time of the Romanian occupation, Odessa's days of glory were long gone, but even years of Soviet neglect and mismanagement had failed to erase all evidence of its erstwhile wealth and sophisticated cosmopolitan culture.[14] From the first days of occupation, the Romanians proceeded to patronize Odessan institutions of high culture and education, which, they felt, belonged to the pan-European treasury. Owing to the massive and enthusiastic support of provincial and municipal administrations, Odessa University and the city's opera theater opened on December 7, 1941. As if demonstrating the Romanians' liberality, the first performance was Peter Tchaikovsky's *Eugene Onegin*, although the program began with German and Romanian anthems by a choir and orchestra from which all Jews had been ruthlessly purged.[15] Through the end of the Romanian occupation, both institutions continued to stage old and new performances, Russian and Western European alike, but increasingly also Romanian.[16] For Romanian and German dignitaries visiting Odessa, attending an opera or a ballet became a matter of course, and some of them noted with surprise the high quality of the productions.[17] In the late fall of 1942, Hermann Binder, a German Lutheran pastor from Transylvania on a mission to Transnistria, attended a performance of Tchaikovsky's *Swan Lake* in Odessa. That day, he wrote in his diary: "Rightly a famous ballet, in which the whole plot, every feeling, is expressed through rhythmic movement. It is really wonderful, the best one can see and hear here, also because the incomprehensible Russian language does not bother you."[18]

Repertory theaters, old and new, also attracted increasingly larger audiences. Some of these companies were formed at the initiative of and with the participation of Russian political émigrés, who came to Romania during the interwar period. The most well-known example is Vasilii Mikhailovich Vronskii, a successful Odessa-born producer and actor who lived and performed in the Russian drama theater in interwar Chişinău, Bessarabia, and then in Bucharest.[19] Under the Romanian occupation, Vronskii founded the Theater of Drama and Comedy and became the most popular and critically acclaimed producer and actor in Odessa. Petr Konstantinovich Leshchenko, a beloved émigré singer of Russian romances, whose smuggled vinyl discs were secretly listened to in the interwar Soviet Union, regularly performed in Odessa during the occupation period. Odessa's lively cultural life presented strong contrast to the situation in the metropolitan centers in the German zone of occupation, where such activity was conspicuous by its absence.[20]

The Romanian army and administration identified "intellectuals," among whom they counted artists, university and college professors, school teachers, as well as engineers and managers, as the most reliable and sympathetic social stratum. They attributed two causes to their exceptional loyalty: first, the material privileges they accorded to them, and second, their "critical discernment," which helped them appreciate the "profoundly humane ideas that animated [the Romanians'] attitude toward them." Romanian observers favorably contrasted the intelligentsia's attitude with the moods of "the masses" who supposedly remained under the noxious influence of communist ideology.[21] Material privileges granted to Odessan creative intelligentsia, especially those bestowed on the higher-ranked "intellectuals," such as university professors and famed artists were indeed considerable. In addition to substantially higher salaries and larger rations, both in comparison to the incomes of the lower classes under the Romanian rule and to their own incomes under the Soviets, they were granted luxurious living quarters, including the former villas of the Russian nobility that lined Odessa's gorgeous boulevards. Under the Soviets, these villas had served as the homes of the *nomenklatura*, but under the Romanian occupation, Romanian officials moved into the best of them, while the rest were allocated to select local "intellectuals."[22] Even if "intellectuals" resented the need to publicly praise everything Romanian and pretend that the provincial Romanian artists sent to Transnistria by the Bucharest bureaucrats could teach them "European culture," it was a relatively low price to pay for the benefits that collaboration with the Romanian authorities afforded them.[23]

The Romanian administration was of two minds as to what line to adopt with respect to the "Russians," by whom they meant not only ethnic Russians

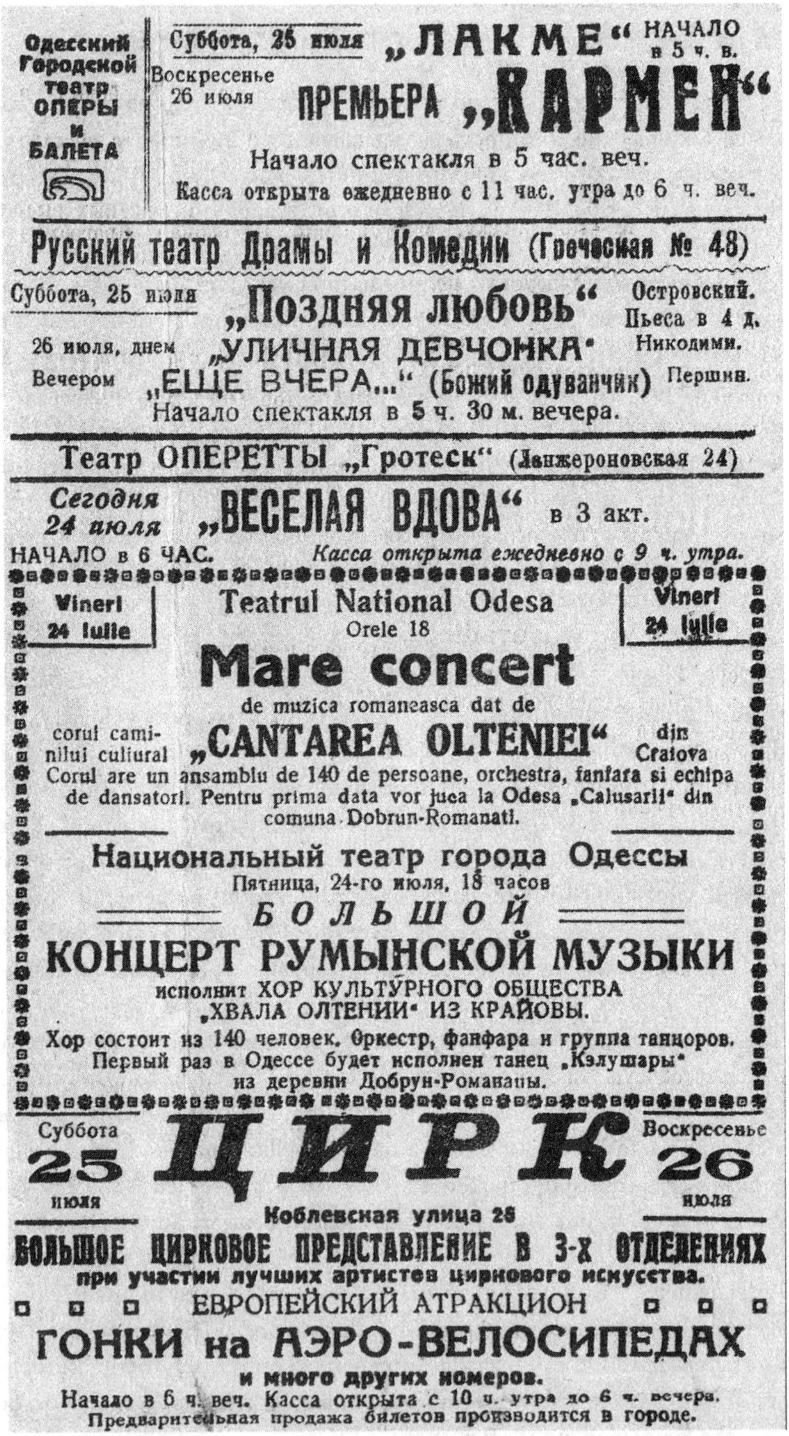
Одесский Городской театр ОПЕРЫ и БАЛЕТА

Суббота, 25 июля „ЛАКМЕ" НАЧАЛО в 5 ч. в.

Воскресенье 26 июля ПРЕМЬЕРА „КАРМЕН"

Начало спектакля в 5 час. веч.

Касса открыта ежедневно с 11 час. утра до 6 ч. веч.

Русский театр Драмы и Комедии (Греческая № 48)

Суббота, 25 июля „Поздняя любовь" Островский. Пьеса в 4 д.

26 июля, днем „УЛИЧНАЯ ДЕВЧОНКА" Никодими.

Вечером „ЕЩЕ ВЧЕРА..." (Божий одуванчик) Першин.

Начало спектакля в 5 ч. 30 м. вечера.

Театр ОПЕРЕТТЫ „Гротеск" (Ланжероновская 24)

Сегодня 24 июля „ВЕСЕЛАЯ ВДОВА" в 3 акт.

НАЧАЛО в 6 ЧАС. Касса открыта ежедневно с 9 ч. утра.

Vineri 24 Iulie

Teatrul National Odesa

Orele 18

Mare concert

de muzica romaneasca dat de

corul caminului cultural „CANTAREA OLTENIEI" din Craiova

Corul are un ansamblu de 140 de persoane, orchestra, fanfara si echipa de dansatori. Pentru prima data vor juca la Odesa „Calusarii" din comuna Dobrun-Romanati.

Национальный театр города Одессы

Пятница, 24-го июля, 18 часов

БОЛЬШОЙ

КОНЦЕРТ РУМЫНСКОЙ МУЗЫКИ

исполнит ХОР КУЛЬТУРНОГО ОБЩЕСТВА „ХВАЛА ОЛТЕНИИ" ИЗ КРАЙОВЫ.

Хор состоит из 140 человек. Оркестр, фанфара и группа танцоров. Первый раз в Одессе будет исполнен танец „Кэлушары" из деревни Добрун-Романацы.

Суббота 25 июля ЦИРК Воскресенье 26 июля

Коблевская улица 26

БОЛЬШОЕ ЦИРКОВОЕ ПРЕДСТАВЛЕНИЕ В 3-х ОТДЕЛЕНИЯХ

при участии лучших артистов циркового искусства.

ЕВРОПЕЙСКИЙ АТРАКЦИОН

ГОНКИ на АЭРО-ВЕЛОСИПЕДАХ

и много других номеров.

Начало в 6 ч. веч. Касса открыта с 10 ч. утра до 6 ч. вечера.

Предварительная продажа билетов производится в городе.

FIGURE 7. Advertisement from an Odessan newspaper containing announcements of one opera, one drama theater show, one operetta, one concert of Romanian music, and one circus performance, in Russian and Romanian during the weekend of July 12–15, 1942. Courtesy Mikhail Borisovich Poizner.

FIGURE 8.   Scene from the show *Serf Actress* produced in Vasilii Vronskii's theater in 1943. Vronskii is in the center. Courtesy Mikhail Borisovich Poizner.

but anybody for whom Russian was the primary language of communication, with the exception of Jews. From this perspective, after the deportation of Jews from Odessa in January 1942, practically the entire population of the city was "Russian." Odessa's mayor Gherman Pântea insisted that the most efficient policy toward "Russians" would be to treat them "with kindness" ("as Bessarabian, I know Russians very well," he wrote to Antonescu, "with calmness, using tender words, one can do anything with them, with brutality, one just hardens their animosity").[24] But the director of the *guvernământ's directia* of culture Traian Herseni advocated a much harder line. In October 1942, Herseni addressed Transnistrians with a long speech that was subsequently published in Russian translation in three installments of *Odesskaia gazeta* of October 30–November 1 of the same year. Titled "Conquerors or Liberators?" he made it sound as if the Romanians' treatment of Russians depended on Russians themselves. The Romanians, intoned Herseni, were "the only people in Europe about whom one cannot say that we came from somewhere. We were born here, on our land, from the ancestors who inhabited it from time immemorial. We endured despite a confrontation with more numerous and powerful people." He went on to say that the Romanians did not wrong the Russians in any way, whereas the latter committed numerous injustices against the former. Communism was the latest and the greatest of their crimes. Although communism was predominantly a Jewish phenomenon, the Russians did not sufficiently resist it and even tried to spread it outside of their country. Now the Axis powers delivered a powerful blow to Russia and thus relieved Romania of Russian terror. The Romanians liberated the Russians from Judeo-communism, and now the Russians' fate was to a large extent in their own hands. If they would help the Axis powers prevail over communism and "take part in the creation of civilization," the Romanians would treat them mildly, because kindness is in their nature. However, if the Russians would support communism, then they would be regarded as a gangrene "that can be treated only surgically." Still, even those Russians who would decide to support the Axis powers' war efforts would have to appreciate that during the war they will have to suffer serious difficulties and that their level of consumption would be kept lower than that of the Romanians. "This is just a harsh law of war," concluded Herseni, apparently forgetting that international law forbade waging wars at the expense of the occupied populations.[25]

Ironically, Herseni aired this speech just before the battles of El-Alamein in North Africa and Stalingrad on the Volga River entered their decisive phases, changing the tide of war against the Axis powers. Tellingly, neither Herseni nor anybody else in the Romanian administration would ever proclaim anything comparable to this speech with all its overconfident self-righteousness and repeated threats of violence in case of deviation from the prescribed and strictly defined course. It nevertheless serves as a sign of the direction the Romanian policy was likely to turn had the war continued according to their government's designs.

Promoting Religious Revival and Homogeneity

The Romanians were predominantly Christian Orthodox, as were most of Transnistria's Slavs. To Ion Antonescu, the Romanian Orthodox Church was "The Church of the Nation," and besides serving as "the spiritual base" of the nation and state, it was duty-bound to identify itself with the aims of his regime.[26] For him, priests were little different from teachers, physicians, military, and public servants, all of whom he considered to be in the service of the nation.[27] In turn, the Conducător vowed to achieve religious homogenization of the Romanian ethnic nation through eradication—both by means of administrative pressure, legal restrictions, and intensified Orthodox missionary activity—of what he called "foreign cults" or "sects."[28]

This same policy was applied in Transnistria. On August 19, 1941, the day Ion Antonescu issued the decree on the creation of the Romanian administration in Transnistria, he also signed Instructions establishing its main principles. Under point 6 (among 9), he ordered rapid "reopening of all Orthodox churches and resumption of the re-Christianizing mission and of propaganda to return to religious tradition. The spiritual and administrative leadership of the Orthodox Church in the province" was to be fulfilled by a newly appointed "Bishop of the Dniester with a seat in Tiraspol."[29] It soon became clear, however, that this instruction contradicted the canon law, which disallowed the creation of bishoprics of an Orthodox church in the canonical territory of another Orthodox church. To the surprise of the government, the Romanian Holy Synod insisted that Transnistria was still under the authority of the Russian Orthodox Church, whether one recognized the Moscow Synod or the Karlowitz Synod as its head. Thus the Patriarch of All Romania could not appoint a "regular" bishop for Transnistria.[30] Even more problematic was Alexianu's idea to extend the Romanian Church's administrative outreach to the east of the Buh River, in the rest of occupied Ukraine. Although it received enthusiastic support from Mihai Antonescu, who presided over the Council of Ministers meeting when this issue was discussed ("a historical moment when Romania and the Orthodox Church could play a great civilizing role, having as their mission the returning to the Christian faith of Russians from the territories, either occupied or marched through by our soldiers," he declared), the synod pointed out the same canonical hindrance: this territory was under the Russian Orthodox Church control and any missionary activity there had to be carried out under the Russian hierarchs' authority. Mihai Antonescu was not ready to accept such an arrangement: "I am not obligated to work for a foreign synod," he said. He also pointed out that since Russian Orthodoxy was historically linked to Russian nationalism, he was not ready to encourage religious revival led by priests and bishops whom he could not control and whom he was not disposed to trust.[31]

Romanian nationalist intellectuals explicitly linked Romanian missionary activity in the occupied Soviet territories with the vision of the country's future great role in the European east. For example, I. P. Prundeni, a virulently anti-Semitic journalist, in December 1942 published in a popular Russian-language Odessan newspaper an article with the telling title "Militant Orthodoxy." He wrote that the Russian Orthodox Church, due to its unsavory inclination toward "orientalist mysticism," was partially responsible for the victory of Bolshevism in the USSR. Nowadays, Orthodoxy was in need of a "unifying center" whose role could be performed solely by the Romanian Orthodox Church, which Prundeni defined as "the most enlightened in theological disciplines, the strongest in its faith, and the most conscious of its responsibility amidst other Orthodox Churches." The Romanian Church had an additional advantage in that it could rely on the "Romanian solidarity" in the occupied territories to perform its duty of "reconquering the eastern world for Orthodoxy."[32]

The Romanian Holy Synod found a solution to the canonical problems by authorizing its own mission into Transnistria, and later by appointing a temporary or "military"—that is for the duration of the occupation—bishopric there. Archimandrite Iuliu Scriban, who in the interwar period taught theology in Chișinău at what might be called a regional campus of the University of Iași, was appointed the bishop.[33] At the time of his appointment, Scriban was a professor of theology at the University of Bucharest and refused to abandon his position. Shuttling between Bucharest and Odessa proved difficult for a sixty-three-year-old hierarch who soon requested a replacement.[34] Nevertheless, he continued in this position through November 1942, when he was removed, following accusations of corruption. His replacement was Metropolitan Visarion Puiu. Puiu remained in this post until mid-December 1943.[35] He was conferred the title of "Bishop of Odessa and all Transnistria" but his bishopric was still considered a temporary military one.[36]

FIGURE 9.   Metropolitan Visarion Puiu "in the Bolsheviks' camp" (the handwritten legend on the back of the photo, probably made by Puiu's secretary). To the left of Puiu, first row, Governor Gheorghe Alexianu. Transnistria, exact date and location unknown. Courtesy DANIC.

According to historian Mikhail Shkarovskii, Romanian missionaries faced a daunting task. During the Soviet rule, by July 1941, only 1 out of 891 prerevolutionary churches was left open: 363 were closed down, 269 partially demolished, and 258 completely demolished; there was not a single functioning monastery or convent left.[37] Although many residents practiced their religion clandestinely, the lack of priests led to the phenomenon of "self-ordination" of laymen unrecognized by the church hierarchy. Those few priests who survived Soviet repressions were divided among the followers of the Moscow Synod, "Renovationist" movement (obnovlenchestvo), and the Ukrainian Autocephalous Orthodox Church, the latter two uncanonical.[38] Upon occupation, many locals, thirsting for spiritual solace, immediately requested the restoration of services and churches; they even sometimes rebuilt church buildings without authorization. These labors quickly brought numerous fruits: by the end of the Romanian domination, about 600 churches were functioning in the province; in addition, there were 135 "prayer houses" in the locales where they failed to restore churches. Further, there were twelve monasteries and convents with about sixty monastics, and two seminaries—in Dubăsari and in Odessa. In the Dubăsari seminary, teaching was in Romanian, in the Odessa one, in Russian. The University of Odessa had department of theology and all public schools had classes in religious instruction. The Romanian mission had its own publishing press and published three bulletins, two in Russian and one in Romanian, as well as numerous calendars, prayer books, and other such materials. All of these were efforts aimed to re-Christenizing the province.[39]

The Romanian administrators believed that their and their local charges' belonging to the same religion would facilitate their "coming together" (apropiere).[40] However, tensions stemmed from the Romanian determination to merge missionary activity with Romanianization. The Romanian clergy wove official propaganda motifs—such as lauding the Romanian administration's supposed benevolence and the liberating mission of the Romanian troops to whom locals had to be grateful—into the pastoral addresses. The bishops favored ethnic Moldovans for appointments to the priesthood and even for distribution of material resources[41] According to data cited by Shkarovskii, in the spring of 1942, there were 203 priests in Transnistria, of whom 115 were either Romanians or Moldovans (they were apparently counted together), and the remaining 88 were either Ukrainians or Russians; all abbots and abbesses were Romanians. In early 1944, there were 617 clerics in Transnistria (counting priests, deacons, and psalmists), of whom almost 400 were Romanians or Moldovans.[42]

Still, Shkarovskii notes substantial differences between the policies of the two longest-serving heads of the mission: Scriban was a much more ardent Romanianizer than Puiu. The latter studied in 1907–1908 at the Spiritual Academy in Kyiv and served as a bishop in Bessarabia between the world wars.[43] Metropolitan Visarion, who was fluent in Russian, was generally more willing to ordain priests from among local Slavs. Well-versed in Moscow Synod church troubles, which witnessed numerous schisms and uncanonical autocephalies following the Bolshevik Revolution, he made it a point to reordain only those self-appointed priests and followers of uncanonical churches who repented, which many of them did willingly. Metropolitan Visarion tried to convince Ion Antonescu, to whom he had direct access, that because more than two-thirds of the Transnistrian parishes had predominantly Slavic populations, they were in need of priests who would be able to communicate in vernacular and celebrate the liturgy in Church Slavonic. Occasionally, Metropolitan Visarion conducted services in that language and sermonized in Russian. Visarion ended the policy, started by his predecessor, of enforcing the use of the "new" (Gregorian) calendar for religious holidays. This calendar had been used in Romania since 1924 but was an unsettling novelty for the most Transnistrian faithful who still considered the old (Julian) calendar the only proper one for determining the dates of most religious holidays. He also advised the Romanian clergy not to annoy local believers by requesting that they adopt every and all Romanian religious practices, which in some details were different from their own. This led to considerable improvement in the relations between the Romanian clergy and their local flock.

Metropolitan Visarion's flexibility and tactfulness should not be interpreted as evidence of his abandoning Romanianization.[44] He continued to plead with Antonescu that more and more priests and missionaries would be sent from Romania into Transnistria (they were supposed to serve there on six-months assignments). Although Metropolitan Visarion insisted that they should be recruited from among those who spoke Russian or Ukrainian, this consideration was not always followed, and the language barrier continued to remain a serious problem for Romanian clerics. Since they received a salary three times as high as that received by their local counterparts (600 RKKS and 200 RKKS, respectively), it is a small wonder that local clergymen were resentful of them. Furthermore, the Romanians suspected the locals in Russophile tendencies, while locals resented the Romanians' perceived haughtiness.

Accusations of corruption, abuse of power, and embezzlement abounded and tarnished the mission's reputation.[45] Tellingly, the Romanian gendarmerie also frequently reported such practices. For example, on March 6, 1942, Gendarmerie Legion Golta reported that "Priests on mission in Transnistria discredit the purpose of their mission by their unbecoming behavior."[46] On October 29, 1943, Gendarmerie Legion Oceacov reported to the higher-ups in Odessa that "priests on the mission from the country [Romania] manage to destroy what the Bolsheviks had failed to destroy, concerning faith in God. This is due to their engaging in illicit business transactions and committing actions which compromise the dignity of their office." They went on to cite a case of a priest "whose only occupation was getting drunk."[47] One Romanian missionary, Paulin Lecca, at the time a novice at a monastery in Romania and later an archimandrite, left a fictionalized biographical account of his life, most of it dedicated to his Transnistrian adventure. Lecca was a Bessarabian and spoke fluent Russian. As such, he was well acquainted with the realities of the province. In his memoir, he describes rampant corruption and the abuses of missionary priests and monks (călugări). In one particularly outrageous scene, he recounts advice given to him by a priest from Romania to rape Jewish women (apparently, from a nearby ghetto) in order "not to get sick [from sexual abstinence]." To Lecca's protestation that such behavior was sinful, Fr. Gurie opined that since Jews were not baptized, a simple prayer to Theotokos (Virgin Mary) would be enough to receive absolution.[48]

One should not rush to condemn the Romanian missionary activity because on par with such criticisms one can cite more positive assessments of their work.[49] Significantly, despite his critical attitude toward Romanianization in Transnistria, Shkarovskii concludes that "in general, the [religious] situation in Transnistria was much better than in the neighboring Reichskommissariat Ukraine," where German authorities tolerated but did not actively promote Orthodox Christian revival.[50] As to the religious situation in Transnistrian ethnic German communities, it was worse than among Orthodox Christians since Einsatzkommando R actively obstructed efforts of Lutheran pastors and Catholic priests to promote religious revival among their Volksdeutschen charges.[51]

There is plenty of evidence that the local population enthusiastically supported the religious revival in the province, at least during the first two years. For example, the Second Army Corps reported to the commander of the Third Army in November 1941, that "propaganda in favor of Orthodoxy made by the missionary priests is being met with great enthusiasm."[52] The Transnistria Gendarmerie Inspectorate agreed, ascertaining in the information bulletin for the first two weeks of the same months that the "religious movement is quickly gaining momentum. Everybody thirsts for exaltation."[53] According to the information bulletin of the Iampol Gendarmerie

Legion dated January 8, 1942, by that time in this județ alone "hundreds of children and youths" had been baptized.[54] One former Odessan émigré memoirist, Mikhail Dmitrievich Manuilov, remembered after the war that following the Soviets' withdrawal, "the population immediately turned to their religious cults and completely restored their rituals . . . believers not only attended services but feverishly and sincerely prayed, being in a state of religious ecstasy and fanaticism . . . neither in the old [prerevolutionary] times nor in emigration did I ever observe such intense religious sentiment among those praying as I saw [back then in Odessa]."[55]

Besides these admittedly impressionist accounts, one can cite the Romanian data on the decline of the number of "sects" and their membership. As I have already noted, the Romanian leaders believed that wider spread of Christian sects in Transnistria, among whom they counted both neoprotestant churches and homegrown cults, was the result of the Bolshevik suppression of the Orthodox Church. Ion Antonescu was even convinced that members of the sects or *sectanți* were in cahoots with the Soviets, serving as their sui generis agents intent on undermining resistance to the communist ideology.[56] Accordingly, and in congruence with the policy of limiting and eventually suppressing the "sects" in Romania, the Romanian authorities registered the sects' members, put pressure on them to (re)convert to Orthodoxy and closed down their houses of worship. By Ordinance #88, issued in late September 1942, Alexianu recognized the traditional cults such as Orthodox, Catholic, Lutheran, and Armenian, and "completely banned" all others.[57] The gendarmerie and police regularly reported on the activities of the sects and noted with satisfaction their decline, attributing it to the missionary activity of Orthodox clerics. For example, the Ananiev Gendarmerie Legion reported in early March 1942 that "religious propaganda is not being conducted due to the lack of priests. [For this reason, the population] tends to adhere to the sects."[58] Already in June 1942, however, the same legion reported that the "arrival of a higher number of priests helped reduce the spread of sects."[59] In September 1942, the Moghilău Gendarmerie Legion assessed that "*Sectanții* no longer foment propaganda and have returned to the true religion. [This development] is due to the priests' missionary activity."[60]

With all their initial optimism with respect to the prospects of re-Christenizing the local population, the authorities soon realized that not all local demographics were equally interested in religion. In particular, young people educated by the Soviets showed little inclination to attend services. For example, the Ananiev Gendarmerie Legion commander opined, in August 1942, that "one can find religion only with those who received education under the tsarist regime, while the youth roams in the dark."[61] The

Transnistria Gendarmerie Subinspectorate tersely noted: "The youth abstains from the churches."[62] The Berezovca Gendarmerie Legion commander expressed the same opinion in April 1943.[63] Another category refractory to religious propaganda were teachers who were predominantly young and educated under the Soviets, although some of them were a little older than "youth," a separate category in the authorities' taxonomy (up to twenty years of age). For example, in September 1942, the Tiraspol siguranța bureau opined: "The teachers do not come to the churches, in this way demonstrating that they are not religious."[64] This observation went hand in hand with the growing Romanian suspicion that Soviet-educated teachers had "communist ideas deeply rooted in their souls"; to their dismay, this was also true of ethnic Moldovan teachers who visited Romania on the *guvernământ*'s account.[65] In March 1943, the Dubăsari Gendarmerie Legion commander bluntly wrote: "The teachers who are in their majority communists, they are all under our surveillance."[66]

As the war dragged on and the situation at the fronts changed in favor of the Soviets, surveillance bodies noted decreasing attendance of religious services and the simultaneous augmentation of communist propaganda influence. In November 1943, the Odessa gendarmerie inspector reported that "attendance at church services has been reduced to virtually zero." And the author added bitterly: "It is safe to conclude that the priests' missionary activity did not yield hoped-for results, either because of their lack of spiritual qualities and moral rectitude, or because of population's preoccupation with material shortages." He then offered other possible reasons for this perceived failure. Besides the fact that "the population was educated in the atheistic spirit under the Soviet regime," "developments at the fronts" also might have influenced the locals' behavior, persuading them that "their attending religious services might be reported to the Soviets upon their return and thus cause them difficulties later on." And so, he summed it up, "the churches are empty and only old people who have nothing to lose still visit them."[67]

As I show in the next chapters, by this time—late 1943—popular moods changed dramatically in favor of the Soviets and away from the purported "liberators," which suggests that those processes were interrelated, and that declining church attendance was indicative of the population readjusting to the idea of soon having to don, again, the identity of loyal Soviet citizens. If this was indeed so, then the report's negative assessment of the Romanian missionary efforts in Transnistria is overdetermined. The powerful resurgence of popular religiosity after the end of communism is an indication that in 1941–1943 the Romanians managed to tap into an enormous reservoir of Christian piety that lingered not too far beneath the surface of Sovietness. Whether, however, and to what extent they succeeded in instrumentalizing this religious revival, which probably was no less and possibly more real than its precipitous decline in late 1943, for the purposes of Romanianizing Transnistrian clergy and population, is another question entirely. It is likely that the answer to it should be "rather negligent or not at all."

Civilizing by Romanianizing

Although the Romanians dreamed of ethnically cleansing Transnistria, they simultaneously pursued a policy of Romanianizing its nonethnic Romanian population, in particular its upper strata. Here, too, the Romanians followed in the footsteps of the European colonial rulers who taught their languages and cultures to the elites in the colonies as a means of "civilizing" them. Efforts to mark Transnistrian public space as Romania resulted in the renaming of streets and, more rarely, some localities, as well as in the mandated use of signs in Romanian. The authorities also invested in teaching some Romanian to the locals employed in various public institutions and enterprises, in order to facilitate and improve collection data and management. According to the activities report of the city administration of Odessa, between August 1941 and August 2943, Romanian language courses were offered in Odessa for "municipal employees and local functionaries."[68] Reports of the administration of the port of Odessa for the same period also mentions such courses, adding that they were not obligatory but achieved good results, "so much so that now most paperwork is done in Romanian."[69] The CBBT director, Lieutenant Colonel Stelian Iamandi, who visited Odessa in early 1942, reported that there were three courses of Romanian in the city with 300 students enrolled.[70] In the rest of the province, teaching of Romanian was sporadic. According to the activities report of the *guvernământ* department of culture, in the summer of 1942, such courses were organized "in the raions and judeţe in which eighty-one teachers from Romania took part." The report does not specify the intended target of these courses, but both their short duration and limited personnel suggest that their effects were insignificant.[71] The Romanian railway administration also organized courses of Romanian for their local employees and boasted, in May 1943, that significant progress had been achieved. The reliability of the latter claim is questionable, however, since it appears in the context of the administration support of the local employees' plea to stop forced migration within the province, which was due to the influx of eastern ethnic Moldovans. Local railway employees supported by the Romanian administration insisted that such forced resettlement was hampering the smooth functioning of the railways. The administrators also claimed that while their employees were loyal, as their supposed willingness to learn Romanian demonstrated, their loyalty was strained by dislocation, which thus had to be suspended.[72] As for teaching Romanian to pupils in non-Romanian schools, it is mentioned only with respect to schools in Odessa, and the veracity of this official claim is impossible to confirm.[73] Odessa radio stations broadcast lessons of Romanian language, but according to at least one source, they were not listened to.[74]

FIGURE 10.   Private photograph taken on Deribasovskaia Street, 23, Odessa, 1942. Note the sign above that reads "Romania," rendering in Cyrillic Romanian pronunciation, with a mistake. Courtesy Mikhail Borisovich Poizner.

It is likely that teaching Romanian to the locals had wider symbolic meaning to the authorities outside of simply facilitating their communication with them. It was supposed to convey the message of the durability of the Romanians' domination in Transnistria and of their cultural superiority. The authorities preferred to ignore the apparently paradoxical nature of their policy aims: if ethnic non-Romanians had to eventually leave Transnistria, it made no sense to teach them Romanian. Making at least some locals speak, or simply learn, Romanian carried symbolic importance well beyond its real value.

The pressure to learn Romanian language and history was stronger in Odessa colleges. At the University of Odessa, faculty members were obligated to study Romanian and those who occupied administrative positions faced the possibility of demotion in case they did not demonstrate sufficient progress.[75] According to one source, Romanian had to be studied for at least four hours per day.[76] Teaching hours for Russian language and history were drastically reduced and required solely of philologists and historians; teaching of Ukrainian history was discontinued. Conversely, history of Romanians and Romanian literature became required courses. Docent Sokolov, dean ad interim of the Philology and History Faculty, who resisted these measures, was forced to resign in 1942. The new appointee, Professor Lazurskii, carried out the requirements faithfully. In June 1943, Sokolov was sacked from his post of the director of the Odessa School of Arts (Khudozhestvennoe uchilishche) because of his unwillingness to learn Romanian. In his postwar deposition, he claimed that starting from mid-1942, many municipal civil servants in Odessa were indeed replaced by newcomers from the Old Kingdom under the same pretext.[77] Still, according to Sokolov, both the low quality of teachers, their lack of enthusiasm—apparently, some of them did not necessarily believe in the longevity of Romanian Transnistria—and especially the skeptical attitude on the part of students and faculty, who ignored these courses, resulted in the "resounding failure" of this program.[78] Nonethnic Romanian students and faculty flaunted even the public lectures of Romanian dignitaries and professors who visited the university. On April 30, 1943, the university's rector, Professor Pavel Chasovnikov, forwarded a circular to the faculty, in which he drew attention to their and their students' conspicuous absence at such events and solicited their cooperation in the future, in order to avoid possible "unpleasant situations."[79]

Alexander Werth, who arrived at Odessa shortly after its liberation by the Red Army, noted that "neither Ukrainians, Russians, nor Romanians could, after all, take (Romanian) Transnistria very seriously. For one year (up until the battle of Stalingrad) it seemed possible that the Romanians had come to stay, but not after that."[80] This observation is supported by many residents of Odessa who noted the visible sagging of Romanianizers' zeal as time progressed.[81] It is thus little wonder that Romanianization left no lasting traces in the region.

Fighting Ukrainian "Irredentism"

Although Romanians showed overt respect toward the high culture of Odessa and patronized the city's Russian-speaking creative intelligentsia, they disparaged Ukrainian culture with its association with the peasantry and poverty. For example, in December 1941, the gendarmerie inspector of Transnistria, Colonel Emil Broşteanu, attributed the majority Ukrainian rural population's failure to understand the Romanians' refusal to disband kolkhozes to their supposedly "low cultural level."[82] In November 1943, Governor Alexianu referred to the ethnic Ukrainians of Bessarabia, whom he proposed to "evacuate" to Transnistria in the expectation of their future transfer to the east, as "an irredentist, lazy, and recalcitrant population."[83] In January 1944, an Odessa police prefect noted that "the level of morality and personal discipline among Ukrainians is extremely low, regardless of age and sex."[84]

What was worse, the Romanians were afraid of what they called Ukrainian *irredenta*, by which they meant the Ukrainian nationalist movement that sought to create a Ukrainian national state. Romanians had a long history of confrontation with this movement, beginning with their battles with the Ukrainian militia in Bukovina over the control of the former Austrian province in 1919 and lasting throughout the interwar period.[85] When the Romanian authorities returned to northern Bukovina after its Soviet occupation in 1940–1941, they resumed the policy of repressing Ukrainian community members suspected of separatist inclinations. The Romanians arrested, harassed, and shot some Ukrainian activists and expelled others into the German-controlled Ukraine. They moderated the level of their repression only after repeated German interventions on the Ukrainians' behalf.[86] Mihai Antonescu insisted that the government policy was "categorically opposed to" Ukrainian "irredentism," even if the Germans supported it.[87]

It should thus come as no surprise that from the beginning of the Romanians' occupation of Transnistria, the authorities closely monitored all signs of the Ukrainian nationalist movement and blocked attempts to spread its influence. There was no policy of cooperation with the Ukrainian nationalists, as there was in the German zone of occupation. Instead, the Romanians repressed any and all Ukrainian nationalist activity. Situation reports by

Romanian gendarmerie, police, army, and the Special Service of Information (SSI) in 1941–1942 invariably identified proponents of Ukrainian nationalism as "intellectuals"—teachers, medical personnel, students, priests, and artists in Ukrainian theaters. I will quote just one. In his note on the "mood" of the population of Odessa on September 26, 1942, an SSI official claimed that the Ukrainian irredentist movement was in the phase of "organizing" and added that its leaders "were waging a vivacious nationalist propaganda among the Ukrainian population . . . Ukrainian intellectuals, the great majority of whom are ardent nationalists, try to promote trusted persons into important public functions in order to conduct activities of public bodies in the interests of their conationals and to impart to the province a Ukrainian character, in this way preparing the ground for their claims."[88]

Romanian officials were sure that "in the soul of every Ukrainian, a feeling of love of an independent Ukrainian state was preserved."[89] They sometimes felt that every Ukrainian hated them. As the intelligence bureau of the Romanian Third Army that was deployed in Transnistria reported: "From the Ukrainians' attitude one detects the hatred that they feel toward us."[90] The Gendarmerie reported even such apparently innocuous manifestations as wearing Ukrainian national shirts (Romanians apparently meant *vyshyvanky*) and singing songs in Ukrainian at wedding parties as noteworthy and disturbing developments.[91] Another sign of "irredentism" supposedly was putting up in one's home a portrait of Taras Shevchenko, the national Ukrainian bard whose populist undertones made him acceptable to the Soviets. A mandatory subject in prewar Ukrainian schools and a darling of the Ukrainian nationalists, Shevchenko's cult-like status was a constant irritant to the Romanian authorities. Typical was the following passage in the June 1942 activities report of the Transnistrian Gendarmerie Inspectorate: "It has been ascertained that the Ukrainian population continues to hope in the eventual establishment of an independent Greater Ukraine. [This hope], however, does not manifest itself other than via putting on in every house of a portrait of Taras Shevchenko, who is their symbol. We have taken measures to remove this portrait everywhere. We also keep under surveillance Ukrainian intellectuals and officers of the former Tsarist army who are instigators of this movement."[92]

Romanian military members were particularly zealous in the fight against "irredentism" to the extent that in December 1942, the Third Army requested that the governor take measures to prevent the further sale of "notebooks with the portraits of Ukrainian poets Shevchenko and Lermontov," which according to their intelligence was taking place in Berezovca județ. Traian Herseni, acting on behalf of the governor, supported this request and as a result, the Berezovka Gendarmerie raided a local stationery shop from which they confiscated "seven notebooks with the portrait of Shevchenko and twelve with the portrait of Lermontov." Although the gendarmes, unlike Herseni, correctly identified Lermontov as a Russian and not a Ukrainian poet, they still reported this action as part of the fight against irredentism.[93]

Perhaps nothing better demonstrates the difference in the Romanians' attitude toward Ukrainian and Russian culture than their decision to close down the Ukrainian Theater in Odessa. A fruit of the Soviet Ukrainianization campaign, this theater was closed on June 1, 1942, on the pretext that its performances were solely commercial (read "lowbrow") and thus deserved no support. A National (Romanian) Theater was opened on its premises.[94]

Still, the Romanians' view of the Ukrainians was more complex. Perhaps it would not be an exaggeration to say that it was schizophrenic. While Romanians saw Ukrainians as ardent nationalists and thus dangerous enemies, they were also inclined to perceive them as docile, peaceful, and grateful to the Romanians for liberating them from communist oppression. For example, in July 1941, the Romanian General Staff summarized the situation in Ukraine: "The Ukrainian population is very satisfied that at last it has been saved from communist terror. German and Romanian troops have been welcomed at the entry points to the localities with bread and salt. Crowds . . . have eyes full of tears. Although they live in great misery, they put at the troops' disposal everything they have. This attitude has to persuade every Romanian soldier to have a dignified attitude [and to behave] as a liberator."[95] In his report on the mood of the population in September 1942, Gendarmerie Legion Commander in Berezovca județ opined that "the Ukrainian population accepted with relief the expulsion of the Bolshevik authorities and the establishment of Romanian rule because this population is refractory to the communist doctrines and reforms and has preserved beautiful Christian traditions."[96]

The belief that virtually no Ukrainians were communists and that the real danger was Ukrainian nationalism framed the Romanians' understanding of the population's mood in the region for more than a year. In the fall of 1942, however, this belief began to weaken, and by the end of 1943, it was shattered. Simply put, the Romanians came to the realization that communism had regained traction among the province's Ukrainians and that "irredentism" had lost its appeal. In October 1943, Colonel Mihai Iliescu, head of the Odessa Gendarmerie Inspectorate, concluded that "in general, the Ukrainian irredentist current is weak, having been overwhelmed by the communist one."[97]

The Romanians identified two main reasons for the precipitous decline in "irredentism" and the increased appeal of communism. The first was the changed course of the war and the increasingly real perspective that the Soviets would soon be back, which made the project of an independent Ukraine unrealizable in the foreseeable future. The second was their own ruthless exploitation of Transnistria's population and plunder of the province's economic assets. It is this latter subject that I address in the next chapter.

The Romanians fell back on Orientalism by default, as the only readily available discursive practice through which to make sense and justify their rule over the Transnistrian population. Previously having had only limited experience of ruling over foreign populations, they resorted to the familiar—from the language of European politics of imperialism—tropes of backwardness and the laziness of the locals—to rationalize their violent and oppressive rule over the Transnistrian countryside and their suppression of Ukrainian culture. Pervasive and exaggerated fear of Ukrainian *irridenta,* however, was rooted not so much in an orientalist mental framework as in the Romanians' own confrontation with the Ukrainian nationalism in Bukovina in the preceding decades. Quite possibly, they might have projected their own ethnic nationalism—a sui generis official ideology of the Romanian ruling class at the time—onto the ethnic majority of Transnistria.

Kulturträger motifs in the Romanian propaganda did not result in any observable action except perhaps limited and largely inconsequential attempts to teach Romanian to the local population. The Romanian largess toward the Odessan creative intelligentsia was most probably self-serving: patronizing high culture they saw as European boosted the Romanians' sense of belonging to pan-European civilizational space. It also spoke to the Romanians' predilection to accord high (one is tempted to say, unduly high) status to intellectuals in their own society. One way or another, this aspect of their policy was quite successful, both in the sense that it helped elicit support from this part of the region's population and create a myth of Odessan cultural revival during the occupation that outlived both the occupiers and the occupied.

Measures to promote the revival of the Orthodox religion starkly distinguish the Romanian rule from the practices in neighboring Reichskommissariat Ukraine, where the Germans tolerated but never encouraged religious activities. Romanian endeavors to reconstitute canonical unity of the Orthodox Church in the region and their drive to suppress Christian "sects" resulted in the resurgence of religious observance among the local Orthodox believers. However, the occupiers' tendency to conflate missionary activity with Romanianization hindered their efforts and sowed tensions between local and Romanian clergy. Nor was the upsurge in religious observance durable:

as soon as prospects of the Soviets' return became certain, most local residents hurried to shed their Christian identity and to don the appearance of ordinary Sovietness.

Overall, it is doubtful that Romanian cultural and religious policy in the province, whether of a more benevolent or purely oppressive character, had any longer-term consequence beyond the period of occupation, with the sole exception of above-noted memory of cultural renaissance in Odessa.

CHAPTER 7

Extracting Economic Resources

Initially, both Ion and Mihai Antonescu defined Romania's goals in Transnistria as military and political. However, beginning in the fall of 1941, the crudely material needs of the Romanian state moved to the top of the government's priorities list in Transnistria. According to the Conducător's statement at the meeting of the Council of Ministers of December 16, 1941: "Ahead of the interests [of the province's residents], there stand interests of the Romanian State, and these interests require that we pull out as much as we can [from Transnistria] for the economic needs of the war, and especially for future operations, so that we could support ourselves by pulling [resources] out from there."[1] Addressing the same audience six months later, Mihai Antonescu acknowledged that: "The purpose of the occupation of Transnistria has been defrayal of expenses and difficulties of the war."[2] A month later he explained: "The war has cost us 230 billion lei so far. If we do not defray this sum from the revenue from the occupied territory, then wherefrom will we get the resources? From false assumptions?"[3] This radical change of priorities was caused by a longer than expected hostilities in the east and a bad harvest in 1941. In response to these challenges, the government cut back on the previously agreed-on deliveries of food supplies to Germany and on rations to the country's citizens.[4]

Exploitation of Transnistria, both of its productive assets and of residents, started from the first day of occupation. The immediate instrument of expropriation of the individuals' wealth was an obligatory exchange of the Soviet rubles into RKKS. The exchange rate of RKKS was established on August 25, 1941, when Romania received 60,000,000 newly minted RKKS from Germany for use in Transnistria at the rate of sixty lei to one RKKS. This rate was used to exchange these currencies for the Romanian military and administrative personnel deployed in Transnistria. Initially, one RKKS was exchanged at a ten-ruble rate but on November 21, 1941, the rate was altered to twenty rubles for one RKKS (the authorities claimed that the population had many more rubles than they originally calculated—not a totally implausible claim) and the maximum exchangeable amount was limited to 5,000 rubles. The exchange could be done solely during fifteen days, from December 10 to 15, 1941.[5] Thus, most citizens of Bessarabia and Bukovina were forced to exchange their ruble savings at the rate of one ruble for three lei.[6] According to the Romanian Ministry of Finance, however, at the beginning of the hostilities, the real value of a ruble was six lei.[7] As a result, most residents of Transnistria saw the value of their ruble savings cut in two or more (if they possessed more than 5,000 rubles).[8] As for the Jews, their rubles were exchanged at the robbers' rate of sixty rubbles for one RKKS, or three times lower than the rest of Transnistria's population and six times lower than its prewar value.[9] On top of this, from the first days of occupation, the authorities resorted to massive buying of precious objects, such as jewelry and anything made of gold, for RKKS. In August 1942, by Ordinance # 79, Alexianu arrogated to the occupying authorities the right of first refusal in transactions involving buying and selling such objects. In December of the same year, by ordinance #103, the same regime was imposed on the sale of jewelry. Although the exact amount of values thus "procured" from the population is still unknown, it is certain that the proceeds were transferred to the coffers of the National Bank of Romania and its Ministry of Finance.[10]

The worst was to come. Contrary to their original promise, in March 1942 the Germans introduced in neighboring Reichskommissariat Ukraine one more quasi-currency, the karbovanets. As a result, Transnistria experienced an influx of RKKS, which led to the vertiginous downfall of the currency's value. In early June 1942, according to the calculations of the Ministry of Finance commission that investigated the situation, the real value of RKKS was only 15.2 lei.[11] The authorities, however, refused to acknowledge the economic reality and continued to pretend that the original value of RKKS had not changed. Their response to RKKS fall in value was a strict ban on the circulation of lei in Transnistria, more severe limitations on the RKKS-lei exchange, and the introduction of ever more draconian price controls.[12] The governor issued ordinances on the "fixation of maximum prices" on May 2,

July 12, and September 19, 1942, and again on April 14, 1943. This frequency alone testifies to the inefficiency of this measure.[13]

Predictably, widespread shortages of basic goods in the government-run "general stores" (also called, inappropriately, coops) that were opened under the aegis of the *preture* in all the raions and in some villages, became a persistent reality.[14] For example, the Ochakov Gendarmerie Legion reported in December 1942: "Practically all travelers who pass from and into Transnistria bring contraband goods such as alcohol, silk, socks, thread, soda, glass chimneys for kerosene lamp, cigarettes, etc. This kind of commerce is especially popular among invalids of the current war who occupy themselves with nothing but contraband. In the town of Oceacov, German sailors also sell some articles [such as saccharine and socks]."[15] In early July 1942, the Iampol Gendarmerie Legion reported that the "Local population was dirty, naked, and ragged . . . [while there was] a total lack of matches, soap, clothes, cooking oil, fabrics, and other sewing materials on the market."[16] Then in April 1943, the Dubăsari Gendarmerie Legion reported that local populations complained of the lack of clothing and shoes. "Local traders have for sale solely secondhand articles, which they have procured on occasion in Odessa or Tiraspol, and then in very small quantities . . . coops . . . have almost nothing for sale."[17] With the local industrial capacities (that had been partially restored after the devastation wrecked by the Soviet scorched-earth policy) directed to manufacture products for the Romanian war needs, the only way for local residents to obtain the much-coveted consumer goods was through the black market, which in the border towns and along the railways was lavishly supplied by contraband goods from Romania and Germany. According to Transnistria subinspectorate's general report of March 1943, contraband of clothes and shoes from Romania was the only way those articles reached the local markets.[18]

Low pay and the unavailability of goods of first necessity at officially controlled prices and their dearth on the black market were day-to-day experiences of the great majority of the Transnistrian population, even of those who were employed in the occupiers' administrative structures. Small wonder then that they strongly resented the double pay and other perks of their Romanian overseers and bosses.[19] Among the perks enjoyed by the latter group, the most important might have been exclusive access to closed distribution centers (*economate*) where they could buy products, including those imported from Romania, at the artificially low prices.[20]

Keeping artificially low prices on locally produced commodities had its rationale in that it offered the Romanians a golden opportunity to procure these products well below their costs. Faced with a predictable refusal of producers to surrender the fruits of their labor on such devastating terms, the authorities responded by decreeing the state's exclusive right to buy such products and interdicting to sell them to private buyers (regulations called *monopol* and *oprire* or *blocare*, respectively). The list of such products grew exponentially, and by the end of 1943 it included fish (introduced in October 1941); sheep hides (February 1942); pharmaceutical products; alcoholic beverages with the exception of homemade wine (March 1942); timber; 70 percent of all harvested agricultural products; all hides (June 1942); tobacco; meats of all kind (March 1943); all silk cocoons; all grapes and fruits (June 1943); most of flour (August 1943); and 25 percent of vegetables and fruits grown in the gardens of residents of Odessa and Tiraspol. Finally, in October 1943, Alexianu established the state's right of first refusal on all locally produced meat, with a maximum consumption of 900 grams per month per person, even in the farming families that grew animals for slaughter.[21] Farmers also suffered from steadily increasing taxes and fees that they had to pay as contributions toward the war effort. For merely symbolic pay or no compensation at all, they had to surrender all available felt boots (*valenki*), bird feathers, pork bristles, horsehair, horns and hooves, field mice fells, as well as significant quantities of sacks, mittens, and other products to the Romanian state.[22] As these lists suggest, by the end of the occupation, the Romanians appropriated—at virtually no cost to themselves—almost all goods produced by farmers on their farms.

Still, most of the agricultural goods pumped out of Transnistria were produced not on the individual but on collective farms, which Romanians, following the German lead, decided to preserve by renaming them from the Soviet kolkhozes intro the Romanian-sounding *obște*. Soviet-style state farms (sovkhozes) were also kept intact while renamed *ferme de stat.*[23] As early as the fall of 1941, the Romanian leaders concluded that stripping Transnistria of most of its agricultural goods was the only way to save the country from severe food shortages. As fate would have it, while 1941 proved to be a year of an exceptionally bad harvest in Romania, it witnessed a bumper harvest in Transnistria. In a statement at the February 26, 1944 meeting of the Commission for the Investigation of the Activities of the Administration of Transnistria (*guvernământ*), Mihai Antonescu revealed that the food situation in the country in 1941–1942 had been so grave that the prefect of Brașov județ called him every day to warn him that supply of flour in his județ would last only one day. Without the deliveries of food from Transnistria, the Romanians could not have coped, Mihai Antonescu concluded.[24]

In 1942–1943, although the harvest in Romania was better, a labor shortage in the countryside because of the unforeseen continuation of hostilities in the east made deliveries from Transnistria indispensable. Ion Antonescu admitted that without the 53,000 railway cars of grain brought from Transnistria from September 1942 through June 1943, the Romanians "would have had an enormous crisis." "To this one should add," he continued, "goods that are kept in [public] warehouses and revenue [to the budget] resulting from the difference on the prices of Transnistrian products which are estimated . . . at 10 billion lei, as well as the fact that [specially created stores for the sale of Transnistrian products such as tobacco, alcohol, and sugar] kept the market saturated and contributed to lowering price levels."[25]

Enormous quantities of agricultural goods could be delivered from the war-ravaged province into Romania only by reneging on the authorities' promises to allocate a higher share of their produce to farmers than the Soviets ever allowed. In the fall of 1941, the Romanian authorities promised to divide crops into two equal parts, one for the farmers and one that they would purchase at fixed prices.[26] However, as soon as the crops were harvested, the authorities ordered that public warehouses be locked, and the distribution of goods stopped. Then, to the locals' outrage, a lion's share of the crops was shipped to Romania. In the spring of 1942, the authorities renewed their promises, and then they reneged on them again in the fall of the same year. By the end of 1942, their credibility had all but vanished. For example, the commander of the Ananiev Gendarmerie Legion described the situation in his report for September 15–October 15, 1942: "Many locals have nothing to eat. They worked [because] they were promised a share in the harvest. And now, they see that everything has been harvested and stored in the kolkhoz warehouses and that [the authorities] issued an order that nothing be given to the population. They treat this measure as dispossessing them of what belongs to them. They say that they have absolutely no incentive [to work] and believe that the work they do is the same as the [forced] labor of a prisoner."[27] According to the gendarmerie political surveillance agency in Tiraspol, the local population received 30 percent of the harvested crops, but a member of the Berezovca județ Gendarmerie Legion reported that locals received only 10 percent.[28]

Predictably, under such conditions, violent enforcement was the only means left to the authorities to extract the resources they needed. In the meeting of the Council of Minister of December 16, 1941, Ion Antonescu pulled no punches in his instruction to Alexianu: "You drag people over to work even with a whip if they do not understand. . . . if a peasant does not come to work, pull him out even with a bullet. For this, you do not need my authorization. We did them a favor by saving them, and if they do not understand, then treat them as animals, with a lash."[29] Sometime in 1942, the Romanians introduced "agrarian gendarmes," who became notorious for their violent methods of "organizing" agricultural work. For example, in June 1943, a member of the SSI related that one of the reasons for the unsatisfactory situation at the state farm named after Mihai Antonescu was that "agrarian gendarmes solve all issues by resorting to beating."[30] Not only the agrarian gendarmes used beating as a primary method of disciplining the local population; many a petty official also used this method to enforce compliance, with impunity, without shame, and often in public. The Romanian geographer Simion Mehedinți, who visited Transnistria in the summer of 1942, was so shocked by the widespread use of violence against the "autochthonous population" that he wrote a memorandum to the government protesting this practice. He cited concrete examples, among which was a pretor's beating a woman with a baby in the presence of a priest and neighbors in the village of Ternovka (Tarnaucă) in the Tiraspol raion.[31] There is no indication that Mehedinți's protest had any effect.

What ultimately tipped the balance against the Romanians was Operation 1111, which amounted to the transfer of virtually all of the region's productive assets into Romania. Officially commenced in the fall of 1943, Operation 1111 had antecedents from the first days of the Romanian occupation. In the initial phase, the plunder of resources was carried out under the pretext that they constituted "trophies." An army commission under the command of Colonel Georghe Cassian defined the term "trophy" so broadly that it permitted the Romanian officials to confiscate anything they found in Transnistria. Accordingly, by June 1942, the Romanians had shipped from the province "trophies" such as 98.5 railcars of "sanitary material, 30 railcars of didactic material (books, museum objects, paper), 164 railcars of army commissariat materials (beds, pillows, etc.), 20 railcars of pianos, 11 railcars of mobile chairs and tables, machines, 22 railcars of technical and automobile materials, 4 railcars of big bed sets, . . . linoleum, etc." Although preliminary and apparently incomplete, these data are the best available since Romanians were loath to keep too detailed a registry of their "trophies."[32] It should be noted that "medical" and "sanitary" materials were shipped from Transnistria at the same time when tens of thousands of Jews were dying of typhus in ghettoes and concentration camps in Transnistria and while the local population was suffering from a breakdown of the health care system.

Notorious was the evacuation of "superfluous" trams, together with the necessary materials such as rails, poles, and depot equipment from Odessa to the Romanian cities. Initiated by Governor Alexianu, the shipment of Odessan trams produced a veritable competition among the Romanian cities intent on getting as many tramcars as possible.[33] While it is true that the decrease in the number of Odessa's residents made some trams unnecessary, the Romanians overkilled in this respect, too. During occupation, the trams were so overcrowded that passengers eager to get on were often hanging over the steps while holding on the outer handles, which led to numerous casualties. One such story was reported in *Odesskaia gazeta* on May 6, 1943, under the telling title "Children! Once again a victim of a tram": a nine-year-boy thus traveling in one of those railcars fell out and was cut in two by a tram moving in the opposite direction.[34]

The Romanians' appetite for plunder upset the German army command, who apparently observed their rapine in Crimea where the Romanian troops were fighting Soviet partisans alongside the Wehrmacht. While it is unknown whether the Germans were concerned about the psychological effects that the Romanian behavior was likely to have on the locals or about their appropriating what the Germans believed to rightfully belong to them, it is prima facie doubtful that considerations of international law per se might have caused the German protests. One way or another, the Germans requested that their allies follow a more restricted definition of "trophies," that is, materials of military character only. In July 1942, the Romanians signed an accord, committing themselves to follow the Germans' demand.[35] Simultaneously, however, the General Staff issued instructions on the implementation of this convention that amounted to nothing less than a requirement to continue plunder regardless, but to hide the theft better from their German allies. The following paragraph is worth citing at length:

> One will try to appropriate (*ridica*) as much pharmaceutical material as possible, preferably raw and finite materials. . . . one will try to gather as discretely as possible all works of art and artistic values. It is preferable that pictures be expedited in their frames. If this is not possible, they will be cut out [from their frames] with a razor and rolled up. Works of art and national values will be expedited solely with the Romanian sanitary trains to the General Staff, which will direct them to destinations according to their importance.[36]

In September 1942, the minister of Munitions and Production for War general Gheorghe Dobre presented a memorandum to Mihai Antonescu, in which he suggested that since Odessa was predestined to lose a good part of its economic potential after the war, it was in the interest of both Odessa and Romania to evacuate a substantial share of its factories and workshops into Romania without delay.[37] From that moment, the Romanian leaders began to prepare for what was later codenamed Operation 1111. It is impossible to establish the exact amount of plunder, since Mihai Antonescu ordered the relevant documentation destroyed in February 1944. However, the following partial list of factories slated for evacuation from Odessa by a commission specially created in April 1943 gives some sense of the nature and scope of the operation. The list includes the "Transporter" factory of mechanical equipment; a workshop of craftsmen school # 1; a workshop for repairing surgical tools; a knitwear factory; a set of spinners from three factories; and installations from a cloth factory.[38] As Ion Antonescu decreed on November 17, 1943: "Future necessities oblige us to bring everything from Transnistria—to stock it, to sell it, and especially to make reserves."[39]

For Alexianu, everything meant literally everything: the products of all factories and workshops, all harvested crops in their entirety, all cattle and agricultural equipment, all seeds, all railway equipment, and all raw materials. Government ministers, the prefects of Romanian județe, and the mayors of the cities to where these materials were sent soon began to complain. They had insufficient storage facilities and not enough personnel to register, stock, and guard the massive deliveries of Transnistrian goods, and they were afraid that they would be held responsible when the goods inevitably deteriorated. The avalanche of complaints about the unsolicited deliveries from Transnistria reached such a level that Ion Antonescu, whose personal protection Alexianu had enjoyed for so long, finally turned against his protégé. On January 3, 1944, the Conducător placed a note in a resolution on a summary of reports about the shipments from Transnistria, stating that they not only overwhelmed the state and local administrators but also created a danger of epizootics because of the poor state in which cattle arrived from Transnistria: "In this way, all fortune collected in Transnistria . . . is squandered. Mr. Alexianu angers me at every step."[40] Governors of Bessarabia and Bucovina were ordered to stop convoys of cattle from entering their provinces. On January 27, 1944, Governor of Bessarabia general Olimpiu Stavrat reported to the Council of Ministers that he had received from Transnistria 29,000 bulls, 106,000 sheep, and 4,800 horses. Besides, he had halted at the border, for lack of manpower and fodder, further shipments of 8,878 bulls and 88,000 sheep. He estimated their value at an astonishing 200 million lei.[41] On January 29, 1944, Ion Antonescu sacked Alexianu, in effect punishing him for faithfully fulfilling his own rushed and destructive orders and placing blame for the resultant disaster onto his appointee. Despite this change, the plunder of the region's resources continued uninterruptedly under General Gheorghe Potopeanu, whom Antonescu put in charge of the reorganized "military administration of the region between the Dniester and Buh rivers," as Transnistria was now officially called, until the end of the Romanian occupation on March 16, 1944.[42]

The Myth of Odessan Prosperity

In the gloomy picture of widespread shortages of basic goods in the province, Odessan markets presented a stunning exception. Abundance of fruits, vegetables, and even dairy products and meats seemed unreal to rare travelers through the occupied Soviet territories accustomed to the horrors of starving urban centers. Nikolai Mikhailovich Fevr, a "first wave" émigré (from 1920) from Soviet Russia and an important journalist on the staff of Berlin pro-Nazi *Novoe slovo*, was allowed to visit the occupied Soviet territories three times—in 1941, 1942, and 1943.[43] It was during his third trip in the fall of 1943 that he arrived in Odessa and was astounded to find a city that looked so much different from anything he saw in the other urban centers. Especially startling was the look of a famous Odessan market "Privoz." He wrote: "one sees piles of various products on both sides of the street. Here is bacon [*salo*], stacked in tiers, ham, sausages, smoked fish, endless rows of baskets with grapes and apples . . . live poultry and piglets . . . agile Odessan boys . . . in eager rivalry offer matches, cigarettes, and lighters."[44]

A collaborationist journalist writing under the pseudonym "S. K." in December 1942 rhapsodized in an article titled "Odessa yesterday and today":

> You stroll along the street and cannot believe your eyes: where there were dirty, empty cooperatives and canteens are now clean stores, snack bars, and restaurants. Where there were pits and bumps are now clean and smooth pavements . . . where there were colossal lines next to a kolkhoz horse-cart with unripe or rotten apples—that is, in the bazaar—one sees boundless piles of all kinds of fruits offered by sellers. And not only there! Fruits and other commodities one can buy everywhere. . . . Soviet peacetime bazaar pales in comparison with our wartime bazar.[45]

Mikhail Dmitrievich Manuilov, who was born and lived most of his life in Odessa, both under the tsarist and Soviet regimes, left a more balanced description of the economic situation in the city. A specialist in the city financial management, he was employed in similar positions in municipal services by the Soviets and the Romanians, both of whom he despised. He fled Odessa with the approach of the Red Army.[46] Although in his postwar memoirs Manuilov made a point that wartime conditions prevented full development of the city's economic potential, he also asserted that under the Romanian rule "life in Odessa gradually improved (*nalazhivalas'*) and its situation was in stark contrast to the situation in the other cities, which were under the German occupation." Manuilov claimed that perception of the

"Odessan miracle" survived the war and constituted a run-of-the-mill topic of small talk in émigré circles.[47]

Contemporaries agreed that the main cause of this "miracle" was the Romanian policy, which encouraged private enterprise. According to Major Paulian Nicolae, in the first month following the city's occupation, the population was starving, mostly due to the disruption of the supply lines and the Soviet scorched-earth policy. Soon, however, Mayor Pântea's decision to start issuing licenses to local entrepreneurs permitting them to open up new small businesses helped alleviate the situation.[48] Manuilov and other eyewitnesses confirm this assessment.[49] According to Odessa's *primaria* department of immovable properties, whose responsibility included "regulation of private commerce," the latter was supposed to serve as "the new basis of the restored economic life [in the city]." By August 31, 1943, this department issued 8,610 licenses for various types of economic activity, among which the greatest number—1,256—were issued to the owners of various types of groceries, such as dairies, butchers, bakeries, and others. The next most numerous category was restaurants and cafes (1,062) followed by barber shops, bath-houses, and laundries (199), and "small industries" such as sausage-makers, soap factories, mineral waters distributors (171), and so on.[50]

Such impressive statistics begs at least two questions. The first concerns provenance of initial capitals. As Manuilov explains, the population lacked sufficient quantities of the only legal tender in the province, RKKS, and could not obtain credits from the banks. A pawn shop, created supposedly on his initiative with the initial capital provided by the Romanian administration, helped solve this problem. Anything of value, saved from either Soviet or pre-Soviet time, could be left as collateral.[51] Major's Nicolae account leaves no doubt that massive looting of abandoned apartments in the first month or two of the occupation helped locals secure such valuables.[52] Among the looted properties were those "abandoned" by Jews, some of them murdered, others interned and later deported to certain death.[53] The Romanian and German soldiers and policemen also participated in looting and quite possibly later sold looted valuables on the Odessan black market.[54] Valuable objects of dubious provenance were also sold via numerous consignment shops.[55]

Odessan commerce was thus lively and largely illegal, or semilegal, and consisted of goods obtained in the manner described above together with merchandise clandestinely "imported" from Romania by Romanian military and state employees. This does not, however, explain the provenance of agricultural goods on the Odessan market, especially if one recalls that Romanian requisitions in the countryside were so thorough that hardly anything was left to farmers that they could sell without endangering the survival of their families. To this, one should add that severe restrictions on travel outside of one's village further impeded the intraprovince trade. The explanation can be found in the existence of a privileged farming community in the province, namely the Volksdeutsche, whose freedom of travel was considerable while the extent of their economic exploitation by the authorities was significantly lower than that of the other local farmers. As fate would have it, a number of their villages were located within a one-day travel distance by a horse cart. Soviet postwar investigative files contain numerous references to the ethnic German farmers' travel to Odessa for sale either of their own or their Jewish victims' belongings.[56] It is obvious that such trips with the purposes of selling and buying were routine to Volksdeutsche and it is certain that deliveries of their agricultural produce were essential for the Odessan "miracle."

No less important a factor contributing to the abundance of products on Odessan markets was the Romanian authorities' refusal to strictly enforce the German policy of price control. Ultimately one more instrument of the economic exploitation of the occupied eastern territories that allowed the German authorities to procure local produce on derisory prices, it was compounded, in the German zones of occupation, by a policy of deliberate cordoning off the bigger cities from the countryside in order to leave more products available to supply the Wehrmacht and continue deliveries to the Reich. This aspect of the Nazi occupation policy was linked to the longer-term aims of murdering millions of supposedly racially inferior Eastern Europeans.[57] The Romanians did not pursue such aims and there is nothing in the extant sources suggesting that they ever discussed such perspectives or thought along these lines. Odessa was never deliberately cordoned off from the surrounding villages, nor was the policy of strict price control ever enforced in the city (as opposed to the rest of the province). In his postwar depositions, Pântea claimed the credit for this deliberate nonenforcement for himself, but it is doubtful that he could have followed this policy and resisted the German pressure without Alexianu's support. As early as December 25, 1941, the head of the German Army Liaison Office in Transnistria (Verbind-ungsstab der deutschen Wehrmacht für Transnsitrien), generalleutnant Friedrich-Wilhelm von Rothkirch und Panthen, complained to Alexianu about the laxity of the Romanian price control, to which a week later the governor responded by blaming the German troops for causing price inflation by buying products at "exaggerated prices."[58] In early July 1942, Hermann Neubacher, a high-ranking German diplomat stationed in Bucharest with extensive powers in the economic sphere who had just visited Transnistria, forwarded to Alexianu a strongly worded memorandum on this issue, referencing the flourishing black market in the city, ostensibly tolerated by the authorities, and demanded actions.[59] No actions followed.

Pântea-Alexianu's "procapitalist" policies (or so they were perceived by the economically better-off Odessans) succeeded in creating the appearance of an island of prosperity amid the sea of misery, but they failed to satisfy the immediate needs of the Odessan working class and lower administrative personnel who comprised the majority of the city's population. Some contemporaries, even those who were generally pro-Romanian, were acutely aware of the narrowness of the economic "revival" of the city and the unhealthy, largely speculative character of its "miracle."[60] The Romanian police and army collected through their network of informers a wealth of information testifying to the widespread economic hardship of the majority population, and their growing anger at the unfulfilled promises. For example, on September 16, 1942, the head of Odessa's police force reported: "When a worker is paid 3 RKKS per day while one kilogram of bread costs 3.5 RKKS, his family is surely dying of hunger. . . . and what will happen to them during the winter, [when they will need] fuel [to keep their houses warm]?" The officer went on to blame the municipal and provincial authorities for their "lack of foresight," thus suggesting that their hands-off-the-market policy benefitted "speculators" and disadvantaged everybody else.[61] On July 25, 1942, surveying the economic situation in Transnistria, the SSI reported matter-of-factly: "Foodstuffs, as well as industrial and textile commodities, are inaccessible for the population. The workers' remuneration is low (max 90 marks) and for this reason, they are greatly disaffected and disinterested in working efficiently."[62] Relentless depreciation of RKKS brought further hardship to workers and laborers because the authorities refused to adjust wages to inflation. On October 23, 1943, the Odessa Gendarmerie Inspectorate ascertained that while the real value of RKKS was 13–14 per leu, salaries and wages were paid to those employed by the *guvernământ* were calculated according to the official exchange rate of 60 RKKS per leu.[63] As in the other urban center of the province, most people survived by selling anything of value they possessed and by further engaging in various types of illegal activity on the black market.[64] One is thus bound to conclude that the Odessan "miracle" was more perceived than real and that the majority of the city's population did not feel much of an improvement in their lives.

In Lieu of Conclusion: Plunder, International Law, and the Romanian Grand Strategy

Ruthless exploitation of the province's resources and plunder of its economic assets was predicated on a peculiar interpretation of international law on the rights of occupiers, shared by both Antonescus. In particular, the Conducător insisted that, according to the law of nations, the occupiers were allowed to seize any resources they wanted in the occupied territory.[65] Mihai Antonescu also insisted that the international law was "categorical" in that everything that the occupier found in the occupied territory belonged to him and if he left anything not seized, such valuables should be counted as the occupier's investments in the region.[66] Instructing members of the investigating commission on the activities of the *guvernământ* on February 26, 1944, Mihai Antonescu revealed that the commission was created not so much to investigate as to destroy documents potentially damaging to the "interests" and "honor" of Romania, since they might reveal various "mistakes" committed in the region. The vice chairman of the Council of Ministers maintained his previous position that the international law gave to the occupier large discretionary powers with regard to the resources of the occupied country that constituted "an usufruct." "Usufruct of sovereignty means," Mihai Antonescu argued, "that one could seize all crops and goods linked to the process of production, circulation, etc. . . . from the time of Khan and through today . . . the wars have been made this way."[67] The debates over the international rules of war following World War I led to the consensus that "the occupier's rights include not only the right for compensation for the costs of war but also the right to limit the military capabilities of its adversary."[68] The rules and customs of war require the occupier neither to keep an exact registry of all goods seized for compensation nor to maintain the previously existing legal regulations.[69]

As it happened, the Antonescus' interpretations of the provisions of international law were in stark contradiction to the agreements on the laws and customs of war signed prior to the Great War. Particularly bewildering is Mihai Antonescu's reference to the supposed unchanged nature of war "from the time of Genghis Khan on" since Antonescu, as professor of law, should have been aware that modern international regulations intended to limit the unnecessary suffering of combatants and noncombatants alike. With the vagueness of these agreements, which stemmed from disagreements between the signatories, Mihai Antonescu violated some of the key provisions of the Convention Respecting the Laws and Customs of War on Land (singed in Hague in 1907). In particular, articles 49 and 52 prohibited collection of taxes and fees, as well as requisitions in kind and services, other than for the needs of the army of occupation and the administration of the occupied territory, which furthermore had to be "in proportion to the resource of the [occupied] country." Moreover, Operation 1111 clearly contradicted articles 53 to 56 that restricted the seizure of goods in the occupied territory to those belonging to the belligerent state and required that the occupying power respected private and municipal property, as well as that belonging to religious institutions and art museums. Although the seizure of means of transportation, even if private, was permitted, they had to be restored on the conclusion of peace, and indemnities paid—something that the Romanians did not intend to do. The rules of usufruct required, contrary to Mihai Antonescu's statements, that the occupying power "safeguarded the capital [of the immovable properties they exploited] and administered [it]," a wording that excluded the possibility of their dismantling.[70]

On one occasion, Mihai Antonescu disclosed the way he arrived at these conclusions. Speaking at the Council of Ministers meeting on August 28, 1942, he referred to the precedent set by the Germans during their occupation of most of the Romanian Old Kingdom in 1916–1918, when they "removed all rolling stock of Romanian railways and brought it into Germany . . . and it was pronounced legitimate on the basis of all principles of international law of that time; they acknowledged the legitimacy of this operation."[71] When, following the liberation of Odessa on April 18, 1944, Radio Moscow accused the Romanian occupation authorities of the illegal plunder of the Transnistrian resources, Mihai Antonescu, while acknowledging that the General Staff's instructions concerning the seizure of works of art constituted an "imprudence" (the Soviets captured them and quoted verbatim), nevertheless insisted that his interpretation of international law was correct, and again referred to the precedents created during the Great War.[72] It is worth noting that following World War I, the Romanian lawyers decried Germany's and its allies' occupation practices, in particular the removal of railway rolling stock and other equipment, as barbaric and unlawful.[73] They tended to interpret the rights of the occupant in a restricted sense following the Western, as opposed to the German, line of reasoning.[74] Still, Mihai Antonescu chose to use the German practices of violating the pre-Great War agreements on the laws and customs of war to justify the Romanians' illegalities on the Eastern Front a quarter century later.

According to Isabel V. Hull's prescient assessment, the Germans' position on the rights of the occupying power was unique in comparison to the other powers in that they refused to accept any limitations, arguing from the standpoint of "military necessity." German practices of occupation during the Great War were clearly in breach of the widely recognized international norms. Nevertheless, despite the initial determination of the Western governments to bring German war criminals to justice, they quickly lost interest in this project in favor of a policy of accommodation of the defeated enemy.[75] The Romanians, too, were frustrated by their inability to receive reparations from the Germans' and their allies' for their abuses during the occupation.[76] It was thus the Western powers' failure to prosecute German war crimes and the Romanians' failure to obtain reparations for the ruthless economic exploitation of their country during World War I that persuaded Ion and Mihai Antonescu that the occupier's powers were virtually unlimited.

Tellingly, in the only area in which the international community did achieve progress toward strengthening the laws of war in the interwar period—the treatment of the prisoners of war—Ion Antonescu demonstrated greater sensitivity.[77] In 1941 and 1942, the Conducător went on record insisting on the humane treatment of the POWs, including the Soviets. In July 1941, the Romanian commanders gave orders to the troops, which provided for humane treatment of the POWs, such as transportation of the wounded to the military hospitals.[78] Perhaps, one is tempted to conclude, had the Western powers been more consistent in punishing war criminals after the Great War, the Romanian leaders would have been more moderate in conducting their occupation policy in 1941–1944.

One more aspect of the Romanian policy of spoliation of the Transnistrian economic assets deserves attention: its radicalization as the war went on. This is in stark contrast to their treatment of Jews in Romania and Transnistria, which underwent de-escalation as soon as they realized that the war was unlikely to end in victory for the Axis powers. Believing that Jews exercised an inordinate influence over the foreign policy of the Western powers, the Romanian leaders decided that it would be unwise to expose Romania to their vindictiveness at the peace conference at the end of the war and refrained from further participation in the Nazis' "Final Solution."[79] That Romanian leaders' calculations about the strategic prospects of Romania had no bearing on the aspects of their policy discussed in this chapter signifies that they did not consider such abuses as having potentially serious consequences for the country' international standing. Quite likely, they did believe that such practice was largely in agreement with international usages.

It is also important to bear in mind that both Antonescus stubbornly refused to face the eventuality of Germany's and its allies' defeat and occupation. On February 10, 1944, Ion Antonescu told Ioan Hundiţa, secretary general of the opposition National Peasants Party, that he simply could not see "how the German army could be destroyed."[80] As the Germans escaped paying the high prize for their abuses in the occupied territories after the World War, so would Romania, the Antonescus reckoned. And so, the reckless plunder of Transnistria accelerated through the end of the Romanian rule there.

If the colossal plunder of Transnistria's economic resources did not benefit Romania, certainly not as much as its leaders envisaged, it did bring an enormous hardship to the local population and break any residual trust that might have existed, in the fall of 1943, between the authorities and their charges. It is to the history of their relations that the next chapters turn.

PART 3

Responding to Romanian Occupation

CHAPTER 8

Accommodating and Collaborating

This chapter explores the changing relations between the majority local population and occupiers. "Majority" here implies two stipulations. First, Jews and Roma are excluded from the chapter's purview for reasons explained in the introduction. Second, most locals' behavior can be described as either accommodation or collaboration with the occupiers. This thesis might still raise a few eyebrows because it stands in stark contradiction to the long-enduring Soviet-era myth about the "all-people's" struggle against the occupiers. Still, the evidence that the overwhelming majority of local residents either accommodated or collaborated with the occupiers is irrefutable. In order to make sense of these massive and diverse phenomena it may be instructive to inquire about taxonomy, namely the differences between accommodation and collaboration and the various forms that collaboration took. The rest of the chapter explores those forms and motivations behind them as well as the changing attitudes of the majority of the local population toward the Romanian authorities.

I believe that one grasps intuitively what kind of behavior belongs to the category "accommodation." It can be defined as "apolitical." Most farmers, laborers, workers, and lower administrative personnel in occupied Transnistria exhibited it. Most of them never felt a need to explain themselves, probably considering their behavior natural and unexceptional. For that reason, their mental world is probably destined to remain a mystery to us. One can only surmise that they tried to live their lives as "normally" as possible, taking care of their own and their families' immediate needs and staying out of harm's way.

The meaning of the category "collaboration" appears somewhat problematic, primarily because its understanding by the Soviet authorities was quite different from the one that had currency in Western Europe in the late stages of the war and immediately following it. Moreover, as Vanessa Voisin writes, the Soviets' own understanding of this term also evolved, from the one that criminalized all forms of cooperation with the occupiers, even the most inconsequential, to the more differentiating and attentive to the realities and hardships of the occupation.[1]

In his book on the collaboration in Nazi-occupied Belarus, Leonid Rein distinguishes several forms of collaboration, some of them common for all occupied Europe, others discernible only in Nazi-occupied Soviet Union. For example, economic collaboration was widespread in the West but could hardly be found in the occupied East, largely because this notion implies mutual profit, and the ruthless exploitation of resources in the East was such that it amounted to extortion without any regard for and thus no significant opportunity for the economic self-interest of the locals.[2] Although this assessment may be correct if one defines economic collaboration as always implying participation in profits, it does not apply to Transnistria. There, most local residents, particularly in the early stages of the occupation, shared with the occupiers a vital interest in restoring, as much and as quickly as possible, a local economy that had been severely damaged by the retreating Soviets. A particularly prominent role in this endeavor was played by those local residents whom Romanian occupiers had employed in the local administration, including managers of various factories, power grids, and municipal services, as well as mayors of villages and heads of kolkhozes (*obşte*). These people comprised the majority of Transnistrian "collaborators" broadly defined.

How different was this behavior from that of those local residents who labored in the factories, tilled the fields, and tended to the animals in the countryside, paying taxes and contributions and fulfilling various labor duties imposed by the Romanians? In the first months and years after the liberation, the answer to this question was highly significant. The Soviet definition of treasonous collaboration, in effect from May 1942, required investigators to prosecute only those persons whose actions were intended "to aid the German army . . . and [in general] the German fascist occupiers," and to refrain from prosecuting those "employees . . . and professionals (such as doctors, agronomists, veterinarians, etc.)" whose actions did not contain such intent.[3] While intent thus defined might have been absent or impossible to establish, it is likely that many local residents who worked as managers and administrators, applying themselves conscientiously to the fulfillment of their duties, did so because they expected to derive—and did receive—benefits and privileges from their performance. Unlike the lower classes—laborers, workers, and farmers—they were driven not only by the fear of punishment and desire to survive but also by some degree of identification with the occupiers' aims.

Rein devotes particular attention to ideologically driven collaborators, who in the context of occupied Belarus were mostly motivated by visions (largely utopian under the circumstances) of attaining, with Nazi support, an independent Belarus. Unlike the Nazis, the Romanians did not support Ukrainian nationalism and suppressed all inklings of Ukrainian irredentism. Nevertheless, the phenomenon of ideological collaboration did exist, in particular in Odessa; its basis constituted pure anticommunism rather than any coherent vision of the future.

Finally, Rein distinguishes "military-police collaboration." This notion is applicable to the Transnistrian situation with a proviso that the Romanians did not create an auxiliary military force manned by the locals, although they did create local police that served under the gendarmerie. Collaborators from this category, their recruitment, motivations, and the tasks they performed are discussed in a separate section of this chapter. Undercover agents recruited by the SSI and siguranța constitute a separate subgroup of this category.

Local Administrators and Managers

The majority of the local population welcomed the German and Romanian troops. On July 23, 1941, Major Bădărău, chief of the SSI information center attached to the Third Army, summarized the situation to the east of the Dniester River as follows: "The Ukrainian population is very satisfied that at last it has been saved from communist terror. German and Romanian troops have been welcomed at the entry points to the localities with bread and salt. Crowds . . . have eyes full of tears. Although they live in great misery, they put at the troops' disposal everything they have."[4]

Bădărău also noted that this population resisted the Soviet authorities' attempts, as part of their scorched-earth policy, to destroy productive facilities, crops, and to drive away cattle. There were neither signs of communist ideology's influence on them nor of any pro-Soviet sentiment among them. As soon as the military situation permitted, farmers proceeded to harvest crops.[5] In the instructions distributed by the second section (information) of the Fourth Army concerning the treatment of the local population, the local Ukrainians' attitude toward the Romanian troops was described as "absolutely friendly."[6] In early August 1941, the German military command affirmed in its instructions to the troops operating in Ukraine, "the attitude of the civil population vis-à-vis German and Romanian troops is friendly, especially in the countryside, and they demonstrate the same by their friendly actions."[7] Upon its arrival in Odessa, an SSI detachment reported on October 21, 1941, that the city's population took notice of the Romanians' efforts to restore order and municipal services and were offering them their concurrence. In particular, "many technicians and specialists of all kinds, especially those in the spheres of water supply and illumination were anxious to extend their assistance [and] workers were showing up at the factories hoping to see them resuming their activities."[8] In November 1941, the same unit reported that "many Christian citizens [of Odessa] manifested their firm determination to assist the authorities in capturing subversive elements [that is, pro-Soviet partisans]."[9] On January 24, 1942, this unit noted that Odessan Christians were helping Romanians to identify and arrest all Jews.[10]

Odessan citizens who fled to the West at the end of the war confirmed the Romanian authorities' information as to the readiness and even eagerness of their compatriots to assist the occupiers in restoring municipal infrastructure

FIGURE 11.   Soviet engineers who designed restoration works on the dam. May 1942. Courtesy Mikhail Borisovich Poizner.

and the economy. Manuilov, for example, wrote: "I do not now recall, whether locals were acting in pursuance of the [new] authorities' order, or on their own initiative, but all workers and clerks started coming to institutions and enterprises where they were previously employed."[11] According to Manuilov, most locals simply did not have any alternative since their pressing needs—providing for themselves and their families—could be attained only in cooperation with the occupiers.[12] In this way, Manuilov's assessment is in tune with Voisin's statement that Soviet citizens in the Nazi-occupied territories faced a "non-choice situation," which made the notion of "collaboration inapplicable to the behavior of most of them."[13] "Gradually," Manuilov continues, "an enormous number of people got employed in private firms and municipal services or opened their own businesses."[14] In the rest of the province's countryside, the most important officials from among the locals were town and village mayors, whom the Romanians called *primari* (singl. *primar*), an equivalent of *starosta* and *burgermeister* in the German zone of occupation. The *primar*'s tasks consisted of controlling the population of the respective village (*comună*), including making sure all residents were registered and no newcomers were allowed to settle without prior permission from the gendarme post chiefs; enforcing restrictions on travel; fulfilling all services imposed by the occupiers; and fully and punctually collecting all taxes and one-time contributions. *Primari* were selected from among the locals. Officially, *primari* were elected by the village's assembly and confirmed by the pretors or prefects, depending on the locality's size, but in reality assemblies often simply rubber-stamped prior decisions of the Romanian officials.[15]

Occupiers preferred to select *primari* and other appointees from among persons repressed by the Soviets. For example, in March 1942, officials from the Ananiev Gendarmerie Legion reported that formerly dekulakized farmers were eager to offer concurrence to the Romanian administration, suggesting that they be placed in various administrative positions since they were reliable.[16] Soviet postliberation investigative files of war crimes also contain anecdotal evidence of the Romanians' preference for the appointment of persons from this category to mayor positions, although high turnover because of the widespread accusations of abuse of power and embezzlement, as well as steadily increasing fear of Soviet reprisals, made following this policy in the latter stages of occupation difficult.[17]

After liberation, the Soviets routinely arrested all former *primari*, considering them traitors. They investigated their actions and sentenced them to different punishments depending on the nature of their offenses.[18] Their investigative files presumably contain a wealth of information for the history of collaboration and conditions under occupation. Unfortunately, so far their accessibility to researchers has been limited and somewhat random. Ukrainian authorities released selected files under foreign pressure, mostly those relevant to Holocaust history. In these files, *primari* often appear as participants in crimes against humanity. In particular, they organized searches, arrests, and guarding of the arrested Jews in the places of their detention, as well as taking them to the places of execution. They also transmitted orders for the execution of Jews to the policemen from the gendarmerie officers, under whose orders policemen served. They took clothes and other belonging from Jewish victims, which they later distributed to the villagers.[19] It would be wrong to extrapolate this evidence over all or even the majority of Transnistrian *primari*. Rather, it is more than probable, that in those localities that did not serve as places of internment and/or massacre of Jews, and such were the great majority of Transnistrian localities, *primari* made themselves guilty of no greater wrongdoings than the collection of taxes and contributions decreed by authorities. Such activity was liable to make them unpopular among the villagers, and traitorous in the eyes of the NKVD but they hardly deserve opprobrium.[20]

Immediately following the *primari*, the heads of the revamped *obşte* were next in the hierarchy of officials in the villages. These were followed by Soviet-educated agronomists, veterinarians, livestock specialists, and others of similar professional backgrounds. Given the nature of collectivized agriculture, their services were indispensable, and on August 28, 1941, Alexianu issued Ordinance #2 requiring "all those who had any post or had been tasked with particular services in kolkhozes or sovkhozes . . . to appear before local authorities to be issued authorization for the resumption of activity."[21] This injunction was repeated in Ordinance #5, issued on September 7 of the same year, with an addition that *obşte* would elect their heads "there where they do not exist," thus making it clear that, as a rule, occupiers preferred Soviet-era leadership to remain in their positions.[22] This prima facie paradox had a simple explanation in that the Romanians accorded priority to the rapid restoration of the region's productive potential, which required avoiding the disruption of the existing economic-administrative apparatus.

The decision to keep ex-Soviet low- and mid-level administrators in their positions caused tremendous resentment on the part of the locals. The gendarmerie and other surveilling entities regularly reported on the popular anger with this state of affairs, as well as demands for the replacement of these administrators. I will cite just a couple of the numerous examples of such reports. In early April 1942, the Balta Gendarmerie Legion reported that the population was dissatisfied with the Romanians' failure to disband the kolkhozes and "did not understand why they still keep former bosses in their posts."[23] In June 1942, the Ananiev Gendarmerie Legion reported that the population "resented that many former communists remain in their commanding posts and say that their current diligence is a tactic designed to protect their people and to show to others that it was not so bad under the communists."[24] Although the Romanians tried to replace some of the petty officials, such as the heads of kolkhozes, these efforts had only limited success.[25] On October 23, 1943, the Odessa Gendarmerie Inspectorate noted that the population persisted in expressing dissatisfaction with the continuous presence of former communists in their posts but, the report went on, there was no alternative to keeping them there, for lack of replacements.[26]

Indeed, the lack of trained cadres who were not members of the Communist Party before the occupation was a common phenomenon not only in the countryside but also in the cities, including in the metropolis of Odessa. There, too, constant complaints of ostensibly anticommunist-inclined members of the citizenry who suspected the former communist administrators and managers of "sabotage" clashed with the harsh reality of personnel shortages and with the highest priority accorded by the occupiers to the restoration of the province's productive potential.[27]

Although reemploying former Soviet-era administrators, the Romanian authorities still considered them a security risk. From the start of the occupation, they demanded that all communists and Komsomol members register with the authorities under penalty of internment in concentration camps.[28] Following registration, they were kept under police surveillance and were required to periodically reregister with police and gendarmerie stations. For example, the Transnistria Gendarmerie Inspectorate reported in August 1942 that "all local public employees (*funcționari localnici*) are former communists and are all to be kept under surveillance."[29]

The overall number of the Communist Party members who remained under the Romanian occupation is unknown, but it was quite high. The Soviets left some of them behind the enemy lines for the purpose of sabotage (for more on this, see the next chapter). Others deliberately escaped mobilization in the army or evacuation into the Soviet rear. According to the strict party rules, communists who found themselves in the occupied territory had to devote themselves wholeheartedly to the fight against the occupiers, either by means of sabotage, or, preferably, armed struggle. Under no conditions could they register, thus self-reporting as security risks with the occupying authorities.

Contrary to these injunctions, and largely as in the other occupied territories, most, probably more than 90 percent of the Communist Party and/or Komsomol members in Transnistria did exactly this. According to the summary drawn by the Central Committee of the Ukrainian Communist Party, by April 25, 1944, Soviet authorities identified 1,224 communists who stayed in occupied Odessa, of whom at least 746 registered with the Romanians.[30] The authors of the report suspected that the latter number was "incomplete," and so it was since, by the end of 1942, Romanians registered 2,093 communists and 4,156 Komsomol members in the city. By that time, they "identified, arrested, and transferred to the court" 69 (unregistered) communists and 27 Komsomol members.[31] As Ivan Emel'ianovich Platov, one of the leaders of Odessa's underground party put it, despite his order not to show up for registration, "almost all those left [for subversive work in behind enemy lines] showed up for registration."[32] Another supposed partisan, Stepan Il'ich Drozdov (who, as it turned out, grossly exaggerated his exploits), testified after the war that "the majority of members of the party and specialists" showed up for registration "because they believed that the Soviet government would be no more."[33]

Massive abandonment by the communists of their duties was a common occurrence throughout the USSR. As Vanessa Voisin put it, this fact proves "the fragility of communists' heroic ethos, in the situation in which pressure of collectives and hierarchy was absent."[34] If one judges by the rate of expulsion from the party ranks of communists who stayed under occupation, it might appear that regional party membership was particularly opportunistic.[35] The more than 90 percent rate in Odessa oblast was the highest in the country. Before these numbers are considered accurate, proper allowance must be made to the randomness and inconsistency of the postliberation purge, so that the rates of expulsion may have had "very weak connection to the reality on the ground."[36]

In general, former communists and Soviet-era managers and administrators proved reliable partners for the Romanian authorities in the latter's efforts to restore the province's productive capacity. For example, the *guvernământ's* department of industry, summarizing its activity in 1941–1944, explained that in its policy of "relaunching of factories" in Transnistria, it was guided by the principle to "utilize wherever possible, Russian [meaning, local] personnel, from a simple laborer all the way up to technical director. As a result, only the overall management of a factory would be carried out by a managing director from Romania who in most cases was the sole Romanian there." Despite numerous and seemingly insurmountable difficulties, the report continued, the department registered continuous successes in reopening factories that had been partially destroyed by the retreating Soviets: 85 upon the establishment of the Romanian administration; 25 more through March 31, 1942; 121 in 1942–1943; and in the final year, March 31, 1943–March 31, 1944, an additional 74 (from the overall number of 946 prewar factories).[37] Another 30 factories were reopened under the aegis of a separate Department of Food Industry, Procurement, and Provisioning (branched off from the department of industry in February 1943). This department alone supplied products to the army in the incredible amount of 925,257.45 RKKS.[38] The proportion of local agricultural specialists, as opposed to those who came from Romania, was also heavily in favor of the former according to official statistics: 3,108 to 418 in the early fall of 1943.[39]

The directorate of the Romanian Railways in Transnistria (CFRT) was particularly incisive in its emphasis on the importance of using local employees for the successful fulfillment of its many missions under the most trying of circumstances. These missions included the restoration of railway lines damaged by the Soviets during their retreat, supplying the Romanian troops at the front, transporting "grains and mineral resources" into Romania from the occupied territories, and providing for the province's economic needs. Judging from the directorate's activity report for 1941–1943 (composed in the fall of 1943), Romanian achievements were indeed impressive: quick restoration of 410 kilometers of double-lane railroad tracks, 718 kilometers of single-lane tracks, and 465 depot-type tracks, as well as the steadily increasing railway traffic. None of this would have been possible but for the massive hiring of local employees, both those formerly employed in the Soviet railways and those newly trained in the specially organized courses. As a result, by the fall of 1943, the number of local employees in the CFRT was 19,499 compared to 3,746 Romanians.[40] The locals' productivity also steadily grew, due to their learning of skills and the Romanian language, as well as the Romanians' efforts to take good care of them and their families' needs. The directorate summed up its observations: "although we found ourselves in the midst of a people alien to us both by their blood and their political ideology, local employees appreciated new conditions of life offered to them by a civilized regime and greatly contributed to our success. This is why our efforts did not encounter any sabotage, for which they had an infinite number of possibilities."[41] (This latter claim, as will be shown in the next chapter, was not exactly correct.)

The Romanians made sure salaries of the local administers and managers were higher than those of their underlings. According to an SSI report from July 1942, at that time wages of workers and laborers (*lucrători*) in Transnistria varied from 20 to 90 RKKS while the clerks' salaries (*funcționari*) were anywhere from 45 to 150.[42] According to the activities report of the Department of Finance of *guvernământ*, however, the upper limit for the latter category was considerably higher, at 400 RKKS (data for the early fall of 1943).[43]

Upon liberation, the Soviets found evidence of the widespread participation of local cadres in the restoration of the provincial economy, to the distinct advantage of the occupying power. For example, Captain Tsymbaliuk, Odessa oblast Third Ukrainian Front Partisan Movement Staff Operational Group chief, having investigated claims of a group of purported partisans who pretended that they sabotaged the activity of the Odessa power distribution network, found that according to the official Romanian statistics, the network performed its tasks reliably and with increasing efficiency. Consequently, occupying troops and industries working toward their needs received a steadily growing volume and share of generated electricity, to the detriment of local residents. All of this was because of the company's local employees' efforts, which were arguably indicative of their being "traitors" rather than "partisans."[44]

Available evidence thus leads to the conclusion that formerly Soviet mid-level administrative and managerial personnel, in their great majority, contributed to the relative success of the Romanian policy of economic restoration and exploitation of the region. Nothing in the sources suggests that the Romanians ever experienced the lack or shortage of volunteers for better-paid administrative or managerial positions, or that the great majority of those employed presented any danger of sabotage to the occupiers. On the contrary, it was their willing and sometimes, no doubt, enthusiastic participation that helped the Romanians achieve their aims of economic exploitation of the region without expanding too many administrative or police resources there. It is thus obvious that Soviet mid-level "professionals" showed themselves ready collaborators who sloughed their Soviet identity without qualms in expectation of personal improvement under the new regime. This should not surprise us since Tanja Penter found evidence of the same phenomenon in the neighboring Donbass region, supposedly much more Sovietized and pro-Russian than Odessa and the eponymous region.[45] This evidence suggests that Voisin's notion of "nonchoice situation" that Soviet citizens displayed in the territories occupied by the Axis powers is not universally applicable.[46]

The Intelligentsia and Ideologically Driven Collaboration

A tiny but highly visible minority of collaborators were motivated by a hatred of communism and a vision of restored bourgeois Russia. As noted above, while the Romanians in Transnistria, unlike Germans in the rest of occupied Ukraine, did not tolerate Ukrainian nationalism, they did encourage the activities of the anti-Soviet and vaguely pro-Russian intellectuals.

The authorities' aim was to harness their writing, polemical, and oratorical skills, their knowledge of Soviet reality and local culture, to their propaganda machine in order to help convince the populace of the beneficial character of their occupation and to induce them to render assistance to the Axis powers' war efforts by faithfully fulfilling tasks imposed on them by the occupiers. The Romanians created several outlets through which these intellectuals could apply their abilities and energy toward serving this cause.

An important tool toward this purpose were Russian-language news-papers published in Odessa, as well as in some judeţe centers, which were mostly organs of the municipal or judeţe authorities, as well as a few private ones. Whether private or not, all were heavily censored, with a good and steadily increasing part of the printed space occupied by official translations of speeches by German and Romanian officials—from Hitler and the Goebbels to the Antonescus and Alexianu—as well as news from the front, announcements of German, Italian, and Romanian information agencies, official decrees and communiqués. The rest of the pages were filled with locally produced texts in various forms—reminiscences from the Soviet past, including memoirs or fictionalized accounts of one's life under the tsarist and Soviet regimes, praise for the efforts of the Romanian authorities, crime reports, reviews of agricultural and industrial production in local enterprises, feuilletons against scaremongers, and so on.

The first newspaper to appear on October 26, 1941 in occupied Transnistria was *Odesskaia gazeta,* an organ of Odessa *primaria.* The following month, the section of culture and propaganda of the *guvernământ's* Department of Culture established *Glasul Nistrului* (The Voice of the Dniester), in Romanian. On March 8, 1942, the newspaper *Odessa* was added to the list, a Russian-language organ of the *guvernămant* that had two versions, one for the city and one for the province. The most controversial and widely read newspaper, titled *Molva* (Rumor or Talk)—name that implied its unofficial character—started to appear on December 1, 1942, as one more propaganda vehicle of the *guvernământ.* Unlike other publications, which had two A2 pages, *Molva* had six. Its run was reported to be the highest, with up to 15,000 copies, while the other newspapers ranged from 4,000 to 10,000.[47] Other newspapers targeting particular readerships, such as *Bug* in Russian and *Bugul* in Romanian for villagers, *Ştiri de pe Bug* (The Bug news, also printed in Ukrainian and called *Pribuz'sky visti)* were published in Golta. There was even a periodical for children called *Detskii listok* (The children's page). By the fall of 1943, the overall number of periodicals was eighteen, which was more than had been available under the Soviets, as the propaganda section self-contentedly assessed.[48]

The Romanian occupying forces tended to put either their own citizens or Transnistrian Moldovans in charge of these media outlets. For example, the editor-in-chief of the newspaper *Odessa* was Semën Dem'ianovich Dumitrashku (Dumitraşcu), who until 1935 was a "scientific worker" at the MASSR's Scientific Committee in Tiraspol when he was arrested by the NKVD (charges not known). Released shortly after his arrest, Dumitrashku subsequently worked at various factories in Odessa until the occupation.[49] *Odessa* was headed by a Pâslaru (no other names indicated) who later also served as chief of the section of propaganda mentioned above.[50] *Glasul Nistrului* was entrusted to Transnistrian intellectuals and priests from Romania.[51] The editor-in-chief of *Molva* was Al. Borşag, who simultaneously served as the *primaria*'s press bureau chief.[52] This latter appointment was apparently intended to conceal the real power as this newspaper belonged to two émigrés from Bolshevik Russia. One was Xenia Balas, daughter of a former head of the Danube port of Chilia, probably a former White Army officer, and Olga Balas, who in 1941–1944 was in Odessa as a correspondent for Berlin-based Russian-language newspaper *Novoe slovo*.[53] (Although likely belonging to the same family, the nature of their relationship is unknown.) Xenia's educational background—graduate of a commercial school (Academia Comercială) in Bucharest—generated doubts as to her suitability to this post, but Alexianu defended her credentials on the basis of her excellent Russian.[54] Xenia Balas was seconded by Marc Bialchovschi (Mark Bialkovskii), a right-wing Russian journalist with more than forty years' experience in various outlets in Russia (including the infamous anti-Semitic *Novoe vremia* in St. Petersburg/Petrograd) and interwar Bessarabia, where he used to edit a number of Russian-language newspapers, among them one with the same title. For a short time during the Russian Civil War, Bialchovschi served as the head of the propaganda bureau under General Anton Denikin, the head of the White Army in southern Russia.[55] Nikolai Fevr, whom otherwise unsympathetic contemporary Russian historian Oleg Vital'evich Budnitskii characterized as "undoubtedly a capable journalist," eulogized Bialchovschi as a "teacher and patriarch" of all the other Odessan journalists of the occupation, all of them young and experienced. Bialchovschi, wrote Fevr, was "a bridge from the old, wonderful traditions of the Russian journalistic world, to the new world of the fledgling Russian press."[56]

A perusal of the texts written by local Transnistrian, mostly Odessan, authors printed in these outlets leaves no doubt that their authors were convinced enemies of the Soviet regime and hoped that they would secure its overthrow by cooperating with the Axis powers. Beyond that, these authors' politics remain largely obscure, probably because of their having no possibility to develop their visions in the heavily censored press. Nevertheless, it is highly likely that their agendas did not coincide with those of the occupiers, whom they hoped to "use" in the same way that the occupiers used them.

Among local journalistic cadres who enthusiastically supported the new regime and played an important role in its propaganda efforts was Andrei Dmitrievich Baliasnyi (or Beliasnyi), docent and later (under the Romanian occupation), a professor at the University of Odessa. His professional background during the interwar Soviet era is identified in some sources as Marxist-Leninist philosophy, while in others as Ukrainian or Russian philology.[57] Judging from the extensive archival materials from *Odesskaia gazeta*, he served on its editorial board and ruthlessly filtered out those submitted materials that he considered poorly written, with the use of "Ukrainianisms and Odessa jargon."[58] Baliasnyi was the most outspoken, hard-hitting, and talented anti-Bolshevik writer who was regularly published in both *Odesskaia gazeta* and *Molva*. Other prominent journalists included Anatolii Kraft, an ethnic German who at one time served as the newspaper's director; Anatolii Maslennikov, who purported to be the grandson of a revered nineteenth-century Russian writer Ivan Sergeevich Turgenev and author of a book about Marshall Ion Antonescu, which was supposedly published in Bulgaria with the approval of the Germans (neither of these claims could be independently verified); journalist Evgenii Adamov; and writer Petr Pershin who was also employed in the *guvernământ*'s department of propaganda.[59] Some of these materials were signed by pen names or initials.

Several themes emerge from their writings. The first is the predominance of obsessive anti-Semitism. These authors equated—again and again—communism and "the essence of Jewishness [*zhidovstvo pejor*]" and emphasized their supposed preeminence in all spheres of life. The Soviet rule was nothing but "Yids' domination," alien to the Russian people's spirit. The frequency and vehemence with which anti-Semitic themes are harped on in these publications leave no doubt that their authors really believed in what they wrote. For them, anti-Semitism was a convenient and convincing way of explaining away the catastrophes of the Soviet era and absolving the Russian nation and, in particular, the intelligentsia with which they identified themselves, from any guilt for this trauma. Also, given that these publications appeared at the time when Odessan Jews were barbarically deported from Odessa, murdered en masse, and exposed to starvation and epidemics in ghettoes and concentration camps, implicates these authors in crimes against humanity.

A second theme was Soviet depredations, such as constant shortages of food and other consumer goods, periodic famines, repressions, confiscations, and executions. Again, these were all blamed on the "Yids'" evil designs. One more theme running through these materials is nostalgia for prerevolutionary Russia, which appears as a much happier era, without much repression and far superior in terms of liberties and material abundance. Liberation from the Bolshevik yoke, brought about by the Axis powers' troops, although it had not yet resulted in complete reversal to that almost-golden age, has already produced an abundance of goods in the stores, the reappearance of free trade and entrepreneurship and, significantly, "removal of yids" from the public space, which they disfigured under the Soviets. These felicitous changes would be harbingers of further improvements after the war.[60] The idealization of tsarist Russia, however, had its limits, so that the lead article in *Odesskaia gazeta* from September 19, 1943, denied that the Axis powers intended to restore the tsarist-era arrangements as "calumny" typical of Soviet propaganda. Instead, aware that "the attitude of most Russians toward tsarism is negative," the belligerents wanted to create in the country "a truly people's (*narodnyi*) state that would take care of their interests."[61] Reprinted from the newspaper *Zaria* (The dawn), published in 1943–1944 in Berlin, this material probably reflected the Nazis' and Romanians' fear that this Soviet propaganda claim might have been indeed effective in driving the wedge between the local population and the occupiers. It is however not clear whether and to what extent such fears were justified, and they certainly were not shared by Odessan collaborationist journalists and writers.

One more important motif can be labeled "the return of the Western culture." The Bolsheviks, or so the argument went, created a wall between Russia and Western Europe. Because Russian culture was considered essentially European, this forced isolation inflicted a severe blow to the cultural and artistic creativity of the Russian intelligentsia. Now, lamented Baliasnyi in the first issue of *Molva* in an article titled, "Western culture and the Bolshevik 'Chinese Wall,'" the majority of former Soviet citizens have no idea about the new artistic and social trends in the West, nor do they know Russian émigré philosophers and writers such as Nikolai Berdiaev and Ivan Bunin. But luckily, the Germans and Romanians have demolished this wall, and the duty of Russian intellectuals is to familiarize the Russian audience with recent achievements in Western, and especially Axis-member nations.[62] What constituted "the West," however, was less than obvious since "plutocratic democracies" were excommunicated from "The New Europe" that was being created under the leadership of Nazi Germany, by the mere fact of their fighting against the Axis powers in an alliance with the communist Soviet Union.[63] The resulting narrowing of the notion of "Western culture" to Germany, Italy, and Romania undermined the cohesiveness of the thesis.

Probably in order to undermine the persuasiveness of trope of "the return to Europe" supposedly accomplished by Germans and Romanians, many Soviet propaganda materials spread by the resistance groups emphasized the Soviet alliance with Great Britain and America.[64]

Many locally produced materials emphasized the paramount importance of the intelligentsia, which was depicted both as a creator and as a bearer of the glorious prerevolutionary Russian culture, as victim of the Soviet regime, and as the only social group capable of helping the Russian nation return to its spiritual and cultural roots.[65] An abundance of materials dedicated to the issues of high-brow culture, including literature, both prose and poetry, music, and theater strengthens the readers' impression that the newspapers' primary intended audience were indeed the educated and cultured strata of the Transnistrian population. Some published materials betray scorn for the lower, less educated classes who due to the coarseness supposedly became unwitting helpers of the "Yids" in their destruction of old Russia. For example, in the first issue of *Molva*, Anatolii Maslennikov wrote: "The International Jew let loose the rabble (*velikogo khama*) from their cage. Together, they trampled culture."[66] It is impossible to say whether and to what extent this visible pro-intelligentsia bias in the collaborationist writers' materials was due to their own class prejudices—many of them did indeed belong to the privileged upper middle classes of prerevolutionary Russia—or stemmed from the "objective" difficulty of constructing a more inclusive message under the continuously deteriorating material conditions of the lower classes in Transnistria.

The occupier-authorized press was not the only outlet through which local anticommunist intellectuals could participate in ideological warfare against the regime that they passionately loathed. Another was the Institute of Anticommunist Research and Propaganda, whose solemn opening took place on May 21, 1943, in the building of the Odessa Conservatory on Peter the Great Street, which before the revolution and after 1995 was called Dvorianskaia (nobility). Its first head was a legal scholar and Odessa University Law Department dean Ivan Iakovlevich Faas, who seemed to have played a leading role in its establishment.[67] A master's degree graduate in law from St. Vladimir University in Kyiv in 1918, he taught law in Odessa from 1921 until 1930, when the law department was liquidated by the Soviets. This fact, as well as his perceived political unreliability, prevented him from defending his doctoral (*kandidat*) dissertation in law, which he had completed by 1930. He was also stripped of his teaching position that year. For the rest of the 1930s through the German-Romanian occupation, Faas and his family (his wife was a medical doctor) lived in abject poverty in an overcrowded communal apartment. The new regime opened new prospects for Faas, who was soon promoted to a full professorship and appointed chair of the restored juridi-cal department at the university.[68] Reportedly because of an illness, Faas was soon replaced by a professor at the Institute of Communications, Nikolai Aleksandrovich Iablonovskii, who was arrested and interrogated in 1938 but was then released after Stalin ordered the end of the purges.[69] Before that, Iablonovskii reportedly helped the German military in Krasnodar, where he found himself at the time of occupation.[70]

The institute's aim was defined as giving the possibility to every intel-lectual interested in "delivering lectures, reports, or publishing books or bro-chures . . . either in the original or in translation intended to undermine the foundations of communism . . . of the Stalinist-Bolshevist regime"; any activity directed toward this goal was labeled "a valuable contribution to the common cause of struggle and construction of the New Europe."[71] The university's *prorector* (vice rector) and professor of chemistry Ivan Gus-tavovich Shettle (Schoetlle?) oversaw drafts of such lectures.[72] Judging from the appeals from the rector and professor of medicine, Pavel Georgievich Chasovnikov, and from Traian Herseni, at the time head of the Department of Culture of *guvernământ*, dated April 30 and May 20, 1943, respectively, the Romanian administration had to resort to pressure, cajoling and even threats of expulsion from the faculty, "regardless of academic merits," in order to secure their participation in anticommunist activity.[73] Despite the unremitting deterioration of the military situation, the institute (from Octo-ber 1943, also referred to as the Institute of Social Studies), continued its activity through the end of January 1944, when it hosted a lecture on the Crimean Tatars by one A. A. Shevelëv.[74]

Many of the same persons mentioned above as particularly active writers in the newspapers made considerable contributions to the institute's activity. For example, Alidin in his note to Khrushchev mentions three public lec-tures delivered at the institute by Baliasnyi on such topics as "The Critique of Lenin's Theory of State," "The Main Moments in the Development of Russian Philosophical Thought," and "Philosophy of History and Marxism." Other sources mention lectures on other similar topics, assessing their over-all number as between ten and twelve.[75] Other notable speakers included Anatolii Kraft ("The History of National Socialism"); university docent in economic geography Konstantin Konstantinovich Stamerov ("Mystery of Soviet Demography"—on population losses resulting from collectivization and dekulakization); philology professor Georgii Petrovich Serbskii (on the Russian poet Sergei Esenin: the lecturer opined that the poet's suicide in 1925 was the result of his depression at seeing the deliberate breakdown of the patriarchal order in the countryside by the Soviet authorities); and art

history professor and occupation-era Academy of Fine Arts director Nikolai Afanas'evich Sokolov ("The Policy of the Soviet Power toward Arts").[76]
A noteworthy poet, Orest Aleksandrovich Nomikos, offered a lecture on the
degradation of the epic genre under the Soviets.[77] Among the speakers, there
were also journalists and Christian Orthodox priests.

It is probable that many an Odessan intellectual refrained from participating in the institute's activity due not so much to their sympathy for the Soviet
regime, to which they, in their great majority, felt none, as to the fear of the
Soviets authorities, whose violent and vindictive nature they knew firsthand
from the interwar period. Thanks to the publication of the NKVD files summaries on various repressed intellectuals, we now have a valuable insight into
the fate of many Odessan intellectuals during the Stalinist terror, when in
their frantic drive to fulfill politburo-approved quotas for arrests, executions,
and GULAG imprisonments, investigators concocted numerous imaginary
"spy networks" and "counterrevolutionary," "nationalistic," and "rebellious"
organizations that involved a significant part, perhaps even a majority, of this
social strata.[78] Several other personalities met a fate similar to Faas. Conservatory professor, Sergei Dmitrievich Kondrat'ev's parents were executed while
he managed to avoid arrest by claiming an incurable illness, which allowed
him to spend fifteen years of his life in his Odessa apartment.[79] At the end of
the occupation, he immigrated to Germany with his new wife, the widow of
Teofil Richter, the NKVD-executed (October 1941) father of the great pianist
Sviatoslav Richter, who during the war was busy making his career in Moscow.[80] The notable historian of Russian theater Professor Boris Vasil'evich
Varneke disclosed, in an interview with *Odesskaia gazeta* on December 21,
1941, that the communist authorities never trusted him, and until 1932 had
even barred him from teaching in colleges. When in 1932 they finally readmit-
ted him to the university faculty, he was put under close police surveillance
and his students were required to write regular reports on him to the NKVD.[81]

The anti-Soviet stance of most of Odessa's creative intelligentsia is understandable not only in light of their suffering at the hands of the NKVD but
also because the Stalinist policy of cultural auto-isolation was particularly
repugnant to them, educated as they were at a time when the Russians felt
themselves belonging to a pan-European cultural space. When in a January 1943 article titled, "Dreams of an Old Professor," seventy-two-year old
philologist Vladimir Fëdorovich Lazurskii praised "liberation" at the hands
of the Germans and Romanians because it allowed reestablishing cultural
exchange with the Western world, he expressed a sentiment that many other
people of the same background and upbringing felt deeply.[82] Nor is there
any reason to doubt the sincerity of the art historian Nikolai Afanasievich

Sokolov, who served under the occupation as director of the Odessa Academy of Arts (Akademiia khudozhestv), and who in his public lecture at the Institute of Anticommunist Research and Propaganda condemned the Soviet heavy-handed censorship and restriction of artistic freedom.[83]

In the eyes of Soviet justice, all such public statements critical of the Soviet regime amounted to treasonous activity during the time of war, and their perpetrators were subject to arrest and severe punishment.[84] Whether they would be criminalized by a democratic Western government (for example, as "aiding and abetting the enemy" of the U.S. Code) is a different question entirely, the detailed examination of which does not belong here.[85] Morally, however, these intellectuals can hardly be condemned for publicly saying something that was so clearly justified, even if their pronouncements supported the occupiers.

Publicly condemning Stalinist crimes was one thing, justifying Nazi crimes quite another. Some collaborators from among Odessan intelligentsia did exactly this. For example, diarist Aleksandr Afanas'evich Shvets summarized the content of Baliasnyi's public lecture on May 26, 1943 thusly: "In contemporary Germany, Hitler's dictatorship enjoys the support of the people (narod). Hitler refused to accept the title of emperor although after Caesar he has been the only one who could rightfully bear it. Germans are pure-blood descendants of Romans. Their language and culture are of the highest quality. As for Russians, they have gotten mixed up with Tatars and thus can be counted as a yellow race."[86] Praising the anti-Slavic Nazi racism in front of a Russian audience was, in the eyes of Shvets, a sign of Baliasnyi's utter depravity. In an article published shortly before this speech, Baliasnyi eulogized the Nazis for "freeing" Russia of Jews, thus making himself an accomplice to their crimes.[87] "The Hymn to Hitler," written by composer Georgii Nikolaevich Fomenko, would also probably be considered a crime by any victorious democratic government.[88] This would also be the case with respect to such authors as Kraft, Maslennikov, Adamov, Pershin, and others who published repugnant anti-Semitic materials in the local press, calling, in a slightly veiled form, for violence against Jews.

The same distinction could be applied to a whole range of artists—producers, actors, singers, musical performers, conductors—who served in various Odessan theaters. Indeed, this rich theatrical life would not have been possible without their enthusiastic participation. There is no reason to doubt the account of a member of the Opera and Ballet Theater troupe concerning the troupe members' sabotage of the Soviets' order to evacuate together with the retreating army, not leaving in the city any decorations and costumes. Most decided to stay, likely expecting greater artistic freedom and new opportunities in life.[89] Nor could the performers and conductor, Nikolai Nikolaevich Cherniatinskii, be judged harshly for occasionally expressing gratitude in public for the "liberation" of their city, and for performing national anthems and other rousing songs of Germany, Italy, and Romania.[90] Their role in purging the orchestra and troupe of their own Jewish colleagues, however, deserves a different assessment. In his December 1942 interview to *Molva*, Nikolai Petrovich Savchenko (the most popular opera singer at the time), related how "a year ago [they] received a categorical order: "not a single Jew [in the orchestra]." The situation was "paradoxical," he continued, since earlier in Odessa "almost all" orchestra players were Jews but due to the common efforts the problem was solved, which constituted one of the greatest achievements of the theater.[91]

It may be legitimate to consider the public expression of support for persecution of Jews, and even more so participation in it, as a litmus test of an individual intelligentsia member's conduct under the occupation as accomodationist or criminally collaborationist. One should not forget that these expressions and actions occurred at a time when Odessa Jews were subjected to the most horrific atrocities imaginable—being expelled from their homes, interned in ghettoes, deported to the camps in eastern judeţe of Golta and Berezovca, left to die in typhus-infected barracks, and murdered en masse— and that all of these atrocities were widely known by Odessa's gentiles. Under such conditions, violent anti-Semitic outbursts amounted to an incitement to endorse the most abominable crimes. Significantly, although anti-Semitic sentiments were widely shared among Odessa's gentile population, and the occupiers' narrative on Judeo-communism was largely accepted at their face value, not everybody among Odessa's anticommunist intelligentsia participated in an anti-Semitic propaganda or activity.[92] Unfortunately, presently accessible sources do not allow further insight into the motivations of those intelligentsia members who refrained from such activity, and there is no way to know whether they were moved by ethical convictions or by strategic calculations not to incur more severe punishment upon the Soviets' return, or by some other considerations. There is, however, no doubt that participation in an anti-Semitic activity in any form was a matter of individual choice.

Local Policemen: Pliable Tools of the Occupiers or Ideological Warriors?

One more category of collaborators deserves a mention here, namely local policemen. This is because some of them took part in the persecution, including mass murder, of Jews. Two approaches have been recently formulated by scholars: one that is inclined to see local policemen as pliable tools of the occupiers because of their facing a "no choice" situation, whereas another views them as particularly vicious perpetrators of crimes against humanity.[93] The former view largely absolves them of responsibility for their actions, the latter puts such responsibility squarely at their door. Only a small minority of Transnistrian local policemen participated in the persecution of Jews since most of them served in the localities in which there were no ghettoes and concentration camps and in which any Jewish residents were either murdered or expelled before the policemen's appointment to their posts. Thus, responsibility for the participation of some policemen in anti-Jewish atrocities cannot be extended to all of them. Local police did not constitute an organization, it had no unified command, and its members did not receive any training.

This being said, the question of policemen's agency still begs itself. According to ordinance #4 from September 3, 1941, local policemen had to be appointed by the mayors; they were under the orders of the latter as well as of the gendarmerie. Local police duties were defined as "supervising and securing public order and tranquility; guaranteeing life and property of the residents "as well as the application of all measures ordered by the civil and military authorities."[94] Ordinance #27 from November 24, 1941, which laid down regulations concerning local police in the urban centers, largely similar to those contained in ordinance #4, added the following provision that referred to local police both in urban and rural areas: "Police service is mandatory. Refusal to fulfill it or unjustified shirking from the duties imposed on the police bodies by the present ordinance constitute acts of sabotage and are punishable by prison terms from five to ten years."[95] Taken together, these provisions suggest that Transnistrian men could not escape appointment into the police force and once appointed had to carry out all orders given to them by the authorities for fear of severe punishment. In fact, in the conditions of arbitrariness and lawlessness characteristic of wartime Transnistria outside of the urban center, dodgers of police duties could have expected even more severe sanctions than those provided by regulations.

On the other hand, local men could not but be aware of the severe consequences they were likely to face in case of the Soviets' return. Thus, it is not surprising that at least some of those selected for service were reluctant to join the police. Most of what we know about the process of appointments in the police force comes from the Soviet postwar investigative files of former policemen. The ones that I was able to consult have been made available to the researchers through the efforts of United States Holocaust Memorial Museum and Yad Vashem staff, who identified and microfilmed files of

Transnistrian policemen who participated in the persecution of Jews. This criterion of selecting files for microfilming may lead one to doubt their representative nature, but the evidence contained in them does prove that some local men were either appointed policemen against their will or escaped the service altogether.[96]

One category of local policemen, which immediately catches one's eye as they start perusing the said files, were former inmates of the German POW camps. As explained in chapter 2, in the fall of 1941, the Germans initiated a policy of mass release of Soviet POWs of Ukrainian nationality who were residents of the areas occupied by the Axis powers. Such POWs had to present proof of their place of origin and nationality, whether in the form of Soviet papers or depositions of eyewitnesses and sometimes to sign a document committing them to refrain from any anti-Axis activity. Afterward, they were issued a pass to their domiciles, which frequently lay in Transnistria.[97] The Romanian administration had no control over this policy and generally considered such persons, especially former Red Army officers, security risks.[98] According to data from the Transnistrian governorship, by August 1, 1943, the Germans had released 74,854 former Soviet POWs, most of whom appear to have been of Ukrainian ethnic origin, who were now residing in their putative places of origin in Transnistria.[99]

As noted in chapter 5, the Romanians clearly preferred ethnic Moldovans to Ukrainians in all appointments to positions of authority. However, given the virtual absence of the former in many Transnistrian localities, they often had to appoint ethnic Ukrainian policemen. They also faced a shortage of able-bodied men, as a consequence of the massive mobilization in the Red Army at the beginning of the war. According to their assessment, females comprised no less than 70 percent of the province's population, whereas among men the "percentage of seniors and invalids [was] very high."[100] Besides, police service might require, if sporadically, elementary skills in the use of arms, which were more readily available among the former Red Army soldiers. Thus it is understandable that the authorities turned, however reluctantly, to this category of people for recruitment for police service. For the recently released POWs who were aware of the precarious nature of their situation and the authorities' suspicion of them, service in the local police may have seemed a guarantee, however weak, of survival and of escape from the imminent danger of persecution.

Indeed, this is exactly how some former policemen explained their reasons for joining the local police force in their postwar depositions during interrogations. For example, Mikhail Stepanskii, who, among others, guarded the Peciora concentration camp for Jews, stated that he agreed to the village mayor's proposal to become a policeman because "he was afraid of being sent [back] to the camp," as well as of "being subjected to beatings."[101] Mikhail Poshtovniuk was taken prisoner in December 1941 and in February 1942 fled from the POW camp in Proskurov (now Khmel'nits'kyi) in western Ukraine, reaching his native village of Kumarovo in Vradievskii raion, Odessa oblast, in March 1942. When in November 1942 the local policeman was fired, the mayor demanded that Poshtovniuk replace him. He threatened to disclose his identity as a fugitive and an unregistered former member of the Komsomol, but Poshtovniuk still refused. It was only after the chief of the kolkhoz joined the mayor and beat Poshtovniuk with a whip that they finally forced him to agree.[102]

If these accounts seem to suggest that when joining the local police some future perpetrators in Ukrainian villages, and in particular Soviet POWs, had limited choice, there are other accounts that indicate that some local men managed to escape service in the police. For example, when Mikhail Tkachuk from the village of Stepanovka in Veselinovskii raion defended himself before Soviet prosecutors, he insisted that he could not have refused to serve in the police because he was elected by the village assembly (*skhod*), but the interrogator countered by citing cases of two other villagers who refused this commission without suffering any consequence.[103] According to Mina Varinitsa from the village of Vradievka in the eponymous raion of Odessa oblast, Aleksandr Roshko, who from the fall of 1941 through the spring of 1942 was pretor of Vradievskii raion, invited him to join the police. Varinitsa refused, preferring instead to serve as the chief of the commercial section of the pretor's office.[104] The interrogators seemed to have accepted this version, which suggests its veracity.

If it was hard, though not impossible, to escape service in the local police in ethnic Ukrainian villages, it was even more difficult in the Volksdeutsche villages, where all able-bodied men were to participate in the Selbstschutz, ethnic German militia organized by SS Sonderkommando-R. Given the exceedingly violent nature of SK-R rule there, especially in the first weeks after its arrival in the region, as well as the extraordinarily strong peer pressure in the tightly knit communities, it is not surprising that the choice of not serving in Selbstschutz was available only at the risk of putting one's own life in danger. So far, I have found only one case of an ethnic German who avoided service. Nikolai Leitner, born in 1921, was mobilized by the Red Army in 1940, taken prisoner in the fall of 1941, and escaped from a POW camp. Having come to his native hamlet of Neu-Amerika (Golta județ), Leitner found out about the Einsatzkommando and probably for fear of his life because he was an escapee, refused to show up and went into hiding. This effectively made him an outlaw in the eyes of the German and Romanian authorities, but with considerable good luck he managed to survive the war. After it, he escaped the fate of his three brothers, all of whom were arrested, tried, and sentenced to death for their role in the massacre of thousands of Jews in the concentration camp Bogdanovca in December 1941–January 1942.[105]

Once recruited, local policemen were under tremendous pressure to fulfill any and all orders, including criminal ones, most infamously mass murder of Jewish civilians. Still, available evidence proves that while some of them carried out their duties willingly and even enthusiastically, others hesitated; still others simply refused, sometimes right at the site of execution. One case of such refusal took place in the ethnic German hamlet of Neu-Amerika whose Selbstschutz killed hundreds of Jewish deportees from Odessa interned by the Romanians in makeshift ghettoes, in the winter and spring of 1942. According to Georg Frank's account, one policeman in the death squad, Robert Waikum, did not shoot. When the police chief ordered him to shoot a child who was sitting in the bathtub next to him, Waikum categorically refused, declaring that he did not shoot adults, nor would he shoot a child. The next day he was summoned to see his commander who verbally abused him, took away his rifle, and expelled him from the police. No other punishment seemed to follow.[106] No less stunning case of moral choice under most trying of circumstances comes from the investigative files on the enormous massacres of Jewish inmates in the Bogdanovca camp, in late December 1941–early spring 1942. There, seventy-one or seventy-two local policemen and Selbstschutz members shot up to 50,000 victims. From among this crew of executioners one Ukrainian policeman, whose name survivors remembered alternatively as Samoliuka, Samoil, or Samoilenko (the survivors did not recall his first name), refused to shoot.[107] It is possible, judging from the transcript of the interrogation of one of the perpetrators, that this person, alongside with the other policemen from Pervomaisk, reported to the camp without knowing the purpose of his assignment, which might explain why he made up his mind at the last minute.[108] As one survivor, Rakhil' Veksel'man, related in 1966, this Samoliuka/Samoil/Samoilenko was still alive and residing in the Donbass region, which suggests that he did not suffer serious consequences for his disobedience.[109]

The evidence thus refutes the notion of local policemen as pliable tools in the hands of the occupiers, at least in Transnistria, and possibly in the other occupied territories as well (a detail of local policemen to whom Samoliuka/Samoil/Samoilenko belonged came from the town of Pervomaisk in the German zone of occupation). It also calls for deeper research in the intragroup dynamic in killing squads. I have studied these issues at some length and, as the other scholars who have studied lower-level perpetrators before me (Christopher Browning's pioneering book on Police Battalion 101 comes inevitably to mind), I have concluded that local participants in the Transnistria mass shooting of Jews can roughly be divided into three ideal type groups: ideology-driven, convinced Jew-haters, who often equated Jews with the maligned Soviet regime; compliers, who carried out the order just because it was an order; and shirkers, who, although they did accept these assignments and did shoot when looked upon by their commanders, preferred to avoid killing unarmed civilians while out of sight and even occasionally extended help to individual victims. Those policemen who refused to murder outright made up a small minority; although scoffed by their superiors and mates, they appear not to have suffered any serious consequences.[110]

Besides the murder of Jews—the most egregious crimes—some policemen were guilty of other offenses—abuse of civilians, whether interned Jews and Roma or local Christians. Abuses of Jews and Roma, who were routinely robbed, subjected to savage beatings, and raped, were largely tolerated by the authorities, but local Christians could and did indeed sometimes find protection from the Romanian authorities. While executing their official duties, such as forcing local residents to perform labor duty or pay various taxes and surrender their produce to the authorities, local policemen inevitably alienated their neighbors some of whom later testified against them to the Soviet investigators and judges. Unfortunately, Soviet jurisprudence did not sufficiently distinguish between such actions on behalf of the occupying powers and those that constituted abuses of power for personal gain. According to the May 1942 order of the USSR procurator general Viktor Mikhailovich Bochkov, all actions of the Soviet citizens contributing "to the execution [of the occupiers'] instructions concerning the collection of food and forage intended for consumption of the [enemy's] troops, for the reconstruction of industrial enterprises and communal service, as well as all other measures assisting the German fascist occupiers were considered 'treason against the motherland.'"[111] As Franziska Exeler writes, Soviet punitive policy in postwar Belarus was "less indiscriminate and less strict" than the Soviet legal acts called for, probably due to the realization that their literal application would result in the wave of repression comparable to the Great Terror of 1936–1938 and hamper efforts to rebuild Soviet economy and society.[112] It seems obvious that most of the policemen's actions in fulfillment of their official duties would not constitute a crime in the legal systems of most democratic nations, unless accompanied by excessive violence and embezzlement.

Economic Exploitation and Changing of Popular Attitude toward the Occupiers

As has already been noted, most residents of Transnistria were neither collaborators, even if one applies the stretched Soviet definition, nor resisters. If one needs a term to describe their attitude toward the changes they were going through, "accommodators" would be the most fitting. Adjusting to the overwhelming force may be the most human of all reactions, and does not require any justification, nor is it susceptible to moral judgment. Belonging to this broad category, which can be seen as largely coterminous with what sociologists call the "general population," does not, however, imply having no attitude, even if inchoate and self-contradictory, toward the controlling regime.

Gaining insight into the ways they saw 1941–1944 developments is not easy because of the lack of access to their own unadulterated voices. So far, just one diary from the occupation period has surfaced, which is already cited journal of Shvets, at the time student at the Odessa Conservatory. It provides a fascinating glimpse into the world of Odessan intelligentsia but it tell very little about the moods outside of that rather narrow circle.[113] There were two types of outside observers who tried to closely follow the local population's "moods." The first was the Soviet resistance groups, whose very survival and success largely depended on the accuracy of their observations. The second group was made up of the Romanian gendarmerie, police, army intelligence gathering units (second bureau of the big army units, that is armies, army corps, and divisions deployed in Transnistria), and the SSI, all of which monitored popular moods through their network of informers (the gendarmerie and police relied on siguranța bureaus, who sometimes presented their own notes if they felt their views were at odds with the ones reported by the legion and company commanders). Of these two groups of sources, Soviet materials seem to be least reliable since, written after the liberation, their authors framed their narratives in the ways designed to fit the official narrative, whatever it was at each particular time, rather than reveal the situation as they experienced it. Nevertheless, all of the sources present a remarkably similar picture of the evolution of popular moods.

As noted at the beginning of this chapter, the sources agree that the Romanians and Germans were enthusiastically welcomed by the local population as liberators from the trepidations of the Soviet regime. In addition to the Romanian sources already cited, the following announcement published by *Odesskaia gazeta* in its third issue on November 2, 1941 suggests that the occupiers were tired of the locals' expressions of gratitude. According to it, the editorial board had been flooded with letters from citizens with "nearly identical content and, in various forms, expounding satisfaction with the collapse of Bolshevik rule and the joy of liberation from Bolshevik oppression." The editors advised the public to refrain from sending such materials to them since publishing "multiple repetitions [of the same message] is inadvisable."

According to both Romanian and Soviet sources, local Christians willingly participated in the hunting down of former communist bosses who were either left in the enemy-occupied territory to conduct a subversive activity or for whatever other reason found themselves there. For example, the chief of the Romanian police in Odessa city and oblast reported to his superiors in January 1942 that members of the Communist Party were "immediately identified with the assistance of the population, which currently demonstrates no interest in maintaining the rigors and expectations of the former regime."[114] The Soviets, too, had to grudgingly admit that their withdrawal from the area was followed by an anticommunist frenzy. For example, a report of the party committee (obkom) of Vinnytsia oblast—which was divided into the German and Romanian zones of occupation—dated February 9, 1944, stated the following about the partisan movement in that region: "From the first days of occupation small groups of partisans appeared; they were not connected to one another, had no unified leadership, no experience of struggle [behind enemy lines]; they were isolated from the people. The population did not support them either morally or materially. . . . The lot of the first partisans was dire. . . . In 1941, it was hard for an armed partisan to get a piece of bread."[115]

The first Soviet victories during the winter of 1941–1942 did not generate the change of attitude among the locals, as the Romanians noted, and even the victory at Stalingrad and subsequent advances of the Red Army during the winter of 1942–1943 produced more panic than joy. Summarizing reports on popular moods all over Transnistria in late March–early April 1942, Transnistrian gendarmerie inspector colonel Broşteanu related to Bucharest that "having acquainted themselves with the character of Romanians, the population . . . manifests sympathy for the Romanians."[116] When news of the Soviet counteroffensive reached Odessa, the population there was "greatly alarmed," opined Odessa police chief.[117] On February 4, 1943, Shvets noted in his diary: "Panic spread in the city that the Jews would return and cut everybody down."[118]

Still, the Transnistrian Christian population, with the exception of ethnic Germans who constituted a highly peculiar case, were not uniform in its attitude toward the Soviets. In particular, the younger generation schooled in Soviet educational institutions tended to be more positively inclined toward the Soviets and more receptive to their propaganda. In late April 1942, the Transnistria Gendarmerie Inspectorate reported that "communist youth searches for news from the front," presumably eager to learn about the

Soviet advances.[119] Other groups of risk from the Romanian perspectives included former POWs, especially officers, and Communist Party members, who lived under the police and gendarmerie supervision.[120] Soviet victory at Stalingrad visibly "enthused" young people, giving them hope of the Soviets' return, while the rest of the population was agitated by the news.[121] The same was true of workers and laborers. For example, in March 1943, commander of Berezovca Gendarmerie Legion noted in his monthly information bulletin that "craftsmen, workers, and laborers [who] made their living from petty trade having no other jobs . . . met last winter's Russian victories with great joy with the result that they joined the partisan gangs."[122] Soviet partisan sources identify the victory at Stalingrad as the turning point in relations between the occupiers and the occupied, but this might have been a tribute to the official Soviet story line.[123] The real change came later, in the summer and fall of 1943, and it proceeded apace with Operation 1111 (see chapter 7). The spectacle of the shameless confiscation of agricultural produce, as well as dismantling and shipment of productive assets of the region into Romania destroyed, by late fall of 1943, the last remnants of good will among the great majority of the population toward the Romanian occupiers. The latter were under no illusion. For example, on August 15, 1943, the Oceacov Gendarmerie Legion commander related that "the Ukrainian and Russian population who work in the obște is highly dissatisfied that they are not getting anything from this year's harvest, such as wheat."[124] On September 23, 1943, the commander of Odessa police force reported that "the population becomes increasing unruly, especially in what concerns mandatory labor duties and [assisting in] the evacuation [of productive assets] as ordered by the mayor."[125] The information bulletin of the Odessa Gendarmerie Inspectorate for November 1943 contained the following assessment of the mood of the Ukrainian population:

> [They] manifest an indifference in all spheres of activity. It is difficult to make them get out for agricultural work and they do not work conscientiously. They look with hostility at the evacuation of grain, beasts, agricultural implements, industrial installations. . . . The population is composed of two parts. One part awaits gladly and with impatience the return of the Bolsheviks. Many others, who were peaceful and even served our regime, now try to commit acts that would prove their devotion to the communist regime in order to protect themselves against future repressions.[126]

In December 1943, the same inspectorate opined that the majority of the local population was on the side of the Soviets.[127] On January 21, 1944, the

Romanian Third Army related that in Northwest Transnistria "the majority of the population is hostile toward the Romanian administration and allied armies. It has been proven that they act in the interests of the partisans, supply them with information, and help them to carry out their attacks."[128] The situation in the southern part of the region was only slightly less dangerous since the Odessa Gendarmerie Inspectorate, which at that time oversaw southern județe, reported in early January 1944 that the Ukrainian population was "passively sabotaging agricultural works" while "Moldovans were drifting away from us," but did not mention active support of the armed pro-Soviet groups.[129] By the end of the Romanian stay in Transnistria, they had lost sympathy of the most local residents.

There was little love lost between the Soviet rulers and their Transnistrian charges. A warm welcome extended to the Romanian and German troops, especially in the countryside, was no doubt genuine. Certainly, people who decided to stay in the occupied territory were to some extent a self-selected group, in particular as far as able-bodied men and women were concerned. Whatever persons of the latter category would claim after the war, most of them could evacuate and if they did not, this was because they decided not to. That staying in the occupied area involved accommodating to and cooperating with the occupiers was obvious. Thus, "the no choice" thesis advanced by Voisin with respect to German-occupied Russia could be rightfully applied to some, but by no means to all, Transnistrian local Christians. That it is applicable to the old-aged, handicapped, or otherwise incapacitated persons, as well as children, is self-evident.

When and under what conditions did accommodation and cooperation become criminal collaboration, in the sense subsumed under the American legal term of "aiding and abetting the enemy in time of war"? It is clear that fulfilling their orders and regulations, carrying out labor duties and paying taxes and various contributions imposed by the occupier do not constitute a crime, even if the residents' activity did help the Romanian war efforts: those occupied persons cannot be held responsible for the infractions of international law committed by the occupiers. Such ordinary activities as running local utilities, administering factories and other enterprises, even running railway trains transporting the German and Romanian troops would by no means constitute crimes in the eyes of a civilized public and of legal opinion, even if the Soviets might have construed them as such. From the types of behavior analyzed in this chapter, only two stand out as either potentially or obviously criminal.

The first was the Odessa intelligentsia's participation in the anti-Soviet propaganda of the Romanian authorities. Although most of the accusations laid by the Romanian occupiers at the door of the Soviet regime were no doubt correct, the simple fact that they were alleged during wartime and in a way that obviously assisted their country's enemies made such activity potentially liable for criminal charges under whatever government would be in place after the war. True, a lot of extenuating circumstances could have been brought by their defense so that a guilty verdict would probably be averted unless their public pronouncements involved appropriating racist and anti-Semitic discourse of the occupiers as their own. The latter aspect would be particularly damning since no Odessan could escape the knowledge of the murderous character of German and Romanian policy toward Jews. Under such circumstances, making anti-Semitic statements was a clear-cut case of justification of mass murder.

The second group was even more egregious. It encompassed local policemen and low-level administrators who participated in the rounding up, interning, and murdering of Jews. Although carried out on the orders of German and Romanian occupiers, such participation was not completely involuntary and could be avoided without them risking their lives. It usually involved some measure of agreement with the occupiers' anti-Semitic aims.

As for the majority of the Transnistrian Christian residents, their romance with the Romanians was short-lived. In a little over two years, the Romanian occupiers disabused local Christians of their illusions as to what kind of order, civilization, and culture they brought to them. Nothing explains this transformation more than the Romanians' own rapacious appetite for the "free resources" they found in the region, in violation of international law and in crass disregard for population's most vital needs. Ironically, as was shown in chapter 7, the Romanians did not benefit from such plunder, which far exceeded their capacity of absorption. That Romanians managed to achieve this outcome is nothing short of extraordinary, in view of the enormous suffering that the local population underwent during Stalinism in the 1930s, and the considerable benefit of the doubt that they willingly granted to the Romanian occupiers at the beginning of their rule. It is also remarkable how little the population's changed attitude was occasioned by the occupiers' feeling of cultural, let alone racial superiority, which according to the scholarly consensus was a hallmark and one of the major causes of the Germans' failure to win the local population to their side in the rest of the occupied territories of the Soviet Union. Greed and brutal plunder alone were enough to produce a similar result among the majority of the residents of Romania-administered Transnistria. Needless to say, to the extent that the Romanians' credit fell, support for the communist-led resistance grew, and it is to this development that the following chapters turn.

CHAPTER 9

Resisting, Phase I

Disasters

Resistance in Transnistria went through two distinct stages, similar to the other occupied Soviet territories. Both its membership and organizational structures changed substantially from one stage to another. During the first stage—late 1941 and most of 1942—resistance was limited to the terrorist groups set up by the party, the NKVD, and the army in the weeks prior to withdrawal to the east. As Kenneth Slepyan points out, during this stage Soviet leaders "discounted and even discouraged popular initiative and participation."[1] Only in the fall of 1942 did Soviet policy change, with Stalin ordering "to include as many as Soviet people in the struggles against the occupiers (particularly behind enemy lines) as possible."[2] This policy shift was engendered by two separate developments. First was the appearance in the areas of mass encirclements of the Red Army troops, which occurred in the initial weeks of the war, of spontaneously created partisan detachments. Taking to the woods rather than surrendering to the enemy, these men constituted the nucleus of the new resistance forces. Second, by the time the Nazi's brutal character became obvious to the residents of the occupied territories, the popularity of the partisan detachments increased considerably. Thus, the more inclusive Soviet strategy of partisan warfare roughly coincided with the shift of the public opinion against the occupiers and led to the exponential strengthening of armed resistance in the subsequent months and years of occupation. This growth accelerated as expectations of the approaching victory soared after the Soviet triumph at Stalingrad.

Resistance in Transnistria was limited both in the number of participants and in its overall impact. This is not surprising given that the Red Army withdrew from Transnistria later than from the other parts of the western USSR and in a more orderly fashion. As a result, there were no large-scale encirclements in this area. Nor did Transnistria have vast and dense forests, like those in Belarus and the Polis'e region of Ukraine. Thus, the essential conditions were lacking for the emergence of a powerful armed resistance there.[3] When during his May 1946 interrogation Alexianu insisted that partisans and saboteurs were practically "nonexistent" in Transnistria, he was exaggerating but he was still closer to reality than were Soviet propagandists, who from the first days after the province's liberation were busy constructing the myth of "partisan glory" in Odessa and the surrounding areas.[4] Still, armed resistance in Transnistria did exist, and although its record is far from justifying wild Soviet claims of an "all-people's struggle with the fascist occupiers," the phenomenon deserves attention. Although its general trajectory broadly coincides with that traced by Slepyan, in some important respects its story differs from the more typical partisan areas of Belarus, western Russia, and the Polis'e region. This chapter focuses on the first phase of resistance in Transnistria, from late 1941 to late 1942.

Catacomb Guerillas: Fanaticism and Betrayal

"Catacombs" is the word commonly used to reference stone quarries underneath Odessa and its vicinity, such as the villages of Kuial'nik and Usatovo. Having been continuously mined from the early nineteenth century on for shell rock (also known as coquina in English or *rakushechnik* in Russian), its overall length is now estimated at whopping 1,400 kilometers under the city alone.[5] Consisting of meandering underground corridors—some interconnected, others blind—with more than 1,000 apertures, since the early twentieth century they presented a serious problem for the authorities, initially tsarist and later Soviet, as a refuge for violent gangs terrorizing the local residents.[6] In the weeks before the final Soviet withdrawal, the Soviets decided to use the catacombs as a base for their own terrorist groups to be left behind enemy lines.

Most catacomb groups were created and commanded by the NKVD officers, some of whom were local cadres, others sent for this mission from Moscow. Catacomb groups created by the Communist Party were led by the local party cadres. Preoccupied with securing the utmost secrecy (*konspiratsiia*), Soviet bosses left group leaders uninformed of each other's existence so that when groups would meet in underground passages, such encounters often led to suspicions and tensions. Groups were supplied with ammunition and provisions. They also were supposed to benefit from a network of spies and liaisons in the city itself. Their combat and military efficiency turned out to be rather low while the human cost extremely high.

Particularly tragic was the story of a group of eighteen members under the leadership of the NKVD officer Aleksandr Soldatenko, whose rank is not mentioned in the available documents. His group's catacomb mission seems to have been improvised after the initial task for which it was created by the party regional committee (obkom)—passing through the enemy lines for sabotage operations prior to the surrender of Odessa—proved impossible to achieve. Shortly before the Romanians' arrival, the group entered the catacomb on Dal'nitskaia Street No. 47. Unfortunately for the group, this catacomb was a blind one, a fact that they had been unaware of, and all their subsequent attempts to establish contacts with their city liaison failed. Tipped off by the locals, the Romanians found the entrance and attempted to enter the catacomb on November 13, 1941; they were met by fire and suffered one fatality. Following this setback, the Romanians sealed the only available entrance, thus dooming the group to death by starvation and famine. Grasping this, some members of the group proposed surrender but Soldatenko categorically forbade even raising this issue and threatened to execute anybody who would attempt to do so. One member of the group was assassinated on his order as a panic-monger. Their food reserves were soon exhausted, and Soldatenko ordered the killing of two members of the group, a husband and wife, who were selected because they were not party members, and have their flesh salted and stored. It was then used to cook borscht and stew, which allowed the group to survive for a couple more weeks. Further sacrifices of this sort followed. Afraid that they would face the same fate, some members of the group decided to try to dodge the bullet. They assassinated Soldatenko and his wife and attempted to exit. Unfortunately for them, it was during that same day that the Romanians attempted—unsuccessfully—to fumigate the catacomb. Failing their attempt to exit, the partisans used the Soldatenkos' flesh to stay alive for the next several days. After the fumes dispersed, they exited the catacombs and surrendered to the Romanians, who photographed them and what was left of their comrades. The Romanians widely publicized this story to discredit armed resistance. According to the Romanian count, from the thirteen members of the group, six had been shot and eaten, seven exited out to the surface, of whom six were captured and one managed to disappear.[7] The story of the Soldatenko group was kept top secret to the end of the communist regime so that even

Soldatenko's family was denied information about the circumstances of their father's demise (initially they were told he was executed by the Romanians, and later that his fate remained unknown).[8]

No less horrific was the fate of another group headed by two NKVD majors, Vsevolod Aleksandrovich Kuznetsov and Vladimir Antonovich Kaloshin. Head of an unidentified department of the Moscow NKVD office, Kaloshin was dispatched to Odessa together with five other NKVD officers in July 1941 to organize a Soviet *rezidentura*, which had to conduct espionage and "sabotage terrorist activity" behind enemy lines in case of the city's surrender. Upon his arrival in the city, Kaloshin brought under his command twenty-six members of the regional NKVD board under the leadership of Kuznetsov, head of its third (counterintelligence) department. They selected catacombs in the district of Moldavanka, famous for its high crime rate and powerful gangs, some of whom might have agreed to collaborate with the chekists. Weapons, food supplies, and radio transmission equipment were stocked in quantities sufficient for up to six months—time within which, Soviet leaders believed, the city would be cleared of the enemy. On the evening of the city's surrender to the Romanians, all the Moscow and thirteen Odessan chekists descended into the catacombs while thirteen other members of the *rezidentura* were to act as their agents and spies on the surface. Unfortunately for them, Evguenia Semeriunik, who was the principal liaison, failed to carry out her duty so that Kaloshin and his group immediately lost contact with the outside world. In November or December 1941, Semeriunik was recruited by the siguranța and, on their orders, renewed her correspondence with the catacomb group attempting to persuade them to exit. Partisans immediately suspected foul play, however, and started their own game. In the end, they managed to persuade Semeriunik to descend into the catacomb, where she was caught, interrogated, and shot.[9]

In the meantime, an intense rivalry arose between Kaloshin and Kuznetsov. This is how USSR NKGB Fourth Directorate head Pavel Sudoplatov summarized the story in his report to the Deputy People's Commissar for State Security, Bogdan Kobulov, in July 1944:

Having support from the employees of the third special department who were more numerous than the Moscow group, Kuznetsov stripped Kaloshin of his commanding position and . . . had Moscow workers shadowed [by his men] and their food rations cut. . . . [U]nder the pretext of the alleged conspiracy against Kuznetsov, all [Moscow workers] were arrested.

In July 1942 [a member of the Moscow group], N. F. Abramov was cleared of charges and released from arrest while [all the other members of the Moscow group] were shot as conspirators against Kuznetsov.

On August 28, 1942, I. M. Molochnyi was shot on suspicion of stealing one loaf of bread and some crackers.

On September 27, 1942, on the order of Kuznetsov, they shot V. M. Pol'shchikov and Anis'ia Koval'chuk "for stealing food and for sexual licentiousness," the latter consisting of Koval'chuk giving birth to Pol'shchikov baby; the baby died in three hours.

On suspicion of conspiracy against himself, Kuznetsov, assisted by Litvinov, shot [five more members of his own group] on October 21, 1942.

The same day the only surviving member of the Moscow group, N. F. Abramov, enraged by Kuznetsov's behavior, shot him twice in the temple while Glushchenko, on the order of Abramov, shot [to death] Kuznetsov's assistant, V. S. Litvinov.

By that time only Abramov and Glushchenko remained alive because G. F. Tkachenko died of typhus in September 1942.

On February 18, 1943, Glushchenko shot Abramov [to death] and then [dug out a new] exit from the catacomb on November 10, 1943, which he left through, leaving behind his diary and all documents of the *rezidentura*.

On the day of Odessa's liberation by the Red Army, April 10, 1944, Glushchenko appeared before [the SMERSH officer] and reported the fate of the NKVD *rezidentura*.

On April 12, 1944, accompanied by the Red Army men, Glushchenko was sent into the catacomb to fetch the documents that he had left there.

After having found the documents, Glushchenko accidentally blew himself up by a grenade and died in the city hospital on April 14, 1942.

The only surviving member of *rezidentura* and participant in the surface group, Nikolai Zenonovich Molukalo, had been arrested by us as an agent of siguranța and transferred with all evidence to the NKVD Odessa regional board for further investigation.[10]

One can hardly escape the observation that Kuznetsov replicated Stalinist purges in the Odessa catacombs. Unlike his Kremlin role model, however, he brought them to their logical finale: total annihilation of his own people and perishing with them in the last act of the tragedy. Extreme hardship of the protracted stay in the catacombs, with little light and fresh air, complete isolation, and uncertainty as to the situation on the surface likely exacerbated

Kuznetsov's inbred suspicion and proclivity to violence so characteristic of the NKVD culture. It is worth noting that since Glushchenko managed to dig out a new exit from the catacombs single-handedly, and then to blend into the Odessa crowd, the same could likely have been achieved by the other members of this group had Kuznetsov allowed them to do so. According to the information the Romanians received from Semeriunik, Kuznetsov forbade his people to even consider this option and instead insisted that members of the network acting on the surface in case they were unable to carry out their mission, join him in the catacombs in the expectation of more propitious circumstances. Needless to say, nobody did. According to the same source, Kuznetsov kept his people in a state of constant nervous strain and fostered the thirst of bloody revenge over the enemy, which in the end proved too much for them.[11] For obvious reasons, the Soviets deemed this inglorious story "unsuitable for popularization in the uncensored press," thus the information did not reach the general public, even though *rezidentura* members' families received state pensions.[12]

A much better known in the postwar period story concerns another group that included members selected by both the Odessa NKVD and the party, headed by the captain of State Security (a rank equivalent to that of colonel in the Red Army) Vladimir Aleksandrovich Badaev (real name Molodtsov), who had also been sent from Moscow.[13] Despite its short existence, this group performed a string of acts of sabotage on the railways and transmitted some valuable military information to the Moscow high command.[14] Badaev group's lifespan also proved short. The Romanians captured Badaev in January 1942 while he was conferring at the home of the chief of his surface network, NKVD officer Petr Boiko (real name Anton Bronislavovich Fedorovich). Boiko's home was closely watched by the Romanians, who had been aware that he was regularly meeting with notorious female chekists left in the city to complete "special tasks." After their arrest, Badaev refused to give any information to the Romanians, whereas Boiko immediately cracked and was eventually recruited by the SSI.[15] Left without leadership, the surviving partisans exhausted their provisions and in May 1942 left the catacombs. Almost all of them were apprehended by the Romanians, others disappeared never to be heard of again. In September 1942, the Odessa martial court heard cases of forty guerillas, most of them from the Badaev group. Twenty-five were sentenced to death and executed, among them Badaev; others received up to twenty-five years of hard labor. Of the latter, few survived to the end of the war.

While virtually nothing is known of Kuznetsov and Kaloshin, Badaev's official biography has been widely disseminated since November 1944 when

FIGURE 12. Vladimir Aleksandrovich Molodtsov-Badaev in chekist uniform with his sons. 1937. Courtesy of Odessa Regional History Museum.

he was posthumously awarded the title of the Hero of the Soviet Union.[16] He was thirty at the time of his arrest and thirty-one at the time of execution (in July 1942). A son of a Tambov gubernia (in central European Russia) railway worker, he joined the Komsomol in 1926 and the party in 1931. A coal miner from 1930, he simultaneously studied at the Moscow Engineering-Economic Institute, which he, according to his official biography, completed in 1934. The same year, he enrolled and graduated from the NKVD school and joined the NKVD directorate for the Moscow region in 1935. Soon he was promoted to the economic section of the Main Board of State Security of the NKVD. Nothing is known about his role in the purges but judging from the fact that by 1940 he was the deputy head of the sixth bureau of the Main Economic Board of the NKVD which oversaw coal and oil industries, it is probable that he was a trusted participant in them. In March 1941, he was appointed to head a section in the foreign intelligence department of the Main Board of State Security of the NKVD focusing on Romania. A perfect case of Stalinist youth, Badaev possessed an abundance of fanatical determination (as one witness reported, before his arrest he often quarreled with Boiko, insisting on more resolute actions against the Romanians), ruthlessness, and resourcefulness, all hallmarks of an ideal communist, as understood at the time.[17] He was also a patriot. According to the Soviet hagiography, which supposedly was based on eyewitnesses' accounts, he refused to sign a request for clemency, stating, "I am Russian and do not ask for pardon on my own land."[18] If true, this saying is a curious case of the discursive blending of Sovietness and Russianness, a common trope in Stalinist wartime propaganda. By his actions and by his martyr's death he delivered important services to the regime to which he devoted himself.

Archival materials offer a glimpse into the other members of the group and how they were recruited. One pool of recruits was made up of the prewar NKVD agents. This was the case with one Elena Gore who, according to a Romanian account, being of exceptional beauty, seduced a Romanian officer and obtained from him useful military information. Gore most probably agreed to work for the NKVD not out of ideological convictions but for fear of persecution since prior to the Bolshevik Revolution her parents owned factories and apartments blocks, while two of her brothers had been dekulakized.[19] Gore might have agreed with another NKVD agent with a similar family background who was left behind enemy lines in neighboring Nikolaev, Elena Polokhova. When asked by an SS officer whom she was afraid of more, the Germans or the Soviets, Polokhova answered: "You and they are all the same to me."[20]

Others were recruited shortly before the occupation or even during it from among the general populace. This is, for example, how Akim Karlikovskii (or Kurliukovskii) described his recruitment process. Karlikovskii served under the Romanians as a mayor of the Odessan suburban village of Usatovo, a site of one of the biggest catacomb networks. Shortly before the city's surrender, he was visited by Afanasii Nikitich Klimenko, a former director of the Usatovo quarry and a member of the party, who suggested that he join his partisan detachment that would later descend into the catacombs. Karlikovskii refused to descend underground but agreed to help them on the surface, and Klimenko concurred, letting him know that he expected him to be appointed a mayor and thus become more useful to the partisans.[21] The recruitment process during the occupation unfolded in a similar manner. For example, when Boiko approached somebody called Shevchenko, a communist and a retired mechanic, with a request to join the detachment, the latter refused, citing his old age, but then agreed to the less onerous task to collect military information. He successfully carried out this mission. Referencing other similar examples, such as a former priest agreeing to serve the partisans, the Romanians suggested that these people could not even conceive of turning such requests down because that would have gone so much against the habits they had learned under the Soviets.[22] This assessment of the SSI seems plausible.

Taken together, the above accounts point to the insignificance of the cata-comb guerilla achievements, despite the efforts and resources poured into organizing them, and notwithstanding the Soviet postwar officially spon-sored partisan mythology. Another inevitable conclusion is that much of their failure was attributable to the lack of popular support and the high incidence of betrayal among the guerilla group members. The latter was due not only to the harsh methods of interrogation used by the Romanians—in fact, torture—but also to the composition of the groups recruited, as a rule, from among former NKVD agents. Many of them collaborated with the secret police out of fear for their lives or because of careerist considerations. The example of Boiko-Fedorovich is a case in point. Not only did he betray Badaev and the group as a whole immediately upon his arrest but was rere-cruited by the SSI and later served as a Romanian officer investigating the partisan activity. Klimenko was also easily recruited by the SSI.[23] Among these men, staunch fighters like Badaev and Kuznetsov were exceptions. The Romanians' harsh sentences of lower-ranking guerillas reflected not so much their loyalty to the Soviets, or the degree of danger they presented, as the occupiers' fears of underground gangs, whose presence was massively exaggerated in their, as well as general population's, imagination.

Party Underground Obkom: Ineptitude or Treason?

Although most catacombs guerillas were organized by the NKVD, the party created its own cells that were tasked to remain behind the enemy lines and serve as nuclei of partisan detachments. Their members were to blend into the general population and live under assumed names. Starting from Octo-ber 1944 through May 1946, the Odessa regional party committee (obkom) collected information from the district party committees (raikoms) on par-tisan activity during the German-Romanian occupation of Odessa oblast in 1941–1944. Based on this and other information, the instructor of the Organizational-Instructional Section of Central Committee of the Commu-nist Party of Ukraine Kolesnikov compiled a summary, according to which from July through September 1941, party leaders selected 200 communists for sabotage activity behind enemy lines. In Odessa in particular, each raion was supposed to have its own underground raikom conducting the activity of three-member cells or troikas. Raikoms were also created in the rural suburbs of Odessa as well as in some outlying rural raions. This network was to be led by an underground obkom headed by the former first secretary of Vodno-transportnyi raion party committee (raikom), of Odessa, Aleksandr Pavlovich Petrovskii. On the third day of occupation, Petrovskii was arrested and, according to the NKVD, recruited by the Romanians so that "as the result of Petrovskii's betrayal, most of the communists were arrested and many annihilated."[24]

Whether the NKVD intended this or not, blaming Petrovskii for this failure concealed an even gloomier reality, a pattern of ubiquitous betrayal, dereliction of duty, greed, and incompetence. According to the same summary, for example, first secretary of the Il'ichëvskii underground raikom, Mukha,

> ran away in the first days of occupation; presently his whereabouts remain unknown. Most communists left for underground work, having no leadership conducted virtually no sabotage activity, showed up for registration at police stations, where many of them were arrested and interned in prisons. [The head of the Kaganovichskii raikom] Shelukha disappeared one day before the occupation, together with all the valuables intended to support underground work . . . [First secretary of Voroshilovskii raikom in Odessa] Klochek did not conduct any sabotage activity under the occupation and offered no leadership to the communist underground members. In October 1942, he left the organization to its fate and departed Odessa together with his liaison Shmidt to Savranskii raion [in the countryside], where he resided through the liberation of the territory by the Red Army."

The only exception among the five Odessa raikoms was Il'ichëvskii under the leadership of Sëmen Fëdorovich Lazarev, whose achievement consisted of surviving through the end of the occupation without being arrested. Throughout most of the occupation period they remained inactive. No better was the situation in the rural raions. For example, in the first days of occupation, first secretary of the Beliaevskii raikom, together with six other communists, were arrested and executed. In Berezovskii raion, "a few days prior to the arrival of the occupiers, leaders of the underground committee, Krishtal', Artem'iev, and Ivanov left the raion and subsequently almost all the communists followed suit, so that, through 1943 in Berezovskii raion, no party antioccupation work was carried out."[25] Subsequent investigations into the records of the party underground in the city and region of Odessa revealed some gaps in Kolesnikov's summary, raising the overall number of communists left for underground work up to 300 but leaving the pattern largely unchanged, just adding further colorful details of the kind cited above.[26]

Soviet official reports hint at the widespread hostility toward the pro-Soviet resistance groups, especially in the first year of the occupation. For example, a 1944 summary of the Vinnytsia oblast obkom, whose territory was divided between the German and Romanian zones, states that initially "the population did not support partisans neither morally nor materially. . . . Awfully hard was the first partisans' lot. . . . In 1941, an armed partisan could hardly count on a piece of bread from the local residents."[27] In the activity report of the partisan detachment Burevestnik, which in 1943 was active in the northern raions of Transnistria, one reads that in the first months of the occupation "the population was disoriented. Former kulaks, those repressed by the Soviet government, and criminal elements supported the occupiers."[28] Romanian observers also noted the locals' hostility toward communist groups, as did for example the SSI Odessa bureau on November 18, 1941, stating, "Many Christian citizens manifest their firm determination to help us identify and exterminate subversive elements."[29] Evaluating the population in Berezovca județ in March 1942, the gendarmerie legion commander noted that the failure of all communist attempts to organize resistance was due to the hostility of the locals toward the communist regime and their refusal to extend any help to its resisters, "without which they cannot survive."[30]

The lack of popular support and the help extended by many locals to the occupiers, compounded by numerous cases of betrayal among the communist underground cells likely were the principal causes for the failure of the party-organized underground network, but there were others. After the war, the Soviets emphasized the poor organization of the gangs, and numerous breaches of the rules of *konspiratsiia*, or the art of conspiratorial organizing, which the party had mastered since the tsarist era. This is how SMERSH's report, composed upon the liberation, described the process of its formation:

> The organization of the party underground was carried out with negligence. . . . During the preparatory period, they did not obey the most elementary rules of *konspiratsiia*. Secretary of the Il'ichëvskii raikom Platov used to summon ten to fifteen communists simultaneously into his office, to have a short conference with them and [following that] to order them, on the spot, to surrender their party membership cards [a sign that they were to stay behind enemy lines on official duty. Otherwise, loss of a party membership card was considered an act of utter disloyalty, sometimes tantamount to treason]. Second obkom secretary Senin, while selecting membership for the Stalinskii underground raikom, summoned into his office all the secretaries and members of the underground raikom and after a conversation [with them] announced: "I ask you to surrender your party membership cards since you will be left behind enemy lines."[31]

It is noteworthy that besides illustrating the point SMERSH was making— thoughtless exposure of future illegals to one another, even before the start of their activity, against all rules and common sense—this scene reveals another flaw in the organization of the party underground: its future members were selected by their bosses, who gave them no choice but to fully and immediately comply with this order. While this procedure was reflective of the ethos of mature Stalinism as it emerged after the Great Terror of 1936–1938, it was hardly conducive to the success of the underground network. Compliance in the Soviet Union was secured by the constant threat of repression, a crucial tool that would inevitably go missing once the Soviet apparatus of repression was withdrawn from the area. That the Soviet leaders apparently believed that fully obedient lower-rank party members would as faithfully carry out their orders in the occupied territories as they did under the Soviet regime is an indication of the extent to which they were removed from the reality on the ground.

In view of the central role Petrovskii played in the tragic history of the Odessa obkom, and the continuous controversy surrounding his name after the war, it is instructive to look more closely at his background and activity under the occupation. Fortunately, we know more on this subject than on any other aspect of the obkom's history. An ethnic Ukrainian born in 1906 in Odessa, he joined the CPSU in 1932 and later graduated from the Higher Party School. Thus, he belonged to the generation of Soviet leaders promoted during Stalinist industrialization and purges (*vydvizhentsy*). Before the war, Petrovskii served as the first secretary of the Vodno-transportnyi raikom.[32] The city's port, the most important economic and strategic unit of the city, was located in this raion, making Petrovskii's post of first-rank importance. His selection as leader of the underground communist network made sense because the port was primarily working-class area of the city and the party considered workers the most reliable social stratum. The decision to entrust Petrovskii with this mission belonged to the first secretary of Odessa's regional party committee Anatolii Georgievich Kolybanov.[33] Simultaneously, Kolybanov appointed Sergei Semënovich Sukharev, who in the summer of 1941 served as the first secretary of the Il'ichëvskii raikom of Odessa, Petrovskii's deputy (or second secretary of the underground obkom). It was Petrovskii and Sukharev who selected raikom secretaries and, together with the latter, the other members.[34]

When on October 21, 1941, the Romanians arrested Petrovskii, they already had in custody or were in hot pursuit of many other leading members of the organization.[35] On October 25, to everybody's surprise, the Romanians released Petrovskii, after he had signed an agreement to become their agent. After the war, Petrovskii claimed that this was a ruse he was expressly allowed to use in order to get the freedom to continue his underground activity. Petrovskii claimed that he received oral instructions in this sense shortly before the Soviets' withdrawal from Odessa from an NKVD officer whose name he could not remember. In order to sound more convincing to the Romanians, he used the name of the first secretary of Il'ichëvskii underground raikom, Ivan Emel'ianovich Platov. Petrovskii claimed after the war that Romanians already knew Platov's name from the confession of another arrestee that he supposedly overheard.[36]

Petrovskii's exposure and quick release understandably alarmed the members of the Odessa underground, who refused to cooperate with him, suspecting foul play. Another aspect of Petrovskii's behavior that raised many an eyebrow was his refusal to follow rules of *konspiratsiia*, which provided that in case of exposure he would transfer all available information on the underground network, together with his commanding role, to Sukharev. Instead, he kept the leadership role to himself and started to rebuild the network, selecting new members from among Odessans whom he trusted and who helped him identify other reliable persons. The progress was slow, being hindered by massive registration of the Communist Party members with the occupying authorities (see chapter 8).[37] Obkom leaders considered registered communists untrustworthy but even among those who failed to register many refused, under different pretexts, to join, and Petrovskii had to change secretaries of various raikoms several times. In April 1942, the Romanians arrested Platov, who under torture (or so he claimed) cracked and turned in almost all of his comrades. In August 1942, the Odessa martial court sentenced Platov to fifteen years of forced labor and his comrades to shorter terms—surprisingly (and suspiciously) lenient sentences given the nature and circumstances of their actions.[38]

From his release from custody on October 25, 1941, and through March 1942, Petrovskii fed the Romanians disinformation. In March 1942, he successfully escaped, as he believed, from under surveillance and intensified his illegal work. While rebuilding the network he instructed its members to refrain from acts of sabotage, which could have exposed the organization prematurely. His strategy seemingly aimed at creating an extensive network of interconnected groups, which would cover Transnistria as a whole. It was only with the approach of the Red Army that they would start an armed uprising.[39]

As it turned out, however, much of obkom's activity following Petrovskii's alleged escape from under surveillance in March 1942 was closely monitored by the SSI. Even if the SSI was unaware of Petrovskii's whereabouts, they planted their agent-provocateurs to smash the recreated obkom in one sweeping blow. Unfortunately for them, however, police and gendarmerie, who were not aware of this extensive undercover operation, arrested the SSI's agent.[40] As a result, the SSI had to carry out what they considered premature arrests, in order to forestall the resisters likely going into hiding. This massive operation, carried out all over Transnistria on March 12–13, 1943, resulted in the detention of 124 members of groups coordinated by the obkom and 171 members of self-created groups, unconnected or only loosely connected to the obkom.[41] More arrests followed soon, delivering a severe, although not a mortal, blow to the pro-Soviet underground.[42]

Petrovskii was among those arrested in the wave. This time, he attempted to commit suicide by cutting his own throat but survived the wounds (convalescence lasted months). The Romanians kept Petrovskii in an Odessa prison through April 1944, when they transferred him to a Bucharest prison, where he was kept through the occupation of Romania by the Red Army in August 1944. Whether he exposed his comrades during this second arrest, in addition to those already arrested on the leads of the Romanian agent-provocateurs, is unclear. Other than that, he refused to cooperate with the SSI, who tried to recruit him for their planned sabotage operations in the Soviet territory.[43] Upon Petrovskii's release from prison, after Romania's occupation by the Soviets in September 1944, he returned to Odessa, where he was arrested by the NKVD, probably on the suggestion of Kolybanov, first secretary of Odessa oblast party committee. He was charged with high treason, tried, sentenced to death, and executed on September 5, 1945.[44]

Leaving Petrovskii's fate for a moment and returning to the time of his arrest by the Romanians in 1943, throughout the spring and summer of that year arrests and executions, sometimes illegal, of the party underground members continued. Among numerous tragedies, the story of the party underground organization in Balta raion stands out because of the particularly savage punishment inflicted. The organization was created by Tat'iana Sergeevna Bragorenko (real name Fridman) in early 1942 on Petrovskii's order. Shortly after the Soviets' surrender of Odessa, Fridman, before the war a lecturer in Russian language and literature at the university, obtained false documents and changed her last name after her ethnic Moldovan step-father to conceal her Jewish identity. She also decided to relocate to the town of Balta. Before her departure, she established contacts with Petrovskii via Karachentsev, at the time secretary of the Vodno-transportnyi raikom, and received a commission to create an underground cell in Balta. Fluent in both Romanian and German, she opened a translation bureau under the *primaria*, and ran a philanthropic agency extending assistance to the POWs, which was permitted by the authorities. This provided her a cover for recruitment of underground members. Bragorenko was arrested in the fall or

December 1942, having been turned in by a traitor. During interrogations, Bragorenko claimed that the only aim of her activity was to secure an "alibi" in case the Soviets returned, and the Romanians apparently believed her, since they released her (her comrades later claimed that the bribe they had collected and paid to the Romanians was the key to her release). Upon her release, she returned to Balta and in the early summer of 1943, summoned a meeting of the organization, which was disguised as a dancing party. It is not surprising that shortly thereafter, numerous arrests followed; the organization was devastated. Tried in Odessa in February 1944, partisans received various prison sentences, were transferred back to Balta, and upon their arrival were shot by the gendarmes. The overall numbers of those murdered has been estimated between twenty-two to as many as fifty. Among them was Bragorenko.[45]

An Exception as a Model: An Unlikely Case of Prigorodnyi raikom

Many, if not most of the party underground members who survived occupation were arrested by the NKVD in the aftermath of Odessa's liberation, and sentenced to various terms. Others escaped persecution by claiming that their cells had nothing to do with the obkom.[46] This development was a public relations disaster for the party, which had severe difficulty portraying its leading role in the resistance in the region, as was a sine qua non of all official histories of the war. Regional party leaders obviated this problem by highlighting the activity of the Prigorodnyi raikom of Odessa, the only one whose leaders survived the war without being arrested by the Romanians, such arrests constituting a definitive proof of their guilt or even treason in the eyes of the paranoid Stalinists. The official *Report on the Underground and Partisan Activity in Odessa Oblast*, published in 1946, praised the purported exploits—rather thin—of the raikom and kept silence over the role and fate of other communist cells, thus portraying this raikom's story as a standing metonymically for the myth of the heroic partisan struggle led by the Communist Party. Extensive accounts of its activity, from 1944 to 1945, are revealing both of the situation on the ground and the reasons the authorities approved its report.[47]

Sëmen Fëdorovich Lazarev, who served as the first secretary of the Prigorogdnyi raikom from 1937 to 1941, was left in the occupied territory as the head of the underground raikom.[48] This raion offered a tremendous advantage to the underground groups since it included several villages in the immediate vicinity of Odessa where catacomb entrances were located. According to Lazarev's detailed account, composed shortly after Odessa's liberation, his group descended into the catacombs on October 14, or two days before the Romanians' entry into the city, which allowed them to avoid arrests during the anticommunist frenzy that followed the city's surrender, when a disgruntled populace enthusiastically assisted the Romanians in hunting down everybody associated with the hated Soviet regime. When the first wave of arrests and executions subsided, Lazarev first sent outside parties on reconnaissance mission. Some members of these parties returned to the catacombs, others disappeared, and nothing was ever heard of them. All attempts to establish contact with the obkom having failed, the Prigorodnyi raikom remained in total isolation from the rest of the city's communist underground.

As the Romanians increasingly discovered most of the entrances into the catacombs, closed them, and put sentries on each of them, the groups' supplies ran out. Lazarev ordered his men to leave the catacombs individually or in small groups and move to Savranskii forest where they supposedly could form armed bands of resisters. Upon leaving the catacombs, some of them were caught by the Romanians, tried, and sentenced to death or forced labor. Lazarev would later find out about their fate from the local newspapers. Still others would never be heard of again. By early July 1942, only three members of the raikom remained in the catacombs, headed by Lazarev. On July 5, 1942, Lazarev sent his last two comrades out, not knowing what would happen to them. Only he and Afanasii Klimenko, together with Klimenko's brother Ivan, remained in the Usatovo catacomb. Their supplies were virtually gone when Lazarev received a written message from his liaison, Anastasiia Porfir'ievna Shcherba (wife of Ivan Nikolaevich Shcherba, member of raikom, and mother of partisan Aleksandr Ivanovich Shcherba, in the same group), saying that they arrived safely to their abode. They found shelter at the home of Praskov'ia Iakovlevna Gorbel', whose two sons served in the Red Army while two other relatives were in the raikom organization. It was here that Lazarev and the other leaders of the raikom passed most of the time until April 1943, living in a hole dug out in the basement. They reduced their contacts with the people outsider their abode to a minimum. As Lazarev explained shortly after the liberation, they were greatly aided by the fact that Gorbel''s neighbors were unaware of the communist identity of her family members. At that time, the raikom's subversive activity was reduced to passing out pro-Soviet leaflets.[49] In April 1943, they decided to return into the catacombs. Their activity remained limited through late 1943, by when the popular mood had changed decisively in favor of the Soviets.

As this account suggests, Prigorodnyi raikom's apparent success was mostly due to its breaking virtually every rule in the book, either by default or by design. First, they failed to establish contact with the obkom, which most certainly would have resulted in the raikom's exposure. Second, during most of 1942 and 1943, when the popularity of the Soviets was at its nadir, their leaders effectively insulated themselves from anybody who did not belong to the inner circles of relatives and friends.[50] This was probably a decisive reason for their survival until the tide of the war and the popular mood changed in the Soviets' favor. It was in these last days of the occupation, when the Red Army was closing in on Odessa and the Germans were hastily retreating from the city that raikom partisans exited the catacombs and engaged the enemy soldiers in a bloody battle (for more on this, see chapter 10). This battle elevated the raikom's reputation to the top of the list of postwar Soviet Odessa heroes and helped conceal their inactivity—contrary to the Soviet government's demands for immediate armed struggle against the occupiers—during most of the occupation.

Traitors into Heroes: Postmortem Carrier of the Underground Obkom

In the post-Stalinist period, the official views of the party underground in Odessa and the eponymous region underwent a thorough revision. This shift was just one case of the deeper transformation of the Soviet political culture. During that time, the cult of the Great Patriotic War emerged as the foundational myth of the reconstructed Soviet polity. Unlike the immediate postwar years, during which victory was almost exclusively ascribed to the "war-hero-in-chief" Joseph Stalin, both the Khrushchevian Thaw, and Brezhnevite partial restoration of Stalinist orthodoxy (1956–1985) witnessed a populist bent in official discursive and commemorative practices. It was marked by the ever-increasing number of officially recognized heroes and progressively more inclusive rhetoric of the "all-people struggle against the occupiers."[51]

As in other parts of the country, veterans of the party underground were active participants in the process of revision. The impetus came from the gradual rehabilitation of the many victims of Stalinist repression, among whom were members of the partisan groups accused of aiding the enemy.[52] In the earlier stages of de-Stalinization through the late 1950s, rehabilitation could but did not necessarily lead to official recognition of a rehabilitated person as a former partisan, with all the attending honors and benefits this status carried.[53] It was only at the beginning of the second stage of de-Stalinization, in the wake of the Twenty-Second Congress of the CPSU (October 1961), that the CC of the CP of Ukraine (CPU) initiated a new review of the former partisans' files. On February 21, 1962, obkom secretary Nikolai Ivanovich Zotov sent letters coded "Top Secret" to raikom secretaries in which he referenced the above-mentioned decision of the CPU CC and explained that it was based on the finding that due to "mistakes and imprecisions committed in the first postwar years concerning the examination of partisan detachments and underground patriotic groups . . . the activity of many honest Soviet citizens has not been recognized."[54] In a true Soviet manner, raikoms were expected not so much to check the accuracy of the official accounts as to find faults in them and acknowledge hitherto unrecognized patriotic exploits of "many honest Soviet citizens." The hectic activity that followed led to the revisiting of many partisan files on raikoms and the obkom in Odessa oblast', including the rehabilitation of Petrovskii.

Zotov was put in charge of the obkom's commission to investigate Odessa's wartime underground obkom. The commission's work lasted from November 1962 to November 1964.[55] The commission found no fault in Petrovskii's record under occupation and praised his activity as denoting "selfless devotion to the Communist Party and Soviet Motherland." It recommended his complete rehabilitation, the popularization of his exploits in the press, as well as his posthumous decoration with the title the Hero of the Soviet Union.[56] The commission's findings, however, came too late to be approved in their totality by the obkom and superior bodies. The removal of Nikita Sergeevich Khrushchev on October 14, 1964, from the Central Committee Plenum marked the end of the most radical phase of de-Stalinization. When on May 22, 1965, the Odessa obkom discussed the commission's recommendations, it approved activity of the underground obkom but refrained from recommending decorating Petrovskii with the Hero of the Soviet Union order. The obkom simultaneously petitioned "competent bodies" to posthumously rehabilitate Petrovskii. The decision of the Military College of the USSR Supreme Court came only on April 23, 1966.[57]

By that time, the conservative nature of the new Brezhnevite regime was clearly discernible, which might explain the temerity of the college decision. The college likely followed the opinion and reasoning of the chief military prosecutor, Lieutenant General Artem Grigor'evich Gornyi, dated April 18, 1966. Having asserted that Petrovskii's file did not contain proof of his treasonous activity, Gornyi nevertheless noted that he "committed a series of mistakes and incorrect actions, which . . . negatively affected the organization and activity of the party underground and to some extent facilitated the activity of Romanian intelligence aimed at liquidating members of the party underground." Among Petrovskii's "mistakes," Gornyi mentioned his violating the rules of work with secret documents, even if unintentional;

his signing a declaration of collaboration with the enemy; and his signing declarations containing names of other partisans during his second arrest. Even though these signatures were obtained after confronting him with the arrestees whom he would then name, this declaration might have helped the Romanians to put additional pressure on the persons concerned and force them to cooperate.[58] These were, indeed, damning facts, which precluded the possibility of decorating Petrovskii with the most exalted Soviet order. Shortly after the Gornyi opinion was issued, the Odessa obkom restored Petrovskii's membership in the party, posthumously.[59]

Thus, Petrovskii's elevation from traitor to hero was stopped halfway. Although a recognized leader of the party underground—his name would become regularly mentioned in propagandistic, celebratory publications on the history of the partisan underground—neither his exploits nor failings would be explained.[60] It was only after the end of the Soviet regime that the Odessan public would become acquainted, due to the efforts of local enthusiasts and despite the continued secretiveness of the local USB office in charge of the former KGB archive, with the unevenness of his record. Besides Petrovskii's "mistakes" enumerated in Gornyi's 1966 opinion, his file contains evidence of his embezzlement of funds allocated for the support of the sabotage activity, which he squandered on his and his mistress's high living while refusing requests for assistance from his comrades in distress. Petrovskii also fed his comrades false information on the situation on the fronts, apparently to boost their moral (this practice might have been secretly permitted by his instructions) and, what was surely worse in the eyes of the party, he kept a false diary of the obkom's exploits, which he intended to present to the Soviets after the war as a proof of his manifold achievements.[61]

Petrovskii's rehabilitation opened the floodgate for the former underground members' petitions for rehabilitation and recognition. In the 1960s and 1970s it was much easier to receive the official status of a former partisan than in the first years after the war; usually a couple of letters from an already recognized former partisan in support of one's claim, absent counterclaims, was enough to pass through the hoops. On October 26, 1972, the Odessa obkom approved a confidential summary of pro-Soviet resistance in Odessa oblast during the war, which had to replace a similar 1946 document.[62] Odessan historian Aleksandr Babich composed the following statistical comparison of two documents: a 1946 summary recognized eight partisan detachments and units, a 1972 document—thirteen; "underground sabotage groups"—two and eight, respectively; "underground Bolshevik organizations"—twelve and twenty-two; underground antifascist groups—eight and forty-eight respectively. The 1946 summary registered 1,981 resisters while in 1972 they listed 4,308, an increase more than two times.[63] Although the 1972 summary was meant to be a definitive account, it soon underwent further revision. On November 27, 1974, the Politburo of the Central Committee of the Communist Party of Ukraine adopted a decision "On Some Issues Concerning Underground and Partisan Movements in Ukraine during the Great Patriotic War, 1941–1945." Judging from the measures taken by the Odessa obkom in its pursuance (I was not able to find this decision), it amounted to a call to revisit and supplement the lists of officially recognized *podpol'shchiki* (members of underground groups) and partisans with new names under the pretext that in previous decades many legitimate claims to such titles were incorrectly denied. In the wake of this decision, the obkom resolved to recognize nine previously unacknowledged groups. Simultaneously, it posthumously bestowed the status of resisters on 573 persons shot or otherwise murdered by the Romanians as well as on 352 persons "who rendered assistance to and helped" partisan and underground groups.[64]

As the previous accounts suggest, the NKVD and party-created-and-led guerrilla and resistance groups met virtually unmitigated disasters. Put in the wider context, they testify to the utter dysfunctionality of the Soviet regime whose functionaries often faced the necessity to fulfill their superiors' orders even if they were fully aware of their unfeasibility and foolishness. When shortly before the Transnistrian territory surrender some party and NKVD apparatchiks, members, and agents were "invited" by their superiors to join the cells, which had to act in the enemy's rear, they knew that they had to either agree or face immediate and severe consequences. Those who agreed, which was the majority, realized the impossibility of the task with which they were entrusted, because of the local population's hostility toward the Soviet regime agents. As soon as the Romanians came, they proceeded to register with the occupying authorities, thus voluntarily submitting to the police surveillance and relinquishing any links to the pro-Soviet resistance. Their actions were rational and unsurprising.

Those few guerrilla groups who lingered for several months in the catacombs were sustained by the unremitting terror imposed on them by their commanding officers who might have acted as much on their ideological fanaticism as on the certainty of their execution in case they would be apprehended by the Romanians. Even so, these groups' achievements were rather slim and the sheer horror of their survival was such that the Soviet authorities made sure neither their families nor the wider public would ever be informed of its enormity.

The story of the underground party obkom was mythologized and revised so many times, always with an eye on political expediency, that it is now impossible to be sure where the falsity ends and the truth begins. Even in its most central element of the story, on which so much depends—the character of Petrovskii and the role he played—one cannot tell with certainty whether the first secretary was "just" an utterly foolish, incompetent, and selfish careerist or an outright traitor. Either way, the damage inflicted by him on the communist underground was enormous.

In the perspective of long-durée of Soviet history, what strikes the observer is how little the officially-sponsored myths of NKVD and party-created guerrillas had in common with the reality of their conditions and activity. This is true of both the late Stalinist, virtually nameless version of the myth, and of its later Soviet counterparts, which contained longer rosters of heroes but were as poor in content. The protagonists in both accounts were cast exclusively in black and white colors and assigned to the categories of either heroes or villains. The conflicting motivations, the contradictory pressures, the excruciating dilemmas to which they were exposed found no place in those accounts. That shrewd time-servers succeeded where the brave failed and staunch fighters achieved little while provoking useless suffering of many were not truths the Soviet propagandists were ready to let out and the Soviet public to stomach.

CHAPTER 10

Resisting, Phase II

Recovery to Resurgence

This chapter traces the evolution of resistance in the last year of the war in the region, from the spring of 1943 to the spring of 1944. Its main theme is the transition from an isolated and largely impotent assortment of guerrilla cells to a movement with considerable support among the local general population and real influence on the situation on the ground.

Autonomous Groups: Idealism and Impatience

While composing its report on the destruction of the obkom underground shortly after the mass arrests in March 1943, the SSI noted the formation of what it branded "accidental groups," which were formed on the independent initiative of Odessans. Though these groups sought to establish contact with the obkom, the latter kept its distance from them for fear of provocations. The SSI noted that they were more dangerous than the obkom: while "official" party resistance was biding its time in expectation of the Red Army's approach, "accidental groups" were ready to commit acts of violence any time.[1] Ironically, after the liberation of the city, the party censored the underground obkom for its "passivity" and failure to resort to armed forms of resistance until its liquidation by the SSI. Combativeness of these groups thus more faithfully reflected the Soviet government's directives than the more cautious approach of the party leaders.

The SSI report offered just a few details about these groups and the identities of their members. Judging from the fact that one of them was led by the former secretary of one of Odessa's Komsomol raikoms, it is likely that young people were prominent in them.[2] One of the organizations created by the komsomols in Transnistria acquired, in the Soviet era, fame comparable to that of the Young Guard (Molodaia gvardiia) in the Donbass region. In 1956, Odessan writer Sergei Pavlovich Poliakov published a novel, commissioned by the obkom, titled after the name of the organization Partisan Spark (Partizanskaia iskra).[3] In the next year, Dovzhenko studio in Kyiv released an eponymous film based on the novel. A museum dedicated to the same was set up, and a local school was named after this organization in the village of Krymka, home to its members. One of the few surviving participants, Ivan Gerasimenko, served as the museum director (after his release from a Stalinist GULAG where he was served his term as a traitor). Gerasimenko also published a book on the history of this organization.[4]

The main contours of the myth about the organization had been laid down by 1947, the time when party officials collected a file of its heavily edited interviews with the war survivors, their kin and friends. Most participants were students in middle or high schools, between the ages of thirteen and eighteen. Edited testimonies depict them as ideal Soviet citizens raised on such Soviet classics as *How the Steel Was Tempered* by Nikolai Ostrovskii, and the 1934 classic movie *Chapaev*. These youngsters also liked to read Pushkin (whom they allegedly recited on the eve of their capture) and Nikolai Gogol, both central characters in the Stalinist cultural pantheon, were indefatigable readers of the *Short Course of the History of the CPSU*, that Soviet bible, as well as of stories about Spartacus and Garibaldi, the perennial heroes of European radicals. Created in January 1942, Partizanskaia iskra borrowed its name from Lenin's famous newspaper *Iskra* (Spark), which helped build the Bolshevik Party. They were organized by the principal and history teacher of their school, who was no less of a Soviet ideal man than any of them, and barely more than thirty years of age, Vladimir Stepanovich Morgunenko.[5] The film and the novel extolled their exploits, which included blowing up trains, assaulting enemy convoys, gathering military intelligence, and other such operations. Betrayed by a turncoat, they refused to confess under beastly torture and died cursing the occupiers and prophesying happy life in liberated Soviet Ukraine.

A different account emerged over time. In 1955, the authorities in Bucharest tried gendarme officers involved in this case and transferred the relevant files to the state archives in Mykolaiv oblast archive. These materials were identified and summarized in an article by the Ukrainian historian Mykola

Shytiuk. To begin with, the organization's real achievements were much less impressive than the hagiographic accounts claimed: a telephone line cut, strewn guns collected, Soviet prisoners of war helped to escape from the camp. Indeed, young partisans planned to blow up a nearby railway bridge but their plans were cut short by the chief of the Romanian gendarme post C(onstantin?) Anuşcu, who noticed suspicious night strolls of the youths in the forest.[6] On February 15, 1943, Anuşcu arrested four members of the organization. He first interrogated the head of the organization, Parfentii Grechanyi, who happened to be its head, and subjected him to harrowing torture. Grechanyi broke down, named some of the organization's members and signed a commitment to secretly collaborate with the gendarmerie, after which he was released. The next day Anuşcu arrested Aleksandr Kucher, who refused to cooperate, however, until Anuşcu showed him Grechanyi's signed declaration. Kucher then signed a similar commitment, though apparently he did not name other members. Released the same day, Kucher met with Grechanyi and suggested to raid the gendarme post in order to free two other arrestees, kill Anuşcu, and destroy the incriminating evidence. The rest of the members adopted this proposal, and on February 18, shortly after midnight, four young partisans assaulted the station. The raid succeeded only partially; they could not find the sought-after papers and Anuşcu escaped through a window. Reinforcements, called by Anuşcu and commanded by the Golta Legion commander major Romulus Ambrus, arrived the same night. In the ensuing shootout, one gendarme was killed. The partisans managed to escape but Grechanyi, acting either in the state of emotional distress or trying to displace his own guilt for giving in under torture, shot Kucher point blank, shouting that he deserved death as a traitor. The next day Anuşcu showed to Kucher's father the dead body of his son. The old man immediately named his son's friends. Further, the Krymka station gendarmes found a bag with the organization's papers apparently lost there by the attackers, which provided them with additional names. One by one, all the members of the organization—with the exception of Grechanyi, who facing an imminent arrest committed suicide—were arrested and convoyed to Pervomaisk prison. There, they were severely beaten and tortured. Eventually, all of them were murdered by the gendarmes as described in chapter 4.

The materials contained in the Soviet 1947 file on this case dwell extensively on the last minutes of the protagonists' lives, recording in particular their declarations to posterity. All of them supposedly expressed utter contempt for the occupiers, selfless love for their motherland, and loyalty to the Soviet regime. To what extent these records reflect the truth and to what extent their sources just regurgitated the Soviet official discourse is anybody's guess. The file also contains a letter, apparently in its original version, from Tamara Kholod, held at the time in the Tiraspol' prison. Dated June 3, 1943, this letter is strikingly at odds with the rest of the materials. Written in simple, beautiful, even though somewhat convoluted language, it contains not a word about the motherland, revolution, Stalin, or a future happy life, all familiar Soviet tropes, just the expressions of utter despair and anguish, together with longing for her family and her parents' hut: "My heart grieves deeply. I have pain in my chest, but who cares? Who cares about somebody else's fate? Whom can I blame? No, I [can] blame only the existing world. And presently, my own fate as well. But why is it so? Just think . . . to come to know prison at eighteen. And still, this is not the real misfortune. The real misfortune is that I cannot be of any use to anybody, even to you."[7] This crie de coeur is perhaps the most authentic expression of the sheer horror of the Krymka story. Young people's naive idealism, their ineptitude, the pointlessness of their sacrifice, as well as the gendarmes' needless savagery all come through clearer in this letter than in any other document from the history of the Transnistrian partisan warfare. Mythologized by the Soviet propagandists, its members decorated by military orders, including three of them receiving the title of the Hero of the Soviet Union, the true story of this tragedy became public only after the end of the regime whose purposes that myth was meant to serve.

The Romanian SSI captured other groups of young men created by individual enthusiasts on their own volition. One such group was headed by Georgii Smirnov in the fall of 1943 in Odessa. As in Krymka, the group had accomplished little before it was discovered. As in Krymka, its leader was largely to blame for its failure. In order to divert the police's attention, he reported a case of a third person allegedly selling a weapon and offered his further services to the police. It ostensibly agreed but simultaneously ordered his shadowing, which soon led to the arrest of the whole group. It is worth quoting from the SSI report's conclusion, in which the authors speculated on the young men's motivations in setting up this group: "Judging from this organization's method of creation, [as well as] from its behavior . . . it seems obvious that this organization was set up not on the order of . . . Soviet authorities but rather as a result of education received in a Soviet school. . . . All of this poisoned these youths, who are still unaware of all the horror embodied in the Soviet regime."[8] Perhaps the author of this report should have added that what these youths had seen for the past two years under the Romanian-occupation regime might have served as another motivating factor for their joining resistance.

More than the other social groups in urban areas, workers and laborers were susceptible for recruitment into the newly formed resistance groups. Tellingly, in Odessa the Romanians singled out the intelligentsia as the only social stratum loyal to them to the very end. For example, in September 1943, the second section of the Romanian General Staff (in practice, the SSI) reported to Ion Antonescu that no one should believe that Transnistrian Russians were positively disposed toward the Romanians. Even though they preferred them to the Germans due to the Romanians' kind-heartedness (the term Romanians routinely applied to themselves) and their belonging to the same religion, "the Russians" (this is what the Romanians called all Odessan citizens with the exception of the Moldovans) still secretly despised them because they were educated in the spirit of "megalomania, characteristic of any great people." The intelligentsia, whom the Romanians saved from starvation that they experienced under the Soviets, favored the former, whereas manual laborers and clerical workers whose salary was very low, "wanted the Soviets to return." Even though they were aware that their incomes would not be higher under the Soviets, they still expected "to be in the dominant position and to play political roles in the Soviet state."[9] In October 1943, the Balta județ gendarmerie legion assessed that the "craftsmen and workers were dissatisfied" because of the worsening economic conditions and "some of them commit small acts of sabotage."[10] When in 1944–1946, the Communist Party collected data and compiled its first statistical assessment of the partisan movement in Transnistria, it calculated that among the 1,774 recognized participants there were 319 workers, 726 "clerical and technical workers," and only 189 "peasant collective farmers."[11] Although it is quite probable that among those whom the Soviets labeled as "clerical and technical workers" many resided in the countryside, the results tend to agree with the Romanians' assessments and seem to jibe with recent findings suggesting that Soviet-educated technical and administrative cadres and manual workers were among the most reliable soldiers in the Red Army.[12]

Ukrainian Activists into Soviet Partisans? The Ambiguity of (Some) Resisters' Identities

The July 1943 SSI report assessed that the occupation regime had become so repugnant to many locals that "even Russian and Ukrainian nationalists were being attracted to the idea of getting rid of 'foreign occupation' at any price." That was one of the reasons why recruitment of members to the underground cells had been gathering pace, the report suggested.[13] If correct, the observation concerning the Russian and Ukrainian nationalists' inflow into the armed resistance may be of significant heuristic value and as such deserves verification against other independent sources.

Let us start with the Russian nationalists. Given the well-documented Russo-centrism and the increasing identification of the Soviet Union with traditional Russia in the Stalinist wartime propaganda, it is not surprising that patriotic sentiment of self-identified Russians in Transnistria motivated them to join pro-Soviet resistance. One finds echoes of Soviet propaganda appealing to such sentiments in leaflets disseminated in Transnistria by underground groups. For example, in October 1943, the Romanian gendarmerie reported that a manifesto was found glued to the doors of the apartment buildings in Odessa, containing the following appeal: "To the Russian People! Germany is destroyed . . . Long Live the Russian Army! Death to the Occupiers!" Another leaflet (the locality is not indicated) called "the Ukrainian people" to join the struggle of "our brother—the Great Russian people" against the common enemy of all Slavic peoples, German fascism.[14] The language of the leaflet was within the confines of the official Stalinist formula of the "Friendship of the Peoples," but the identification of the Red Army as the Russian army seemingly transgressed the official discourse, perhaps suggesting that it was not authorized by the communist leaders but belonged to an autonomous group.

Other observers also noted the increasing strength of the Russian patriotic sentiment in Transnistria. For example, in a note to the Ministry of Defense of March 12, 1943, a commandant of the Border Guards Corps opined that the Transnistrian population was becoming increasingly convinced that "the war was being waged not against communism and yids but against Russia as a nation and as a state" (the guards attributed this state of affairs to the inefficiency of Romanian propaganda in the province).[15] Diarist Aleksandr Shvets noted on February 21, 1943 that the public reacted to the performance of patriotic music by Alexander Borodin (aria of Prince Igor from the eponymous opera) and Petr Tchaikovsky (*Marche Slave* and *1812 Overture*) during a concert in the Theater of Opera and Ballet with a spontaneous manifestation of "protest against the foreign rule," shouting "Long Live Liberated Russia!" Subsequent performances of the Romanian national anthem, meant to quell the fury of the attending Germans, looked "laughable and silly," Shvets added.[16] At least one other likewise public reaction to the patriotic monologue of a character in a play was mentioned by another Odessan resident.[17]

As to the inflow of Ukrainian nationalists into the gangs of Soviet partisans, this statement looks, at the first glance, highly doubtful given the intense Soviet hostility toward Ukrainian independence and the Soviet portrayal of Ukrainian nationalists as Nazi lackeys. Nevertheless, there is evidence to support that assessment. As has been noted in chapter 3, during the first two years of occupation the Romanians considered what they dubbed "Ukrainian irredentism" to be a greater security threat than communist resistance. They viewed any and all manifestations of Ukrainian national identity, such as the singing of Ukrainian songs during family celebrations, hanging on the walls of peasant huts portraits of Ukrainian national poet Taras Shevchenko, and wearing of national costumes as sure signs of irredentism's growing appeal. Believing that Ukrainian village intelligentsia—teachers, priests, agronomists, and administrators—tended to be exponents of this current, they suspected that deep down in his soul every Ukrainian peasant supported the idea of independent Ukraine. The Transnistrian gendarmerie, police, and SSI closely followed the Ukrainian nationalists' actions and asserted that they were guided by the Organization of Ukrainian Nationalist centers—both the Banderist and Melnikist factions—located in the German zones of occupation, such as Lviv, Kyiv, Vinnytsia, and Melitopol'. The Ukrainian nationalists' primary aims were to create a network of supporters, to infiltrate local administrative institutions, schools, and economic establishments, and to sow nationalist ideas among ethnic Ukrainians in the hopes to "impart the province a Ukrainian character and in this way prepare the basis for Ukrainian national claims."[18] Despite intense surveillance activity, the Romanians failed to detect any signs of the nationalists gaining strength. Even in the northern Tulcin, Jugastru, and Moghilău județe where, according to their assessments, "irredentism" was the strongest, nothing but futile arrests and confiscation of some kind of "manifestos" (no information as to the exact content provided) was ever reported. Typical was the following report of the Tulcin Gendarmerie Legion: "On August 4, 1942, we have arrested nineteen banderists. Although we failed to find any evidence, we remain convinced that a well-disguised movement exists and has its nuclei everywhere."[19]

From early 1943 on, the gendarmes noted with increasing frequency the disappearance of even the symbolic presence of Ukrainian nationalism in public spaces, attributing this development to the changing fortunes of war. In 1943, for example, the Golta Gendarmerie Legion observed in its monthly activity report that "the Ukrainian irredentism had not manifested any symptom, probably because of the Soviet offensive at the front that put the Ukrainian nationalism at the totally secondary level."[20] To the extent that the appeal of the Ukrainian nationalism was falling, Soviet propaganda was finding a more receptive audience. In December 1943, the Odessa Gendarmerie Inspectorate noted in its information bulletin that "Ukrainian irredentism finds no response among the population, having been overwhelmed by the communist current."[21] In the context of shifting popular moods, the SSI's April 1942 observation that the Ukrainian nationalists' (they referred specifically to the banderist faction) and communist partisans' aims in Ukraine were largely identical and that the banderist cells were being used by the communists as recruiting ground appears particular illuminating.[22] In July 1942, in an information bulletin on the situation in Transnistria, the SSI again noted that a banderist cell in Moghilău judeţ was "infiltrated by the communists."[23]

The SSI assertion that the partisans' and banderists's aims were identical should be understood as referring to their immediate aims—expulsion of German and Romanian troops from Ukraine. The only difference between the two, the SSI opined, was the banderists' insistence on postponing the uprising until the "right" moment (probably exhaustion of the Germans and Soviets in the war), whereas the communists aimed at an immediate armed struggle.[24] Indeed, the slogans advocated by nationalist and communist propaganda were so similar that the Romanians had difficulty correctly attributing propagandistic materials.[25] Some members of the Ukrainian nationalist cells claimed after the war, with some plausibility, that they had joined these cells wishing to contribute to the struggle against the occupiers, and they saw little difference between them and the communist partisans.[26]

These observations open an intriguing possibility that the political identities of some resisters in Transnistria were fluid and that some residents changed their allegiance depending on their assessment of the war prospects. The case of Evgenii Artëmovich Blagodar', an organizer of the most successful partisan detachment in Transnistria that was called from August 1943 "Burevestnik" (stormy petrel; after Maxim Gorky's 1901 poem "The Song of the Stormy Petrel," a symbol of revolutionary élan) may be particularly illustrative. Proclaimed after the war a great hero of the partisan movement and an ardent Soviet patriot, Blagodar' was killed under murky circumstances by friendly fire in September 1943, just one day following his ousting from the commanding position in the group under the accusation that he was a Ukrainian nationalist. According to at least one eyewitness, a member of the detachment, Iosif Ivanovich Vykhodtsev, Blagodar' was assassinated on the orders of his replacement, Nikolai Antonovich Khranovskii.[27] Whether Vykhodtsev's account was correct or Blagodar''s death was an accident, Blagodar''s background does suggest his involvement with Ukrainian nationalist movement.

A graduate of Odessa University in 1940, majoring in history, Blagodar' was that same year sent to the newly Soviet-annexed Galicia, a center of the Ukrainian nationalist movement. Both his profession and his stint in Galicia make him a likely recruit of the Organization of Ukrainian Nationalists that preserved much of its underground network during the Soviet occupation of 1940–1941 and actively recruited new members from among Ukrainians sent to the province from eastern Ukraine. Upon Ukraine's occupation by the Germans, Blagodar′ returned to his native village of Savran′, Balta județ, where he worked as a school history teacher. These and subsequent of Blagodar′'s actions also followed the organization's familiar script designed to spread influence outside of its stronghold in Galicia. Shortly upon his return, Blagodar′ initiated the creation of a cell, involving in it mostly local members of the intelligentsia. In school, he used textbooks by Ukrainian nationalist historian Mikhailo Sergi′iovich Hrushevskii proscribed in Soviet schools; when later confronted with this fact by his pro-Soviet detractors, he explained it by saying that it was a ruse designed to deceive the occupiers. This claim, however, is not persuasive given that the Romanians persecuted Ukrainian nationalists with no less severity than communists, especially in the first two years of the occupation.[28] During late 1941 and the first half of 1942, when his cell was created, the public opinion was decidedly anti-communist while the fortunes of the Ukrainian nationalist project seemed sound, a fact that also suggests the cell's initial nationalist orientation. One of Blagodar′'s first recruits was Aleksei Alekseevich Shelkovnikov, a former officer in the Tsarist army and thus an unlikely survivor of Stalinist purges (Shelkovnikov would later be murdered by the gendarmes). That a man with such background would put his life on the line to fight for the restoration of the regime that zealously persecuted his own ilk overstretches credulity. Blagodar′'s reluctance to engage in armed resistance also likely reflected the organization's strategy to organize a rebellion at the end of the war, when both the Soviets and Nazis would be, as they hoped, exhausted. According to Vykhodtsev, it was only when Blagodar′ realized that the Red Army was likely to return in a short while, that he changed his orientation and decided to try "to expiate his crimes before the Soviet power by engaging in armed resistance." Vykhodtsev's suggestion that among the members of Blagodar′-Shelkovnikov's group were "some of the best patriotic [pro-Soviet] people who were unaware of these machinations," also looks plausible.[29]

It may appear ironyic that the most consequential partisan detachment in Transnistria was created by the Ukrainian nationalists, although eventually pro-Soviet members ousted them and took the situation under their control. In June 1942, the Soviets parachuted a group of three intelligence officers and saboteurs close to Pervomaisk (Golta) raion, among whom only one, the former first secretary of the Pervomaisk city committee, Nikolai Stepanovich Kostiuk, proceeded to fulfill the mission (the fate of other officers remains unknown—a rather ordinary episode in the Soviet sabotage efforts). In October 1942, he managed to bring together the leaders of several cells in the northern areas of Transnistria and establish a unified underground organization Pribuzhskaia (of the Buh region). Little changed, however, in northern Transnistria, the activity of partisans being still limited to the dissemination of leaflets and recruitment of new members. Mass arrests in early 1943, probably the result of the obkom's exposure, delivered a severe blow to the organization, but its key members survived. It was only in August 1943, that is after the Soviets won the Battle of Kursk and moved speedily into eastern and central Ukraine, that the organization decided to commence armed struggle by relocating the center of its activity into local forests. The same month, another group of intelligence and military officers under the command of Ivan Afanas'evich Kukharenko were parachuted by the Fourth Ukrainian Front of the Red Army into the "northern raions" of Transnistria. It took them three months to establish contacts with the organization and other groups, all of which were now brought together into the newly created Burevestnik partisan detachment. From that moment on, the detachment, numbering about 250 men, hiding in Savran' and other local forests, and enjoying considerable support in the villages, resorted to attacks on the gendarme posts, horse-drawn and auto-truck convoys with provisions and ammunition, and organized derailments of trains, as well as other acts of sabotage. In their postliberation reports these partisans exaggerated their exploits, including the number of enemies killed, equipment destroyed, and kettle seized: in the final tally, 3,000 soldiers and officers killed in action, three locomotives and twenty-two railcars destroyed, among other achievements.[30]

Romanian reports paint a substantially more subdued picture, although they also document a considerable increase in sabotage activity and damage inflicted by it. For example, according to the partisans' report, the train crash organized by them in late November 1943 led to the destruction of one locomotive and the death of seventy enemy soldiers; however, the Romanians reported only the wreckage of railways but no victims.[31] Both Soviet and Romanian sources mention partisan attacks on a horse-drawn Romanian column in the Savranskii forest in mid-December 1943, but the former source cites twenty enemies killed with only one partisan wounded, while the Romanian report mentions two agrarian gendarmes killed and one wounded.[32] On December 17, 1943, Romanian losses in the fight against the partisans amounted to two men killed and two wounded, while among the "bandits" four men were killed and eighty-six arrested (their further whereabouts unknown).[33]

From the Fall of 1943 On: The Mass Movement

Romanian sources agree with the Soviet ones that in late 1943–early 1944 the partisan movement in the north of the region grew, relying on the massive support of the local farmers. Led by professional military officers parachuted in by the Soviets and sometimes merging together with the other partisan groups and even the Red Army detachments crossing the Buh River from the north into Transnistria, these groups, among which Burevestnik was the biggest and the most prominent, harassed mayors and policemen, attacked gendarmerie and police stations, transports, prisoners' of war camps and prisons (with the aim of liberating the inmates), damaged communication lines, and sometimes battled whole battalions and even larger enemy detachments. Typical was the following SSI report of January 22, 1944:

> The population in the north of Transnistria is nearly hostile and favorably disposed to the partisans, in the rest of the province the population is calm. During the night of January 21–22, Tarcov Gendarmerie Post was attacked by the partisans, one gendarme was killed. In the forest of Timanovka twelve kilometers from Tulchin, three German vehicles were attacked and all occupants, eight in total, were killed. This band mined a bridge and a railway . . . causing serious damage. The patrol and security office of Tulchin garrison were attacked. In the village of Capustiany, Tulcin judeţ, two German vehicles were attacked: eight killed, two wounded. Partisan bands . . . entered the village of Kopaigorod, arrested its mayor and committed lootings. They are approximately 300-strong. . . . Other bands wander and reconnoiter the territory. A vehicle belonging to the German 311th artillery company was attacked while exiting the village of Timanovka: three men killed . . . At Capustiany, a medical transport carrying fifty wounded men and ten orderlies was attacked: two orderlies killed and some of the wounded disappeared.[34]

In January–February 1944, to the extent that the front approached, evacuations of everything of value on which the Romanians and Germans could put their hands accelerated, and the locals' anxieties heightened. The Romanian assessments of the "moods of the population" changed from "nearly hostile" to "hostile" and "very hostile," while information reports painted a picture of continuous battles with intermittent results. The Germans had to send in tanks and airplane bombers by diverting them from the front to reinforce the Romanian troops.[35] Romanian and German losses mounted, although they were likely lower than the partisans' reports claimed. Still, antipartisan operations were frequently unsuccessful, their bands managing to escape total destruction by breaking through the encirclement and blending into the general population. That was the outcome of the German-Romanian attempt to destroy a group of about 500 partisans in early February 1944 in the forest next to the village of Shpikov, Tulcin judeṭ, in which German tanks and bombers were engaged. Despite the initially successful encirclement, partisans managed to break through during the night of February 2–3. Although they suffered serious losses—the Romanians assessed them as forty-eight—they inflicted comparable damage on the enemy: thirty Romanian soldiers unaccounted for and three wounded, three Germans killed and four wounded, vehicles and weapons destroyed. Escapees from the encirclement dispersed into the surrounding villages, distributing grain stockpiled by the Romanians for transportation into the country, and recruiting new members for their gangs from among the local youth.[36] As the SSI observed in the January 21, 1944 information report: "The population's mood in the northwest of Transnistria is hostile to the Romanian administration and allied troops. It has been proven that they act in the partisans' interests, supplying them with information and helping them in armed actions."[37]

So convinced, the Romanians, following the German lead, resorted to reprisals against the locals. In the early fall of 1943 (the exact date is not indicated in the extant copy), the Third Army Corps (commander general de divizie Hugo Schwab) issued an order that provided for "complete destruction" of the villages in which partisans dwelled or an attempt on the life of a Romanian or German officer took place; "execution by firing squad of families who sheltered partisans"; arrest and transfer to gendarmes of all foreign persons entering a village; execution of those guilty of breaching these provisions and destruction of their villages.[38]

Abundant evidence proves that this order was followed, although perhaps not everywhere and with some hesitation on the part of individual officers. When in mid-November 1943, the partisans carried out an attack on a gendarmerie station in Tulcin judeṭ, killing one or two gendarmes, the reserve colonel (rank in the Romanian army at the time), Nicolae Pătrășcoiu, who served as commander of rear troops deployed in the area, responded by ordering reprisals against local civilians. As a result, several of the nearby villages were set on fire, including the large village of Bandurovo where, according to Soviet sources, up to 500 houses were burned to the ground. Soldiers were ordered to kill suspected "partisans" on the spot, which they proceeded to do while officers scolded the shirkers. Some officers apparently protested such brutally, which might have spared the further loss of life.[39] Eventually, the Romanians apprehended one hundred suspects and interned about sixty of them in prison in the town of Balta. The latter group was murdered on March 3, 1944, by the Germans.[40] When in December 1943, a series of sabotage acts were carried out on the railway lines near Râbnița, Gendarmerie Legion commander major Popescu ordered the execution of thirteen local residents suspected of being the partisans' liaisons; this order was carried out.[41] When in January 1944, in the village of Holubovka partisans attacked a gendarme patrol, killing two officers and seven soldiers, the Romanians responded by setting the whole village on fire and murdering forty-eight residents.[42] These are just some examples from a substantially longer list.

Even so, the Romanian policy seems to have remained somewhat less brutal than that of the Germans, while partisan leaders also preferred not to escalate violence. In some cases, they refrained from murdering the captured gendarmes and instead ordered their disarmament and release.[43] After the burning of Bandurovo, however, the partisan behavior radicalized, although they continued to treat captured Romanians with more leniency than the Germans.[44] With the arrival of the parachuted Soviet military officers and their taking charge of the partisan groups, their militancy and the brutality of both sides grew exponentially. Pătrășcoiu remained convinced that his policy was the only correct response to the partisan menace and continued to advocate toughness German-style, at one point even suggesting expelling the population of the villages suspected of supporting the partisans to the east, across the Buh River into the German zone. If the Romanians were to lose Transnistria, he insisted, it should not be for lack of toughness in dealings with the partisans.[45]

There is little doubt that increasing efficacy of the partisans' actions in northern Transnistria in late 1943 and through the arrival of the Red Army in March 1944, was caused by the tectonic shift in the local public opinion in favor of the Soviets. As the SSI noted in its February 1944 report on the partisan movement in Golovanevskii raion (northern Transnistria): "The same population that met us with open arms now fights against us."[46] In addition to the spectacle of the occupiers' ruthless plunder of all and every stock of provisions and economic asset, other factors infuriated local population in the late 1943. German policy of forcible recruitment of local youth for work in Germany or for the construction of fortifications drove youngsters into the woods and straight into the partisans' ranks. For example, on January 23, 1944, the Tulcin Gendarmerie Legion reported:

This județ's population, mainly men and in particular youngsters, abandoned their domiciles and took to the woods for fear of being rounded up by the retreating German and Romanian troops, as it happened in the territory to the east of the Buh River. For this reason their houses are empty, and no work is being done in the kolkhozes. Some of them have even enrolled in the partisan gangs whom they help as guides and informers, while others are impressed in the gangs, which are growing more numerous and more powerful in this județ.[47]

Indeed, the quick growth of the partisan movement, in its own turn, helped them recruit new members, sometimes forcibly.[48] The swift approach of the Red Army added to the excitement and strengthened the incentive to join the winning side, including and possibly in particular among those who in the previous months discredited themselves in the eyes of the Soviets by collaborating with the enemy. As commander of the Odessa Gendarmerie Inspectorate summed it up in December 1943, the province's population was divided into two parts, the majority was on the side of the Soviets, while those who had served the Romanians, "were concerned with their fate" and some of them "were even trying to commit acts of devotion to the Soviet regime."[49] The partisans sometimes called on the collaborators to join them if they wanted to "expiate their sins before the motherland."[50] Recalling his conversation with a local resident serving in the town mayor's office, one former partisan from Tulchin addressed the collaborator thus: "Listen Matveev, how do you imagine justifying your behavior before the Soviet authorities?" Hearing this, Matveev replied, "I will do anything you will tell me."[51] Persistent rumors of the returning Soviets' repression of anybody who did not join the resistance no doubt also influenced the locals' choices in the last months before the liberation.[52]

Besides joining armed resistance, other, less risky options were open to local residents willing to inflict some damage on the occupiers. Among them was the destruction of foods and machinery gathered for shipment into Romania. The partisans regularly called on the locals to impede such shipments and to destroy machinery and other assets en route to Romania, as well as to distribute cereals collected for shipment among local farmers.[53] Both Romanian reports on the situation all over Transnistria and partisan reports after the liberation are peppered with accounts of machinery damaged or destroyed, railways dismantled (usually causing delay, more rarely derailment of railcars), cattle contaminated with rinderpest and swine fever, haystacks and cereal and milk collection centers put on fire, tractors wrecked and abandoned by their drivers en route to Romania, kolkhoz harvests distributed among the farmers, and other similar occurrences. By the end of 1943, the Romanians concluded that the rural population as a whole, and even those generally well-disposed toward them, resisted their efforts to strip the province of its food reserves and productive efforts. As the Odessa Gendarmerie Inspector colonel Iliescu opined in his monthly December 1943 report: "Passivity and negligence manifested by the population in fulfillment of their work duties seem to be acts of sabotage meant to hinder shipment of resources into the country." Concrete cases gathered in support of this statement came from all over the province, thus suggesting that resistance activity extended far beyond the forested northern județe.[54]

By late January 1944, the Romanians had lost control over Transnistria's northern județe. As the detailed report of the Balta județ prefect demonstrates, partisans remained a major concern, but the massive influx of refugees from the east, as well as of the retreating German troops and their auxiliaries, including the Cossacks, further added to the pressure on the local authorities. Massive looting of food reserves and frequent attacks on the Romanian officials of all ranks by the partisans, Germans, and Cossack auxiliaries (for example, the pretor of Trostineț raion was murdered by the German soldiers) made further shipment of goods into Romania impossible. Massively outnumbered and fearing for their lives, the gendarmes stayed put in their quarters while officials on business trips were routinely attacked and their vehicles commandeered by the Germans and Cossacks.[55] Under such conditions, General Potopeanu, who by that time had replaced Alexianu and bore the title of the chief of the Military Administration of the Territory between the Dniester and Buh Rivers opined that, since further transport of agricultural goods from there had become impossible, the authorities should focus on the transfer of tractors into Romania.[56] On February 18, 1944, he calculated that the overall quantity of tractors to be "evacuated" was between 800 and 1,200, an astonishingly high number.[57] Predictably, such a policy that was bound to leave the province without any means to conduct the spring sowing only further aggravated the local population, who looked to the partisans as their protectors.[58] Soon after, Potopeanu related to Bucharest that "ravages" made by the partisans in the northern part of Transnistria "had almost totally annihilated the Romanian administration there," and that two columns of an estimated 3,000 partisans were preparing to cross the Dniester River into Bessarabia.[59] (Northern Transnistria was occupied by the Red Army in little more than a month.)

In Odessa, too, public opinion was quickly shifting in favor of the Soviets. While the intelligentsia remained pro-Romanian, petitioning the authorities for permission to immigrate into this country (Ion Antonescu was receptive to their requests, eventually allowing several hundreds of them to do so), the lower classes and especially youngsters fearing forcible recruitment for work in Germany tried to hide anywhere they could.[60] They often descended into the catacombs, which by now were not guarded as thoroughly as they were in 1941–1942. In the fall of 1943, the surviving core of the leadership of the Prigorodnyi underground raikom, the only one from those left for sabotage in the occupied city, saw their stocks soaring in the eyes of ordinary Odessans. Having returned in April 1943 to the catacombs from their hideouts, raikom leaders presided over an enormously increased group.

By January 1944, this group numbered one hundred members. In March–April 1944, partisan detachments loosely subordinated to the raikom conducted operations from the catacomb exits in the nearby villages of Usatovo, Kuial′nik and Nerubaiskoie. On April 9, when the Red Army was approaching Odessa with the German retreating, partisans launched a surprise attack on a column of Germans at Kuial′nik. The same day, another partisan detachment attacked a group of German engineers in Usatovo when they were laying down explosives to blow up the Hadzhibei dam to slow the Red Army advance, even at the cost of flooding Odessa. The partisans managed to drive the engineers out of the village and away from the dam. Only with the arrival of a German infantry battalion were they forced to retreat from the village, but the continued advance of the Red Army forced the Germans to withdraw, preventing the dam's destruction. According to Soviet data, in the battle in Usatovo thirty-two Germans were killed and many more wounded.[61] The commander of the German engineers' infantry battalion, Captain Luthke, also reported to his superiors the "heavy losses" among the German infantry, plus one of his men killed and two wounded.[62] The partisans subordinated to the raikom offered shelter to up to 7,000 local citizens (mostly men, hiding to avoid deportation to Germany for forced labor), as well as to cattle concealed from requisitioning.[63]

Preventing the destruction of the Hadzhibei dam might have been the partisans' most important achievement. Other resistance groups were instrumental in saving Odessa's vital industrial assets. For example, a group of locals employed at the port, many of whom collaborated with the Romanians during the occupation, carried out a successful sabotage action against the destruction of their facility by cutting the wires that connected the explosives installed by the Germans with the aim of blowing up the port just hours before their withdrawal. Since this group was not in any way connected to the party underground, its achievement was not recognized until the late 1960s, when its exploits were finally publicized in the Soviet press.[64]

As the previous account suggests, the history of resistance in Transnistria fits neither the Soviet-era grand narrative of the "all-people's struggle against

FIGURE 13.   Soviet troops and partisans in front of the monument to the fifth Duke de Richelieu (locally known as "Diuk"), governor of the New Russia Province in 1804–1815. Odessa, April 1944, Soviet photo. Courtesy of Odessa Regional History Museum.

the fascist occupiers," nor the Cold War–era Western view of the partisans as "the long arm of Moscow."[65] It also implies that most postwar accounts of the resistance fighters should be approached with skepticism, as they were influenced by the official Soviet narrative and in full awareness of the stakes involved in official recognition or denial of their self-ascribed identities as members of the Soviet underground. This latter point seems to be particularly relevant since even after the downfall of the Soviet Union those accounts continue to be accepted as a significant source of partisan history.[66] Romanian contemporary sources, and in particular the SSI and gendarmerie sources, still underutilized, seem more reliable for the reconstruction of this story, although they too are sometimes skewed by the perceived need to sway the higher-ups toward one or another perspective and to inflate the importance of the surveilling institution.

Taken together with the Soviet documents, these sources show that the resistance's fortunes were largely a function of the general population's attitude toward the occupiers. Their initial hostility toward the hated Soviet regime goes a long way toward explaining both the inefficiency and the quick exposure of terrorist groups left in the occupied territory by the retreating Soviets. To the extent that the population's attitude toward the occupiers changed from friendly to strongly negative, and the expectation of the Soviets' return boosted the incentive to prove one's Sovietness by participating in the resistance, the detachments' ranks swelled and their efficiency vastly increased.

Another observation that follows from the preceding account suggests considerable fluidity of the resisters' identities. Despite their postwar narratives that present them as dedicated to the Soviet cause throughout the occupation, it is very likely that their orientations changed throughout the period and that among those who would be officially celebrated as Soviet partisans were quite a few initially favorably disposed to the new regime, including former collaborators, as well as Ukrainian nationalists, who either in late 1942 or in early to mid-1943, reoriented themselves to the Soviet course. While such trajectories were signs of untrustworthiness in the eyes of the Soviets, it is likely that they were the norm rather than the exception among the province's population and maybe even among the majority of the partisans themselves. Christopher Gilley, who studies the history of Ukraine during the Russian Civil War, has suggested that some leaders of the pro-independence gangs tended to define their identity based on the conditions they found themselves in, even though those identities might not have fully accorded with their own ideological or political preferences. Gilley suggests that such changes of identities should not be dismissed as pure falsehoods since, as he explained by quoting Sheila Fitzpatrick, "impersonation is an inevitable part of self-formation" and in any case, such identity changes often entailed the transformation of the actors' behavior.[67] This insight jibes well with Slepyan's findings that Soviet partisans actively sought and participated in the formation of their public image, navigating between the rigid confines of Stalinist speak and folkloric repertoires of social bandits and people's avengers against their oppressors.[68]

People who found themselves, in 1941, under the Romanian occupation had to make strategic choices that not only affected their chances of survival through the end of the war but also offered them ways of finding their place in the postwar world. It should come as no surprise that their understanding of the contours of that future world were changing with dizzying rapidity and that those changes powerfully affected their strategic choices and ways of self-definition. Disenchantment with the Romanian regime was an important variable affecting their behavior, but in and of itself it does not fully explain the way they elected to act. Their decisions were likely based on the evaluation of a host of factors, among which the Romanians' record was but one.

Conclusion

Romania's occupation of Transnistria was due to the unlikely combination of circumstances. Without going too far into the pre–World War II history, it is more than probable that had the USSR not annexed Bessarabia and northern Bukovina in 1940—in itself a consequence of the Stalin-Hitler pact of the previous year—Romania would not have joined Nazi Germany in its anti-Soviet war. Once, however, the Romanian army found itself on the territory east of the Dniester River, occupation and eventual annexation of Transnistria appeared to the country's leaders as a natural next step. The lore of European statecraft and diplomacy and the basic values of European statesmanship conditioned them to see territorial expansion as a sign of political success, power, and prestige. Opposition parties, while critical of the troops' performance in Odessa, later acquiesced with the occupation for fear of being seen as unpatriotic.

Although the Romanian leaders did not announce the annexation of Transnistria, they intended to do it later in case the war ended in the Axis powers' victory. Though administering it mostly as a Romanian province, they did not extend the Romanian law into its territory. They had to contend with the German claims on the territory's resources and to make considerable concessions to its hegemonic ally. Although pretending to comply with the provisions of the international law concerning the rights of the occupier, they interpreted them so loosely that they became basically meaningless, especially where the limitations—vague as they were—on the exploitation of local resources were concerned. While ostensibly civil, the Romanian administration in the province was subordinated to the Conducător, Ion Antonescu, as commander-in-chief of the Romanian army rather than as head of state, an arrangement that created legal incongruities the Romanians proved unable to resolve. Transnistria's institutional setup and place within the government apparatus to some extent followed the German patterns of administration in occupied Eastern Central Europe, but ultimately the long-standing Romanian traditions and governmentalities prevailed over the Germans' advice. Run to a large extent as Antonescu's personal fiefdom, Transnistria was a region of lawlessness and administrative arbitrariness. Double standards, patron-client networks of loyalties, illegal oral orders, evasion of responsibility, and official cover-ups were ubiquitous.

The institutional and legal breaks on abuses, although not completely inexistent, were feeble. For one, Bucharest governmental bureaucrats, concerned with fiscal accountability and Antonescu's desire to avoid domestic corruption scandals and international condemnation for barbarity, imposed (weak) restrictions on the rapacity of the Transnistrian administrators. Furthermore, military magistrates who manned the Transnistrian courts and who in their great majority were former civilian lawyers were unwilling to brazenly disregard all appearances of legality and proved reluctant to rubberstamp some of Antonescu's most brutal orders, such as the execution of all suspected partisans without proof of actual guilt. Other repressive bodies, such as gendarmerie, steeped in the culture of double standards and impunity, proved a pliable instrument of extra-legal repression, so that the end result might have been the same. Personal loyalties and connections at various levels, in particular between governor Alexianu and prefects, gendarmerie inspectors Broşteanu and Iliescu, and legion commanders were channels through which illegal and sometimes murderous orders were communicated and enforced.

The Romanians' visions of the annexed and transformed Transnistria stemmed from the powerful tradition of ethnic nationalism, to which the country's rulers during World War II subscribed. Convinced that temporary victories of fascist Italy and Nazi Germany proved that ethnic purity would be the norm in the future world of European nation-states, the Romanian leaders planned ethnic purification of the province by means of massive population transfers. However, the attempted resettlement on a limited scale during the war proved so difficult logistically and costly politically that these plans were shelved and remained largely inconsequential. Mostly unsuccessful, probably due to the short span of the occupation, turned out to be efforts to raise the level of "national consciousness" among the Transnistrian Moldovans and to transform them into reliable members of the Romanian ethnic nation.

In the meantime, Western discourses on European "east" in general, and "Russian steppe" in particular, as the oriental other of European civilization also influenced the Romanian administrators' mentalities and understanding of their own role in the region. Most evident in the Romanian view of Ukrainian peasants as benighted, backward, and in need of a benevolent but stern fatherly rule, this discourse in practice served to legitimize violent rule over the countryside and the shameless exploitation of its population. The Romanians were hostile to any manifestation of Ukrainian nationalism; yet racial undertones, although present, were rather weak in their propaganda and official documents. The fact that most lower-ranking Romanian troops were peasants themselves, whose way of life did not differ greatly from that of the Transnistrian farmers, and that the majority of the Romanians belonged to the same Christian Orthodox religion as their local charges, further helped to diminish tension between the occupiers and the occupied. The Romanian self-imposed mission of re-Christianization initially produced spectacular results, largely because of the local population's thirst for religious solace. As soon as the Soviets' return became imminent, the locals retreated back into the Soviet-type secularism, for fear of being seen as disloyal and thus re-Christianization turned out short-lived.

One of the several ways that the Romanian rule differed from the German rule was the respect and comfort they accorded to the Russian-speaking Odessan intelligentsia. Partially a function of ingrained social norms in Romania, in which "intellectuals"—understood as members of liberal professions, professors, artists, and writers—carried an inordinately high status and dominated political and social life, this respect was also the result of the strong impression that Odessan cultural treasures had on Romanian officials. A thriving commercial hub with sophisticated artistic and cultural elite under the tsars, Odessa experienced steep decline under the Soviets but still boasted high-quality theaters and museums, a number of colleges with the faculty of high, sometimes international repute. In a paradoxical twist of orientalizing fantasy, Romanian officials saw their patronizing of Odessan high European-style culture as proof of their own Europeanness and civilizational worthiness. This policy resulted in the largely cordial relationship between Odessan intelligentsia and the Romanian authorities and produced the city's spectacular cultural renaissance during the war.

The authorities also tolerated free trade and private economic initiatives in Odessa which, together with the presence of a privileged farming community of ethnic Germans in the vicinity, helped supply the city with foods in amounts unparalleled to any other occupied Soviet urban area. In this respect, too, the Romanian policy was in stark contrast with the German policy of starving the urban cities in the occupied Soviet Union in order to appropriate as much local agricultural goods as possible. The ensuing "prosperity" benefitted only a tiny portion of the city's population, consisting largely of black market profiteers, Romanian administrators, and privileged intelligentsia. Workers and laborers had to make do with starvation-level wages. Lively cultural life and ostensible prosperity of the privileged few produced a strong impression on rare journalists and even some locals, who created a myth of the Odessan economic miracle—which endured inside (as an unofficial memory) and outside the Soviet Union—a myth that remained popular in immigrant circles long after the war. The suffering of the lower-laboring strata was purged from such accounts but was emphasized in the official Soviet memory of the war.

The conditions of the overwhelming majority of the local population, who rejoiced at the sight of the Red Army's movements farther to the east in late fall 1941, steadily deteriorated from the beginning of 1942 on. The main reason for the growing impoverishment was the Romanian determination to pump out as much agricultural resources and other economic assets from the region as possible, irrespective of the cost to the locals. Driven by the combination of pressing needs to feed the army and to fulfill agreements with Germany concerning the delivery of agricultural goods, particularly against the background of bad harvests in 1941 and 1942, this policy quickly alienated Transnistria's lower classes. Failure to live up to the promise to disband the hated kolkhozes further increased the steadily growing disappointment. Dismantling and shipping into Romania of Transnistria's productive assets, including industrial machinery, railway stock, draft and pedigree kettle, art and other museum objects accelerated during 1943 and continued through the Romanians' withdrawal in March 1944. As the Romanians became painfully aware, by the fall of 1943, the clear majority of the province's population were eager to see them out and many impatiently awaited the Red Army's return. Turning the majority of an initially welcoming local population against themselves in just two years constitutes the most striking outcome of the short-lived Romanian occupation.

Although the Soviet state criminalized most forms of employment in local administration, industrial and agricultural managerial positions, and any participation in local police units, in the first year of the occupation the Romanians did not experience any shortage of volunteers for such positions. Soviet-era party and state apparatchiks and low- and mid-level managers showed up at the recruitment centers and were reemployed for their previous posts, often to the chagrin of ordinary citizens who continuously lobbied for their removal. Party members, whether they left for sabotage activity or stayed there for other reasons, answered the summons to register with the local authorities and showed no sign of loyalty to the Soviet cause, with only rare exceptions. Nor was it difficult to find those willing to serve as village mayors or policemen, except in the last months of the occupation. During that period, many local managers and administrators supported pro-Soviet resistance as a way to earn absolution or to mitigate their guilt.

It is not surprising, nor is it morally reprehensible that many an intellectual in Odessa found the temptation irresistible to actively participate in anticommunist propaganda campaigns encouraged by the occupiers. Memories of the Stalinist regime's depredations were still fresh while indignation against them too strong for this to be otherwise. When denunciation of Stalinist era-crimes was coupled with the propaganda of racial hate and anti-Semitic worldviews equating communism with Jewishness and justifying eliminationist violence against Jews, then their activity entered a drastically different moral universe. Although not directly responsible for the murderous violence and other monstrous abuses against Jews, such discourses contributed to their normalization and possibly encouraged them. In the postwar world, this part of the story has been almost completely glossed over. Although the Soviets considered participation in anti-Jewish violence a crime deserving the most severe punishment, including the death penalty and although, they punished anybody guilty of anti-Soviet propaganda, practicing anti-Semitic discourses during the war was not in and of itself a subject of their particular attention. In some instances at least, Odessan intellectuals guilty of such behavior slipped through the Soviet clutches unscathed. The memory of the betrayal of Jews by their Soviet non-Jewish neighbors was not preserved in the public space of the postwar Soviet Union. Neither has post-Soviet Ukraine nor, for that matter, the city of Odessa, been particularly interested in excavating these pages of its wartime history. This dark past still awaits its revealing and the public's coming to terms with it.

It was the profound change in the populace's attitude toward the occupiers and their regime that primarily determined the changing fortunes of pro-Soviet resistance. Deeply unpopular at the beginning of the occupation, sabotage groups selected, trained, and equipped by the Soviets shortly before their retreat were quickly discovered and destroyed by the Romanians, with the enthusiastic support of local residents resentful of their former bosses, whom they easily recognized and reported to the newly installed authorities. For a time, until early 1942, the Romanians considered, no doubt correctly, that the only serious threat to their control was presented by the Ukrainian nationalist underground, whose strategy was to prepare an uprising after the end of the anti-Soviet war, in order to reclaim Ukrainian independence from the Germans and Romanians. However, to the extent that the prospects of the Axis powers' victory looked increasingly unlikely while the expectations of a rapid Soviet return intensified, pro-Soviet resistance groups reappeared and some of the former nationalist activists changed their identity to that of pro-Soviet partisans. The latter became the main conduit for the growing resentment of the local residents against the occupiers. Other factors that explained the increasing buoyancy of resistance groups included an upsurge of patriotic feelings and an urge to join the winning side, in particular among the Soviet POWs residing in many villages and even among lower-ranking collaborators who were desperate to join the partisans in order to acquit themselves in the eyes of vengeful Soviets. Soviet-parachuted sabotage and military groups often served as nuclei of the newly formed partisan detachments recruiting their ranks from among the locals. In response to the growing armed resistance, the Romanian antipartisan policy quickly radicalized although it probably never reached the level of brutality characteristic of German antipartisan warfare in other parts of the Soviet Union.

This brings us to the question of how important were the differences between the German and the Romanian occupation regimes and policies for the overall dynamic of occupier-occupied relations. Unlike the Germans, Romanian officials were not driven by racial hatred toward Slavs and feelings of their own superiority over Transnistrian peasantry lacked that "biological" aspect that was so characteristic of the Nazi worldview. Romanian patronage of Odessan high-brow arts and culture had no analog in the German-occupied part of the Soviet Union. Throughout most of the occupation, Romanian surveillance bodies noted fears among the locals that the province would be transferred to the Germans, which they expected would cause significant additional hardship.[1] Nevertheless, by the end of the occupation, the populace's attitude toward the Romanians was probably not much different from that in most of the neighboring Reichskomissariat Ukraine toward the Germans, as the strength of the popular support to the partisan groups in northern județe suggests.[2] Conversely, scarcity of partisan violence in the southern part of the region until the Germans' withdrawal is explicable by the virtual absence of forested areas and the abundance of open spaces ill-suited for partisan activity. It thus appears that the difference between the German and Romanian occupiers' mentalities and policies had only a limited effect on their relations with the locals. While it had taken longer for the Romanians to turn the population against them, the end result was quite similar in both zones of occupation. The progressive radicalization of

Romanian policies in Transnistria despite the relative weakness of anti-Slavic racist prejudices also suggests that perceived military necessity and brazen disregard for the international law in a war against a country seen as barbaric might have been a more important factor in determining the policy of the Axis powers' occupation than anti-Slavic racism per se. It was only among the privileged stratum of Odessa intelligentsia that support for the Romanians was never shattered, and that may well constitute another notable difference from the developments in other areas of the occupied Soviet Union within its 1939 borders.

NOTES

Introduction

1. Finland occupied a tiny part of eastern Karelia whose population was, in December 1941, according to the official Finnish count, a little more than 86,000 people (some historians believe that the actual number might have further declined shortly afterward to just above 67,000). See Hel'he Siappelia, "Finliandiia kak okkupant v 1941–1944 godakh," *Sever*, nos. 3, 4, 5 (1995), http://www.aroundspb.ru/finnish/sepp/sepp0.php.

2. Alexander Dallin, *Odessa, 1941–1944: A Case Study of Soviet Territory under Foreign Rule* (Santa Monica, CA: Rand Corporation, 1957).

3. Alexander Dallin, *German Rule in Russia, 1941–1945: A Study of Occupation Policies* (New York: St. Martin's Press, 1957).

4. Ekkehard Völkl, *Transnistrien und Odessa (1941–1944)*, Schriftenreihe des Osteuropainstituts Regensburg-Passau; Bd. 14 (Kallmünz: Lassleben, 1996).

5. Herwig Baum, *Varianten des Terrors: Ein Vergleich zwischen der deutschen und rumänischen Besatzungsverwaltung in der Sowjetunion 1941–1944* (Berlin: Metropol, 2011).

6. See, for example, Ia. H. Horburov, Iu. V. Kotliar, and M. M. Shytiuk, *Povstan'sko-partizans'kyi rukh na Pivdni Ukraïnyv 1917–1945 rr.* (Kherson: OLDI-plius, 2003). This book contains accounts of nationalist and pro-communist resistance movements in World War II southern Ukraine. In its first part, nationalist rhetoric and viewpoint are adopted, in the second, Soviet clichés are employed, without any visible effort to reconcile mutually exclusive myths.

7. Alexandr Anatol'evich Cherkasov, *Okkupatsiia Odessy: God 1941* (Odessa: "Optimum," 2007); Cherkasov, *Okkupatsiia Odessy: God 1942, Ianvar'–mai* (Odessa: Optimum, 2008); Cherkasov, *Okkupatsiia Odessy: God 1943, Ianvar'–mai* (Odessa: Optimum, 2010). For an example of a negative review from the "patriotic" standpoint, see Evgenii Maliar, "Knigi ob okkupatsii Odessy. Dva podkhoda," *Porto-Franko* no. 17 (1064), May 13, 2011, http://porto-fr.odessa.ua/index.php?art_num=art018&year=2011&nnumb=17. Cherkasov's books are based on the local press collection of posters and leaflets in Russian from the period of occupation, as well as recollections of Odessa citizens.

8. Knut Stang, *Kollaboration und Massenmord: Die litauische Hilfspolizei, das Rollkommando Hamann und die Ermordung der litauischen Juden* (Frankfurt am Mein: Peter Lang, 1996); Bernhard Chiari, *Alltag hinter der Front. Besatzung, Kollaboration und Widerstand in Weißrussland 1941–1944*, Schriften des Bundesarchivs, BD. 53 (Düsseldorf: Droste Verlag, 1998); Christian Gerlach, *Kalkulierte Morde. Die deutsche*

Wirtschafts- und Vernichtungspolitik in Weißrussland 1941 bis 1944 (Hamburg: Hanburger Edition, 1999); Karel C. Berkhoff, *Harvest of Despair: Life and Death in Ukraine under Nazi Rule* (Cambridge, MA: Belknap Press of Harvard University Press, 2004); Manfred Oldenburg, *Ideologie und militärisches Kalkül. Die Besatzungspolitik der Wehrmacht in der Sowjetunion 1942* (Cologne: Böhlau-Verlag, 2004); Norbert Kunz, *Die Krim unter deutscher Herrschaft (1941–1944): Germanisierungsutopie und Besatzungsrealität*, Veröffentlichungen der Forschungsstelle Ludwigsburg der Universität Stuttgart, Bd. 5 (Darmstadt: Wissenschaftliche Buchgesellschaft, 2005); Dieter Pohl, *Die Herrschaft der Wehrmacht: Deutsche Militärbesatzung und einheimische Bevölkerung in der Sowjetunion 1941–1944* (Munich: Oldenburg, 2008); Sven Jüngerkers, *Deutsche Besatzungsverwaltung in Lettland 1941–1945. Eine Kommunikations- und Kulturgeschichte nationalsozialistischer Organisationen* (Konstanz: UVK, 2010); Leonid Rein, *The Kings and the Pawns: Collaboration in Byelorussia during World War II* (New York: Berghahn Books, 2011); Laurie R Cohen, *Smolensk under the Nazis: Everyday Life in Occupied Russia* (Rochester, NY: University of Rochester Press, 2013).

9. See Nina Tumarkin, *The Living and the Dead: The Rise and Fall of the Cult of World War II in Russia* (New York: Basic Books, 1994); Amir Weiner, *Making Sense of War: The Second World War and the Fate of the Bolshevik Revolution* (Princeton, NJ: Princeton University Press, 2000); Mark Edele, *Soviet Veterans of the Second World War: A Popular Movement in an Authoritarian Society, 1941–1991* (Oxford: Oxford University Press, 2008).

10. I have already explained my views on these subjects elsewhere. See "A Conspiracy to Murder: Explaining the Dynamics of Romanian 'Policy' towards Jews in Transnistria," *Journal of Genocide Research* 19, no. 1 (2017): 1–21; "Hating Soviets— Killing Jews: How Antisemitic Were Local Perpetrators in Southern Ukraine, 1941– 42?" *Kritika: Explorations in Russian and Eurasian History* 15, no. 3 (Fall 2014), 505–533. The best book on the persecution of Jews in Transnistria is Jean Ancel's *Transnistria, 1941–1942: The Romanian Mass Murder Campaigns*, vol. 1: *History and Document Summaries*, trans. Rachel Garfinkel and Karen Gold (Tel Aviv: Goldstein-Goren Research Center, Tel Aviv University, 2003). Volumes 2 and 3 o contain primary documents. A summary of Ancel's argument is available in Jean Ancel, *The History of the Holocaust in Romania*, ed. Leon Volovici and Miriam Caloianu, trans. Yaffah Murciano (Lincoln: University of Nebraska Press, 2011), 315–429.

11. Among the works that focus on the persecution of Jews in individual regions are Dieter Pohl, *Von der "Judenpolitik" zum "Judenmord." Der Distrikt Lublin des Generalgouvernements 1939–1944* (Frankfurt a/Mein: Peter Lang, 1993); Dieter Pohl, *Nationalsozialistische Judenverfolgung in Ostgalizien 1941–1944. Organisation und Durchführung eines staatlichen Massenverbrechens* (Munich: Oldenburg, 1996); Wendy Lower, *Nazi Empire-Building and the Holocaust in Ukraine* (Chapel Hill: University of North Carolina Press, 2005); Anton Weiss-Wendt, *Murder without Hatred: Estonians and the Holocaust* (New York: Syracuse University Press, 2009).

12. On the limited scale of war criminals' prosecution and their often inadequate punishment in communist Romania, see International Commission on the Holocaust in Romania, *Final Report* (Iaşi: POLIROM, 2005, 313–332. On the Soviet prosecution of war criminals, see Tanja Penter, "Collaboration on Trial: New Source Material on Soviet Postwar Trials of Collaborators," *Slavic Review* 64, no. 4 (Winter 2005): 782–790 and Martin Dean, "Where Did All the Collaborators Go?" *Slavic Review* 64, no. 4 (Winter 2005): 791–798.

13. See Diana Dumitru, "An Analysis of Soviet Postwar Investigation and Trial Documents and Their Relevance for Holocaust Studies," in *The Holocaust in the East: Local Perpetrators and Soviet Responses*, ed. Michael David-Fox, Peter Holquist, and Alexander M. Martin (Pittsburgh: University of Pittsburgh Press, 2014), 142–157. See also Martin Dean, "Schutzmannschaften in Ukraine and Belarus: Profiles of Local Police Collaboration," in *Lessons and Legacies: The Holocaust in International Perspective*, ed. Dagmar Herzog (Evanston: Northwestern University Press, 2006), 7:226–229.

14. On the Soviet definition of high treason with respect to collaborators with the enemy during World War II, see Tanja Penter, "Die Lokale Gesellschaft im Donbass unter deutscher Okkupation 1941–1943," in *Kooperation und Verbrechen: Formen der "Kolaboration" im östlichen Europa 1939–1945*, ed. Christoph Dieckmann, Babette Quinkert, Tatjana Tönsmeyer, Beiträge zur Geschichte des Nationalsozialismus Bd. 19 (Hamburg: Wallstein Verlag, 2005), 189–192.

1. Conquering and Delimiting Transnistria

1. Sebastian Balta, *Rumänien und die Großmächte in der Ära Antonescu (1940–1944)* (Stuttgart: Franz Steiner Verlag, 2005), 122–135.

2. Balta, *Rumänien und die Großmächte in der Ära Antonescu*, 60–122.

3. For more on this decision and how it was perceived by the Romanian contemporaries, see Solonari, *Purifying*, 142–149.

4. See relevant documents from the German and Romanian archives in Vasile Arimia, Ion Ardeleanu, and Ştefan Lache, eds., *Antonescu-Hitler: Corespondenţa şi întâlniri inedite (1940–1944)* (Bucharest: Cozia, 1991), 103–114. See also Balta, *Rumänien und die Großmächte in der Ära Antonescu*, 183–203. Mark Axworthy, *Third Axis, Fourth Ally: Romanian Armed Forces in the European War, 1941–1945* (London: Arms and Armour, 1995), 43–49

5. Arimia et al., eds., *Antonescu-Hitler*, 115. Hitler referred to the previous message by Antonescu as containing such assurances but surviving Antonescu's letters to Hitler from this period do not lend themselves to such interpretation. It is possible, however, that the dictators discussed this issue during one of their previous encounters and the minutes were not taken, as was the case with their discussing particularly sensitive issues. (Hildrun Glass discusses evidence of such practice in her recent book at some lengths, see Glass, *Deutschland und die Verfolgung der Juden im rumänischen Machtbereich* [Munich: Oldenburg Verlag, 2014], esp. 41–48 and passim).

6. Arimia et al., eds., *Antonescu-Hitler*, vol. 1, 118.

7. Andreas Hillgruber, ed., *Staatsmänner und Diplomaten bei Hitler: Vertrauliche Aufzeichnungen über Unterredungen mit Vertretern des Auslandes 1939–1941* (Frankfurt am Mein: Bernard & Graefe Verlag für Wehrwesen, 1967), vol. 1, 619–620.

8. According to the Romanian assessment, at the peak of the battle in early October, the Romanian troops numbered 150,000 men. See Emanuel Stănescu, *Odessa: Gustul amar al victoriei (august-octombrie 1941)* (Târgovişte: Cetatea de Scaun, 2016), 56–57.

9. Quoted in Stănescu, *Odessa*, 137; italicized text is underlined in the original note to von Schobert.

10. See Axworthy, *Third Axis, Fourth Ally*, 49–52

11. Quoted in Axworthy, *Third Axis, Fourth Ally*, 52.

12. See Stănescu, *Odessa*, 84–112.

13. More on the relations between German and Romanian military during the battle of Odessa, see in Stănescu, *Odessa*, 133–158.

14. See Stănescu, *Odessa*, 110–111. Dinu C. Giurescu cites slightly different numbers, which do not change the general picture. See Giurescu, *Romania in the Second World War (1939–1945)* (Boulder, CO: East European Monographs, 2000), 145.

15. Ioan Hudiţa, *Jurnal politic 22 iunie 1941–28 februarie 1942*, ed. Dan Berindei (Bucharest: Editura Lucman, 2005), 81. Hudiţa regularly acquainted himself with Jienescu's views via his wife, PNŢ's active sympathizer; General Jienescu was also close to PNŢ. The Romanian top brass were often quite lax about official secrets so that Jienescu's sharing news and opinions with his wife, while she spread them throughout Bucharest, should not be surprising.

16. Stănescu, *Odessa*, 129.

17. Hudiţa, *Jurnal politic 22 iunie 1941–28 februarie 1942*, 84.

18. Hudiţa, *Jurnal politic 22 iunie 1941–28 februarie 1942*, 116.

19. Ion Calafeteanu, ed., *Iuliu Maniu-Ion Antonescu. Opinii şi confruntări politice, 1940–1944*. Cuvânt înainte, îngrijire de ediţie, note şi comentarii de Ion Calafeteanu (Cluj-Napoca: Editura Dacia, 1994), 79.

20. Hudiţa, *Jurnal politic 22 iunie 1941–28 februarie 1942*, 144, September 30, 1941.

21. Balta, *Rumänien und die Großmächte in der Ära Antonescu*, 234–239. Under the German pressure, Romania declared war on the United States on December 12, 1941.

22. Hudiţa, *Jurnal politic 22 iunie 1941–28 februarie 1942*, 255–256. See the entry on Iacobici in Alesandru Duţu, Florica Dobre, and Leonida Loghin, *Armata română în al doilea război mondial (1941–1945): Dicţionar enciclopedic* (Bucharest: Editura enciclopedică, 1999), 241.

23. Hudiţa, *Jurnal politic 22 iunie 1941–28 februarie 1942*, 176ff.

24. The Romanian losses at Stalingrad were between 170,00 and 182,000 dead, missing, and wounded, far surpassing those at Odessa. See Giurescu, *Romania in the Second World War*, 149–150.

25. The term "occupation zone" was not in use at the time in reference to Transnistria. I use it as a generic, not a proper name.

26. Hillgruber, ed., *Staatsmänner und Diplomaten bei Hitler* vol. 1, 591.

27. Herwig Baum, *Varianten des Terrors: ein Vergleich zwischen der deutschen und rumänischen Besatzungsverwaltung in der Sowjetunion 1941–1944* (Berlin: Metropol, 2011), 68–69.

28. Cited after Baum, *Varianten des Terrors*, 69. My account of negotiations over the establishment of Transnistria as a Romanian zone closely follows Baum's detailed and persuasive reconstruction of the events.

29. Baum, *Varianten des Terrors*, 70–71.

30. Arimia et al., eds., *Antonescu-Hitler*, 120. Hitler requested support of the Cavalry Corps, Mechanized Brigade, and Mountain Shooters east of the Dniester.

31. Arimia et al., eds., *Antonescu-Hitler*, 122.

32. Marcel-Dumitru Ciucă and Maria Ignat, eds., *Stenogramele şedinţelor Consiului de Miniştri. Guvernarea Ion Antonescu*, vol. 3 (Bucharest, 1999), 570.

33. Ciucă and Ignat, eds., *Stenogramele*, vol. 3, 632.

34. Hudiţa, *Jurnal politic 22 iunie 1941–28 februarie 1942*, 64.

35. One such leaker was the Minister of National Education and Cults general Rudu R. Rossetti. See Hudiţa, *Jurnal politic 22 iunie 1941–28 februarie 1942*, 64–65.

36. The memorandum was published in Arimia et al., eds., *Antonescu-Hitler,* vol. 1, 75–80.

37. On such rumors, see Hudiţa, *Jurnal politic 22 iunie 1941–28 februarie 1942*, 6–69 (August 1, 1941). During his meeting with Nicolae Lupu on August 27 Ion Antonescu confirmed the validity of such rumors (Hudiţa, *Jurnal politic 22 iunie 1941–28 februarie 1942*, 101).

38. See, for example, Hudiţa, *Jurnal politic 22 iunie 1941–28 fenbruarie 1942*, 64–65.

39. Hudiţa, *Jurnal politic 22 iunie 1941–28 februarie 1942*, 98.

40. Hudiţa, *Jurnal politic 22 iunie 1941–28 februarie 1942*, 101.

41. Hudiţa, *Jurnal politic 22 iunie 1941–28 februarie 1942*, 101.

42. Holly Case, *Between States: The Transylvanian Question and the European Idea during World War II* (Stanford: Stanford University Press, 2009), esp. chap. 2, "Why We Fight," 67–96.

43. Katherine Verdery, *National Ideology under Socialism: Identity and Cultural Politics in Ceausescu's Romania* (Berkeley: University of California Press, 1991). Chapter 1 is devoted to interwar Romania.

44. For a critical overview of the dominant Romanian nationalist historiography and mythology, see Lucian Boia, *History and Myth in Romanian Consciousness* (Budapest: Central European University Press, 2001), esp. 83–128.

45. See Mihai Antonescu's report on Romanian relations with Hungary and Germany in Ciucă and Ignat, eds., *Stenogramele*, vol. 7, 404–430, esp. 413 (June 25, 1942) and Glass, *Deutschland und die Verfolgung der Juden*, 45–46, 149–151.

46. Ciucă and Ignat, eds., *Stenogramele*, vol. 4, 342–343.

47. Ciucă and Ignat, eds., *Stenogramele*, vol. 4, 345. Romanian word *neam* cannot be adequately translated into English. Its overall meaning is close to German *das Volk* and especially to Bulgarian, Serbian, Russian, Ukrainian, and Belorussian *narod*, in that its first meaning is "kin" as in the Slavic *rod*. *Neam* is thus an ethnic nation with a strong connotation of blood kinship of its members. Romanian nationalists prefer to speak of Neamul Româneasc, while Romanian liberals use Naţiunea Română— both are translated as "Romanian nation." The former notion connotes a community from which nonethnic Romanians are excluded, whereas the latter is of a more inclusive or ethnically neutral character.

48. On regional differences in Greater Romania, see Irina Livezeanu, *Cultural Politics in Greater Romania: Regionalism, Nation Building and Ethnic Struggle, 1918–1930* (Ithaca: Cornell University Press, 1995). For more on Maniu, see Apostol Stan, *Iuliu Maniu: nationalism şi democraţie: biografia unui mare român* (Bucharest: Editura Saeculum I.O., 1997). On the political history of Greater Romania, see Keith Hitchins, *Rumania, 1866–1947* (Oxford: Clarendon Press, 1994).

49. According to official Romanian data, in June 1941 there were 140,000 refugees from northern Transylvania in the country. See Ciucă and Ignat, eds., *Stenogramele*, vol. 3, 632, General Eugen Zwiedeneck, under secretary of state for Romanianization, Colonization, and Inventory. Their numbers grew and reached more than 200,000 by December 1943. See Ciucă and Ignat, eds., *Stenogramele*, vol. 9, 606. The government, whose resources were overstretched, could afford but an inadequate support to refugees who, in turn, mistrusted it and protested what they saw as its bad

faith. See angry exchange between Ion Antonescu and Grigore Forțu, general commissar for refugees from Transylvania, in Ciucă and Ignat, eds., *Stenogramele*, vol. 9, 603–623 (December 8, 1943). During this exchange, Ion Antonescu made it clear that he saw these refugees as potentially disloyal.

50. Ciucă and Ignat, eds., *Stenogramele*, vol. 5, 718 and 716–717 (January 23, 1942).

51. Ciucă and Ignat, eds., *Stenogramele*, vol. 5, 490–491 (December 16, 1941).

52. Arimia et el., eds., *Antonescu-Hitler*, vol. 1, 166–178.

53. Ciucă and Ignat, eds., *Stenogramele*, vol. 4, 343 (August 20, 1941).

54. Ciucă and Ignat, eds., *Stenogramele*, vol. 4, 344 (August 10, 1941).

55. Hudiţa, *Jurnal politic 22 iunie 1941–28 februarie 1942*, 184–185.

56. Hudiţa, *Jurnal politic 22 iunie 1941–28 februarie 1942*, 65–188, esp. 188.

57. Hudiţa, *Jurnal politic 22 iunie 1941–28 februarie 1942*, 134 (September 24, 1941).

58. Ciucă and Ignat, eds., *Stenogramele*, vol. 5, 718.

59. Ciucă and Ignat, eds., *Stenogramele*, vol. 5, 490–491 (December 16, 1941).

60. Ciucă and Ignat, eds., *Stenogramele*, vol. 5, 714–717.

61. Ciucă and Ignat, eds., *Stenogramele*, vol. 5, 490 (December 16, 1941).

62. Ciucă and Ignat, eds., *Stenogramele*, vol. 6, 205 (February 26, 1942).

63. This ruling summed up the discussion of the return of property issues. See Ciucă and Ignat, eds., *Stenogramele*, vol. 6, 712–715 (January 23, 1942).

2. Defining Aims and Experiencing the Limits of Occupation

1. Ciucă and Ignat, eds., *Stenogramele*, vol. 6, 297. With respect to Germans, he was indeed correct. Cf. Mark Mazower, *Hitler's Empire: How the Nazis Ruled Europe* (New York: Penguin, 2008), 319.

2. See his pronouncement "really we are Abyssinia of Europe" in Ciucă and Ignat, eds., *Stenogramele*, vol. 1, 149 (October 3, 1940).

3. Ciucă and Ignat, eds., *Stenogramele*, vol. 5, 103.

4. ANRM F. 706 Inventar 1 dosar 632 vol. 1, f. 68.

5. Ciucă and Ignat, eds., *Stenogramele*, vol. 5, 109.

6. On Romania's population on January 1, 1941, see Anton Golopenţia, "Populaţia teritoriilor româneşti desprinse în 1940," in *Anton Golopenţia. Opere complete*, ed. Sanda Golopenţia, Vladimir Trebici, eds., vol. 2: *Statistică, demografie şi geopolitică* (Bucharest: Editura Encclopedică, 2002), 549. On Transnistria population in 1943, see ANRM F. 706 Inventar 1 dosar 518 vol. 1, f. 219, activity report of the Department of Health of the Governor's Office (*guvernământ*) for August 19, 1941–August 1, 1943.

7. Ciucă and Ignat, eds., *Stenogramele*, vol. 5, 491.

8. Vasile Armia, Ion Ardeleanu, and Ştefan Lache, eds., *Antonescu-Hitler: Corespondenţă şi întîlniri inedite (1940–1944)* (Bucharest: Cozia, 1991), vol. 1, 138, 152.

9. See Baum, *Varianten des Terrors*, 76–86 and Ancel, *Transnistria*, 19–20. Ancel indicates October 3 as the date when the final decision was reached but fails to provide the reference to support it.

10. Baum, *Varianten des Terrors*, 75.

11. Two versions of this convention—a copy of a Romanian original and translation from German—are available in Valeriu Florin Dobrinescu, Ion Pătroiu, and Gheorghe Nicolescu, eds., *Relaţii militare româno-germane 1939–1944. Documente*

(Bucharest: Europa nova, 2000), 143. For the German copy of the original, see Ancel, *Documents*, vol. 5, 59–63.

12. See Ancel, *Transnistria*, vol. 1, 20.

13. Ciucă and Ignat, eds., *Stenogramele*, vol. 5, 107–108.

14. On December 10, 1941, Alexianu related to Antonescu that although the Romanians have already requested such transfer, he was unaware of the answer. See DAOO F. 2247 Op. 1 spr. 677, ark. 196–196 USHMM RG-31.004M reel 1. On March 30, the protocol on the transfer of railways to the Romanian administration was read in the meeting of the Liaison Office for the Administration of Bessarabia, Bukovina, and Transnistria, an inter-ministerial body in which representatives of various ministries discussed and "coordinated" the policies toward the provinces. See ANRM F. Inventar 1 dosar 580, f. 132. On March 17, 1942, Alexianu complained to the head of the German Liaison Office in Transnistria, Generalleutnant von Rothkirch und Panthen, that in expectation of the railways transfer into Romanian hands the Germans were preparing to ship locomotives, cars, and other materials to the east of the Buh River, that is in the German zone of occupation and asked to intervene to stop it. See DAOO F. 2242 Op. 1 spr. 1085, ark. 56 USHMM RG-31.004M reel 2.

15. See the *guvernământ*'s Department of Railways Activity Report for August 19, 1941–August 1, 1943, in ANRM F. 706 Inventar 1 dosar 518 vol. 1, f. 353.

16. Ciucă and Ignat, eds., *Stenogramele*, vol. 6, 386, 400.

17. See the activity report of the Romanian Board of the Port of Odessa for the period August 19, 1941–August 1943, in ANRM F. 706 Inventar 1 dosar 518 vol. 1, f. 134.

18. See the activity report of the Romanian Board of the Port of Odessa for the period August 19, 1941–August 1943, in ANRM F. 706 Inventar 1 dosar 518 vol. 1, f. 135.

19. Ciucă and Ignat, eds., *Stenogramele*, vol. 8, 113.

20. Ciucă and Ignat, eds., *Stenogramele*, vol. 8, 112. "Condominium with equal participation" is my translation of Mihai Antonescu's formula "un fel de asociație în participație egală."

21. Ciucă and Ignat, eds., *Stenogramele*, vol. 8, 166, 232.

22. Ciucă and Ignat, eds., *Stenogramele*, vol. 8, 244, 252. On page 252 the officer is identified as "Commodore Oswald" but most likely this is the same person as Commadore Astmann of the port of Odessa. Note-takers of the Council of Ministers meetings frequently misspelled foreign names.

23. Two most important recent books on this topic are Götz Aly, *Hitler's Beneficiaries: Plunder, Racial War, and the Nazi Welfare State*, trans. from German (New York: Metropolitan, 2007) and J Adam Tooze, *Wages of Destruction: The Making and Breaking of the Nazi Economy* (New York: Viking, 2007).

24. On the Eleventh Army regulations in Romanian translation, see AMAN F. Armata a 3-a Inventar # 6776 din 1976 dosar 481, ff. 111–118 USHMM RG-25.003M reel 19 citation is from 113, n.d. For the regulations of the Romanian General Headquarters, see AMAN F. Armata a 3-a Inventar # 6776 din 1976 dosar 509, ff. 175–180, esp. 179 September 6, 1941.

25. See DAOO F. 2242 Op. 1 spr. 1b, no pagination USHMM RG-31.004M reel 1.

26. Baum, *Varianten des Terrors*, 259–261.

27. DAOO F. 2242 Op. 1 spr. 1083, ark. 34 USHMM RG-31.004M reel 2.

28. See esp. DAOO F. 2242 Op. 1 spr. 1083, ark. 18 USHMM RG-31.004M reel 2. Governor Alexianu's response to the complaint of a group of peasants from Tiraspol județ, November 17, 1941.

29. Ciucă and Ignat, eds., *Stenogramele*, vol. 5, 494.

30. Ciucă and Ignat, eds., *Stenogramele*, vol. 5, 503.

31. On Neubacher, see Glass, *Deutschland und die Verfolgung der Juden*, 25–26.

32. Ciucă and Ignat, eds., *Stenogramele*, vol. 7, 78, 82, 84 (May 16, 1942).

33. Ciucă and Ignat, eds., *Stenogramele*, vol. 8, 112 (August 28, 1942).

34. Ciucă and Ignat, eds., *Stenogramele*, vol. 6, 398 (March 27, 1942).

35. Ciucă and Ignat, eds., *Stenogramele*, vol. 8, 112–115; see also 161 (September 16, 1942). Mihai Antonescu probably meant confidential German-Romanian protocol on economic matters of January 17, 1942. See Balta, *Rumänien und die Großmächte*, 266–267.

36. Ciucă and Ignat, eds., *Stenogramele*, vol. 8, 230–232, 252–253 (September 29, 1942). During that meeting, the Germans refused the Romanians' request to sign a treaty of friendship, thus raising Romania's status among Germany's satellites. See German-language transcript of the meeting in *Akten zur detschen auswärtigen Politik 1918–1945* Serie E: 1941–1943, vol. 3 (Göttingen: Vandenhoeck & Ruprecht, 1974), 539–540. German recognition of the Romanian "unquestionable rights" over Transnistria thus might have been a way of sweetening a bitter pill administered to their purported ally.

37. Ciucă and Ignat, eds., *Stenogramele*, vol. 8, 330–331 (October 10, 1942).

38. See Ion Antonescu's and Governor Alexianu's exchange in the Council of Ministers meeting of January 26, 1941 (Ciucă and Ignat, eds., *Stenogramele*, vol. 10, 35).

39. Ciucă and Ignat, eds., *Stenogramele*, vol. 10, 171.

40. Ciucă and Ignat, eds., *Stenogramele*, vol. 10, 171.

41. Arimia et al., eds., *Antonescu-Hitler*, vol. 2, 120–136.

42. More on this shift in German policy, see in Balta, *Rumänien und die Großmächte in der Ära Antonescu*, 330–345; 364–374.

43. Ciucă and Ignat, eds., *Stenogramele*, vol. 10, 186 (March 3, 1944).

44. On discussions in the council of ministers and Ion Antonescu's motivations for replacing Alexianu, see Ciucă and Ignat, eds., *Stenogramele*, vol. 10, 35–63 (January 27, 1944).

45. Ciucă and Ignat, eds., *Stenogramele*, vol. 10, 36.

46. On Ion Antonescu's decree, see in ASRI dosar 40013 vol. 6, f. 440 USHMM RG-25.004M reel 30.

47. See Alexianu's report on this "operation" to Concător, mentioning Potopeanu's commission and instructions he received to that effect from Mihai Antonescu and himself, in ANRM F. 706 Inventar 1, dosar 52, ff. 6–10, n.d.

48. See Potopeanu's order to that effect on in ASRI dosar 40013 vol. 6, f. 339 USHMM RG-25.004M reel 30.

49. See Baum, *Varianten des Terrors*, 131–134.

50. This is a German assessment. See Eric Conrad Steinhart, "Creating Killers: The Nazification of the Black Sea Germans and the Holocaust in Southern Ukraine, 1941–1944" (Ph.D. diss., University of North Carolina Chapel Hill, 2010), 131.

51. DAOO F. F. 2242 Op. 1 spr. 1087/942, ark. 133–160 USHMM RG-31.004M reel 2.

52. In all probability, SK arrived at Transnistria in mid to late September 1941. See correspondence to that effect between the Romanian Ministry of Foreign Affairs, Alexianu, and prefects in Transnistria in DAOO F. 2242 Op. 1 spr. 1081/1942, ark. 10–12, 16 USHMM RG-31.004M reel 2. Steinhart indicated early September 1941. See Steinhart, "Creating Killers," 131.

53. Steinhart, "Creating Killers," 404.
54. Steinhart, "Creating Killers," 36–55, 401–406.
55. Steinhart, "Creating Killers," 130–132.
56. See Steinhart, "Creating Killers," 125–289.
57. Steinhart, "Creating Killers," 62–64;
58. Steinhart, "Creating Killers," 136.
59. DAOO F. 2242 Op. 1 spr. 1081, ark. 28 USHMM RG-31.004M reel 2.
60. DAOO F. 2242 Op. 1 spr. 1081, ark. 30–32 USHMM RG-31.004M reel 2
61. DAOO F. 2242 Op. 1 spr. 1081, ark. 27 USHMM RG-31.004M reel 2.
62. DAOO F. 2242 Op. 1 spr. 1081, ark. 33–35v USHMM RG-31.004M reel 2, September 29, 1041.
63. On Tiraspol judeţ, see DAOO F. 2242 Op. 1 spr. 1081, ark. 47–48 USHMM RG-31.004M reel 2, October 8, 1941, Alexianu to Mihai Antonescu; see also ark. 73 Tiraspol prefect to Alexianu, n.d., probably October 1941.
64. Pretor of Grosulovo raion to Tiraspol judeţ prefect, November 26, 1941, in DAOO F. 2242 Op. 1 spr. 1083, ark. 64 USHMM RG-32.004M reel 2.
65. See the report from a gendarmerie company commandant to a gendarmerie battalion commandant October 1, 1941, the village of Victorovca, judeţ not indicated, in DAOO F. 2242 Op. 1 spr. 1081, ark. 59 USHMM RG-31.004M reel 2.
66. DAOO F. 2242 Op. 1 spr. 1081, ark. 24–25 USHMM RG-31.004M reel 2.
67. Ciucă and Ignat, eds. *Stenogramele*, vol. 5, 114.
68. DAOO F. 2242 Op. 1 spr. 1083, ark. 63 USHMM RG-31.004M reel 2.
69. DAOO F. 2242 Op. 1 spr. 1085, ark. 123 USHMM RG-31.004M reel 2.
70. DAOO F. 2242 Op. 1 spr. 1081, ark. 84 USHMM RG-31.004M reel 2.
71. See Antonescu's letter to Schobert in Valeriu Florin Dobrinescu, Ion Pătroiu, and Gheorghe Nicolescu, eds., *Relaţii militare româno-germane 1939–1944. Documente* (Bucharest: Europa nova, 2000), 143.
72. See the report of Berezovca judeţ prefect to Governor Alexianu, September 29, 1941, in DAOO F. 2242 Op. 1 spr. 1081, ark. 22 and Alexianu's letter to General Headquarters, no date, DAOO F. 2242 Op. 1 spr. 1081, ark. 124–128 USHMM RG-31.004M reel 2.
73. Copies of the Romanian documents are available in DAOO F. F. 2357 Op. 1 spr. 5. Prefectura Olgopol, 1942, no pagination USHMM RG-31.004M reel 15.
74. Ciucă and Ignat, eds., *Stenogramele*, vol. 5, 503.
75. ASRI dosar 38891 vol. 7, ff. 26–29 USHMM RG-25.004M reel 27.
76. DANIC F. IGJ dosar 80/1943, f. 26 USHMM RG-25.010M reel 26.
77. ANRM F. 706 Op. 1 dosar 52, f. 32.
78. ANRM F. 706 Op. 1 dosar 52, f. 32.
79. The province of Bukovina was enlarged in October 1941 by the inclusion of Dorohoi judeţ, part of the historical province of Moldova of the Old Kingdom or *regat*; Dorohoi Jews were also deported and are included in the number cited. On the

calculation of the number of deported Jews, see International Commission on the Holocaust in Romania, *Final Report* (Iaşi: Polirom, 2005), 177.

80. See Ciucă and Ignat, eds., *Stenogramele*, vol. 5, 2 October 6, 1941.

81. See Steinhart, "Creating Killers," 298–299; Baum, *Varianten des Terrors*, 483–485.

82. Dobrinescu, Pătroiu, and Nicolescu, eds., *Relaţii militare româno-germane 1939–1944*, 154.

83. ASRI dosar 40010 vol. 28, f. 7v. USHMM RG-25.004M reel 33.

84. ANRM F. 706 Op. 1 dosar 819, f. 115 Alexianu report to Antonescu, November 1, 1941.

85. DAOO F. 2242 Op. 1 spr. 677, ark. 24–26.

86. On these "solutions," see Jean Ancel, *Transnistria, 1941–1942: The Romanian Mass Murder Campaigns*, vol. 1: *History and Document Summaries*, trans. Rachel Garfinkel and Karen Gold (Tel Aviv: Goldstein-Goren Diaspora Research Center, Tel Aviv University, 2003).

87. See Valdis O. Lumans, *Himmler's Auxiliaries: The Volksdeutsche Mittelstelle and the German National Minorities of Europe, 1933–1945* (Chapel Hill: University of North Carolina Press, 1993), 157–179.

88. See the report on their plight and desire to return, with Ion Antonescu's note in resolution in ANRM F. 706 Op. 1 dosar 10 vol. 1, ff. 81–82 USHMM RG-54.004M reel 2.

89. See the correspondence between various Romanian authorities with the summary of German position and Ion Antonescu's note in resolution in ANRM F. 706 Op. 1 dosar 14 vol. 2, f. 320–386, October 1941–September 1942 USHMM RG-54.004M reel 5 September 1942; Antonescu's note in resolution is on 385.

90. ANRM F. 706 Op. 1 dosar 14 vol. 2, f. 378 USHMM RG-54.004M reel 5, n.d., no signature.

91. ANRM F. 706 Op. 1 dosar 14 vol. 2, ff. 360–361 USHMM RG-54.004M reel 5 unsigned.

92. Ciucă and Ignat, eds., *Stenogramele*, vol. 9, 148.

93. See Ion Antonescu's note in the resolution of February 12, 1943, in ANRM F. 706 Inventar 1 dosar 52, f. 18.

94. See Alexianu's undated report, probably from the spring of 1942, in ANRM F. 706 Inventar 1 dosar 18 vol. 1, f. 114 USHMM RG-54.002M reel 6.

95. See instructions on the establishment of military control, security, and administration in the territory to the east of the Dniester River, the German Eleventh Army, August 1941, in Romanian translation in AMAN F. Armata a 3-a Inventar #S/6776, dosar 481, f. 117 USHMM RG-25.003M reel 19.

96. This follows from the correspondence of the chief of the general headquarters General Alexandru Ioaniţiu, his Deputy General Gheorghe Tătăranu, Minister of National Defense General Iosif Iacobici, and Ion Antonescu from July 6–7 1941, in AMAN F. Marele Cartier General Inventar #019269 file 3828, ff. 131–134 USHMM RG-25.003M reel 5. On August 21, 1941, Ion Antonescu ordered that "All Russian [probably meaning Russian and Ukrainian] POWs will remain in internment." See AMAN F. Marele Cartier General Inventar Nr 019269 dosar 3827, f. 419 USHMM RG-25.003M reel 4.

97. See the address of the Romanian general staff (Marele Stat Major) to the Office of the President of the Council of Ministers (Preşedenţia Consiliului de Miniştri) of

February 7, 1942 concerning German military's protests to that effect in ANRM F. 706 Inventar 1 dosar 12 vol. 1, f. 4 USHMM RG-54.004 reel 3.

98. Transnistria Gendarmerie Inspectorate acknowledged as much in its activity report for March–April 1942, see DANIC F. IGJ dosar 122/1942, f. 264 USHMM RG-25.010M reel 16.

99. See the Second Army Corps' circular of October 30, 1941, in AMAP F. Brigada 1 Fortificații dosar 399, ff. 41–42 USHMM RG-25.003M reel 394.

100. See Dubăsari judeţ Gendarmerie Legion activity report for September 1942, DANIC F. IGJ dosar 147/1942, f. 137 USHMM RG-25.010M reel 20.

101. See ANRM F. 706 Op.' 1 dosar 518 vol. 1, f. 32. The Romanians suspected that many of these released POWs were actually not from Transnistria and thus settled in the region illegally. Such persons were arrested and interned in Romanian concentration camps. See, for example, DANIC F. IGJ dosar 18/1942, f. 57 USHMM RG-25.010M reel 13.

102. DANIC F. IGJ dosar 122/1942, f. 312 USHMM RG-25.010M reel 16.

103. See the Transnistria Gendarmerie Inspectorate situation report for March 1943, signed by Colonel Mihai Iliescu in DANIC F. IGJ 80/1943, ff. 99, 101–102 USHMM RG-25.101M reel 26.

104. See the Odessa Gendarmerie Inspectorate activity report for October 1943, DANIC F. IGJ dosar 84/94,3 f. 149USHMM RG-25.010M reel 27.

105. See AMAN F. Armata a 3-a Inventar N S/6776 dosar 2208, f. 122.

3. Configuring Transnistrian Administration

1. Glass, *Deutschland und die Verfolgung der Juden im rumänischen Machtbereich 1940–1944*, 120–121.

2. Glass, *Deutschland und die Verfolgung der Juden im rumänischen Machtbereich 1940–1944*, 123, 130 and Dietmar Süß, "Steuerung durch Informationen? Joseph Goebbels als 'Kommissar für Heimatfront' und die Reichsinspektion für die zivilen Luftschutz," in *Hitlers Kommissare. Sondergewalten in nationalsozialistischen Diktatur.* Beiträge zur Geschichte des Nationalsozialismus Band 22, ed. Rüdiger Hachtmann and Winfried Süß (Göttingen: Wallstein Verlag, 2006), 191.

3. See a copy of Pflaumer's memorandum to the Governor of Bukovina, Colonel Alexandru Rioşanu, forwarded to Mihai Antonescu, July 15, 1941, in DANIC F. PCM-CM dosar 559/1941, ff. 55–59. Pflaumer's memorandum contains a summary of his proposals.

4. See Glass, *Deutschland und die Verfolgung der Juden im rumänischen Machtbereich 1940–1944*, 124–125. See also Mihai Antonescu's explanation of the rationale and design of the local administration reform in Ciucă and Ignat, eds., *Stenogramele*, vol. 3, 581–595, Council of Ministers meetings of June 17 and 19, 1941.

5. See Mihai Antonescu's explanations in the meeting of the Council of Ministers on July 25, 1941, in Ciucă and Ignat, eds., *Stenogramele*, vol. 4, 204.

6. See the memorandum signed by Paul Sterian, an official at the Ministry of National Economy and poet, and another dignitary, whose name is not decipherable, on an official mission to Bessarabia, in DANIC F. PCM-CM dosar 559/1941, ff. 107–108, July 26, 1941.

7. See Mihai Antonescu, *Reforma administrativă*. De domnul Profesor Mihai Antonescu Vice-Președintele Consiliului de Miniștri (făcută in fața Comisiei pentru reforma administrativă in zilele de 5 și 18 decembrie 1941) (Bucharest: Imprimeria centrală; Monitorul Official și Imprimeriile Statului 1942), citation is from 18.

8. DANIC F. PCM-CM dosar 559/1941, f. 55. Pflaumer forwarded a copy of this memorandum to Ion and Mihai Antonescu.

9. This is according to Ion Antonescu's order as read by General Voculescu on the first administrative conference in Cernăuți, the capital of Bukovina, on July 25, 1941; see DANIC F. PCM-CM dosar 559/1941, f. 122.

10. ASRI dosar 40011 vol. 5, f. 64 USHMM RG-25.004 reel 19.

11. See his order of July 25 in DANIC F. PCM-CM dosar 559/1941, f. 122. See also Law # 790 of September 3, 1941 "Concerning the organization of Bessarabia and Bukovina," in *Monitorul official,* Partea I, # 209 September 4, 1941, 5192–5195.

12. DANIC F. PCM CC dosar 365 (year is not indicated), citation is from 2.

13. See also Ion Antonescu's comment at the Council of Ministers meeting of February 28, 1941: "We have arrived the road the Romanian Nation [*neam*] has to take . . . integral nationalism." In Ciucă and Ignat, *Stenogramele*, vol. 2, 438.

14. Ciucăand Ignat, *Stenogramele*, vol. 5, 7.

15. For more on this, see Solonari, *Purifying the Nation,* 227.

16. See Cuică and Ignat, eds., *Stenogramele*, vol. 4, 56 and 244. Council of Ministers meetings of July 8, 1941 and August 1, 1941, respectively.

17. See Vasile N. Florescu's testimony in ASRI dosar 40011 vol. 5, f. 64 USHMM RG-25.004 reel 19 and Popovici's memoir (*Spovedania,* ed. Th. Wexler (n.p: Fundația Dr. W. Filderman, n.d.), 19, esp. note. In 1969, Popovici was the first Romanian bestowed the title of Righteous among the Nations by Yad Vashem for his role in the salvation of up to 20,000 of Bukovina's Jews from deportation.

18. On the role of German consul, see Solonari, *Purifying the Nation,* 215–216. For Ellgering's report, see Ottmar Trașcă and Dennis Deletant, eds., *Al III-lea Reich și Holocaustul din România 1940–1944. Documente din arhivele germane* (Bucharest: Editura Institutului Național pentru Studierea Holocaustului din România " Elie Wiesel," 2007), 324–330, esp. 325–328 followed by Romanian translation, with useful information in the footnotes, 330–338, esp. 332–336.

19. See Alexianu's declaration during the 1945 trial investigation in ASRI dosar 40010 vol. 45, f. 225 USHMM RG-25.004M reel 34.

20. See Alexianu's declaration in the 1945 pretrial investigations in ASRI dosar 40010 vol. 41, f. 235 USHMM RG-25.004 reel 34. Alexianu mistakenly claimed that Marinescu suggested his candidacy during the Council of Ministers meeting in Tighina. Since this meeting took place on August 27, 1941 (see communique published in Ciucă and Ignat, eds., *Stenogramele*, vol. 4, 449), the conversation should have taken place earlier.

21. See Ion Antonescu's Decree # 1 of August 1941 issued in Tighina in ANRM F. 706 Inventar 1 dosar 556 USHMM RG-54 reel 10.

22. See Alexianu's farewell in DAOO F. 2242 Op. 1 spr. 1083, ark. 58 ASRI dosar 40010 vol. 45, f. 225 USHMM RG-31.004M reel 2.

23. See an information note from Alexianu to CBBT to that effect in ANRM F. 706 Inventar 1 dosar 53, f. 31

24. ASRI dosar 40010 vol. 45, f. 225 USHMM RG-25.004M reel 34.

25. DAOO F. 2242 Op. 1 spr. 677, ark. 18–19a USHMM RG-31.004 reel 1 [in German in the original].

26. ASRI dosar 40010 vol. 45, f. 235 USHMM RG-25.004M reel 34.

27. In the memorandum of October 17, 1941, Ellgering complained that the extension of Romanian laws—which he believed were too numerous and complicated to serve as a basis for meaningful management of local and provincial affairs—over reconquered Bessarabia and northern Bukovina would have the effect of nullifying provincial autonomy as provided for by the law of September 3, 1941. See Traşcă and Deletant, eds., *Al III-lea Reich şi Holocaustul în România*, 331.

28. Ciucă and Ignat, eds. *Stenogramele*, vol. 5, 110–111.

29. A copy of the statute, undated and unsigned, is available in ANRM F. 706 Inventar 1 dosar 556, ff. 89–90. See Mihai Antonescu's instruction on the creation of the CBBT in Cuică and Ignat, eds., *Stenogramele*, vol. 4, 202–203.

30. ANRM F. 706 Inventar 1 dosar 556, ff. 89–90. The Law of September 3, 1941, is available in *Monitorul oficial* Partea I, # 209 September 4, 1941, 5192–5195.

31. Ciucă and Ignat, *Stenogramele*, vol. 6, 439–458.

32. Ciucă and Ignat. *Stenogramele*, vol. 8, 202.

33. This fact follows from the debates in the council of ministers, see Ciucă and Ignat. *Stenogramele*, vol. 8, 197–203.

34. See ANRM F. 706 Inventar 1 dosar 1123, ff. 283–294 USHMM RG-54.004 reel 17.

35. *Guvernământe* existed until the very end of Antonescu regime overthrown by the coup d'état on August 23, 1944. In June 1944 an unsigned memorandum proposed transformation of the Council of Coordination into the committee on the transfer of *guvernămâint*'s prerogatives to the ministries. (See ANRM F. 776 Inventar 1 dosar 556, ff. 91–95.) As late as August 3, 1944 this committee still debated the transfer. See ARM F. 706 Inventar 1 dosar 594, ff. 141–155.

36. The dismissal was announced in Romanian press on April 12, 1943. See Ioan Hudiţa, *Jurnal politic 1 februarie 1943–31 decembrie 1943*, ed. Dan Berindei (Bucharest: Comunicare.ro, 2010), 149. They were replaced by generals Olimpiu Stavrat and Alexandru Dragalina, respectively.

37. See Ion Antonescu's angry accusations of Voiculescu and Calotescu at the Council of Ministers meeting of May 13, 1942.

38. ANRM F. 706 Inventar 1 dosar 52, f. 105.

39. Ciucă and Ignat, eds., *Stenogramele*, vol. 9, 159.

40. That the Conducător was indeed alarmed by Neagu's (erroneous) accusations that Transnistria had become a burden on Romania's budget and economy follows from the the the note he added to Alexianu's report on the Transnistrian budget showing substantial surpluses (in fact, payments to the national budget and economy): "These numbers seem to be far-fetched. The Secretariat will investigate and show whether this is a real contribution. Mr. Minister [of Finance Alexandru] Neagu affirmed to me today that Transnistria is a burden on us. It would be tragic. Transnistria has to help the national economy and budget. If it is a burden on us, we will renounce its exploitation" (ANRM F. 706 Inventar 1 dosar 52, f. 105).

41. Ciucă and Ignat, eds., *Stenogramele*, vol. 9, 157–158.

42. Ciucă and Ignat, eds., *Stenogramele*, vol. 9, 156.

43. Ciucă and Ignat, eds., *Stenogramele*, vol. 9, 161–162.

44. ANRM F. 706 Inventar 1 dosar 52, f. 84.

45. ANRM F. 706 Inventar 1 dosar 837, f. 69. For the commission's report, see ANRM F. 706 Inventar 1 dosar 837, ff. 99–116.

46. On June 21, the chief of the Transnistria Gendarmerie Inspectorate colonel Mihai Iliescu reported that "the population of Odessa comments with great enthusiasm Marshal Ion Antonescu's visit to the city" (ANRM F. 706 Inventar 1 dosar 59, f. 252).

47. ANRM F. 706 Inventar 1 dosar 52, f. 110, July 2, 1943.

48. Ciucă and Ignat, eds., *Stenogramele*, vol. 9, 259.

49. Nichita Smochină, *Memorii*, ed. Ediție îngrijită de Gorin-Colini Vlad (Bucharest: Editura Academiei Române, 2009), 526.

50. DAOO F. 2359 Op. 1 spr. 9 ark. 28–31.

51. ANRM F. 706 Inventar 1 dosar 10 vol. 2, ff. 309–311 USHMM RG-54.004 (?) reel 2.

52. ANRM F. 706 Inventar 1 dosar 18 vol. 1, ff. 17–24 USHMM RG-54.004 reel 6.

53. QANRM F. 706 Inventar 1 dosar 16 vol. 1, f. 12. Denunciation which provoked this response was received by the CBBT in April 1942, see ANRM F. 706 Inventar 1 dosar 16 vol. 1, f. 14.

54. ANRM F. 706 Inventar 1 dosar 52, f. 9.

55. ANRM F. 706 Inventar 1 dosar 837, ff. 40–42.

56. *Monitorul oficial*, N 135 (13 iunie 1942), 4924 (art. 2, pt. a).

57. In 1946, she was charged and convicted of embezzlement when serving as Maria Antonescu's deputy. She managed to obtain commutation of her prison sentence to forced domicile at her own villa in the village of Ciucea, due to her friendship with the communist prime-minister Petru Groza. See Mircea Goga, *Veturia Goga, "Privighetoarea lui Hitler"* (Bucharest: RAO, 2007), 283. Mircea Goga, the grandson of Octavian Goga's cousin, claims in this book that Veturia spied for various intelligence services, including the Nazi SD and communist Securitate.

58. See his response to the report of the deplorable state in which the grain mill "România Mare" (Greater Romania), a previous Jewish property, was at the end of 1942, after "expropriation" by the Legionaries at the time of the National Legionary State and subsequent mismanagement by an ethnic Romanian leaser: "Had the mill been transferred to the administration of the Council of Patronage, the proceeds would have been channeled to soup kitchens and to the assistance to the poor. The mill would have been a model [institution], such as 'Victoria' restaurant and all other institutions financed by [the Council]." Ion Antonescu, *Secretele guvernări. Rezoluții ale conducătorului statului (septembrie 1940–august 1941)*, ed. Vasile Arima (Bucharest: Editura "Românul," 1992), 155. This note is dated December 2, 1942.

59. I borrow the term "deserving poor" from Sheila Fitzpatrick, *Everyday Stalinism: Ordinary Life in Extraordinary Times: Soviet Russia in the 1930s* (New York: Oxford University Press, 1999), 227.

60. ANRM F. 706 Inventar 1 dosar 52, f. 107.

61. ANRM F. 706 Inventar 1 dosar 52, ff. 125–126.

62. ANRM F. 706 Inventar 1 dosar 52, ff. 499, 507–508 (emphasis added).

63. Baum, *Varianten des Terrors*, 135–146, esp. 142–145.

64. Baum dates Pflaumer's departure to Germany to the summer of 1941 while in reality he was recalled in March 1942 (see Baum, *Varianten des Terrors*, 145 and

Glass, *Deutschland und die Verfolgung der Juden im rumänischen Machtbereich 1940–1944,* 121) and in the fall of 1941, he advised Alexianu on the design of the provincial administration in Transnistria.

65. Perhaps the Warthegau (mostly upper Silesia) ruled by "model Nazi" Arthur Greiser, as Catherine Epstein has aptly dubbed him, presents the most (in)famous case of a provincial autonomy dependent on the fortune of its governor. See Catherine Epstein, *Model Nazi: Arthur Greiser and the Occupation of Western Poland* (Oxford: Oxford University Press, 2012).

4. Ruling Transnistria

1. See this decree in ANRM F. 706 Inventar 1 dosar 556, f. 84.

2. See activity reports of various departments of the *guvernământ* in ANRM F. 706 dosar 518 vol. 1. See also Baum, *Varianten des Terrors,* 86.

3. Baum, *Varianten des Terrors,* 85.

4. Baum, *Varianten des Terrors,* 86.

5. In Romania, the title of engineer was conferred by professional associations and carried some social weight.

6. See Ordinance # 8, September 12, 1941, in DAOO F. 2242 Op. 1 spr. 1, f. 9v. USHMM RG-31.004M reel 1.

7. See Alexianu's address to the CBBT concerning mobilization of civil servants from Romania for the work in Transnistria, February 17, 1942, in DAOO F. 2242 Op. 4c spr. 3 USHMM RG-31.004M reel 1. See also *guvernământ*'s note "Realizări Românești în Transnistria," dated March 3, 1943, unsigned, in ANRM F. 706 Op. dosar 53, 39.

8. This ordinance cited eleven departments and nine sections. See DAOO F. 2242 Op. 1 spr. 1, ark. 9–9v. USHMM RG-31.004M reel 1.

9. DAOO F. 2242 Op. 1 spr. 1, ark. 9v. USHMM RG-31.004M reel 1.

10. DAOO F. 2242 Op. 1 spr. 1, ark. 9v. USHMM RG-31.004M reel 1.

11. See Odessa mayor's office activity report, August 19, 1941–August 1, 1943, in ANRM F. 706 Inventar 1 dosar 518 vol. 1, f. 242.

12. For biographical data on Alexianu, see in Şerban Alexianu, "Gheorghe Alexianu" in *Trecutul la judecata istoriei: Mareşalul Antonescu—pro şi contra,* ed. Gheorghe Buzatu. Colecţia "Românii în sitoria universală / The Romanians in World History" vol. 117 (Bucharest: Editura "Mica Valahie," 2006), 245–260.

13. For the law-decree content, see Ioan Scurtu, ed., *Ideologie şi formaţiuni de dreapta în România 7 iulie 1943–30 martie 1938.* Vol. 4 (Bucharest: Institutul naţional pentru studiul totalitarismului, 2003), 394–398. For its effect, see International Commission on the Holocaust in Romania, *Final Report* (Iaşi: Polirom, 2005), 41. On Alexianu's excess of zeal in implementing this law-decree (he supposedly put pressure on Jews stripped of their citizenship to dispose of their properties in fourteen days), see Ştefan Borcea, "Gheorghe Alexianu, un personaj atât de puternic, pe cât de controversat în istorie," *Adevărul,* April 30, 2013, http://adevarul.ro/locale/focsani/foto-gheorghe-alexianu-personaj-puternic-atat-controversat-istorie-1_51714e18053c7dd83f261eda/index.html.

14. Şerban Alexianu, "Gheorghe Alexianu," 249.

15. Ion Constantin, *Gherman Pântea între mit și realitate*. Cuvând inainte de Mircea Druc (Bucharest: Editura Biblioteca Bucureștilor, 2010), 75–76.

16. Constantin, *Gherman Pântea*, 86–88.

17. Constantin, *Gherman Pântea*, 95–96.

18. See the inspector general's letter to Alexianu suggesting a list of officers to be appointed as prefects, January 12, 1942, in DAOO F. 2242 Op. 1 spr. 331, ark. 41–42.

19. DAOO F. 2242 Op. 1 spr. 1, ark. 9–10 USHMM RG-31.004M reel 1.

20. The text of decree is available in ANRM F. 706 Inventar 1 dosar 556, f. 84, art. 5.

21. See ANRM F. 706 Inventar 1 dosar 26 vol. 2, f. 280. See also the activity report of the financial directorate of *guvernământ*, August 19, 1941–August 1, 1943, in ANRM F. 706 Inventar 1 dosar 518 vol. 1, f. 42.

22. See the activity report of the *guvernământ* directorate of food industries, acquisitions, and provisioning, August 19, 1941–August 1, 1943, in ANRM F. 706 Inventar 1 dosar 518 vol. 1, f. 163.

23. Those canteens are mentioned in the activity report for August 13, 1941–August 1, 1943 of the *guvernământ* directorate of the fishing industry in ANRM F. 706 Inventar 1 dosar 518 vol. 1, f. 169.

24. See the activity report of the directorate of labor for August 13, 1941–August 1, 1943, in ANRM F. 706 Inventar 1 dosar 518 vol. 1, f. 212.

25. See the activity report of the *guvernământ* directorate of the villas, parks, and gardens for August 19, 1941–August 1, 1943, in ANRM F. 706 Inventar 1 dosar 518 vol. 1, f. 279.

26. See Alexianu's request and Antonescu's order to that effect in ANRM F. 706 Op. 1 dosar 61, f. 79. In February 1943, Ion Antonescu repeated the same order in ANRM F. 706 Op. 1 dosar 61, f. 7.

27. For the summary of Alexianu's proposal, see in ANRM F. 706 Op. 1 dosar 2, f. 79.

28. In May 1942, Alexianu requested the decoration of civil servants *detașați* in Transnistria with a medal "Crusade against Communism" (see ANRM F. 706 Op. 1 dosar 18 vol. 2, f. 443 USHMM RG-54.004 reel 7). In November of the same year Ion Antonescu approved (or renewed) this request for decoration (see ANRM F. 706 Op. 1 dosar 54, f. 87). In September 1942, Ion Antonescu turned down Alexianu's initiative to honor high-ranking Transnistrian civil servants "who via their devotion and service raised the province," with double-size monthly salary in RKKS (see ANRM F. 706 Op. 1 dosar 26, ff. 166–167).

29. See a petition from a retired colonel from Bessarabia expressing such sentiments, 1942, in ANRM F. 706 Op. 1 dosar 18 vol. 1, f. 68 USHMM RG-54.004M reel 5.

30. See ANRM F. 706 Op. 1 dosar 52, f. 119.

31. DAOO F. 2242 Op. 1 spr. 677, ark. 22–23v. USHMM RG-31.004M reel 1.

32. DAOO F. 2242 Op. 1 spr. 331, ark. 41–42 (January 12, 1942).

33. DAOO F. 2242 Op. 1 spr. 331, ark. 42a.

34. See Alexianu's activity report of September 23, 1941, in DAOO F. 2242 Op. 1 spr. 677, ark. 24v. USHMM RG-31.004 reel 1. Alexianu referred to these appointees as *notars*.

35. Pavel Moraru, *România și bătălia informațiilor între Prut și Nistru (1940–1944)* (Bucharest: Editura militară, 2011), 188.

36. I was not able to find the criteria for appointment of subprefects, except that two of them are identified in their investigation files as lawyers, and more specifically, Aristide Pădure (*județul* Golta), as *avocat* (see ASRI dosar 40011 vol. 6, f. 111 USHMM RG-25.004M reel 19), and Alexandru Moisev (județul Moghilău) as *licențiat în drept* and employee in the Ministry of National Economy *detașat* in Transnistria (DAOO F. 2242 spr. 1514, ark. 51 USHMM RG-31.004M reel 5).

37. For Alexianu's complaint see DAOO F. 2242 Op. 1 spr. 677, ark. 24 USHMM RG-31.004M reel 1.

38. ANRM F. 706 Op. 1 dosar 53, f. 339.

39. DAOO F. 22442 Op. 4 spr. 4, ark. 153–154.

40. DAOO F. 2242 Op. 1 spr. 329, ark. 10–11.

41. See DAOO F. 2242 Op. 1 spr. 316; F. 2242 Op. 1 spr. 329; F. 2242 Op. 1 spr. 331; F. 2242 Op. 1 spr. 361; F. 2242 Op. 4 spr. 4 passim.

42. DAOO F. 2242 op. 1 spr. 331, ark. 73. The only qualification Alexianu added was that a forester's candidacy was to be approved by his forestry department.

43. DAOO F. 2242 Op. 1 spr. 316, ark. 110.

44. DAOO F. 2242 op. 1 spr. 109, January 14, 1942.

45. DAOO F. 2242 op. 1 spr. 157–159, no date provided, signature illegible.

46. DAOO F. 2242 Op. 4 spr. 4, ark. 87–90.

47. ASRI dosar 40011 vol. 20, ff. 152–157 USHMM RG-25.004M reel 21.

48. ASRI dosar 40011 vol. 20 f. 169v. The text is partially illegible. USHMM RG-25.004M reel 21.

49. ANRM F. 706 Op. 1 dosar 58, ff. 181–201

50. Cited in Pavel Moraru, *România și bătălia informațiilor între Prut și Bug (1940–1944)* (Bucharest: Editura militară, 2011), 194.

51. ANRM F. 706 Inventar 1 dosar 8 vol. 2, ff. 455–456.

52. DAOO F. 2242 Op. 1 spr. 1, ark. 186–187 USHMM RG-31.004M reel 1.

53. ANRM F. 706 Inventar 1 dosar 518 vol. 1 ff. 150,–151, activity report of the department of domestic commerce for August 17, 1941–August 1, 1943.

54. ANRM F. 706 Inventar 1 dosar 52, f. 9. CBBT summary of this case, with Ion Antonescu's order.

55. See Transnitrian General Inspectorate of Gendarmerie report for March 1943 in DANIC F. IGJ dosar 80/1943, f. 90 USHMM RG-25.101M reel 26. See also Odessa Inspectorate of Gendarmerie report for October 1943, in DANIC IGJ dosar 84/1943, f. 142 USHMM RG-25.010M reel 27.

56. Alexander Werth, *Russia at War, 1941–1945* (New York: E.P. Dutton, 1964), 818.

57. Werth, *Russia at War,* 820.

58. Werth, *Russia at War,* 820.

59. GARF F. P-7021 Op. 69 delo 343, l. 25v. YV JM-19.969.

60. Cited in Pavel Moraru, *România și bătălia informațiilor între Prut și Bug (1940–1944)* (Bucharest: Editura militară, 2011), 193.

61. See the 1946 deposition of Nicoale Dumitrescu, former chief of the Tiraspol police who ordered the investigation of the case and court-martialing of the accused in ASRI dosar 40011 vol. 20, ff. 138–140v. USHMM RG-25.004M reel 21.

62. See Pădure's deposition in ASRI dosar 40010 vol. 20, f. 67 USHMM RG-21.004M reel 21.

63. See Alexianu's deposition in ASRI dosar 40010 vol. 45, f. 243 USHMM RG-25.004M reel 34.

64. See Ion Antonescu's marginal note on Alexianu's report on the increased number of unauthorized persons from Romania showing up in Transnistria: "Unverified but increasingly numerous reports indicate the Odessa's mayor's office as the nest of illegal commercial activity." ANRM F. 706 Op. 1 dosar 52, f. 78, August 1942.

65. See ASRI dosar 21401 vol. 2, ff. 254–254v. USHMM RG-25.004M reel 30.

66. ASRI dosar 40010 vol. 45, ff. 227–228 USHMM RG-25.004M reel 34.

67. DAOO F. 2242 F. 2242 Op. 4c spr. 5, ark. 1–2 USHMM RG-31.004M reel 1 (report on the organization of gendarmerie in Transnistria, signed Gendarmerie Inspector M. Petala) and ASRI dosar 38881 vol. 3, ff. 97–97v, 99 USHMM RG-25.004M reel 27 (information note prepared for the People's Tribunal by the staff of the General Inspectorate of Gendarmerie, October 1946).

68. DAOO F. 2242 Op. 4c spr. 5, ark. 1–2 USHMM RG-31.004M reel 1.

69. ASRI dosar 39181 vol. 3, ff. 152–159 USHMM RG-25.004M reel 26.

70. See, for example, Ananiev legion commander activity report for March 1942, DANIC F. IGJ dosar 18/1942, f. 53 USHMM RG-25.10M reel 13.

71. ANRM F. 706 Op. 1 dosar 540, ff. 6–7, *guvernământ* activity report for October–December 1943.

72. DANIC F. IGJ dosar 199/1042, ff. 173–175 USHMM RG-25.010M reel 22.

73. DANIC F. IGJ dosar 199/1942, ff. 167–169 USHMM RG-25.010M reel 22. Response to the accusation of the Corps of Border Guards that gendarmerie failed in their duty to provide sufficient oversight over concentration camps of Jews.

74. See the activity report of the *guvernământ* for October–December 1943 in ANRM F. 706 Inventar 1 dosar 540, ff. 6–7.

75. See Alexianu's Ordinance # 8, September 12, 1941, and #27 November 24, 1941, in DAOO F. 2242 Op. 1 spr. 1, ark. 9–10 and 33–34 USHMM RG-31.004M reel 1.

76. See a note signed by a police subinspector (name illegible) in DAOO F. 2242 Op. 4c spr. 5/1941, ark. 8.

77. See the request for such subordination from Odessa police chief, Amy 1942, in DAOO F. 2351 Op. 1s spr. 1, ark. 31–31v. USHMM RG-31.004M reel 20.

78. See the reference signed by the chief of such bureau in DAOO F. 2242 Op. 4 spr. 36, ark. 10.

79. See gendarmerie inspector colonel M. Petala report on the establishment of gendarmerie service in Transnistria, December 3, 1941, in DAOO F. 2242 Op. 4c spr. 5/1941, ark. 1–7 USHMM RG-31.004M reel 1.

80. See Vasiliu's letter to the Transnistrian Inspectorate reminding of the rules of camouflage, which supposedly were not strictly followed in DANIC F. IGJ dosar 199/1942, ff. 135–136 USHMM RG-25.010M reel 22.

81. See Golta Legion information report dated March 6, 1942, in DANIC F. IGJ dosar 122/1942, f. 314 USHMM RG-25.101M reel 16.

82. See Pavel Moraru, *Serviciile secrete și Basarabia: 1918–1950: Dicționar* (Bucharest: Editura militară, 2008), 257–261 and Ioan Eșan, *Maeștrii culiselor secrete: file din istria spionajului* (Bucharest: Logos, n.d.,), 120–128.

83. Imprisoned and awaiting trial on charges of abuse of power, he was assassinated, together with other political prisoners by the Legionaries, who considered them their sworn enemies, on November 26, 1940. For more on Moruzov, see Pavel Moraru, *România și bătălia informațiilor între Prut și Bug (1940–1944)* (Bucharest: Editura militară, 2011), 47–50.

84. See Moraru, *România și bătălia informațiilor între Prut și Bug*, 154–160.

85. See Pavel Moraru, *România și bătălia informațiilor între Prut și Bug*, 160–246.

86. See V. Pantilimonescu, ed., *Codul justiției miltare "Regele Mihai I"* (cu ultimele modificări). Legislație, trimiteri și modificări (Bucharest: Editira ziarului "Universul," 1941).

87. Ordinance #37 is available in DAOO F. 2242 Op. 1 spr. 1, ark. 49–50 USHMM RG-31.004 reel 1. I was unable to find Ordinance #10, but detailed instructions on its application signed by the head of the division of justice and administrative litigation of military administration of the territory between the Dniester and Buh rivers (successor to *guvernământ*) can be found in DAOO F. 2242 Op. 1 spr. 1569, ark. 624–627 USHMM RG-31.004M reel 6.

88. This ordinance is available in DAOO F. 2242 Op. 1 spr. 1a, no pagination. Instructions in the application of Ordinance #10/944 referred to in the previous note (DAOO F. 2242 Op. 1 spr. 1569, ark. 624–627 USHMM RG-31.004M reel 6) contain an informative discussion of legal difficulties arising from these provisions.

89. DAOO F. 2242 Op. 3 spr. 4, ark. 19v–20 (pagination inconsistent) USHMM RG-31.004M reel 7. On October 8, 1941, Alexianu demanded his newly created *direcții* "to collect all documentary materials regarding the Soviet laws and regulations." These materials had to be studied in order "to make our rule in these territories as close to the local traditions, social organization, and legislative system as possible." DAOO F. 2242 Op. 2 spr. 76, ark. 3 USHMM RG-31.004M reel 7.

90. Ciucă and Ignat, eds., *Stenogramele*, vol. 5, 712–715.

91. GARF F. P-7021 Op. 69 delo 343, ll. 17–22v. YV JM 19.969. Brodskii was of Jewish ethnic origin but practiced Christian Orthodox religion. It was because of this that Brodskii, although imprisoned for several months as an undisclosed Jew—a capital offence in occupied Odessa—was able to obtain release and continue to practice under the Romanian law. This account comes from his deposition with ChGK. For more on Brodskii, see his son's memoirs, Mikhail Brodskii, *Mama, nas ne ub'iut . . . Vospominaniia*, http://bookscafe.net/read/brodskiy_mihail-mama_nas_ne_ubyut_vospominaniya-239121.html#p1.

92. GARF F. P-7021 Op. 69 delo 343, ll. 24–24v. YV JM 19.969.

93. GARF F. P-7021 Op. 69 delo 343, ll. 18v.–20 YV JM 19.969.

94. Alexandr Nikolaevich Lebedinskii, identified in a ChGK file as "a scientist," asserted that Ionescu arrested him because a group of unidentified "Ukrainian nationalists" paid him a bribe for this arrest; half of it Ionescu had to transfer to his boss, prosecutor Soltan. GARF F. P-7021 Op. 69 delo 434, l. 1ob YV JM 19.971.

95. See GARF F. P-7021 Op. 69 delo 343, l. 21 YV JM 19.969 for Brodskii's testimony. Practically all members of the Soviet resistance "processed" by the SSI or siguranța mention torture in their recollections.

96. For example, Vladimir Il'ich Trofimovskii, who was the editor of an underground pro-Soviet bulletin in Odessa, mentioned such fact in his autobiography

submitted to the Odessa obkom in 1967. See DAOO F. 92 Op. 1 spr. 18, ark. 25. Another member of resistance, Pantelei Nikolaevich Kozyrev, mentions another similar episode (see the transcript of his interview in DAOO F. 92 Op. 1 spr. 135, ark. 9–10).

97. See the transcript of his interrogation in DAOO F. 92 Op. 1, ark. 10–11.

98. TsDAHOU F. 1 Op. 22 spr. 450, ark. 30.

99. See Zoltan's 1949 deposition in ASRI dosar 38891 vol. 4, f. 205–205v. USHMM RG-25.004M reel 27.

100. ASRI dosar 38891 vol. 4, f. 323–323v. USHMM RG-25.004M reel 27.

101. Ion Lissievici, "Amintirile unui fost lucrător în serviciul de informații al statu-lui," in *Glorie și tragedii. Momente din storia Serviciilor de informații și contrainformații pe Frontul de Est (1941–1944)*, ed. Cristian Troncotă (Bucharest: Nemira, 2003), 158–159.

102. See the summary of the Soviet investigation in TsDAHOU F. 1 op. 22 spr. 472. Romanians investigated the gendarmes who perpetrated this crime in 1955. Some materials from this investigative file were then transferred to the archive of the Mykalev oblast of Ukraine; they are summarized in Mykola Mykolaiovych Shyt-iuk, "Pidpil'na organizatsiia 'Partizans'ka iskra' v svitli novykh istorychnykh dzherel i dokumentiv," in *Mykolaïvshchyna v roky Velykoï Vitchyznianoï viiny: 1941–1944: do 60-richchia vyzvolennia oblasti vid nimets'ko-rumuns'kykh okupantiv*, ed. O M Harkusha, ed. (Mykolaiv: [Vyd-vo ta drukarnia "Kvit"], 2004), 92–102.

103. According to the postwar trial deposition of Plutonier Nicolae Melinescu, who in December 1941–January 1942 was șef de post (chief of the gendarmerie post) in Bogdanovca sector, a site of a monstrous massacre of Jews (around 50,000) in the fall of 1942, pretor Vasile Mânescu and some other local officials and gendarmes were investigated and tried by the Tiraspol Martial Court "for massacring the Jews in Bogdanovca." Melinescu testified that the chairman of the court, colonel Constan-tin, "adjoined the meeting saying that this affair is an old way and that martial court has been aware of it." Melinescu undoubtedly meant that Constantin closed the case and refused to follow on the available evidence. See Melinescu's deposition in ASRI dosar 40011 vol. 20, f. 54. USHMM RG-25.004M reel 21.

104. See his bill of indictment and sentence in ASRI dosar 40013 vol. 6, ff. 72–73 (USHMM RG-25.004M Reel 29) and f. 335 (USHMM RG-25.004M reel 30), respectively.

105. See his defense in ASRI vol. 40013 vol. 4, ff. 284–287 USHMM RG-25.004M reel 29.

106. See Gotz Aly, *Hitler's Beneficiaries: Plunder, Racial War, and the Nazi Welfare State* (New York: Metropolitan, 2005).

5. Making Transnistria "Romanian"

1. Ernest Gellner, *Nationalism* (New York: New York University Press, 1997), 3–4.

2. I more fully developed my interpretation of the evolution of the official Romanian definition of the nation from one based more on citizenship to one based more on ethnicity during the 1930s–early 1940s in Vladimir Solonari, *Purifying the Nation: Population Exchange and Ethnic Cleansing in Nazi-Allied Romania* (Washington, DC: Woodrow Wilson Center Press with Johns Hopkins University Press, 2010), pt. 1, 7–114. See also Vladimir Solonari, "In the Shadow of Ethnic Nationalism:

Racial Science in Romania," in *Racial Science in Hitler's New Europe, 1939–1945*, ed. Rory Yeomans and Anton Weiss-Wendt (Lincoln: Nebraska University Press, 2013), 259–286.

3. Edward W. Said, *Orientalism* (New York: Pantheon Books, 1978), esp. 16–19. Said defined Orientalism as "a Western style for dominating, restructuring, and having authority over the Orient" (3).

4. See in particular Larry Wolff, *Inventing Eastern Europe: The Map of Civilization in the Mind of the Enlightenment* (Stanford: Stanford University Press, 1994).

5. Vejas Gabriel Liulevicius, *The German Myth of the East: 1800 to the Present* (Oxford: Oxford University Press, 2009), 1–10.

6. One of the important books on Russian orientalism is David Schimmelpenninck van der Oye, *Russian Orientalism: Asia in the Russian Mind from Peter the Great to the Emigration* (New Haven: Yale University Press, 2010).

7. This issue has only recently become the object of scholarly attention. Andrei Cușco discusses it with great sensitivity in *A Contested Borderland: Competing Russian and Romanian Visions of Bessarabia in the Late Nineteenth and Early Twentieth Century* (Budapest: Central European University Press, 2017).

8. Ciucă and Ignat, *Stenogramele*, vol. 6, 205.

9. Among recent studies of the ethnic cleansing as a technique of nation-building in modern Europe, the book by Philipp Ther stands out by the forcefulness and clarity of its argument: Ther, *The Dark Side of Nation States: Ethnic Cleansing in Modern Europe,* trans. from the German by Charlotte Kreutzmüller (New York: Berghahn Books, 2014).

10. The Romanians acquired northern Dobrogea (Bulgarian Dobrudža) following the war with the Ottoman Empire, in which they fought alongside Russia in 1877–1878. The southern part of the same region was annexed by Romania in 1913, at the end of the Second Balkan War, in which it fought against Bulgaria alongside Serbia, Greece, and the Ottoman Empire. It lost it in 1916 and regained it in 1918, only to lose it again in 1940, this time definitively, to Bulgaria. Throughout this period, Romania pursued a policy of Romanianization of both northern Dobrogea and southern Dobrogea. Following the Treaty of Craiova of September 6, 1941, which transferred southern Dobrogea to Bulgaria, the Romanians expelled 63,000 ethnic Bulgarians from northern Dobrogea and accepted 109,000 ethnic Romanians, expelled from southern Dobrogea. As the result of these developments, northern Dobrogea, where ethnic Romanians initially comprised but a small minority, became a "pure" ethnic Romanian territory. See Constantin Iordachi, *Citizenship, Nation- and State-Building: The Integration of Northern Dobrogea into Romania, 1940–1944.* Carl Beck Papers in Russian and East European Studies (Pittsburgh: University of Pittsburgh Press, 2002) and Solonari, *Purifying the Nation*, 95–114.

11. I developed my understanding of these aspects of the Romanian wartime policy in *Purifying the Nation*, see esp. pts. 1 and 2.

12. Dorel Bancoș, *Social și național în politica guvernului Ion Antonescu* (Bucharest: Editura Eminescu, 2000), 108–112.

13. See Solonari, *Purifying the Nation*, 256–263, 318–330.

14. See Solonari, *Purifying the Nation*, 1–3 and Vorel Achim, "Proiectul guvernului de la București privind schimbul de populație româno-ruso-ucrainean (1943)," *Revista istorică* 11, no. 9 (2000): 395–421; Achim, "The Romanian Population Exchange Project Elaborated by Sabin Manuilă in October 1941," *Annali dell'Instituto storico*

italo-germanico in Trento 27 (2001): 593–617; "Schimbul de populaţie în viziunea lui Sabin Manuilă," *Revista istorică* 13, no. 5–6 (2002), 133–150.

15. Ciucă and Ignat, eds., *Stenogramele*, vol. 5, 131.

16. Ciucă and Ignat, eds., *Stenogramele*, vol. 6, 205.

17. See ANRM, 706/1123, voil. 2, f. 443 USHMM RG-54.004M reel 17.

18. An earlier, less developed version of this story can be found in Solonari, *Purifying the Nation*, 314–318.

19. See Solonari, *Purifying the Nation*, 315.

20. This is what, according to the professor of history at the University of Bucharest and an important National Peasants politician, Teofil Sauciuc Săveanu, Minister of National Education and of Cults general Radu Rosetti told him shortly before Săveanu's meeting with Ioan Hudiţa on July 28, 1941 (Hudiţa, *Jurnal politic 22 iunie 1941–28 februarie 1942*, 65).

21. See Smochină's report on his fact-finding mission to Transnistria effected immediately following its conquest by the Romanian army in ANRM F. 706 Inventar 1 dosar 559 vol. 2, f. 307.

22. See his mid-October 1941 memorandum to Antonescu, DANIC F. Sabin Manuilă, XII/211/1941, f. 10.

23. On MASSR, see Charles King, *The Moldovans: Romania, Russia, and the Politics of Culture* (Stanford: Hoover Institution Press, 2000), 63–88 and Igor Caşu, *Duşmanul de Clasă. Represiuni politice, violenţ ăşi rezistenţă în R(A)SS Moldovenească, 1924–1956* (Chişinău: Cartier, 2014), 21–118.

24. See Anton Golopenţia, "Cifra Românilor din Transnistria. Analiză a rezultatelor inventarierii din decembrie 1941 şi confruntarea lor cu evaluările româneşti anterioare şi cu recensămintele ruseşti," in *Anton Golopenţia. Românii de la este de Bug*, ed. Sanda Golopenţia (Bucharest: Editura enciclopedică, 2006) vol. 1, 24–39, esp. 25–26. Excerpts from this ordinance can be found on 26.

25. Anton Golopenţia, "Cifra Românilor din Transnistria," 33–34.

26. On the work of this group, see [Anton Golopenţia], "Lucrarile de înscriere a moldovenilor effectuate peste Bug de Institutul Central de Statistică în 1941–1943," in Golopenţia, ed., *Anton Golopenţia*, vol. 1, 109–113, as well as many other documents in this collection.

27. On the schedule and areas investigated, see Gheorghe Bucurescu, "Identificarea românilor de peste Bug (31.12.1943)," in Golopenţia, ed., *Anton Golopenţia*, vol. 1, 100–102.

28. Anton Golopenţia, "Notă despre lucrările de identificare a românilor de peste Bug" [November 16, 1942], in Golopenţia, ed., *Anton Golopenţia*, vol. 1, 58–60, citation is from 59. For the questionnaire, see Anton Golopenţia, "Raport către Directorul general al Institutului Central de Statistică," in *Anton Golopenţia*, ed. Golopenţia, vol. 1, 41–42.

29. See the interview with Gheorghe Retigan in Zoltán Rostás, *Parcurs întrerupt. Discipoli din anii '30 ai Şcolii gustiene* (Bucharest: Paideia, 2005), 393.

30. See Bucurescu, "Identificarea românilor de peste Bug," 101. In his report to Manuilă from February 1943, Golopenţia mentioned that the work also started in Podolia but there is no further evidence that the census takers ever reached this region; see Anton Golopenţia, "Am găsit acolo un însemnat număr de Români," in Golopenţia, ed., *Anton Golopenţia*, vol. 1, 71.

31. See Golopenţia, "Lucrarile de înscriere a moldovenilor effectuate peste Bug," 112.

32. Golopenția, "Cifra Românilor din Transnistria," 31–32. Golopenția was especially incisive vis-à-vis Smochină's assessments which, he claimed, were "flagrant arithmetical errors" (38).

33. See Domitrie Gusti, "Cercetări monorgfice Românești (iulie–decembrie 1942)," in Golopenția, ed., *Anton Golopenția*, vol. 1, 65–66. First published in *Sociologie Românească* 4, no. 7–12 (1942): 659–670.

34. More on Dmitrie Gusti and his school, see Solonari, *Purifying the Nation*, 80–88 and Zoltán Rostás, *Dimitrie Gusti and the Bucharest School of Sociology* (Iași: Center for Romanian Studies, 2007); Zoltán Rostás, *O istorie orala a Scolii Sociologice de la Bucuresti* (Bucharest: Printech, 2001).

35. Gusti, "Cercetări monorgfice Românești (iulie–decembrie 1942)," 65.

36. Gusti, "Cercetări monorgfice Românești (iulie–decembrie 1942)," 66. On Golopenția's disagreements with Gusti, his mentor, over the methodology of sociological research, see Golopenția, "Introducere" in Sanda Golopenția, ed., *Anton Golopenția*, vol. 1, xi, n. 7.

37. Gusti, "Cercetări monorgfice Românești (iulie–decembrie 1942)," 66.

38. Much of the available materials can be found in Golopenția, ed., *Anton Golopenția*, vols. 1–2 and Florin Rotaru, ed., *Românitatea transnistriană. Anthologie* (Bucharest: Editura Semne, 1996).

39. Golopenția, ed., *Anton Golopenția*, vol. 1, 360–361.

40. DANIC F. PCM-CM dosar 140/1943, f. 46.

41. Anton Golopenția, "Memoriu cu privire la problemele practice pe care le ridică în toamna și iarna 1942 Românii de peste Buh," in Golopenția, ed., *Anton Golopenția*, vol. 1, 61 (notes for the conference on the Romanians from across the Buh, Odessa, November 16, 1942). See also his report to Manuilă and the PCM, February 1943, in Golopenția, ed., *Anton Golopenția*, vol. 1, 71–74.

42. For more on Herseni, see Valentin Săndulescu, "Academic Elites and Their Trajectories in Troubled Times: The Case of Traian Herseni," *Studii și materiale de istorie contemporană* 16 (2017): 84–101. I thank one of the anonymous reviewers for this valuable reference. A cynical and ruthless opportunist and careerist, Herseni would successfully reintegrate into the Romanian academic establishment in the 1960s and 1970s after serving a sentence in communist prisons.

43. See I. Făcăoaru, "Rezultatul unor cercetări antropologice în Transnistria," *Buletin egenic și politic* 13, no. 1–4 (1942): 141–142 and I. Făcăoaru, "Valoarea biorasilă a națiunilor europene și a provinciilor Românești," *Buletin eugenic și biopolitic* 14, no. 9–10 (1943): 278–310. Făcăoaru's selection consisted of 700 males and 45 females from four predominantly ethnic Romanian villages: three located along the Dniester River and one in the center of Transnistria. The first part of Făcăoaru's more detailed manuscript can be found in DAOO F. 2242 Op. 1 spr. 1214 USHMM RG-31.004M reel 2. For more on Făcăoaru, see in Marius Turda, "The Nation as Object: Race, Blood, and Biopolitics in Interwar Romania," *Slavic Review* 66 no. 3 (Fall 2007): 413–442 and Vladimir Solonari, "In the Shadow of Ethnic Nationalism: Racial Science in Romania," in *Racial Science in Hitler's New Europe*, ed. Weiss-Wendt and Yeomans, 259–286, esp. 268–273.

44. M. Vestemeanu, Alexandru Manuilă, and Mircea Vlad, "Recheres sur les groupes sanguins des roumains d'au-delà du Nistrou," *Comptes rendus dea séances de l'Academie des Sciences de Roumanie* 6, no. 1–4 (1942): 271–281.

45. See Vladimir Solonari, "In the Shadow of Ethnic Nationalism: Racial Science in Romania," in in Weiss-Wendt and Yeomans, eds., *Racial Science in Hitler's New Europe*, 259–286.

46. Herseni joined the legionary movement in 1936 and soon reached the rank of a commander of a legion. (See Roland Clark, *Holy Legionary Youth: Fascist Activism in Inter-War Romania* [Ithaca, NY: Cornell University Press, 2015], 131, 233; Herseni's memorandum from April 1945 in ASRI dosar 38880 vol. 1, ff. 21–20 USHMM RG-25.004M reel 92; and his personal data sheet in ASRI dosar 16495 vol. 2, f. 269 USHMM RG-25.004M reel 118). From the fall of 1940 until early 1942, he served as secretary general in the Ministry of Education and as a member of the commission set up to purge the university of politically "unreliable, mostly left-wing faculty." Although in his 1945 memorandum Herseni claimed that he occupied a "moderate" position and helped some of the suspected left-wingers keep their positions (ASRI dosar 38880 vol. 1, f. 24 USHMM RG-25.004M reel 92), at least one other of Gusti's disciples remembered otherwise. According to Gheorghe Retigan, Herseni sacked "thousands" of faculty and made it clear he intended to sack Gusti, too, for his being married to a Jewess; even if Gusti divorced her, Herseni still believed he had to be sacked "for lack of character" (interview with Retigan in Zoltán Rostás, *Parcurs întrerupt. Discipoli din anii '30 ai Şcolii gustiene* [Bucharest: Paideia, 2005], 379–380).

47. See correspondence between the general staff, the office of the chairman of the council of ministers, Herseni, and Alexianu concerning this issue (February 1943) in ANRM F. 706 Inventar 1 dosar 59, ff. 671–682.

48. See the certificate concerning the destruction of those files on Herseni's order in DAOO F. 2361 Op. 1s spr. 52 1944, 18 USHMM RG-31.004M reel 20.

49. Ciucă and Ignat, eds., *Stenogramele*, vol. 9, 543–545, 560.

50. One such enthusiast was an influential agronomist and member of the Academy of Sciences, professor Agricola Cardaş. See his brochure "O pagină din economia Transnistriei," *Buletinul al Academiei de Ştiinţa din România* 10 (1942), 334. Golopenţia and Alexianu, as I show later, were strong advocates of immediate actions.

51. See Manoliu's report in ANRM F. 706 vol. 1, f. 66 USHMMM RG-54.004M reel 6.

52. See transcripts of Pantazi's interrogation in Moscow in June 1945 in Tsentral'nyi Arkhiv Federal'noi sluzhby bezopasnosti Rossiiskoi Federatsii (TsAFS-BRF), delo H-18767, vol. 1, ll. 116–117, USHMM RG-06.025M reel 43. See also the gendarmerie reports on the transfer in DANIC F. IGJ dosar 78/1943, ff. 30ff.; and Anton Golopenţia's deposition in Golopenţia, ed., *Anton Golopenţia*, vol. 1, 106–107, 114. According to Gheorghe Retegan, member of Golopenţia's team, the army brought Moldovans from three villages in the Kuban region—Moldavanska, Grozovatka, and another one whose name he could not remember. Retegan believed that they were settled in Bessarabia but he probably confused this group with later refugees (Zoltán Rostás apparently conducted this interview in the 2000s, without indicating the date or even the year. See Zoltán Rostás, *Parcurs întrerupt*, 395). According to Gheorghe Alexianu, ethnic Romanians from Crimea came to the border with Transnistria having been forced by the Germans to sell most of their possessions to them at derisory prices. See Ciucă and Ignat, *Stenogramele*, vol. 9, 43 (February 4, 1943).

53. See the note from the SSSCRI to Alexianu, relating this decision of Ion Antonescu from November 6, 1942, in ANRM F 706 Inventar 1 dosar 651, f. 386.

54. See his marginal note on a report concerning problems of repatriation in ANRM F. 706 Invetar 1 dosar 52, ff. 63–64. The author of the report is not indicated.

55. See Ciucă and Ignat, eds., *Stenogramele*, vol. 9, 43.

56. See the SSSRCI instructions, January 28, 1943, in DAOO F. 2264 Op. 1 spr. 5, ark. 190–196 USHMM RG-31.004M reel 13.

57. DAOO F. 2242 Op. 1 spr. 1561, ark. 185 USHMM RG-31.004M reel 6. Data for Varvarovca subcommission and Tiraspol commission are even less transparent and meaningful.

58. DAOO F. 2264 Op. 1 spr. 5, ark. 4 USHMM RG-31.004M reel 5, August 16, 1943.

59. See the commission's report to Alexianu, August 7, 1943, in DAOO F. 2264 Op. 1 spr. 9, ark. 23–24 USHMM RG-31.004M reel 9.

60. See the SSSRCI letter to ANRM F. 706 Invetar 1 dosar 651, ff. 385–385v. All quotes in the paragraph are from this document.

61. For Golopenția's note, see in Sanda Golopenția, ed., *Anton Golopenția: Românii de la est de Bug*, vol. 1, 67–69.

62. ANRM F. 706 Inventar 1 dosar 52, f. 66.

63. See his resolution of April 19, 1943, in ANRM F. 706 Inventar 1 dosar 52, f. 16.

64. See the summary of the German proposal and Antonescu's decision in ANRM F. 706 Inventar 1 dosar 52, f. 18. No date provided in the file, attribution is based on the order of documents.

65. For correspondence between the governor and the prefects of Râbnița and Moghilău *județe*, see DAOO F. P-2242 Op. 1 spr. 293.

66. DAOO F. P-2242 Op. 1 spr. 293, ark. 10–11, 19.

67. ANRM F. 706 Inventar 1 dosar 16 vol. 3, ff. 428–29, 440.

68. ANRM F. 706 Inventar 1 dosar 16 vol. 3, f. 88.

69. DAOO F. 2264 Op. 1 spr. 5, ark. 273–274 USHMM RG-31.004N reel 13.

70. On the Moldovans' fear of recruitment for work in Germany as a motive for requesting permission to migrate into the Romanian territory, see interview with Retegan, 392, and declarations of other members of Golopenția's group in Golopenția, ed., *Anton Golopenția*, vol. 2, 262, 373. On the other motives, see Titu Răduleascu-Pogoneanu's memorandum on the issue of population transfers of July 8, 1943, in Hoover Institution Archive, Dumitru G. Popescu Papers, box 2, ff. 5, 7.

71. See Viorel Achim, "Proiectul guvernului de la București privind schimbul de populație româno-ruso-ucrainean (1943)," *Revista istorică* 11 (2000): 395–421 and Solonari, *Purifying the Nation*, 319–321. I corrected arithmetical mistakes that creeped into the cited publication.

72. Ciucă and Ignat, *Stenogramele*, vol. 9, 449. See also his marginal note on Alexianu's report on the increasing numbers of such refugees from the east in ANRM dosar 52, f. 25 (September 19, 1941).

73. See Ion Antonescu's marginal note on an (unavailable) CIS paper on the issues of refugees in ANRM F. 706 Inventar 1 dosar 52, f. 26.

74. See Alexianu's request to the CSI in ANRM F. 706 Inventar 1 dosar 52, f. 26 (September 19, 1943). For a summay of Golopenția's second mission group to Transnistria, see in Golopenția, ed., *Anton Golopenția* 113–114. Anton Golopenția's declaration submitted during the investigation of his own activity by communist authorities, January 21, 1950.

75. Golopenția, ed., *Anton Golopenția*, vol. 1, 113–114.

76. Golopenția, ed., *Anton Golopenția*, vol. 1, 286.

77. See Manuilă's relation to the CBBT (read Ion Antonescu) of November 12, 1943, summarizing Golopenția's findings and arguments in ANRM F. 706 Inventar 1 dosar 648 ff. 93–95.

78. ANRM F. 706 Inventar 1 dosar 648, f. 96. Dated November 5, 1943.

79. ANRM F. 706 Inventar 1 dosar 648, ff. 93–95.

80. ANRM F. 706 Inventar 1 dosar 648, ff. 114–116.

81. ANRM F. 706 Inventar 1 dosar 52, f. 100.

82. Ciucă and Ignat, eds., *Stenogramele*, vol. 9, 543–545, 560, citation is from 560.

83. Golopenția, ed., *Anton Golopenția*, vol. 1, 114.

84. See Veaceslav Stavilă, *De la Basarabia românească la Basarabia sovietică 1939–1945* (Chișinău: Tipografia Centrală, 2000), 53.

85. On the dissemination of ethnonationalist ideas among the lower classes of East-Central Europe, see Miroslav Hroch, *Social Preconditions of National Revival in Europe: A Comparative Analysis of the Social Composition of Patriotic Groups among the Smaller European Nations* (New York: Cambridge University Press, 1985).

86. ANRM F. 706 Inventar 1 dosar 518 vol. 1, ff. 174–180.

87. ANRM F. 706 Inventar 1 dosar 53, f. 48. Activities report of the *guvernământ*, March 1943, no signature.

88. ANRM F. 706 Inventar 1 dosar 518 vol. 1, f. 195. In the eyes of the authorities, the Ukrainian theater performed plays "of purely commercial interest."

89. AMAN F. Ministerul Apărării Naționale Armata a 4-a Inventar 06777 din 1976 dosar 957, f. 20 USHMM RG-25.003M reel 13.

90. On the German army's issuing of such certificates, which irritated the Romanians, see the information bulletin of the Gendarmerie Inspectorate of Transnistria for November 15–December 15, 1941, in AMAN F. Armata a 3-a Inventar N S/6776 din 1976 dosar 410, f. 208 USHMM RG-25.003M reel 17.

91. See Governor Gheorghe Alexianu's report on the policy toward the Transnistrian Moldovans, September 1943, DAOO F. 2242 Op. 1 spr. 692/1943, ark. 230–233, USHMM RG-31.004 reel 1.

92. See General Constantin Vasiliu, inspector general of Gendarmerie, to Ion Antonescu, August 12, 1941, relating his instructions on the organization of the Service of the Police in AMAN F. Marele Cartier General, Inventar N 019269 din 1972 dosar 41, f. 397, USHMM RG-25.003M reel 4; and report of Ananiev Gendarmerie Legion March 1942, DANIC F. IGJ dosar 18/1942, f. 55v. USHMM RG-25.010M reel 13.

93. See Mikhail Reshetnikov et al.'s report on their partisan activity in DAOO F. 92 spr. 13, ark. 46, containing a description of Romanianization policy (probably 1944).

94. *Transnistria*, May 28, 1942.

95. *Odesskaia gazeta*, February 12, 1942.

96. Smochină, *Memorii*, esp. 201–412. On the Romanian governments' instrumentalization of the "Transnistrian problem," see 416–418.

97. Smochină's biographical data are recounted after his *Memorii*. On his appointment as Antonescu's liaison officer for refugees from the east, see Smochină, *Memorii*, 424.

98. Smochină, *Memorii*, 441.

99. Smochină, *Memorii*, 449.

100. See minutes of this meeting in Smochină, *Memorii*, 458–460.

101. Smochină, *Memorii*, 461.

102. Smochină, *Memorii*, 463.

103. By February 1942, he had already been removed from this position. See the address of Prefect Colonel C. Loghin to the governor, about problems created by the inclination of subprefects of the Transnistrian origin to focus exclusively on the Moldovans, see DAOO F. 2242 Op. 1 spr. 331, ark. 3.

104. See postwar deposition of the former director of the department of culture, Axente Popovici, in ASRI dosar 40010 vol. 124, ff. 21, 22 USHMM RG-25.004M reel 34.

105. ANRM F. 706 Inventory 1 dosar 9, f. 39. Official note to Smochină informing him of Mihai Antonescu's decision.

106. ANRM F. 706 Inventar 1 dosar 18 vol. 1, ff. 249–250 USHMM RG-54.004M reel 6. The only account of the behind-the-scenes intrigues that surrounded the congress comes from Smochină, *Memorii*, 468ff.

107. DAOO F. 2241 Op. 1 spr. 1098, ark. 15.

108. DAOO F. 2241 Op. 1 spr. 1098, ark. 14.

109. DAOO F. 3949 Op. 1 spr. 8, ark. 3.

110. See statutes and minutes of the meetings at which chapters' statutes were adopted, together with Bulat's correspondence with subprefects about the same in DAOO F. P-3949 Op. 1 spr. 8.

111. DAOO F. 2242 Op. 1 spr. 1040, ark. 64.

112. The 1943 memoranda can be found in DAOO F. 2242 Op. 1 spr. 1099.

113. DAOO F. 2242 Op. 1 spr. 1099, ark. 3–5 (error in pagination) USHMM RG-31.004M reel 2. The memorandum was signed by Bulat's deputy, Ilie Zaftur.

114. DAOO F. 2242 Op. 1 spr. 1099, ark. 5 (page mistakenly numbered 15) USHMM RG-31.004M reel 2.

115. DAOO F. 2242 Op. 1 spr. 1099, ark. 1.

116. See correspondence to that effect in DAOO F. 2242 Op. 1 spr. 1099, ark. 40–48. The Institute initiated the creation of this office in August 1942.

117. ANRM F. 706 Inventar 1 dosar 837, ff. 870–871.

118. ANRM F. 706 Inventar 1 dosar 837, ff. 884–885. Registered September 28, 1943.

119. ANRM F. 706 Inventar 1 dosar 837, ff. 884–887, citation is from f. 887.

120. See Bulat's letter to Antonescu, ANRM F. 706 Inventar 1 dosar 837, f. 933.

121. ANRM F. 706 Inventar 1 dosar 837, f. 940.

122. On the National Peasants Party's position on population exchange in Bessarabia, Bukovina, and Transnistria, see Ion Hudiţa, *Jurnal politic (22 iunie 1941–28 februarie 1942)* (Bucharest: LUCMAN, 2005), 65, 67, 88. On the opposition's protests against anti-Jewish violence, see Solonari, *Purifying the Nation*, 217, 231, 290.

6. "Civilizing" Transnistria

1. See Katherine Verdery, *National Ideology under Socialism: Identity and Cultural Politics in Ceauşescu's Romania* (Berkeley: University of California Press, 1995), esp. 27–71. Since 1878, Romania ruled over northern Dobrogea, initially sparsely populated and ethnically alien. Fast economic development and government measures quickly changed this situation in favor of ethnic Romanians who migrated into the new province. From 1913 to 1915 and then again from 1918 to 1940, Romania ruled over southern Dobrogea, and tried to change its ethnic composition, but with less

success. In 1940, Romania lost southern Dobrogea to Bulgaria. Population exchanges with Bulgaria that followed this cession completed the "nationalization" of northern Dobrogea's population. See Constatin Iordachi, *Citizenship, Nation- and State-Building: The Integration of Northern Dobrogea into Romania, 1878–1913*, The Carl Beck Papers in Russian & East European Studies (Pittsburgh: University of Pittsburgh Press, 2002) and Vladimir Solonari, *Purifying the Nation*, 33–45.

2. Agricola Cardaş, *Colonizare românească*, Academia de ştiinţe din România. Seria conferinţelor de documentare: problemele războiului şi ştiinţa (n.p., [1941]); Cardaş, "O pagină din economia Transnistriei," *Buletinul al Academiei de Ştiinţa din România* 10 (1942): 323–334; Aurel Talasesco, *L'agriculture et la colonisation italienne en Libye* (n.p., 1941).

3. ANRM F.706 Inventar 1 dosar 632 vol. 1, f. 68.

4. DAOO F.2359 Op. 1 spr. 9, 1941, ark. 28–31, USHMM RG-31.004M reel 18.

5. See Andrei Cusco, *A Contested Borderland: Competing Russian and Romanian Visions of Bessarabia in the Late Nineteenth and Early Twentieth Century* (New York: Central European University Press, 2017), esp. chaps. 1 and 4.

6. Quoted in *Molva*, December 25, 1942. *Molva* (Chat) was a Russian-language newspaper that was officially allowed in Odessa.

7. *Odesskaia gazeta*, September 4, 1942.

8. *Odesskaia gazeta*, October 21, 1942.

9. ANRM F.706 Inventar 1 dosar 518, f. 194.

10. See "Osvobozhdennaia intelligentsia," *Odesskaia gazeta*, December 13, 1941; Vasilii K. Dumitresku, "Novyi poriadok v Evrope," *Odesskaia gazeta*, January 16, 1942; A. K-ku, "Vozrozhdennaia Rumyniia i novaia Evropa," *Odesskaia gazeta*, September 1, 1942; "Bol'shoi rumynskii prazdnik: ob otkrytii zhenskogo litseia v Odesse," *Odesskaia gazeta*, October 29, 1940 (a summary of a speech by Princess Alexandra Contacuzino); and Troian Herseni, "Zavoievateli ili osvoboditeli," *Odesskaia gazeta*, October 31, 1942.

11. GARF R-7021 Op. 69 delo 342 l.101v. YV JM-19.969. Testimony for the Extraordinary State Commission, taken shortly after liberation.

12. Sokolov's testimony, l. 8v.

13. GARF R-7021 Op. 69 delo 343 ll. 21v.–22. Dimitrie Cantemir (1672–1723), prince (*hospodar'*) in 1693 and 1710–1711, signed a treaty with Peter the Great, aligning his country with Russia and against the Ottoman Empire. After the allies lost the war, he immigrated, together with his son Antioch, to Russia. Both were important men of letters and wrote in several languages, including Russian. Petru Mohyla (Movilă in Romanian tradition) (1596–1647) was an aristocrat born in the medieval principality of Moldova (or Moldavia) who emigrated to the Polish-Lithuanian Commonwealth, where he received an excellent education. Tonsured as a monk, he became Metropolitan of Kyiv where he founded the Collegium, which later became known as the Kyiv-Mohyla Academy, an important center of enlightenment and Orthodox Christian cultural resistance to Catholic proselytizing pressure.

14. On the social and cultural history of Odessa, see Charles King, *Odessa: Genius and Death in a City of Dreams* (New York: Norton, 2011).

15. See "Pervaia godovshchina plodotvornoi i tvorcheskoi raboty Odesskogo teatra Opery i Baleta," *Molva*, December 10, 1942.

16. See "Pervaia godovshchina."

17. On Ion and Mihai Antonescu attending shows in the Odessa Opera with their spouses, see *Molva*, December 10, 1942. On German Minister Pflaumer's attendance, see *Odesskaia gazeta*, February 20, 1942.

18. Hermann Binder, *Aufzeichnungen aus Transnistrien (September–December 1942)*, foreword by Hans Bergel (Munich: Verlag Siidostdeutsches Kulturwerk, 1996), 91.

19. See interview with Vronskii in *Molva*, December 9, 1942.

20. See Karel C. Berkhoff, *Harvest of Despair: Life and Death in Ukraine under the Nazi Rule* (Cambridge, MA: Belknap Press of Harvard University Press, 2004), esp. 157–160.

21. See, for example, the General Staff's note on the "moods" of the population of Transnistria and Governor Alexianu's comment on it ANRM F.706 Inventar 1 dosar 16 vol. 5, ff. 522–525, August–September 1943.

22. One finds echoes of the resentment the lower classes felt toward this new privileged group in the activity reports of some Soviet partisans. See, e.g., DAOO F.92 Op. 1 spr. 13, ark. 46.

23. See such praise of the Romanian opera *Wedding in the Carpathian Mountains*, staged in Odessa in *Molva*, December 10, 1942, and N. Borsaru's disparaging reference on July 30, 1942, to the quality of theater troupes from Romania performing in Transnistria. Borsaru was the interim chief of the *guvernământ*'s press. DAOO F. 2242 Op. 1 spr. 1644, ark. 162–163.

24. See Pântea's letter to Antonescu tending his resignation because of his disagreements with the military concerning the treatment of the city's population, in particular anti-Jewish atrocities, October 21, 1941, in ASRI dosar 21401 vol. 1, f. 200U (inconsistent pagination) USHMM RG-25.004M reel 30.

25. Traian Herseni, "Zavoevateli ili osvoboditeli" *Odesskaia gazeta*, October 30, 31, and November 1, 1942.

26. See his addresses to Patriarch Nicodim and clerics from September 1940 in General Ion Antonescu, *Către Români. Chemări—cuvântări—documente. La o răscruce a istoriei. Adunate de amiral Dan Zaharia* (Bucharest: Socec & Co., 1941), 48–53. See also his declaration in the Council of Ministers of December 10, 1941, in Ciucă and Ignat, eds., *Stenogramele*, vol. 5, 433. For more on the close relationship between Christian Orthodox hierarchy and Antonescu regime, see Ion Popa, *The Romanian Orthodox Church and the Holocaust* (Bloomington: Indiana University Press, 2017), esp. 41–71.

27. See his declaration in the Council of Ministers meeting of April 17, 1942, in Ciucă and Ignat, eds., *Stenogramele*, vol. 6, 441.

28. See his statements in the Council of Ministers meeting of September 18, 1940, Ciucă and Ignat, eds., *Stenogramele*, vol. 1, 55 and December 10, 1941 in Ciucă and Ignat, eds., *Stenogramele*, vol. 5, 430.

29. ANRM F. 706 Inventar 1 dosar 556, ff. 85–86.

30. See the discussion between Ion Antonescu and Ion Sandu, state under secretary for cults and the arts at the Ministry of National Culture and Cults, during the Council of Ministers meeting of November 27, 1941, in Ciucă and Ignat, eds., *Stenogramele*, vol. 5, 214–215.

31. See discussion in the Council of Ministers meeting of January 23, 1942, in Ciucă and Ignat, eds., *Stenogramele*, vol. 5, 718–719.

32. *Molva*, December 25, 1942. On Prundeni, see Radu Ioanid, "The Romanian Press: Preparing the Ground for the Holocaust and Reporting on Its Implementation,"

in *Why Didn't the Press Shout? American & International Journalism During the Holocaust,* ed. Robert Moses Shapiro, A Collection of Papers Originally Presented at an International Conference Sponsored by the Eli and Diana Zborowski Professorial Chair in Interdisciplinary Holocaust Studies, Yeshiva University, October 1995 (Jersey City, NJ: Yeshiva University Press, 2003), 391–408, esp. 401, 403, 404.

33. See the entry on Scriban in Mircea Păcurariu, *Dicționarul teologilor români* (Bucharest: Univers encyclopedic, 1996), available at the website of the Romanian Orthodox Church of the Holy Trinity, Los Angeles, California, http://biserica.org/WhosWho/DTR/S/IuliuScriban.html.

34. See Sandu Ion Antonescu exchange in the Council of Ministers meeting of November 27, 1941, Ciucă and Ignat, eds., *Stenogramele,* vol. 5, 215–216.

35. See Ion Antonescu's report on *guvernământ*'s investigation into the irregularities committed in the management of the Orthodox Mission in Transnistria in ANRM F. 706 Inventar 1 dosar 61, f. 50 February 1, 1943. Ion Antonescu attributed these irregularities on Scriban's leadership.

36. See Mikhail Vital'evich Shkarovskii, "Deiatel'nost' rumynskoi dukhovnoi missii na iugo-zapade Ukrainy i v Pridnestrov'e v 1941–1944 gg.," *Revista moldovenească de drept internațional și relații internaționale* 4 (2002): 177.

37. Shkarovskii, "Deiatel'nost' rumynskoi dukhovnoi missii," 164.

38. On "Renovationist" movement in the Russian Orthodox Church, see Michael A. Meerson, "The Renovationist Schism in the Russian Orthodox Church," *Canadian-American Slavic Studies* 26, no. 1–3 (1992): 293–314. On the Ukrainian Autocephalous Orthodox Church, see Sophia Senyk, "The Orthodox Church in Ukraine in the Twentieth Century," in *The Orthodox Church in Eastern Europe in the Twentieth Century,* ed. Christine Chaillot (Oxford: Peter Lang, 2012), 323–354.

39. Shkarovskii, "Deiatel'nost' rumynskoi dukhovnoi missii," 169–171.

40. This opinion was expressed, for example, in the activities report of the Gendarmerie Legion Berezovca for March 1942, see DANIC F. IGJ dosar 122/1942, f. 133 USHMM RG-21.010M reel 16.

41. See, for example, summaries of Scriban's addresses on solemn occasions in *Odesskaia gazeta,* July 25, 1942 and October 20, 1942. According to the 1944 deposition of Boris Vasil'evich Varneke, philologist and theater critic, in the spring of 1943, Metropolitan Vissarion distributed various gifts to ethnically Moldovan female students of Odessa University, which engendered strong resentment on the part of their non-Moldovan classmates GARF F. R. 7021 Op. 69 delo 434 l. 16 YV JM-19.971.

42. Shkarovskii, "Deiatel'nost'rumynskoi dukhovnoi missii," 170. In the following account of the mission's activity, I mostly follow Shkarovskii's interpretation and use his data. I refer to other sources whenever I use them.

43. See the entry on Visarion Puiu in Păcurariu, *Dicționarul teologilor români.*

44. Nor did it spare him persecution at the hands of authorities in communist Romania. See Ion Popa, *The Romanian Orthodox Church and the Holocaust* (BloomingtonN: Indiana University Press, 2017), 50, 99, 108–110, 134–137.

45. In addition to the complaints of the local priests mentioned by Shkarovskii, one can also cite Werth's conversation with the dean of the Assumption Cathedral in Odessa, priest Vasilii, in *Russia at War,* 819–820, depositions of psalmist Nikolaev from Mogilev, and an unidentified priest from the village of Nemii, Vinnytsia oblast

of Ukraine, collected by ChGK (1944) in GARF F. 7021 Op. 62 delo 1341 ll. 146–146v and 155–156 YV JM-19.689.

46. DANIC F. IGJ dosar 122/1942, f. 311 USHMM RG-25.010M reel 16.

47. DANIC F. IGJ dosar 84/943, f. 322 USHMM RG-25.010M reel 27.

48. Paulin Lecca, *De la moartea la viață*, Prefață de Valeriu Cristea (Bucharest: Paideia, 1997), 156, see also 127, 136. According to his own account, later in the war, he was arrested and condemned to death for his refusal to bear arms during the war. I was not able to independently verify his claims.

49. See, for example, the assessment of the Gendarmerie Inspectorate Balta, September 1943: "Missionary priests are conscientious" (DANIC F. IGJ dosar 86/1943, f. 271 USHMM RG-25.010M reel 27). See also Lecca, *De la moarte la viață*, 158.

50. Shkarovskii, "Deiatel'nost' rumynskoi dukhovnoi missii," 181.

51. Memoir of the Lutheran pastor Hermann Binder, who in September–December 1942 conducted missionary activities in Transnistria, is filled with evidence of such obstructionism. In particular, he cites Sonderkommando-R's commanding officer, SS-Obersturmführer Dr. Klaus Siebert: "We have one thing in common with the Bolsheviks: we intend to close churches." See Binder, *Aufzeichnungen aus Transnistrien*, 27.

52. See AMAN Inventar N S/6776 din 1976 dosar 410, f. 18 USHMM RG-25.003M reel 17.

53. See AMAN Inventar N S/6776 din 1976 dosar 410, f. 29 USHMM RG-25.003M reel 17.

54. DANIC F. IGJ dosar 120/1942, f. 6 USHMM RG-25.003M reel 16.

55. M. D. Manuilov, "Odessa v period vtoroi mirovoi voiny 1941–1944 gg.," in *Odessa. Zhizn' v okkupatsii. 1941–1944*, O. V. Budnitskii et al., eds. (Moscow: Rosspen, 2013), 183.

56. See his declaration in the Council of Ministers meeting of November 27, 1941, in Ciucă and Ignat, eds., *Stenogramele*, vol. 5, 214.

57. For the text of the ordinance, see in DAOO F. 2242 Op. 1 spr. 1, ark. 137–138 USHMM RG-31.004M reel 1.

58. DANIC F. IGJ dosar 122/1942, f. 140 USHMM RG-25.101M reel 16.

59. DANIC F. IGJ dosar 124/1942, f. 198v USHMM RG-25.010M reel 17.

60. DANIC F. IGJ dosar 147/1942, f. 145 USHMM RG-25–010M reel 20.

61. DANIC F. IGJ dosar 125/1942, f. 172–174 USHMM RG-25.010M reel 17.

62. DANIC F. IGJ dosar 166/1942, f. 162 USHMM RG-25.010M reel 21.

63. DANIC F. IGJ dosar 80/1943, f. 31 USHMM RG-25.010M reel 26.

64. DANIC F. IGJ dosar 147/1942, f. 86–86 USHMM RG-25.010M reel 20.

65. The quote comes from the Râbnița Gendarmerie Legion information report for September 1942, see DANIC F. IGJ dosar 147/1942, f. 116 USHMM RG-25.010M reel 20.

66. DANIC F. IGJ dosar 80/1943, f. 43 USHMM RG-25.010M reel 26.

67. DANIC F. IGJ dosar 84/1943, ff. 235–236 USHMM RG-25.010M reel 27.

68. ANRM F. 706 Inventar 1 dosar 519 vol. 1, ff. 245, 254.

69. ANRM F. 706 Inventar 1 dosar 519 vol. 1, f. 139.

70. ANRM F. 706 Inventar 1 dosar 572 vol. 2, f. 341 USHMM RG-54.004M reel 12. Minutes of the CBBT meeting of March 13, 1942.

71. ANRM F. 706 Inventar 1 dosar 519 vol. 1, f. 178.

72. ANRM F. 706 Inventar 1 dosar 518 vol. 1, f. 354.

73. ANRM F. 706 Inventar 1 dosar 519 vol. 1, f. 254.

74. GARF F. 7021 Op. 69 delo 343, l. 5 YV JM 19.969. Testimony of docent Sokolov in 1944, shortly after the liberation of the city.

75. See Sokolov's testimony in GARF F. P-7021 Op. 69 delo 343, l. 8v. YV JM 19.969. My reconstruction of Romanianization at the university and colleges of Odessa is based on the testimonies of Nikolai Sokolov and another philologist, Boris Varneke, both collected by the ChGk, probably in 1944. Both testimonies can be found in GARF F. P-7021 Op. 69 delo 343, ll. 4–12 and delo 344, ll. 4–16 YV JM 19.969. Shortly after submitting this testimony, Varneke was arrested, charged, and sentenced for high treason. He died in a prison hospital in Kyiv in 1944. See Budnitsky et al., eds., Odessa, 10. I was not able to locate additional information on Sokolov.

76. Verneke, l. 12v.

77. GARF F. 7021 Op. 69 delo 343, l. 8.

78. "Resounding failure" is Sokolov's expression, l. 8.

79. See TsDAHOU F. 1 Op. 22 spr. 450, ark. 24–25. Chasovnikov was a famous surgeon. In 1944 he was evacuated to Bucharest where he was later arrested by the Soviet occupying authorities. Charged with high treason, he was condemned to ten years in labor camps where he died in 1954. See Budnitsky et al., eds., Odessa, 217 n. 150.

80. Werth, Russia at War, 822.

81. See the testimonies of Sokolov, ll. 7–8, and of lawyer N. Lange, F. R- 7021 Op. 69 delo 343 l. 14v. YV JM 19.969

82. AMAN Inventar N, S/6776, din 1976 dosar 410, f. 215 USHMM RG-25.003M reel 17.

83. ANRM F.706 Inventar 1 dosar 648, f. 116.

84. ANRM F.706 Inventar 1 dosar 540, f. 13.

85. On the Romanian suppression of Ukrainian nationalists in Bukovina, see Marianna Hausleitner, Die Rumänisierung der Bukowina: Die Durchsetzung des Nationalstaatlichen Anspruchs Grossrumäniens, 1918–1944 (Munich: Oldenbourg, 2001), 156–157, 180, 344.

86. Andrej Angrick, "Im Wechselspiel der Kräfte. Impressionen zur deutschen Einflussnahmene bei der Volkstumspolitk in Czernowitz vor 'Barbarossa' und nach Beginn des Überfalls auf die Sowjetunion," in NS-Gewaltherrschaft: Beiträge zur historischen Forschung und juristischen Aufarbeitung, ed. Alfred Gottwald, Norbert Kampe, and Peter Klein (Berlin: Edition Hentrich, 2005), 318–358.

87. See his note in the resolution of February 18, 1942, on a report by the General Inspectorate of the Gendarmerie on the problem of Ukrainian irredentism in DAOO F.2377 Op. 2 spr. 2, ark. 33, USHMM RG-31.004M reel 20.

88. ANRM F.706 Inventar 1 dosar 8, ff. 318–320.

89. DANIC F. IGJ dosar 124/1942, f. 181, USHMM RG-25.010M reel 17.

90. AMAN F. Armata a 3-a, Inventar N S/6776, din 1976 dosar 410, f. 119 USHMM RG-25.003M reel 17.

91. On national costumes as "tacit propaganda" of irredentism, see DANIC F. Ministerul de Interne, IGJ dosar 24/1942 II vol. 1, f. 203, USHMM RG-25.002M reel 5. On "national songs" as a sign of the same, see DANIC F.IGJ dosar 18/1942, f. 56v, USHMM RG-25.010M reel 13.

92. DANIC F. IGJ dosar 184/1942, f. 10 USHMM RG-25.010M reel 22.

93. DAOO F. 2361 Op. 1 spr. 42v, ark. 294–296 USHMM RG-31.004M reel 18.

94. ANRM F.706, Inventar 1 dosar 518 vol. 1, ff. 198–201.

95. AMAN F. Marele Cartier General Inventar N 019269 din 1972 dosar 3827, f. 247, USHMM RG-25.003M reel 4.

96. DANIC F. IGJ dosar 147/1942, f. 76, USHMM RG-25.10M reel 20.

97. DANIC F.IGJ dosar 84/1943, f. 153, USHMM RG-25.010M reel 27. The author's signature is hardly legible.

7. Extracting Economic Resources

1. Ciucă and Ignat, eds., *Stenogramele*, vol. 5, 491 (December 16, 1941).

2. Ciucă and Ignat, eds., *Stenogramele*, vol. 7, 442 (June 30, 1942).

3. Ciucă and Ignat, eds., *Stenogramele*, vol. 8, 113 (August 28, 1942).

4. Baum, *Varianten des Terrors*, 264–265; Balta, *Rumänien und die Großmächte in der Ära Antonescu (1940–1944)* (Stuttgart: Franz Stuttgart Verlag, 2005), 224–225. According to Mihai Antonescu's data, bread rations in Romania in September 1942 were lower than in Germany by 20 grams per person per day. In 1941, they were 700 grams per person per day, but by September 1942, they had decreased to 250 grams per day. See the German transcript of Antonescu's conversation with Hitler on September 26, 1942, in ADAP, Series E, Band 3, 541.

5. See Ordinance #24 on the currency regime in Transnistria and rules of exchange, November 21, in DAOO F. 2242 Op. 1 spr. 1, ark. 31 USHMM RG-31.004M reel 1. See also the transcript of the discussion of these issues in the meeting of the CBBT Liaison Committee of June 7, 1943, in ANRM F. 706 Inventar 1 dosar 582 vol. 2, ff. 297–299 USHMM RG-54.004M reel 13. On the official exchange rate of the leu to RKKS, see document "Information from Transnistria," unsigned and undated but certainly from Transnistria Gendarmerie Inspectorate early spring 1942, in DANIC F. IGJ dosar 122/942, f. 51 USHMM RG-25.010M reel 16.

6. See Alexianu's report to Ion Antonescu, January 19, 1942, in ANRM F. 706 Op. 1 dosar 482, ff. 23–24.

7. See the Ministry of Finance note for the meeting of the Council of Ministers of February 4, 1943, ANRM F. 706 Op. 1 dosar 586 vol. 1, f. 135 USHMM RG-54.004M reel 13.

8. According to the summary report of the Third Army on the situation in Transnistria, as a result of ruble/RKKS exchange, "the value of ruble was cut in two." See AMAN F. Armata a 3-a Inventar N S/6776 din 1976 dosar 410, f. 118 USHMM RG-25.003M reel 17.

9. On the separate exchange rate for Jews, see Alexianu's report to Ion Antonescu, January 19, 1942, in ANRM F. 706 Op. 1 dosar 482, ff. 23–24.

10. For the text of Ordinances #79 and #103, see DAOO F. 2242 Op. 1 spr. 1, ark. 123–124 and 171, respectively; USHMM RG-31.004M reel 1. On the campaign of procurement and the deposition of proceeds, see the correspondence between Alexianu and governor of the National Bank Alexandru Ottulescu and Minister of Finance Alexandru D. Neagu, in ANRM F. 706 Inventar 1 dosar 53, ff. 156–171, August 1943. For further details, see on the "collections of valuable objects," as it was

officially called in bureaucratic correspondence, in the first weeks of the occupation, in ANRM F. 706 Inventar 1 dosar 818, ff. 23–24 USHMM RG-54.004M reel 14.

11. ANRM F. 706 Inventar 1 dosar 59, f. 169.

12. See Ordinance #69 from June 11, 1942, on the ban of the circulation of lei in Transnistria, and the punishments of black traffickers (up to three months in prison), in DAOO F. 2242 Op. 1 spr. 1 ark. 101–101v USHMM RG-31.004 reel 1. Lei salaries of the Romanian functionaries deployed in Transnistria were deposited in their accounts in Romania and could not be brought into Transnistria. They could exchange no more than two RKKS salaries they received in Transnistria into lei, but those lei were deposited into their families' accounts in Romania. See Alexianu's explanatory note of September 3, 1942, in ANRM F. 706 Inventar 1 dosar 772, f. 280.

13. DAOO F. 2242 Op. 1 spr. 1 Ordinances #60, #71, #86, and #114, ark. 86–97, 105–106, 133–134, and 195–195v USHMM RG-31.004 reel 1.

14. On the general stores (*magazine generale*), see the activities report of the direcția of commerce of the *guvernământ*, August 19, 1942–December 31, 1942, in ANRM F. 706 Inventar 1 dosar 529, f. 37.

15. DANIC F. IGJ dosar 130/1942, f. 123v USHMM RG-25.002M reel 31.

16. DANIC F, IJG dosar 124/1942, ff. 198–198v. USHMM RG-25.010M reel 17. Activities report for June 1942.

17. DANIC F. IGJ dosar 80/1943 f. 43 USHMM RG-25.010M reel 26. Activities report for March 1943.

18. DANI F. IGJ dosar 80/1943 f. 90 USHMM RG-25.010M reel 26.

19. On January 23, 1942, the Odessa SSI bureau reported that local administrative employees (*functionari*) "were surprised and disaffected by the contrast between their and their Romanian counterparts' salaries." See AMAN F. Armata a 3-a Inventar N S/6776 din 1976 dosar 410, f. 302 USHMM RG-25.003M reel 17.

20. Service of *economate* functioned as a subdivision of the Romanian Railways in Transnistria (CFRT), subordinated to the CFR management in Bucharest. See CFRT activities report, August 19, 1941–August 1, 1943, in ANRM dosar 518 vol. 1, f. 351.

21. See relevant ordinances in DAOO F. 2242 Op. 1 spr. 1, ark. 24, 48, 55, 57–58, 84–85, 98–99, 102–103v, 107–108v, 139–140, 159, 211–213, 220, 221–223 USHMM RG-31.004M reel 1.

22. See regulations for Transnistria issued by the *guvernământ* in DAOO F. 22442 Op. 1 spr. 1, ark. 130, 136, 143–144, 193–194 USHMM RG-31.004M reel 1; F. 2359 Op. 1 spr. 3, ark. 34 USHMM RG-31.004M reel 18.

23. See Ordinance #5 on the preservation—or, better to say, restoration, after their spontaneous dismemberment after Soviet withdrawal—of kolkhozes in DAOO F. 2242 Op. 1 spr. 1, ark. 5–6 (September 1941) USHMM RG-31.004M reel 1.

24. ANRM F. 706 Inventar 1 dosar 58, ff. 213–216.

25. ANRM F. 706 Inventar 1 dosar 52, ff. 106–107.

26. See Ordinances #5 and #18, September–October in DAOO F. 2242 Op. 1 spr. 1, ark. 5–6 and 23 (USHMM RG-31.004M reel 1).

27. DANIC F. IGJ dosar 125/1942, f. 168 USHMM RG-25.10M reel 17.

28. DANIC F. IGJ dosar 125/1942, f. 200 USHMM RG-25.10M reel 17, and dosar 147/1942 f. 78, USHMM RG-25.10M reel 20.

29. Ciucă and Ignat, eds., *Stenogramele*, vol. 5, 491 (December 16, 1941).

30. ANRM F. 706 Inventar 1 dosar 16 vol. 3, f. 474.

31. ANRM F. 706 Inventar 1 dosar 16 vol. 1, ff. 43–46, a summary of Mehedinți's paper prepared by clerks of the Ministry of Internal Affairs.

32. Weekly report of the General Staff, June 21, 1941, in ANRM F. 706 Inventar 1 dosar 18 vol. 1, ff. 31–34.

33. For materials about shipments of trams and their distribution among various Romanian cities, see ANRM F. 706 Inventar 1 dosar 19 vol. 3, esp. ff. 253ff.

34. Title in the original Russian "Deti! Opiat' zhertva tramvaia."

35. ANRM F. 706 Inventar 1 dosar 505, ff. 27–29.

36. ANRM F. 706 Inventar 1 dosar 505, ff. 93v–94.

37. ANRM F. 706 Inventar 1 dosar 19, ff. 352–359.

38. See the list in ANRM F. 706 Inventar 1 dosar 837, ff. 14–16. Mihai Antonescu issued the order to destroy documents related to the "evacuation" of goods from Transnistria at the Commission of Inquiry, which met to inquire into the activities of the Transnistrian *guvernământ* on February 26, 1944 because, as he put it, the Russians and Hungarians could use them "to discredit Romania after the end of hostilities." See ANRM F. 706 Inventar 1 dosar 58, ff. 213–239.

39. ANRM F. 706 Inventar 1 dosar 52, f. 113.

40. ANRM F. 706 Inventar 1 dosar 896, f. 72.

41. See Ciucă and Ignat, eds., *Stenogramele*, vol. 10, 90.

42. For Ion Antonescu's order to replace Alexianu with Potopeanu, see Arhiva Serviciului Român de Informații (ASRI) dosar 40013 vol. 6, f. 440 USHMM RG-25.004M reel 29. See Potopeanu's March 15, 1944 order to withdraw from the region and stop Operation 1111 in ASRI dosar 40013 vol. 6, f. 339 USHMM RG-25.004M reel 30.

43. On Fevr, see Budnitskii, "Odessa v period rumynskoi okkupatsii," in Budnitskii et al., eds., *Odessa* 29–34.,

44. N. Fevr, "Odessa v gody Vtoroi mirovoi voiny," in Budnitskii et al., eds., *Odessa*, 45.

45. "Odessa vchera i segodnia," *Odesskaia gazeta*, December 13, 1942.

46. For more on Manuilov, see Budnitskii, "Odessa v period rumynskoi okkupatsii," 35–40.

47. Mikhail Dmitrievich Manuilov, "Odessa v period Vtoroi mirovoi voiny 1941–1944," in Budnitskii et al., eds., *Odessa*, 149, 154.

48. See ASRI dosar 21401 vol. 1, f. 260v. USHMM RG-25.004M reel 30. Statement of October 1945.

49. Manuilov, "Odessa v period Vtoroi mirovoi voiny," 149–151. See also I. A. Peterle, "Odessa—stolitsa Transnistrii (materialy dlia budushchego istorika)," in Budnitskii et al., eds., *Odessa*, 73–74.

50. F. 706 Inventar 1 dosar 518 vol. 1, ff. 276–277.

51. Manuilov, "Odessa v period Vtoroi mirovoi voiny," 141–143.

52. ASRI dosar 21401 vol. 1, f. 260v. USHMM RG-25.004M reel 30. Statement of October 1945.

53. Many Jewish survivors mentioned in their testimonies such looting of their and other Jews' apartments. See, for example, Leonid Dusman, "Kak my borolis' i vyzhili," in *Istoriia Kholokosta v Odesskom regione. Sbornik statel i dokumentov*, ed. Mikhail Rashkovetskii et al. (Odessa: Migdal', 2006), 142; testimonies of Tat'iana Gurevich in YV Righteous of the Nations file # 6484.

54. See various official documents of the Third Army in AMAN Inventar N S/6776 din 1976 dosar 410, ff. 228, 302, 328 USHMM RG-25.003M reel 17 and dosar 481, f. 158, late fall 1941–early 1942, Odessa. The Romanians tended to emphasize the violence of the German troops against civilians, and the Germans did the same with respect to the Romanians. See Herwig Baum, *Varianten des Terrors*, 224–225.

55. See Paulian Nicolae's testimony in ASRI dosar 21401 vol. 1, f. 260v. USHMM RG-25.004M reel 30. Statement of October 1945.

56. See the transcripts of the interrogation of Florian Frantsevich Kokh (Koch?), January 12, 1967, in DGASBU spr. 13189 vol. 5, ark. 9–10 USHMM RG-31.018M reel 17 and of Grigorii Anton, April 1965 in GDASBU spr. 13153 vol. 20, ark. 115.

57. The literature on this subject is enormous. See Christian Gerlach, *Krieg, Ernährung, Völkermord: Forschungen zur deutschen Vernichtungspolitik im Zweiten Weltkrieg* (Hamburg: Hamburger Edition, 1998); Adam Tooze, *The Wages of Destruction: The Making and Breaking of the Nazi Economy* (New York: Viking, 2007), esp. 429–551; Alex J. Kay, "'The Purpose of the Russian Campaign Is the Decimation of the Slavic Population by Thirty Million': The Radicalization of German Food Policy in Early 1941," in *Nazi Policy on the Eastern Front, 1941: Total War, Genocide, and Radicalization*, ed. Alex J. Kay, Jeff Rutherford, and David Stahel (Rochester, NY: University of Rochester Press, 2012), 101–129. Timothy Snyder has recently restated this argument in his *Black Earth: The Holocaust as History and Warning* (New York: Tim Duggan Books, 2015).

58. See DAOO F. 2242 Op. 1 spr. 1084, ark. 13–14 and 28 USHMM RG-31.004M reel 2.

59. See Neubacher's memorandum in DAOO F. 2242 Op. 1 spr. 1088, ark. 180–181 USHMM RG-31.004M reel 2.

60. Manuilov, "Odessa v period Vtoroi mirovoi voiny," 153–154.

61. DANIC F. IGJ dosar 125/1942, f. 346 USHMM RG-25.010M reel 17.

62. ANRM F. 706 Inventar 1 dosar 8, ff. 102–103 USHMM RG-54.004 M reel 1.

63. DANIC F. GIJ dosar 84/1943, f. 147 USHMM RG-25.010M reel 27.

64. See Transnistria General Subinspectorate situation report for July 15–August 15, 1942: "Odessan population experiences great [economic] difficulties. Some of them sell their household objects to make their ends meet." DANI F. IGJ dosar 166/1942, f. 157 USHMM RG-25.004M reel 20.

65. Ciucă and Ignat, eds., *Stenogramele*, vol. 6, 398 (March 27, 1942).

66. Ciucă and Ignat, eds., *Stenogramele*, vol. 8, 112 (August 28, 1942).

67. ANRM F. 706 Inventar 1 dosar 58, f. 234.

68. ANRM F. 706 Inventar 1 dosar 58, ff. 233–234.

69. ANRM F. 706 Inventar 1 dosar 58, ff. 199–200, 202.

70. See the text in Leon Friedman, ed., *The Law of War: A Documentary History*, vol. 1, with a foreword by Telford Taylor (New York: Random House, 1972), 321–323. For a further illuminating discussion of the evolution of international law before the Great War, see Geoffrey Best, *Humanity in Warfare* (New York: Columbia University Press, 1980), 128–215.

71. Ciucă and Ignat, eds., *Stenogramele*, vol. 8, 112.

72. Ciucă and Ignat, eds., *Stenogramele*, vol. 8, 111–113 (May 15, 1944).

73. See Grigore Antipa, *L'Occupation ennemie de la Roumanie et ses consequences économiques et sociales* (New Haven: Yale University Press, 1929). See also David Mitrany, *The Effect of the War in South-Eastern Europe* (New York: Howard Fertig,

[1936] 1973), esp. 138–154. Mihai Antonescu chose to remain oblivious to the Romanians' occupation of Hungary in 1919 when they confiscated and shipped into their own country Hungarian rolling stock. This caused the Romanians significant difficulties with the Allies, who forced them to return part of this plunder to Hungary. See Keith Hitchins, *Rumania 1866–1947* (Oxford: Clarendon Press, 1994), 287–288.

74. See George Plastara, *Manual de drept internațional public în curent cu nouile tratate și convețiuni internaționale cuprinzând și o expunere a conflictelor de legi (Drept Internațional privat) pentru uzul studenților Faciltăților de drept, Academiilor de Comerț și Școalelor Superioare de Științe de Stat, etc.* (Bucharest: Socec & Co., 1928), 358–452; C(onstatin) Manolache and Ed. Konya, *Manual de Drept Internațional Public pentru uzul Ofiţerilor Armatei Române* (n.p., 1934), 73–91. At the time of publication, George Plastara was professor of law at the University of Bucharest; General Constantin Manolache was the chief military justice at the Ministry of National Defense and Inspector of Military Tribunals, as well as professor of law at the High School of Criminal Studies at the University of Bucharest; Ed Konya was the royal commissar at the Council of War of the Second Army Corps. It is safe to conclude that their voices were among the most authoritative among the Romanian academic and military law establishments.

75. Victorious powers committed themselves to the prosecution and punishment of war crimes in articles 227–230 of the Treaty of Versailles. See Friedman, ed., *The Law of War*, vol. 1, 431–433. On the quick abandonment of the project, see Isabel V. Hull, *A Scrap of Paper: Breaking and Making International Law during the Great War* (Ithaca: Cornell University Press, 2014), 1–16.

76. See Antipa, *L'Occupation ennemie de la Roumanie*, 163–164 and Paul Sterian, *La Roumanie et la réparation des dommages de guerre* (Paris: Librairie générale de droit & de jurisprudence, 1929).

77. See the 1929 Hague Convention for the treatment of the POWS in Friedman, ed., *The Law of War: A Documentary History*, vol. 1, 488–522.

78. For Ion Antonescu's instruction on the treatment of POWs, see Ciucă and Ignat, eds., *Stenogramele*, vol. 5, 453–454: "This is a humanitarian issue . . . We have an international responsibility" (December 16, 1941). See also his pronouncement in Ciucă and Ignat, eds., *Stenogramele*, vol. 6, 386 (March 27, 1942). See also instructions and orders of the Third Army and the Fourteenth Infantry Division on this issue, June–early July 1941, in AMAN F. Divizia a 14-a dosar 1015 ff. 416, 500 USHMM RG-25.003 reel 92.

79. I developed my understanding of this evolution in Solonari, *Purifying the Nation* and "A Conspiracy to Murder: Explaining the Dynamic of Romanian 'Policy' towards Jews in Transnistria."

80. See Ioan Hudiţa, *Jurnal politic: 1 ianuarie–24 august 1944*, ed. Dan Berindei (Bucharest: Editura Roza Vânturilor, 1997), 99. On July 5, 1944, Mihai Antonescu told Hudiţa practically the same thing. See Hudiţa, *Jurnal politic*, 346.

8. Accommodating and Collaborating

1. Vanessa Voisin, *L'URSS contre ses traîtres. L'Épuration soviétique (1941–1955)* (Paris: Publications de la Sorbonne, 2015), esp. 213–261.

2. Leonid Rein, *The Kings and the Pawns: Collaboration in Byelorussia during World War II* (New York: Berghahn Books, 2011), 34–37.

3. Order of the USSR's procurator Viktor Bochkov, May 1942, cited in Voisin, *L'URSS contre ses traîtres,* 233.

4. AMAN F. Marele Cartier General Inventar N 019269 din 1972 dosar 3827, f. 247 USHMM RG-25.003M reel 4.

5. AMAN F. Marele Cartier General Inventar N 019269 din 1972 dosar 3827, f. 247 USHMM RG-25.003M reel 4.

6. AMAN F. Armata a 4-a 06777 din 1975 dosar 957, f. 18 USHMM RG-25.003M reel 13.

7. AMAN Armata a 4-a Inventar 06777 din 1975 dosar 1079, ff. 99–100 USHMM RG-25.003M reel 14.

8. DANIC F. MAI IGJ dosar 402/1941 PCM, ff. 32–33 USHMM RG-25.002 reel 16.

9. DANIC F. MAI IGJ dosar 402/1941 PCM, ff. 91–92 USHMM RG-25.002 reel 16.

10. DANIC F. PCM-CM 319/1942 f. 418 USHMM RG-25.002M reel 16.

11. Manuilov, "Odessa v period," 131.

12. Manuilov, "Odessa v period," 130.

13. Voisin, *L'URSS contre ses traîtres,* 72.

14. Manuilov, "Odessa v period," 150.

15. See Alexianu's ordinances #4, 8, 16, 27 ff. 4–4v, 9–10, 21, 33–34 (September–November 1941) in DAOO F. 2242 Op. 1 spr. 1 USHMM RG-31.004M reel 1.

16. DANIC F. IGJ dosar 18/1942, f. 55v. USHMM RG-25.010M reel 13.

17. This is a tentative conclusion I came to from the study of dozens of files, many of them multivolume, from the GDASBU, whose copies are held in USHMM RG-31.018M and YA TR-18. The files released were selected by the representatives of the aforementioned institutions based on their relevance for the study of the Holocaust. For that reason, it remains unclear to what extent data on mayors featured in these files is representative of all the local residents who served in this capacity under the Romanian occupation. Even so, a high incidence of persons with a history of repression confirms evidence from the Romanian sources on Romanian preferences.

18. See the excellent analysis of the profoundly ambivalent Soviet punitive policy with regard to former collaborators, including mayors and other administrators, as well as policemen in Franziska Exeler, "The Ambivalent State: Determining Guilt in the Post-World War II Soviet Union," *Slavic Review* 75, no. 3 (2016): 606–629.

19. See note 16. I have explained some of my findings in "Hating Soviets—Killing Jews: How Antisemitic Were Local Perpetrators in Southern Ukraine, 1941–42?" *Kritika: Explorations in Russian and Eurasian History* 15, no. 3 (Summer 2014): 505–533.

20. For more on such petty collaborators and their fate under the returning Soviets, see Voisin, *L'URSS contre ses traîtres,* esp. 344–370.

21. DAOO F. 2242 Op. 1 spr. 1, ark. 2 USHMM RG-31.004M reel 1.

22. DAOO F. 2242 Op. 1 spr. 1, ark. 5–6 USHMM RG-31.004M reel 1.

23. DANIC F. IGJ dosar 122/1942, f.298 USHMM RG-25.010M reel 16.

24. DANIC F. IGJ dosar 125/1942, f. 168 USHMM RG-25.010M reel 17.

25. On the efforts to replace the heads of kolkhozes, see the information bulletin of the Transnistria Gendarmerie Inspectorate for the period of January 15–February 15, 1942, in DANIC F. MAI IGJ dosar 24/1942 II vol. 1, f. 172 USHMM RG-25.002M reel 5.

26. DANIC F. IGJ dosar 84/1943, f. 142 USHMM RG-25.101M reel 27.

27. See, for example, SSI Subcenter #5 of Odessa județ, note of December 30, 1941, in AMAN F. Armata a 3-a Inventar N S/6776 din 1976 dosar 410, f. 225–226 USHMM RG-25.003M reel 17.

28. See "Ob'iavlenie voennogo komandovaniia" (An announcement of the military commandant), *Odesskaia gazeta*, November 8, 1941.

29. DANIC F. IGJ dosar 166/1942, f. 160 USHMM RG-25.10M reel 21. Information bulletin for July 15–August 15, 1942.

30. TsDAHOU F. 1 Op. 52 spr. 450, ark. 5.

31. ANRM F. 706 Op. 1 dosar 529, f. 21

32. TsDAHOU F. 1 Op. 52 spr. 451, ark. 178, 180.

33. TsDAHOU F. 1 Op. 52 spr. 451, ark. 70. "Conversation" of Drozdov with the CC CPU instructor Vaksman (no first name and patronymic indicated), probably 1944 or 1945.

34. Voisin, *L'URSS contre ses traîtres*, 464.

35. Voisin, *L'URSS contre ses traîtres*, 401.

36. See Voisin, *L'URSS contre ses traîtres*, 464, n. 103.

37. ANRM F. 706 Inventar 1 dosar 518 vol. 1, ff. 156–160.

38. ANRM F. 706 Inventar 1 dosar 518 vol. 1, ff. 163–165.

39. ANRM F. 706 Inventar 1 dosar 518 vol. 1, ff. 38–40, activities report of the *guvernământ*'s department of agriculture through August 15, 1943.

40. ANRM F. 706 Inventar 1 dosar 518 vol. 1, ff. 299–363, statistics from ff. 326, 354.

41. ANRM F. 706 Inventar 1 dosar 518 vol. 1, ff. 354–355.

42. ANRM F. 706 Inventar 1 dosar 8, ff. 103–105 USHMM RG-54.004M reel 1.

43. ANRM F. 706 Inventar 1 dosar 518 vol. 1, f. 46.

44. TsDAHOU F. 1 Op. 22 spr. 456, ark. 4–8. n.d. (probably the spring or summer of 1944).

45. Tanja Penter, *Kohle für Stalin und Hitler: Die Bergleute im Donbass, 1929 bis 1953* (Essen: Klartext, 2010), esp. 279–282.

46. Voisin, *L'URSS contre ses traîtres*, 72.

47. See the activities report of the section of propaganda, through August 15, 1943, in ANRM F. 706 Inventar 1 dosar 518 vol. 1, ff. 185–187.

48. ANRM F. 706 Inventar 1 dosar 518 vol. 1, f. 187.

49. See "Kratkii obzor struktury gosudarstvennogo apparata na okkupirovannoi territorii mezhdu Bugom i Dnestrom, tak nazyvaemoi 'Transnsitrii'" (A short overview of the structure of the state apparatus in the occupied territory between the Buh and Dniester rivers, the so called Transnistria, material composed on the basis of reports of the underground organization "Im. VMF," 1944), in GARF F. 7021 Op. 69 delo 343, l. 30v YV JM-19.969.

50. See "Kratkii obzor," in GARF F. 7021 Op. 69 delo 343 l. 31 YV JM-19.969 and deposition of Aleksandr Nikolaevich Lebedinskii, identified as a "scientific worker," 1944, in GARF F. 7021 Op. 69 delo 434, l. 2 YV JM-19.971.

51. See the activities report of the subdepartment of propaganda through the fall of 1943, in ANRM F. 706 Inventar 1 dosar 518 vol. 1, f. 185.

52. See Alexianu's response to the SSI insinuation that some publications in this newspaper were not sufficiently orthodox, March–April 1943, in ANRM F. 706 Inventar 1 dosar 8 vol. 2, ff. 478–481.

53. Soviet partisan sources referred to Xenia Balas's father as a general killed in the Civil War, see "Kratkii obzor," in GARF F. 7021 Op. 69 delo 343, l. 30v. YV JM-19.969. On *Novoe slovo*, see Oleg Anatol'evich Korostelev, "Gazety russkogo zarubezh'ia 30–40kh godov: 'Novoe slovo,' Berlin, 1933–1944), and 'Parizhskii vestnik' (1941–1944)," in *Sotsial'nye i gumanitarnye nauki. Otechestvennaia i zarubezhnaia literatura*, Seriia 7: Literaturovedenie no. 2 (1999): 188–202.

54. Soviet partisan sources ("Kratkii obzor") claims that Xenia Balas published a newspaper with the same title in Bessarabia and that she (or Olga) possessed knowledge of several foreign languages.

55. See Nikolai Mikhailovich Fevr, "Odessa v gody vtoroi mirovoi voiny," in Budnitskii, et al., eds., *Odessa*, 48 and n. 49, 63 (author of this note is T. L. Voronina).

56. Fevr, "Odessa," 48.

57. See Alidin to Khrushchev, April 30, 1944, f. 23; Paulin Lecca, *Dela moarte la viața*. Postfață de Valeriu Cristea (Bucharest: Paideia, 1997), 202; and Vladimir Alexandrovich Smirnov, "Kul'turnaia zhizn' Odessy v period okkupatsii," *Iuzhnoe siianie*, no. 10, December 3, 2015, http://litbook.ru/article/7812/. Smirnov cites V. A. Shvets's occupation-era diary.

58. See Baliasnyi's opinion on one such manuscript, in DAOO F. 4093 Op. 1 spr. 3, ark. 1–11v.

59. Most information about these authors comes from Smirnov, "Kul'turnaia zhizn' Odessy." On Anatolii Kraft, see Vladimir Alexandrovich Smirnov, ed., *Rekviem XX veka, V piati chastiakh*, 2nd ed., augmented and corrected (Odessa: Astroprint, 2009), pt. 1, 212 and 216. Kraft was a skilled and prolific author with strong anticommunist and anti-Semitic convictions. Information about him in the sources is scant and his postwar fate unknown. Most of the other journalists were arrested by the Soviets at the end of the war and perished in the GULAG, except for Maslennikov who seemed to have escaped to Argentina where he published, in 1975, a book of fictionalized memoirs under the name of Anatolii Maslennikov-Marlenko, *"Za chto-o-o?!!": iz sovetskoi deistvitel'nosti* (Buenos Aires: O. Marlenko, 1975). Before the war, Petr Pershin was a teacher of chemistry in middle and high school. He wrote a play depicting Stalinist prisons, which was staged only four times in 1943, reportedly because the public was afraid to show up. Pershin allegedly committed suicide in 1945. See Smirnov, *Rekviem XX veka*, pt. 3, 53, 58, 206, 224 (on the basis of SBU files #24179-ІІ and #8082-ІІ).

60. An article signed S. K. and titled "Odessa yesterday and today" in *Odesskaia gazeta* on December 13, 1943 seems to develop this train of thought to its utmost.

61. "Nikakoi restavratsii," *Odesskaia gazeta*, September 19, 1943.

62. Baliasnyi, "Zapadnaia kul'tura i 'kitaiskaia stena' vremen bol'shevisma," *Molva*, December 1, 1942; V. I. Selinov, "Pered zavesoi novoi zhizni" (Before the curtain of the new life), *Molva*, December 4, 1942.

63. See, e.g., lead articles "Novyi front" (The New Front), *Odesskaia gazeta*, December 16, 1941, and "Ëkonomicheskii potentsial" (Economic Potential), *Odesskaia gazeta*, November 6, 1942. See also Anatolii Kraft, "Trud i capital" (Labor and Capital), *Odesskaia gazeta*, August 16, 1942.

64. For spreading information about the Grand Alliance see the activities report of the "Commanding Council of the underground and partisan movement in Bershadskii raion," in TsDAHOU F. 1 Op. 22 spr. 166, ark. 17, and the activities report of

the partisan detachment "Burevestnik," which existed in 1943–1944 in the northern raions of Transnistria, see TsDAHOU F. 1 Op. 22 spr. 444, ark. 61.

65. See the lead article "Osvobozhdennaia intelligentsia," *Odesskaia gazeta*, December 13, 1941; Anatolii Maslennikov, "Poet i grazhdanin," *Molva*, December 1942, and Selinov, "Pered zavesoi novoi zhizni."

66. Maslennikov, "Velikoe slovo" (The great word), *Molva*, December 1, 1942.

67. Officially, however, the initiative to create the institute was ascribed to the *guvernământ's* department of culture. See "Pervyi doklad v institute antikommunis- ticheskikh issledovanii i propagandy," *Odesskaia gazeta*, May 18, 1943.

68. Information on Faas from A. Myzychko, "Ivan Iakovlevich Faas: dekan iuridicheskogo fakul'teta Odesskogo universiteta v gody rumynskoi okkupatsii," available on the website of the Odessa historical regional museum, http://www. history.odessa.ua/publication9/stat06.htm.

69. Iablonovskii was arrested and interrogated together with another professor from the same institute, Boris Fedorovich Tsomakion. Iablonovskii was rumored to have played a negative role in Tsomakion's fate but the surviving transcript of Iablo- novskii's interrogation does not seem to bear out the charge. Iablonovskii was one of the very few who managed to immigrate to Germany at the end of the occupation, where he died. See Smirnov, ed., *Rekviem XX veka*, pt. 1, 125–127 (summary of SBU file #7630-П, 13936-П DGA USB).

70. See Myzychko, "Ivan Iakovlevich Faas"; Smirnov, "Kul'turnaia zhizn' Odessy." On Iablonovskii's appointment, see "V institute antikommunisticheskoi propagandy," *Odesskaia gazeta*, June 23, 1943.

71. "Torzhestvennoie osveshchenie instituta antikommunisticheskikh issledova- nii i propagandy" (A solemn opening of the Institute of Anticommunist Research and Propaganda), *Odesskaia gazeta*, May 23, 1943.

72. See Smirnov, *Rekviem XX veka*, pt. 1, 168 (on the basis of USB file #1140-П). Shettle was also one of those few who managed to immigrate to Germany at the end of the occupation. See V. Faitel'berg-Blank and B. Razumnyi, "Vinovny li? Arkhivy KGB #507, 0398703," *Porto-Franko* no. 42 (938), November 7, 2008, http://porto-fr. odessa.ua/index.php?art_num=art035&year=2008&nnumb=42.

73. These texts are included in Alidin's report to Khrushchev, 25–27.

74. See note on this lecture in *Odesskaia gazeta*, January 29, 1944.

75. See Smirnov, "Kul'turnaia zhizn' Odessy v period okkupatsii."

76. On Stamerov, see Smirnov, *Rekviem XX veka*, pt. 2, 74–87 (on the basis of USB file #28537-П). Stamerov developed the same ideas in his university lectures. In 1947, he was sentenced to ten years in the camps, returning to Odessa in 1955. On Serbskii, see Smirnov, *Rekviem XX veka*, pt. 1, 197–210. Serbskii was sentenced to ten years in labor camps, released in 1954, and settled in Uzbekistan where he taught Russian literature at a pedagogical institute. On Sokolov, see Smirnov, *Rekviem XX veka*, pt. 1, 172–188. Sentenced to an unknown term in labor camps in December 1944 (the full text of the sentence is lacking in the file), Sokolov died while still an inmate in 1953.

77. Alidin lists this lecture among those delivered, but during an investigation, Nomikos claimed that although he did compose it, the unidentified supervisors deemed it insufficiently "anti-Soviet," so he was never offered a chance to deliver. See Smirnov, *Rekviem XX veka*, pt. 1, 244. For more on Nomikos, see Smirnov, 238–275 (on the basis of the USB file #28470-П).

78. Most of these files on the 1930s repression are summarized in Smirnov, *Rekviem XX veka*, pt. 1, 5. On the persecution of Odessan intellectuals in the 1920s, see Viktor Anatol'evich Savchenko, *Neofitisal'naia Odessa epokhi NEPA. Mart 1921–sentiabr' 1929* (Moscow: Rosspen, 2012), esp. 55–96, and 170–186.

79. On Kondrat'ev's background, see "Zhizn' i deiatel'nost' Vladimira Aleksandrovicha Shvetsa, opisannaia v ego dnevnikakh i dokumentakh" (henceforth Shvets's diary), in Smirnov ed., *Rekviem XX veka*, pt 4, 882, May 23, 1976. On Kondrat'ev's simulated illness, see Shvets's diary, pt. 1, 451, February 6, 1942, and 283, May 22, 1942.

80. On Kondrat'ev's immigration and postwar life in Germany, see Smirnov, "Dnevnik Shvetsa o professorakh konservatorii S. Kondrat'eve i Molchanove," in *Rekviem XX veka*, pt. 1, 296–306.

81. *Odesskaia gazeta* December 21, 1941.

82. *Molva*, January 10, 1943.

83. See excerpt from the transcript of his NKVD interrogation (1944), in which he describes the content of this lecture in Smirnov, *Rekviem XX veka*, pt. 1, 178 (summary of USB archival file #26277-ΙΙ).

84. For example, Professors Varneke and Petrovskii died in prison in 1944, Sokolov in the GULAG in 1953. See the summary of their file in Smirnov, *Rekviem XX veka*, pt. 1, 172–189.

85. In Western Europe immediately following the liberation from Nazi oppression, treasonous activity was defined both by public opinion and by the courts in a much wider sense than would be practiced after the complete reestablishment of legal order. See Voisin, *L'URSS contre ses traîtres*, 23–24.

86. Shvets's diary, pt. I, 486.

87. "Kaleidoskop godov," *Molva*, January 1, 1943.

88. See the summary of his USB file (#2559-ΙΙ), in Smirnov, *Rekviem XX veka*, pt. I, 46–48. Fomenko's case was combined with that of orchestra conductor Nikolai Nikolaevich Cherniatinskii.

89. Iu. Petrovsky, "V opernom teatre," *Odesskaia gazeta*, November 26, 1941.

90. See the summary of combined Cherniatinslii-Fomenko USB file #25559-ΙΙ in Smirnov, *Rekviem XX veka*, pt. 1, 46–58.

91. *Molva*, December 10, 1942. Savchenko was arrested by the NKVD in May 1944 but soon released, see the summary of his file #8592-ΙΙ in Smirnov, *Rekviem XX veka*, pt. 1, 276–295.

92. Even Shvets, otherwise averse to the new regime, wrote on February 1, 1942: "These people deserve their own present suffering" (Shvets's diary, vol. 1, 450). That, however, was his only anti-Semitic entry and generally he wrote down news of the Jews' persecution implying at least some sympathy to their plight.

93. For the former approach, see Timothy Snyder, *Bloodlands: Europe between Hitler and Stalin* (New York: Basic Books, 2010), esp. 397. For the latter, see Martin Dean, *Collaboration in the Holocaust: Crimes of the Local Police in Belorussia and Ukraine, 1941–44* (New York: Palgrave Macmillan, 1999).

94. DAOO F. 2242 Op. 1 spr. 1, ark. 4–5 USHMM RG-31.004M reel 1.

95. DAOO F. 2242 Op. 1 spr. 1, ark. 33v USHMM RG-31.004M reel 1.

96. I more fully developed my findings in Solonari, "Hating Soviets—Killing Jews," 505–533.

97. See the Romanian translation of the instructions on the establishment of military control, security, and administration in the territory to the east of the

Dniester River, German Eleventh Army, August 1941, in AMAN F. Armata a 3-a Inventar no. S/6776 dosar 481, f. 117 USHMM RG-25.003M reel 19.

98. See the Second Army Corps circular of October 30, 1941, in AMAN F. Brigada 1 Fortificaţii dosar 399, ff. 41–42 USHMM RG-25.003M reel 394. See also the address of the Romanian General Staff (Marele Stat Major) to the Office of the President of the Council of Ministers (Preşedenţia Consiliului de Miniştri) of February 7, 1942, concerning the German military's protests regarding the arrests by the Romanian police in Transnistria of POWs of Ukrainian ethnic origin released from the German concentration camps, in ANRM F. 706 Inventar 1 dosar 12 vol. 1, f. 11 USHMM RG-54.004M reel 3. See also Golta Gendarmerie Legion current events report, March 6, 1942, requesting internment in concentration camps of POWs released by the Germans (DANIC F. IGJ, dos. 122/1942, f. 312 USHMM RG-25.010M reel 16). In January 1944, former Soviet officer POWs released by the Germans and residing in Transnistria were rearrested by the Romanian gendarmes and interned in concentration camps (AMAN F. Armata a 3-a Inventar no. S/6776 dosar 2208, f. 122 USHMM RG-25.003M reel 20).

99. See ANRM F. 706 Op. 1 dosar 518 vol. 1, f. 32.

100. See the Transnistrian governor's activity report for August 19, 1941–August 1, 1943, in ANRM F. 706 Inventar 1 dosar 518 vol. 1, f. 209.

101. GDASBU spr. 0408724/1427/8495 YV T-3 93, ark. 41.

102. GDASBU spr. 3809, ark. 12v.–13 USHMM RG-31.018M reel 23.

103. See GDASBU spr. 11670, ark. 27v. USHMM RG-31.018M reel 22.

104. See GDASBU spr. 5776, ark. 169–70 USHMM RG-31.108M reel 22.

105. See Solonari, "Hating Soviets—Killing Jews," 518–519.

106. See GDASBU spr. 023834 vol. 1, ark. 164 (YV JM 29.892). To the interrogator's question as to whether he knew of other instances of refusal to shoot, Frank asserted that Waikum's case was the only one (GDASBU spr. 023834 vol. 1, ark. 169).

107. See Kogan, first name illegible, 1945 and Iosif Bronstein, 1945 in ASRI dos. 40011 vol. 20, ff. 73–75v. and 131 in USHMM RG-25.004M reel 21; and Rakhil' Veksel'man, 1966 in GDASBU spr. 13189 vol. 20, ark. 62 v. USHMM RG-31.018M reel 18.

108. GDASBU no. 13189 vol. 25, ark. 280–82 USHMM RG-32.018M reel 19, eyewitness Vladimir Kamenskii.

109. GDASBU no. 13189 vol. 20, ark. 62v. USHMM RG-31.018M reel 18.

110. See Christopher Browning, *Ordinary Men: Reserve Police Battalion 101 and the Final Solution in Poland* (New York: HarperCollins, 1992). A useful review of the historiography on the Nazi perpetrators can be found in Claus-Christian W. Szejnmann, "Perpetrators of the Holocaust: A Historiography," in *Ordinary People as Mass Murderers,* ed. Olaf Jensen and W. Szejnmann (New York: Palgrave Macmillan, 2008), 25–54. I developed my ideas and argumentation in "Hating Soviets-Killing Jews."

111. Cited after Voisin, *L'URSS contre ses traîtres*, 233.

112. Exeler, "The Ambivalent State: Determining Guilt in the Post-World War II Soviet Union," 606–629.

113. Published in Smirnov, *Rekviem XX veka*, pt. 1, 307–646; and pt. 2, 345–794.

114. DANIC F. IGJ dosar 134/1942, f. 48 USHMM RG-25.25.002M reel 15.

115. TsDAHOU F. 1 Op. 22 spr. 164, ark 40.

116. DANIC F. MAI IGJ dosar 24-II vol. 2, f. 261 USHMM RG-25.002 reel 5.

117. DANIC IGJ dosar 199/1942, ff. 191–192, 196, 227, 244–245.

118. Shvets's diary, vol. 1, 572.

119. DANIC F. IGJ dosar 122/1942, f. 281 USHMM RG-25.002M reel 16.

120. For example, in March 1943, the gendarmerie legion commander from Berezovca judeţ identified prisoners of war as the basis for partisan recruitment. See DANIC IGJ dosar 80/1943, f. 31 USHMM RG-25.002M reel 26.

121. The assessment of the population mood in Golta judeţ was done in February 1943 by the commander of the local gendarmerie legion, DANIC F. IGJ dosar 80/1943, f. 209 USHMM RG-25.002M reel 26.

122. DANIC F. IGJ dosar 80/1943, f. 33 USHMM RG-25.010M reel 26.

123. See, for example, deposition of Il'ia Nikolaevich Vedeneev, secretary of an underground party raikom in Odessa, in TsDAHOU F. 1 Op. 22 spr. 462, ark. 24.

124. DANIC F. IGJ dosar 83/1943, f. 163 USHMM RG-25.002 reel 26.

125. DANIC F. IGJ dosar 83/1943, f. 201 USHMM RG-25.002M reel 26.

126. DANIC F. IGJ dosar 84/1943, f. 233 USHMM RG-25.010M reel 27.

127. DANIC F. IGJ dosar 84/1943, f. 432 USHMM RG-25.010M reel 27.

128. AMAN F. Armata a 3-a Inventar N S/6776 din 1976 dosar 2208, f. 205–205v USHMM RG-25.003M reel 20.

129. DANIC IGJ dosar 83/1943, f. 431–432 USHMM RG-25.010M reel 26.

9. Resisting, Phase I: Disasters

1. Slepyan, *Stalin's Guerrillas*, 24.

2. Transcript of Stalin's speech to the partisan leaders in Kremlin, September 1, 1942, cited in Kenneth Slepyan, *Stalin's Guerrillas*, 45.

3. Data on the extent of wooded territories in Transnistria is available in the activity report of the *guvernământ*'s department of forest service for August 16, 1941 through August 1, 1943; see ANRM F. 706 Inventar I dosar 518 vol. 1, ff. 228–229.

4. For Alexianu's statement, see in ASRI dosar 4001, vol. 45, ff. 242–243 USHMM RG-25.004M reel 34.

5. See G. Iablonskii, "K istorii odesskikh katakomb," in *Odesskiie katakomby*, ed. Anna Nikolaevna Dolzhenkova (Odessa: Maiak, [1970] 1973), 145.

6. On the catacombs' history as a nest of criminal gangs before World War II, see Savchenko, *Neofitsial'naia Odessa epokhi NEPa*, 270.

7. See TsDAHOU F. 57 Op. 4 spr. 103, esp. ark. 21–23 and Galuzevyi Derzhavnyi Arkhiv Sluzhby Bezpeki Ukrainy (GDASBU) F. 62 Op. 3 spr. 43, ark. 66–67. See also Ottmar Traşcă, "Serviciul special de informaţii şi mişcare de partizani din Odessa, 1941–1942," in *Armata şi Mass-Media: Studii şi comunicări prezentate la sesiunea ştiinţifică dedicată Zilei Arhivelor Militare şi aniversării a 93 de ani de la înfiinţarea Centrului de Studii s şi Păstrare a Arhivelor Militare Istorice: Brăila, 28 iulie 2013*, ed. Arian Moşneagu, Florea Petrişor, and Cornel Ţucă (Brăaila : Editura Istros a Muzeului Brăailei, 2013), 253–290.

8. See correspondence between Soldatenko's daughter and Odessan NKVD, May 1949, April 1971 in GDASBU F. 62 Op. 3 spr. 43, ark. 81 ff. (pagination inconsistent).

9. See GDASBU F. 62 Op. 3 spr. 43, ark. 45–50.

10. GDASBU F. 62 Op. 3 spr. 43, ark. 50–52.

11. GDASBU F. 62 Op. 3 spr. 43, ark. 21.

12. See correspondence between the heads of the Odessa party archive I. Grechikha and NKVD departmental archive in Moscow Colonel Detinin, January–March 1967 in GDASBU F. 62 Op. 3 spr. 43, ark. 78–79.

13. On the NKVD ranks, see Aleksandr Nikolaevich Iakovlev et al., eds., *Lubianka: Organy VChK-OGPU-NKRB-MGB-MVD-KGB. 1917–1991. Spravochnik* (Moscow: MFD, 2003), 61. Some Romanian sources identify Badaev's rank as major (see, for example, SSI note of December 14, 1942 DANIC F. IGJ dosar 199/1942, f. 91 USHMM RG-25.010M reel 22).

14. See the Romanian summary of their activity in TsDAHOU F. 57 Op. 4 delo 103, ark. 9, 79. For the Soviet summary, see in TsDAHOU F. 1 Op. 22 spr. 444, ark. 18–21, recto and verso. However, the Soviet accounts are exaggerated. For example, a train crash in December 1941, which supposedly killed a number of Romanian and German top brass and which the Soviets attributed to this group is never mentioned in Romanian documents.

15. TsDAHOU F. 1 Op. 22 spr. 444, ark. 18–21, l. 5 and GDASBU F. 62 Op.3 spr. 43, ark. 34.

16. See Vladimir Antonov and Vladimir Karpov, *Razvedchiki: geroi Sovetskogo Soiuza i geroi Rossii* (Moscow: Molodaia gvardiia, 2004), 26–28; Pavel Moraru, *Serviciile secrete și Basarabia (1918–1991): dicționar* (Bucharest: Editura militară, 2008), 160–162. Moraru, however, confuses Molodtsov partisan group's story with that of Kuznetsov's. On the responsibility of various bureaus of the Main Economic Board, see Iakovlev et al., eds., *Lubianka*, 71.

17. On Badaev's altercations with Boiko, see GDASBU F. 62 Op. 3 spr. 32, ark. 8.

18. Quoted in the official summary of partisan activity prepared by the Odessa obkom in 1944–1945 in TsDAHOU F. 1 Op. 22 spr. 444, ark. 20.

19. See GDASBU F. 62 Op. 3 spr. 32, ark. 9.

20. See TsDAHOU F. 1 Op. 22 spr. 430, ark. 74.

21. See TsDAHOU F. 1 Op. 22 spr. 467, ark. 72–73v.

22. TsDAHOU F. 57 Op. 4 spr. 103, ark. 12–13.

23. On Klimento's betrayal, see the official Soviet summary in TsDAHOU F. 1 Op. 22 spr. 44, ark. 21.

24. TsDAHOU F. 1 Op. 42 spr. 450, ark. 47.

25. TsDAHOU F. 1 Op. 42 spr.450, ark. 47–49.

26. See reports of the individual raikoms presented in 1945–1946, that is after Kolesnikov's summary was complied, in DAOO F. 92 Op. 1 spr. 13.

27. TsDAHOU F. 1 Op. 22 spr. 164, ark. 40.

28. TsDAHOU F. 1 Op. 22 spr. 444, ark. 55.

29. DANIC F. MI IGJ dosar 402/1941, ff. 91–92 USHMM RG-25.002M reel 16.

30. DANIC F. MI IGJ dosar 24 vol. 2, f. 322 USHMM RG-25.002M reel 5.

31. TsDAHOU F. 1 Op. 22 spr. 450, ark. 70. Information on the preliminary results in the causes of the exposure of Odessa party underground, no date and signature provided, probably 1944 or 1945.

32. This biographical data come from the 1966 summary of the Odessa region obkom's investigation into the activity of the underground obkom. See DAOO F. 92 Op. 1 spr. 10, ark. 6.

33. On August 18, 1941, Kolybanov relieved Petrovskii from his duties as the first secretary of the Vodno-transportnyi raion of Odessa; see DAOO F. 92 Op. 1 spr. 9, ark.

22, document titled "Conversation of com. Zotov N[ikolai] I[vanovich] secretary of Odessa regional CP(b)U committee with former secretary of Odessa regional CP(b) U committee com. Kolybanov in the Institute of the Party History under CC of the CP of Ukraine, in early 1967" (hereinafter referred to as "Conversation of com. Zotov").

34. Good summaries of the numerous SMERSH, NKVD, and party investigations into the obkom activity can be found in "Deputy head of organizational-instructional department of the CC of CP(b)U [Victor Ivanovich] Alidin to [the first secretary of the CC CP(b)U Nikita Sergeevich] Khrushchev, April 30, 1944 in TsDA-HOU F. 1 Op. 22 spr. 450, ark. 3–11 and "Conversation of com. Zotov"; DAOO F. 92 Op. 1, ark. 18–66.

35. The following reconstruction of Petrovskii's story is based on materials—mostly transcripts of interrogations of surviving members of the obkom and of the former Romanian SSI case officers of the obkom—contained in the following file: DAOO F. 92 Op. 1 spr. 9. His 1945 bill of indictment and letter to Kalinin see in DAOO F. 92 Op. 1 spr. ark. 5–8v. Important additional information can be found in Vera Aleksandrovna Fabianskaia, "Dvoinaia igra," in *Iz nebytiia; ocherki o repressiiakh 20–50kh godov* (Odessa: Druk, 2003), 81–101. Fabianskaia was allowed access, which was denied me, to the NKVD/KGB Petrovskii file in the regional USB archive. The cited chapter is the summary of that file.

36. See Petrovskii's petition for clemency to Mikhail Ivanovich Kalinin, Soviet nominal head of state, dated June 30, 1945, in DAOO F. 92 Op. 1 spr. 135, ark 3. The existence of such instructions was implied by the secretary of Odessa regional party committee Nikolai Ivanovich Zotov in early 1967. See DAOO F. 92 Op. 1 spr. 9, ark. 36, "Conversation of com. Zotov."

37. See TsDAHOU F. 1 op. 22 spr. 450 ark. 5. Alidin cites German data for April 1944 (the Germans took over the administration of Transnistria from the Romanians on March 18, 1944). The Romanian order of November 7, 1941, to all communists to register with the local authorities is mentioned in the summary of the activity of the Prigorodnyi raikom of Odessa, organized by SMERSH or NKVD shortly after Odessa's liberation in April 1945, TsDAHOU F. 1 Op. 2 spr. 467, ark. 7. According to the data provided by Voisin, in July 1945, Odessa oblast led the rest of the USSR in the percentage of communists (more than ninety of the files were subjected to verification) expelled from the party's ranks for reprehensible behavior during the war; see Voisin, *L'URSS contre ses traîtres*, 401.

38. Since Platov's court file has not surfaced so far, one cannot be sure as to the court's reasoning. Platov, as he later claimed, escaped from his escort on March 27, 1944, two days before the Romanians left the province, a claim that the Soviets found implausible. The NKVD arrested Platov in 1944 and in 1945; he was sentenced to ten years in the GULAG for high treason, once again a strangely soft sentence, much softer than the law called for (twenty-five years or the death penalty). As the court explained, it took into consideration Platov's public persona and "inexpediency of applying the full measure of the law under the present conditions"—an explanation that conceals more than it reveals.

39. See SSI report TsDAHOU F. 57 Op. 4 spr. 103, ark. 87, July 3, 1943.

40. See SSI report TsDAHOU F. 57 Op. 4 spr. 103, ark. 70–71, July 3, 1943. See also the correspondence between the Berezovca Gendarmerie Legion, the Martial

Court Odessa Police, and the Odessa Gendarmerie Legion on the bogus resistance organization "Odessa Red Banner Partisans," in TsDAHOU F. 57 Op. 4 spr. 103, ark. 132–140.

41. TsDAHOU F. 57 Op. 4 spr. 103, ark. 59.

42. TsDAHOU F. 57 Op. 4 spr. 103, ark. 69, 88

43. See his bill of the 1945 indictment (DAOO F. 92 Op. 1 spr. 135, ark. 7v.–8) and Zotov's claim in 1967 that further investigation demonstrated the falsity of this charge in DAOO F. 92 Op. 1 spr. 9, ark. 38–39, 46–47, "Conversation of com. Zotov."

44. On the date of Petrovskii's execution, see the decision of the Odessa obkom bureau on the rehabilitation of Petrovskii, August 6, 1966, in DAOO F. 92 Op. 1 spr. 10, ark. 6.

45. Initially assessed by the NKVD investigator as a likely agent-provocateur, Bragorenko was in 1956–1957 absolved of the accusations against her and her name added to the roster of partisan martyrs. The account of the Balta party underground and Bragorenko's role in it is based on investigative files from the epochs of Stalin, Khrushchev, and Brezhnev, which contains interviews and depositions of (alleged) former members of the organization as well as copies of Romanian trophy documents. See TsDAHOU F. 1 Op. 22 spr. 470; DAOO F. 92 Op. 1 spr. 9, 10, 137, 138. The most informative is the *spravka* (information) on Bragorenko group signed by the assistant to the Collegium in Party Affairs of the CC of the CP(B)U Korkhov, 1945 in TsDAHOU F. 1 Op. 22 spr. 470, ark. 3–6, and the deposition of V. P. Osokina, the wife of a murdered member of the Bragorenko group, March 1944, in DAOO F. 92 Op. 1 spr. 137, ark. 104–104v.–105. See also Vasilii Fëdorovich Egorov, Nikolai Ivanovich Zotov and Aleksei Nikolaevich Rogozhin, *Parol'-bessmertie* (Odessa: Maiak, 1968), 62.

46. See "Conversation of com. Zotov" in DAOO F. 92 Op. 1 spr. 9, ark. 56.

47. TsDAHOU F. 1 Op. 22 spr. 467, esp. ark. 6–15 and 45–62, official summary and activity report by Sëmen Fëdorovich Lazarev.

48. See Lazarev's account in TsDAHOU F. 1 Op. 22 spr. 467, ark. 45–62.

49. TsDAHOU F. 1 Op. 22 spr. 467, ark. 55–56.

50. According to the historian Aleksander Babich, who apparently had access to the documents I was not able to consult, the core of the group, including Lazarev, Gorbel', and Shcherba, were relatives, and acted "as a family." See Aleksandr Bachin, "Otriad," available at http://www.tudoy-sudoy.od.ua/pro-istoriiy-i-odessu/vov/partizanskoe-dvijenie-v-odesse/405-posle-aresta.html.

51. See Nina Tumarkin, *The Living and the Dead: The Rise and Fall of the Cult of World War II in Russia* (New York: Basic Books, 1994); Amir Weiner, *Making Sense of War: The Second World War and the Fate of the Bolshevik Revolution* (Princeton: Princeton University Press, 2000); Lisa A. Kirschenbaum, *The Legacy of the Siege of Leningrad, 1941–1995: Myth, Memories, and Monuments* (Cambridge: Cambridge University Press, 2006); Mark Edele, *Soviet Veterans of World War II: A Popular Movement in an Authoritarian Society, 1941–1991* (Oxford: Oxford University Press, 2008). The term "war hero-in chief" belongs to Denise Youngblood, see *Russian War Films: On the Cinema Front, 1914–2005* (Lawrence: University Press of Kansas, 2007), 95, cited by Edele in his *Soviet Veterans of World War II*, 8.

52. See, for example, certificate of rehabilitation of Vera Ivanovna Dzhurilo, one of Petrovskii's liaisons, by the Odessa Military District Tribunal, "for lack of corpus delicti" on November 23, 1954 (see DAOO F. 92 Op. 1 spr. 10, ark. 229–230). See also

information of the vacation of a sentence of Pavel Vasil'evich Sveshnikov, member of the Molodtsov-Badaev group, condemned to eight years of camp labor for high treason; there is no indication as to who vacated the sentence. See DAOO F. 92 Op. 1 spr. 23, ark. 2–5.

53. For example, Sveshnikov's request for the readmission to the CPSU was denied in 1962 (see DAOO F. 92 Op. 1 spr. 23, ark. 2–5) while in the same year Odessa obkom recommended Alxandr Osipovich Tret'iak, a member of underground obkom, for decoration by the order of the Great Patriotic War Second Degree. In May or June 1944, Odessa NKGB board arrested Tret'iak and charged him with high treason for betraying his comrades while in a Romanian prison. Sentenced for labor camps the same year, he was rehabilitated in 1945 "for lack of corpus delicti." Such early rehabilitations of accused partisans were not completely unknown. By the time obkom recommended Tret'iak for decoration, he had been already rehabilitated as a member of the party, which also most probably meant recognition of him as a former partisan. See DAOO F. 92 Op. 1 spr. 15, ark. 59–63.

54. DAOO F. 92 Op. 1 spr. 151, ark. 23.

55. The only copy of its decision I found is not dated. The suggested time range in based in the reference to the "industrial obkom," one of the ill-conceived structures created in the final period of Khrushchev's reign and abolished shortly after his deposition on October 14, 1964.

56. See DAOO F. 92 Op. 1 spr. 10, ark. 22.

57. See *spravka* on Petrovskii signed by the Odessa obkom secretary M. Sinitsa, August 6, 1966, in DAOO F. 92 Op. 1 spr. 10, ark. 6.

58. See Gornyi's petition to the college requesting rehabilitation of Petrovskii, in DAOO F. 92 Op. 1 spr. 10, ark. 30–39, esp. 38–39.

59. See Zotov's "conversation" with Kolybanov, in DAOO F. 92 Op. 1 spr. 9, ark. 19.

60. See, for example, Egorov et al., *Parol'-bessmertiie.*

61. See Fabianskaia, "Dvoinaia igra," passim.

62. See DAOO F. 92 Op. 1 spr. 1 (1946) and 5 (1972).

63. Aleksandr Babich, "Kak organizovyvalos' odesskoie podpol'e," http://www.odessitclub.org/publications/almanac/alm_54/alm_54-53-66.pdf.

64. DAOO F. 92 Op. 1 spr. 137, esp. ark. 1–2, 21.

10. Resisting, Phase II: Recovery to Resurgence

1. TsDAHOU F. 57 Op. 4 spr. 103, ark. 87. Mykola Mykolaïovich Shytiuk, "Pidpil'na organizatsiia 'Partyzan'ska iskra' v svitli novykh istorichnykh dzherel i dokumentiv," in *Mykolaïvshchyna v roky Velykoï Vitchyznianoï viiny: 1941–1944: do 60-richchia vyzvolennia oblasti vid nimets'ko-rumuns'kykh okupantiv,* ed. O. M. Harkusha and M. O. Bahmet (Mykolaïv: [Vyd-vo ta drukarnia "Kvit"], 2004), 92–102.

2. TsDAHOU F. 57 Op. 4 spr. 103, ark. 75–76.

3. Odesskoe obl. izditel'stvo, 1956. For Kirichenko's letter to Khrushchev, see TsDAHOU, Fond 1 Op. 22 spr. 472, ark. 1–2.

4. Ivan Pavlovich Gerasimenko, *Partyzans'ka iskra; spohady uchastnyka* (Kyiv: Molod', 1961).

5. TsDAHOU F. 1 Op. 22 spr. 472.

6. Shytiuk, "Pidpil'na organizatsiia," 92–102.

7. TsDAHOU F. 1 Op. 22 spr. 472, ark. 73–74.

8. TsDAHOU F. 57 Op. 4 spr. 103, ark. 183–187. The report is dated October 31, 1943.

9. ANRM F. 706 Op. 1 dosar 16 vol. 3, ff. 524–525.

10. DANIC F. IGJ dosar 86/1943, f. 291 USHMM RG-25.010M reel 27.

11. TsDAHOU F. 1 Op. 22 spr. 444, ark. 100. Document titled "Report on the underground and partisan activity in the Odessa region," no authors or date provided.

12. Roger R. Reese, *Why Stalin's Soldiers Fought: The Red Army's Military Effectiveness in World War II* (Modern War Studies) (Lawrence: University Press of Kansas, 2011)

13. TsDAHOU F. 57 Op. 4 spr. 103, ark. 82. This is the Russian translation from the Romanian original. It does not reference Stalingrad by name but rather says "November 1941 Soviet offensive," which is obviously a mistake.

14. DANIC F. IGJ dosar 83/1943, ff. 254–255, 264 USHMM RG-25.010M reel 26.

15. ANRM F. 706 Inventar 1 dosar 59, f. 221–230.

16. Shvets's diary, in Smirnov, *Rekviem*, pt. 1, 579.

17. Deposition of Varneke to ChGK, GARF F. P-7021 Op. 69 delo 434, ll. 8–9 YV JM-19.971.

18. See the SSI information note on the moods of Odessa population, September 29, 1942, in ANRM F. 706 Inventar 1 dosar 8. ff. 318–320 USHMM RG-54.002M reel 1.

19. DANIC F. ICJ dosar 125/1942, f. 155–156 USHMM RG-25.010M reel 17. See also gendarmerie legion's report from Iampol, September 1942, in DANIC F. IJG dosar 147/1942 f. 68v. USHMM RG-25.010M reel 20.

20. DANIC F. IGJ dosar 80/1943, f. 215 USHMM RG-25.010M reel 26.

21. DANIC F. IGJ dosar 84/1943, f. 443 USHMM RG-25.010M reel 27.

22. TsDAHOU F. 57 Op. 4 spr. 103, ark. 50–51. Russian translation from the Romanian original.

23. DAOO F. 2242 Op. 4c spr. 23, ark. 76 USHMM RG-31.004 reel 1.

24. TsDAHOU F. 57 Op. 4 spr. 103, ark. 50–51. Russian translation from the Romanian original. The "right moment" for the banderists is my own supposition.

25. See a peculiar case of a leaflet in support of the Red Army misattributed by the Romanians to the Ukrainian nationalists, Odessa, June 1942, information report on the situation in Transnistria of the Odessa Gendarmerie Inspectorate in DANIC F. IGJ dosar 20/1942, f. 8 USHMM RG-25.101M reel 7.

26. This was the case with Anna Vital'evna Ivio, an Odessa resident, sentenced after the war to ten years in GULAG and rehabilitated after the war "due to lack of corpus delicti." See Fabianskaia, *Iz nebytiia*, 128–130 (summary of the USB file # 7774-П).

27. On Blagodar's leading role in organizing this band and his replacement in September 1943, see the document titled "Activity report of the underground organization of Savranskii *raion*," in TsDAHOU F. 1 Op. 22 spr. 473, ark. 71. See also the SSI report on the partisan movement in the Golta raion, TsDAHOU F. 57 Op. 4 spr. 103, ark. 150 and the Balta Gendarmerie Legion report on the partisan activity in the vicinity of the town of Berşadi, DANIC F. IGJ dosar 86/1943, ff. 313–313v (pagination inconsistent) USHMM RG-25.010M reel 27. How awkward this situation seemed to the party leaders one can judge from the fact that while the report of underground party organization Pribugskaia, Savranskii raion identified Blagodar' as among "the best underground workers (*podpol'shchiki*)" (TsDAHOU F. 1 Op. 22 spr. 473, ark. 76), summary of the partisan activity in Odessa oblast approved by the obkom barely

mentioned his name at all (TsDAHOU F. 1 Op. 22 spr. 473, ark. 53–70). On his assassination on the orders of his replacement, see the report of Iosif Ivanovich Vykhodtsev in TsDAHOU F. 1 Op. 22 spr. 473, ark. 85v. For more biographical information, see in Odessa obkom answer to the CC CPU, 1966, in DAOO F. 92 Op. 1 spr. 174, ark. 2–4.

28. On Hrushevski's textbook, see Egorov et al., *Parol'-bessmertiie*, 52–53.

29. Report of Iosif Ivanovich Vykhodtsev, in TsDAHOU F. 1 Op. 22 spr. 473, ark.84.

30. Numbers cited in the obkom-approved final report on the partisan activity in Odessa oblast, in TsDAHOU F. 1 Op. 22 spr. 444, ark. 64.

31. See TsDAHOU F. 1 Op. 22 spr. 444, ark. 64 and AMAP F. F. Armata a 3-a Inventar N S/6776 din 1976 dosar 2208, f. 9 USHMM RG-25.002M reel 20.

32. AMAP F. F. Armata a 3-a Inventar N S/6776 din 1976 dosar 2208 f. 20, Report of the general staff of the Third Army, section 2 (informations), December 15, 1943, USHMM RG-25.002M reel 20.

33. AMAP F. F. Armata a 3-a Inventar N S/6776 din 1976 dosar 2208, f. 24 report of general staff of the Third Army, section 2 (informations), December 15, 1943, USHMM RG-25.002M reel 20.

34. AMAP F. F. Armata a 3-a Inventar N S/6776 din 1976 dosar 2208, ff. 170–171 USHMM RG-25.101M reel 20.

35. See the SSI report on the February 3, 1944 battle with the partisans in the vicinity of the village of Vinocurnaia, Tulcin județ, in AMAP F. Armata a 3-a Inventar N S/6776 din 1976 dosar 2208, f. 286–286v. USHMM RG-25.101M reel 20.

36. See daily reports of the Romanian military, gendarmerie, and SSI to that effect, in AMAP F. F. Armata a 3-a Inventar N S/6776 din 1976 dosar 2208, f. 286–313 USHMM RG-25.101M reel 20.

37. AMAP F. F. Armata a 3-a Inventar N S/6776 din 1976 dosar 2208, f. 220–205v USHMM RG-25.101M reel 20.

38. See instructions issued in pursuance of this order (# 32.656/1943) by the prefect of Oceacov județ colonel I. D. Constantinescu in DAOO F. 2341 Op. 1s spr. 45/1943, ark. 398 USHMM RG-31.004M reel 20.

39. See the transcripts of interrogations of Pătrășcoiu and key eyewitnesses in these events, in ASRI dosar 40011 vol. 24, ff. 1–50 USHMM RG-25.004 reel 22 (April 1945).

40. On detention and triage of the supposed "partisans," see the transcript of confrontation of Pătrășcoiu and commander of the Balta Gendarmerie Legion Lieutenant Colonel Ștefan Gavăț, in ASRI dosar 40011 vol. 24, f. 12 USHMM RG-25.004 reel 22 (April 1945). On their murder by the Germans, see eyewitness accounts collected by the Soviet Extraordinary State Commission in GARF F. P-7021 Op. 69 delo 84, l. 260 in YV JM-19.969 (May 1944).

41. This is according to the sworn account of a former gendarmerie officer Ștefan Botezatu, see ASRI dosar 21535 vol. 1, ff. 332–335 USHMM RG-25.004M reel 124.

42. AMAP F. F. Armata a 3-a Inventar N S/6776 din 1976 dosar 2208, ff. 196–197 USHMM RG-25.101M reel 20; SSI notes of January 19, 1944.

43. See, for example, Gavăț's report on such partisan actions in DANIC F. IGJ dosar 86/1943, f. 188 USHMM RG-25.010M reel 27. Partisan reports also mention such actions; see, for example, the activity report of the Chechelnitskii underground

committee, in TsDAHOU F. 1 Op. 22 spr. 156, ark. 173–175. Both relations refer to events in November 1943.

44. See leaflet of the Berşad underground organization announcing a change of treatment of the captured gendarmes after executions of civilians in the village of Malaia Kirievka (near to Bandurovo, in the same Romanian operation of reprisals) in November 1943, in TsDAHOU F. 1 Op. 22 spr. 155, ark. 28. That leaflet threatened to kill ten Romanians for each Transnistrian civilian. However, as late as February 16, 1944, Colonel Iliescu reported that in Moghilev vicinity partisans captured a railway station guarded by the Germans. They killed the German guards but released Romanian railway administrators, having stripped them of their closes. See AMAN F. Armata a 3-a Inventar N S/6776 din 1976 dosar 2208, f. 387 USHMM RG-25.003M reel 20.

45. See excerpts from his memos and diaries in dosar 40011 vol. 24, after f. 50, pagination inconsistent USHMM RG-25.004 reel 22.

46. TsDAHOU F. 1 Op. 22 spr. ark. 145. Russian translation from Romanian original.

47. AMAN F. Armata a 3-a Inventar N S/6776 din 1976 dosar 2208, f. 253 USHMM RG-25.003M reel 20.

48. For example, in November 1943, the Balta Gendarmerie Legion commander reported that a gang of partisans active in his judeţ "created a center of forcible recruitment threatening people with the destruction of their property and death if they would not submit." DANIC F. IGJ dosar 86/1943, f. 233 (inconsistent pagination) USHMM RG-25.004M reel 27. On February 7, 1944, the SSI reported to the Third Army command that a partisan gang acting in the vicinity of Vapniarka in the north of the province was impressing local men into their ranks. See AMAN F. Armata a 3-a Inventar N S/6776 din 1976 dosar 2208, f. 308 USHMM RG-25.003M reel 20.

49. See DANIC F. IGJ dosar 84/1943, f. 432 USHMM RG-25.004M reel 27.

50. See, for example, the Romanian translation of a manifest spread by the partisans in Oceacov judeţ that is contained in a report of the gendarmerie legion commander of the same judeţ on the partisan activity, October 27, 1943, in DANIC F. IGJ dosar 84/1943, f. 87 USHMM RG-25.004M reel 27.

51. See TsDAHOU F. 1 Op. 22 spr. 166, ark. 52.

52. Such rumors were being brought by refugees from the east. See reports to that effect from the Tulcin Gendarmerie Legion, September 1943, in DANIC F. IGJ dosar 86/1943, ff. 24–26 USHMM RG-25.004M reel 27.

53. See, for example, the SSI report on partisan commander Koval' (nomme de guerre) addresses to the locals, in TSADAHOU F. 57 Op. 4 Spr. 103, ark. 144. Reverse translation into Russian of the Romanian original. See also the report on the program and activity of Iasinovska underground organization, in TsDAHOU F. 1 Op. 22 spr. 474, ark. 9–10.

54. DANIC F. IGJ dosar 84/1943, f. 444 USHMM RG-25.004M reel 27.

55. See DAOO F. 2358 Op. 1 spr. 102/1943, ark. 7–8v. USHMM RG-31.004M reel 15 (January 21, 1944).

56. ANRM F. 706 Inventar 1 dosar 929, f. 12–13. Telegram to PCM.

57. ANRM F. 706 Inventar 1 dosar 929, f. 12–13. Telegram to PCM.

58. See telegram in ANRM F. 706 Inventar 1 dosar 929, f. 12–13.

59. See ANRM F. 706 Inventar 1 dosar 929, f. 12–13.

60. In the meeting of the Council of Ministers of November 17, 1943, he established a limit of "5,000–6,000 Russians," with their families who collaborated with the Romanians and thus discredited themselves in the eyes of the Soviets; he was particularly well-disposed towards intellectuals (see Ciucă and Ignat, eds., *Stenogramele*, vol. 9, 564). Later on he set the number at 5,000; this included not only ethnic Russians but virtually all potential immigrants from the east deemed particularly useful. On March 6, 1944, Vasiliu reported to the Council of Ministers that up until that moment 1,870 persons approved by Alexianu and his ministry were allowed to relocate to Romania. (See Ciucă and Ignat, eds., *Stenogramele*, vol. 9, 564.)

61. See TsDAHOU F. 1 Op. 22 spr. 444, ark. 14v–15v. Official summary of verified activity reports, 1946.

62. Bundesarchiv-Militärarchiv-Freiburg, RH 24–72/33 Gen. Kdo. LXXII A.K. Abt. Ia Anlagen zum K.T.B. Gefechtsberichte Odessa, April 1944, 3. (Battle reports in the vicinity of Odessa, April 1944, 72nd Infantry Division, report by the 742nd infantry [Landschutz] battalion commander Captain Luthke, April 28, 1944.)

63. See TsDAHOU F. 1 Op. 22 spr. 444, ark. 14v–15v. An official summary of the verified activity reports, 1946.

64. See the transcript of Voinov's interview, correspondent of *Komsomol'skaia pravda*, with members of the group conducted in May 1966, in GDASBU F. 62 Op. 3 spr. 31.

65. John Armstrong, *Soviet Partisans in World War II* (Madison: University of Wisconsin Press, 1964), 40. See the further discussion of this issue in Kenneth Slepyan, *Stalin's Guerrillas: Soviet Partisans in World War II* (Lawrence: University Press of Kansas, 2006), 4–5. Slepyan cites this definition of partisan activity by Armstrong.

66. See Ievhen Hryhorovych Horbunov, Iurĭi Vadimovich Kotliar, and Mykola Mykolaïovych Shytiuk, *Povstans'ko-partyzans'kyi rukh na Pivdni Ukraïny v 1917–1944 rr.* (Kherson: OLDI-plius, 2003), 121–183.

67. Christopher Gilley, "Fighters for Ukrainian Independence? Imposture and Identity among Ukrainian Warlords, 1917–22," *Historical Research* 90, no. 247 (February 2017): 172–190, the citation is from 190. Gilley is inspired by Sheila Fitzpatrick, *Tear Off the Masks! Identity and Imposture in 20th-Century Russia* (Princeton, NJ: Princeton University Press, 2005), esp. 3–18.

68. Slepyan, *Stalin's Guerrillas*, esp. chaps. 4–6.

Conclusion

1. For example, the information bulletin of the Balta Gendarmerie Inspectorate for October 1943 assessed that "the population is extremely upset by the rumors that Transnistria would be transferred under the German jurisdiction, being aware of the regime to which residents to the east of the Buh River are subjected." See DANIC F. IGJ dosar 86/1943, f. 289 USHMM RG-25.010M reel 27.

2. See Berkhoff, *Harvest of Despair*.

ARCHIVAL SOURCES

Archives consulted

Romania

Arhiva Ministerului Apărării Naţionale (AMAN)
Direcţia Arhivei Naţionale Istorice Centrale (DANIC)

COLLECTIONS (*FONDURI*)

Ministerul de Interne. Inspectoratul General al Jandarmeriei (MI IGJ)
Inspectoratul General al Jandarmeriei (IGJ—a separate collection from the preceding one)
Preşedenţia Consiliului de Miniştri—Cabitetul Militar Ion Antonescu (PCM-CM)
Preşedenţia Consiliului de Miniştri—Cabitetul Civil Mihai Antonescu (PCM-CC)
Arhiva Serviciului Român de Infomaţii (ASRI)

Russian Federation

Gosudarstvennyĭ Arkhiv Rossiĭskoĭ Federatsii (GARF)
Tsentral'nyi Arkhiv Federal'noi sluzhby bezopasnosti Rossiiskoi Federatsii (TsAFSBRF)

Ukraine

Tsentral'yĭ Derzhavnyĭ Arkhiv Hromad'skykh Ob'ėdnan 'Ukraïny (TsDAHOU)
Galuzevyĭ Derzhavnyĭ Arkhiv Sluzhby Bezpeki Ukraïny (GDASBU)
Derzhavnyĭ Arkhiv Odes'koĭ Oblasti (DAOO)

Moldova

Arhiva Naţională a Republicii Moldova (ANRM)
Arhiva Serviciului de Informaţii şi Securitate (ASIS)

Germany

Bundesarchiv-Militärarchiv-Freiburg (BA-MA-Freiburg)

Note 1: I list archival collections (*fonduri*) in cases when they are identifiable by their name only, viz. in the National Archive of Romania in Bucharest. I refrain from doing so when collections are identifiable by their codes.

Note 2: Some of the archival materials consulted come from the original archives in the countries indicated above. I consulted other materials in the microfilm/ microfiche copies in the archival holdings of the US Holocaust Memorial Museum in Washington, DC (USHMM) and in Yad Vashem—The World Holocaust Remembrance Center in Jerusalem, Israel (YV). In the latter cases, I reference original archival holdings followed by coded names of collections of microfilms or microfiches as well as of institutions that house them.

Note 3: I referred to archival locations using abbreviations in national languages of the respective countries. F. stands for Fond (Romanian, Ukrainian, and Russian); Op. for Opys' in Ukrainian and Opis' in Russian; f. for filă in Romanian; l. for list in Russian; and ark. for arkush in Ukrainian.

INDEX

Abramov, N. F., 195–196

Abuse of power, 89, 90, 92, 134, 135, 159, 160, 167, 185, 186, 232, 235, 257n83

"Abyssinia of Europe", 31, 244n2

Academy of Fine Arts, Odessa, 179

Accommodation, 4, 6, 9, 159, 163, 187, 190

Activists: Moldovan, 116, 118, 141; Ukrainian, 217, 236

Adamov, Evgenii, 175, 180

Administration: military, of the territory between the Dniester and Buh Rivers, 44, 45, 153, 227, 257n87; of Romania in general, 31, 32; Romanian in Transnistria, 2, 3, 6, 20–22, 26, 33, 35–36, 41–45, 50–62, 65–67, 70–83, 87, 93, 94, 104, 106, 113, 117, 121, 127, 130–133, 149, 155, 158, 164, 167, 170, 178, 183, 190, 224, 227, 232, 234, 249n95, 253n64, 280n97, 284n37; Romanian railways, 37, 38, 245n14

Administrators, 1, 4, 8, 32, 34, 36, 44, 66, 73, 74, 76, 78, 79, 86, 90, 93, 103, 104, 110, 112, 113, 125, 127, 134, 138, 142, 147, 153, 157, 163, 164, 165, 168–172, 219, 232–235, 276n18, 189n44; salaries of, 72, 78, 79, 81, 127, 157, 171, 254n28, 272n12, 272n19

Africa, 4, 130

Agriculture, 65, 72, 168, 277n39

Air force: Soviet, 16; German, 17

Alcohol, 17, 148, 150

Alexianu, Gheorghe, 29, 32, 33, 37, 39, 40, 42, 49–52, 59–61, 64–71, 73–82, 84, 88, 91, 103, 106, 108, 109, 110, 112, 113, 118–122, 125, 132, 136, 141, 147, 149–151, 143, 156, 168, 173, 174, 193, 227, 232, 245n14, 246n44, 147n52, 147n63, 147n72, 248n84, 250n20, 255n42, 257n89, 262n47, 262n50, 262n53, 263n59, 272n10, 273n42, 290n60; anti-Legionary stance of, 75; anti-Semitism of, 74; appointed governor

on the proposal of Mihai Antonescu, 59; conflict with the Scientific Institute of Transnistria, 119–122; dismissed, 44; Pântea-Alexianu "pro-capitalist" policies, 155–157; professor of law, 59; special relations with Ion Antonescu, 65–70

Alidin, Viktor Ivanovich, 90–91, 178, 278n57, 279n77, 284n34, 284n37

Aliens, 22, 29, 46, 98, 171, 175, 265n1

Alliances of Romania and Germany, 14, 18, 20, 27; of the Soviet Union with Great Britain and America, 176, 177, 178n64

Allies: of Romania, 31, 40, 44, 54, 55, 275n73; of Germany, including Romania, 21, 24, 44, 55, 152, 159, 160

Alsace, 56, 58, 70

Ambrus, Romulus, 215

Ananiev: județ, 104; town of, 83

Ananiev Gendarmerie Legion, 136, 150, 167, 169, 256n70, 264n92

Annexation, 98; plans of, 116, 123, 231; Romanian of Transnistria, considered but postponed, 22, 24–30; Soviet, of Bessarabia and northern Bukovina, 14, 116

Anti-Semitic: legislation, 74; policy, 191; propaganda, 131, 144, 175, 180, 181, 191, 235; violence, 46; worldview, 278n59, 280n92

Antonescu, Ion: agreement with Hitler on the Transnistrian borders, 35; appointment as dictator and ousting King Carol II, 14; and the battle of Odessa, 16–20; Consiliu de Patronaj al Operei Sociale as personal fief, 68; coup d'état against, 251n35; decided against settling eastern Romania west of the Dniester River, 99, 100, 107, 112; decision to align Romania with Nazi Germany, 14–15; decision to occupy Transnistria, 16; determined to keep Transnistria under Romanian